Praise for the Open Day

What the Press is Saying

"Exploring is an act that is very much a part of the Open Days Program. Treat the *Directory* as you would a spinning globe, letting your finger land randomly on its surface; it has the same qualities of serendipity and promise—the difference here being that the *Directory* can satisfy your spontaneous urge to explore forbidden, beguiling worlds."

—*Country Living*

"Just show up and pay a small entrance fee. From sweet tea olives to Feng Shui to a gardener holding sway over his guests, the diverse array reflects America's creative, enthusiastic horticultural love affair."

—*Veranda*

"Have you ever coveted your neighbor's garden?. . . .The Garden Conservancy. . .has introduced a way for you to take a peek at some of those impressive gardens, meet the gardeners, maybe even snap a picture or scribble notes."

—*Valley News*

"I had a great time in other people's gardens. I learned, had fun, and brought ideas home. I could not have done this without the information provided in *The Garden Conservancy's Open Days Directory*."

—*The Ryder*

What Our Garden Hosts are Saying

"Beautiful day. Fabulous weather. Great crowd."

—*Falls Village, CT*

"It was a wonderful day. The weather was perfect, the visitors delightful and uniformly admiring—why wouldn't we like that?"

—*Cortlandt Manor, NY*

"The visitors were interested, interesting, and appreciative. . . . It was a lovely time—as good as it gets gardenwise. Congratulations to the Garden Conservancy for making it all possible."

—*Evanston, IL*

"I enjoyed sharing my love of gardening with appreciative people."

—*Sands Point, NY*

"We so enjoyed the day!. . . .My husband and I really enjoyed showing people our garden and all the visitors seemed to enjoy it immeasurably."

—*Houston, TX*

"The guests have always been as pleasant and considerate as anyone invited to my home."

—*Amagansett, NY*

"We thoroughly enjoyed our first Open Day and look forward to participating again."

—*Farmington, CT*

THE GARDEN CONSERVANCY'S

OPEN DAYS DIRECTORY

The Guide to Visiting America's
Best Private Gardens

THE GARDEN CONSERVANCY'S

OPEN DAYS DIRECTORY

The Guide to Visiting America's Best Private Gardens

Foreword by Starr Ockenga

EDITION

Published by The Garden Conservancy, Inc.
Distributed by Harry N. Abrams, Inc.

Distributed by Harry N. Abrams, Inc., New York
Book design by Richard Deon Graphic Art

Publisher's Cataloging-in-Publication
(provided by Quality Books, Inc.)
The Garden Conservancy's open days directory: the guide to visiting hundreds of America's best private gardens, 2002 ed., 8th ed.
     p. cm.
     Includes index.
     ISSN: 1087-7738
     ISBN: 0-8109-6744-8
1. Gardens—United States—Directories.
2. Botanical gardens—United States—Directories.
3. Arboretums—United States—Directories.
  I. Garden Conservancy.
  II. Title: Open days directory
  SB466.U65G37 2001   712'.07473
                QBI00-836

This book is printed on recycled paper
Manufactured in the United States of America

Cover photo: Bella Madrona, Portland, OR. Copyright ©Starr Ockenga, *Eden on Their Minds: American Gardeners with Bold Visions* (New York: Clarkson Potter, 2001).

CONTENTS

. . . .

Sponsors

The Garden Conservancy gratefully acknowledges
Sara Lee Corporation for its generous sponsorship
of the 2002 Open Days Program.

We also extend our appreciation to the fine
garden businesses and public gardens that have
supported this publication through their advertising.
Please consult these pages for all your gardening
needs and tell our advertisers you saw them in
The Garden Conservancy's Open Days Directory.

Acknowledgments

· ·

Since our inception in 1995, 138 Regional Representatives have volunteered their time and energy to the development of the Garden Conservancy's Open Days Program. We are grateful for their ongoing commitment and efforts.

Alabama

Birmingham
    Mrs. A. Jack Allison (1998-2000, 2002)
    Mrs. John N. Wrinkle (1998-2000, 2002)

Arizona

Phoenix
    Mrs. Scott Crozier (2000-2002)
    Mary Irish (2002)
    Carolyn O'Malley (2000-2001)
    Nancy Swanson (1999)
    Gregory S. Trutza (2000-2001)
    Mrs. Donald C. Williams (1998-1999)

California

Carmel
    Mrs. Lee Meneice (1997-1998)
Los Angeles
    Judy Horton (2001-2002)
Pasadena
    Mrs. Donivee Nash (1999-2000, 2002)
San Francisco Bay Area
    Sonny Garcia (1998-2000)
    Charmain Giuliani (1998-2000)
    Laurie Jake (2000-2002)
    Richard G. Turner, Jr. (1998-2000)
    Tom Valva (1998-2000)
San Francisco Peninsula
    Mrs. Harvey D. Hinman (1998-2002)
    Joan Sanders (2000-2002)

Colorado

Colorado Springs
    Mrs. Terence Lilly (2000-2002)
    Mrs. Gene Moore (1998-2002)

Denver
    Mrs. William B. Harvey (2001)
    Mrs. Moses Taylor (1998, 1999, 2001)

Connecticut

    Page Dickey (co-founder)
    Penelope Maynard (co-founder)
    Jane Havemeyer (1995-2002)
    Sara M. Knight (1995-2002)
    Enid Munroe (1995-2002)
    Melissa Orme (1995-2002)
    Pam Peck (1995-2002)

Delaware

Wilmington
    Mrs. George P. Bissell, Jr. (1998-1999)
    Mrs. Sidney Scott, Jr. (1998-1999)

District of Columbia

    Mrs. John Macomber (1997-2001)
    Joanne Seale Wilson (1997-2000)

Florida

Jacksonville
    Carolyn Marsh Lindsay (1998)
Vero Beach
    Mrs. Thomas S. Morse (1998, 1999, 2001)
    Mrs. Bruce Roberts (2002)
    Mrs. Henry N. Tifft (1998, 1999, 2001)
    Mrs. Stephen Wyer (2002)

Georgia

Atlanta
    Virginia Almand (1998)
    George E.N. de Man (2000)
    Mrs. William Huger (1999-2000)

HAWAII

Honolulu
  Mrs. E. Chipman Higgins (1997-1998)

ILLINOIS

Barrington Hills
  Mrs. David C. Earl (2002)
Chicago
  Brooks Hartley-Leonard (2001-2002)
  Mrs. Charles E. Schroeder (1997-2000)
  Melissa Shennan (2001-2002)
Hinsdale
  Susan Beard (2000-2002)
Saint Charles, Naperville, & Rockford
  Mrs. David C. Earl (2000-2002)
Western Chicago
  Mrs. David C. Earl (2002)

INDIANA

Indianapolis
  Dr. Gilbert S. Daniels (1997, 1998)

LOUISIANA

New Orleans
  Ann Hobson Haack (1998-2001)

MAINE

York Harbor
  Mrs. Calvin Hosmer III (2001-2002)

MARYLAND

Annapolis
  Mrs. John A. Baldwin (2000-2001)
Baltimore
  Nan Paternotte (1997)
  Mrs. Frances Huber (1998)
  Mrs. Clark MacKenzie (1999)
  Mrs. Thomas G. McCausland (2000)
Chestertown
  Mrs. Adrian P. Reed (1999)

MASSACHUSETTS

Boston
  Diane Dalton (2001-2002)
  Mrs. Henry S. Streeter (1997-2000)
Chatham
  Mrs. Prescott Dunbar (2001-2002)
Nantucket
  Mrs. Coleman Burke (2002)
Osterville
  Mrs. David Cole (2001)
South Dartmouth
  Mrs. Helen Goddard (2002)
  Mrs. Thomas S. Morse (1998)
  Mrs. Robert G. Walker (1999-2000, 2002)
Worcester
  John W. Trexler (1998-1999, 2002)

MICHIGAN

Ann Arbor
  Marie Cochrane (1999)
  George Papadalos (1998)
Bloomfield Hills
  Virginia Berberian (2001)
  Norm Bodine (2001-2002)
  Lynne Clippert (2000)
  Mary Sue Ewing (2001-2002)
  Starr Foster (1998-1999)
  Lois Gamble (2000)
  Judy Knutson (2000-2002)
Grosse Pointe
  Mrs. John Ford (1997-1998)
  Mrs. Bragaw Vanderzee (1999)
Harbor Springs
  Mrs. John Ford (1998)
  Mrs. Frank Hightower (2000)

MINNESOTA

Minneapolis
  Mrs. John Winsor (1997)
  Mrs. Henry L. Sweatt (1997, 1999)

MISSOURI

Kansas City
  Mrs. George Powell III (1997)
  Mrs. Dwight Sutherland (1997)
Saint Louis
  Mrs. William H. T. Bush (1998, 2001)

New Hampshire

Monadnock
  Mrs. Story Wright (2000, 2002)
New London
  Mrs. Gusta Teach (2000)
Sea Coast
  Ms. Beth Hume (2002)
Squam Lake
  George Carr (2000)

New Jersey

Joan Kram (2001-2002)
Mrs. J. Duncan Pitney (1997-2002)

New York

Albany & Schenectady
  Joanne Lenden (1998-2001)
  Mrs. Henry Ferguson (1999-2000)
Cooperstown
  Mrs. H. Rodney Hartman (1998)
  Patricia Thorpe (1998, 2002)
Eastern Long Island
  Lalitte Scott (1996-2002)
Lake Champlain
  Mrs. James T. Flynn (1999-2002)
Mountain Top/Greene County
  Mr. & Mrs. Alan T. Wenzell (2002)
Oneonta
  Heleen Heyning (2002)
Saratoga Springs
  Mrs. Robert Ducas (2000, 2002)
  Mr. Bruce Solenski (2000, 2002)
Westchester, Putnam, Dutchess,
and Ulster Counties
  Page Dickey (co-founder)
  Penelope Maynard (co-founder)
  Jane Havemeyer (1995-2002)
  Sara M. Knight (1995-2002)
  Enid Munroe (1995-2002)
  Melissa Orme (1995-2002)

North Carolina

Asheville
  Hunter Stubbs (2001-2002)
Chapel Hill & Hillsborough
  Taimie Anderson (2001)
  Stepheny Houghtlin (2002)
Charlotte
  Mary Lindeman Wilson (2002)

Ohio

Akron
  Mrs. W. Stuver Parry (1998-1999)
Cincinnati
  Ms. Julie Mahlin (2002)
  Mrs. William R. Seaman (1999-2000)
Columbus
  Mrs. Roger Blair (2000)
  Mrs. Robert F. Hoffman, Jr. (2000)
  Karen K. Meyer (1999)
  Connie Page (1998)
Dayton
  Mrs. James Woodhull (1997-2002)
  Barbara Rion (1997-2002)
Granville
  Mrs. James Murr (2001)
  Janet Oberleissen (1998)

Oklahoma

Tulsa
  Breniss O'Neal (2002)

Oregon

Portland
  Pat Walker (2002)
Salem
  Bobbie Dolp (2002)

Pennsylvania

Philadelphia
Mrs. Frank H. Goodyear (1998-1999)
Mrs. Morris Lloyd, Jr. (2000-2002)
Mrs. Edward Starr III (1998-1999)
Pittsburgh
Bernita Buncher Duber (2000)
Mrs. Joshua C. Whetzel, Jr. (1998, 2000)
State College
Rae Chambers (2001-2002)
Dr. Richard Morgan (2000)
Swarthmore
Mrs. Benjamin H. Heckscher (2001)

South Carolina

Greenville
Mrs. Nelson B. Arrington (1997-1998, 2001)
Mrs. Samuel M. Beattie (1997-1998, 2001)

Tennessee

Chattanooga/Lookout Mountain
Mrs. Halbert Law (1999-2000, 2002)
Mrs. Edward Mitchell (2002)
Mrs. John Stout (1999-2000)
Memphis
Mrs. Albert M. Austin III (1999)
Barbara Keathley, ASLA (2001)
Mrs. David B. Martin (1999)
Nashville
Mr. Bob Brackman (2000-2002)
Mrs. Robert C. H. Mathews, Jr. (2000-2002)
Mr. Ben Page (2000-2002)

Texas

Austin
James DeGrey David (1998-1999)
Deborah Hornickel (2000, 2002)
Jennifer Staub Meyers (1998-2000)
Dr. Gordon L. White (1998-2000)
Dallas
Peter Schaar (2002)
Houston
Mrs. J. Taft Symonds (1998-2002)
Mrs. Sellers J. Thomas, Jr. (1998-2002)
Mrs. Joanne Wilson (2002)

Vermont

Lake Champlain
Mrs. James T. Flynn (1999-2001)
Manchester
Mrs. A. V. S. Olcott (1998-2002)

Virginia

Arlington
Tom Mannion (2002)
Charlottesville
Mrs. Mario di Valmarana (1997)
Middleburg
Mrs. Charles H. Seilheimer, Jr. (1997)
Richmond
Mrs. Robert A. Bristow II (1997)

Washington

Seattle
Barbara Flynn (1999)
Keith Geller (2002)
Mrs. Bruce McIvor (1999-2000)

West Virginia

Charleston
Mrs. Herbert Jones (1997)
Mr. & Mrs. James Rufus Thomas II (1998-2000, 2002)

Wisconsin

Lake Country
Mrs. Anthony Meyer (2000)
Mrs. Henry Quadracci (2000)
Milwaukee
Mrs. William Allis (1998, 1999, 2002)
Mrs. Robert W. Braeger (1998, 1999, 2002)

Foreword

. . . .

Now is the time to travel across America. This is the moment to celebrate America's gardens, those diverse, eclectic, even eccentric gardens that we call our own. Whether your trip is a Sunday afternoon or a summer-long vacation, go and see first hand what America's gardeners have wrought.

What will you find on your adventure? I can only refer to my experience over the last years as I have documented some of America's private gardens. But, I believe America is the most exciting place in the world to be a gardener today—at the beginning of this twenty-first century.

I have crisscrossed the country by car and plane, and I have been welcomed warmly at every garden gate. Spending time with gardeners has been one of my life's great privileges. American gardeners are generous. Seek them out. Ask questions about the hows and whys of their garden-making. Note the unique treatment of a potting shed, the length and graduated width of an axial line, or the trees that form an allée. Observe the plants that blanket arbors and pergolas or those that are woven into woodland carpets. Record the practical methods of fencing against the deer. You will be energized; you will be dizzy with ideas to bring back to enhance your own garden.

You will discover that no two gardens are alike, or even similar, and that each area of this country is rich in gardens. Some gardens, those with grand profiles, we have heard of through the gardening grapevine; others are unknown, unsung horticultural secrets, ripe for exploration.

Our gardeners take risks, push boundaries, make their own rules—and then break them with confidence. Sophisticated in their knowledge of gardening traditions, they interpret international design principles, mix them with American traditions, and add personal touches to create fresh, new gardens. And these gardeners love our land. Each has a deep concern for the fragility of our environment and the endangerment of specific plant species. While exotic plants of wild color and sky-reaching stature are sought with passionate zeal, the natives, too, are harbored and nourished.

So, put on your sun hat, grab a notebook and a camera, and slip behind the wheel of your car. Head off across America the Beautiful. Let these pages be your guide. And thank the Garden Conservancy for having the vision to make all this visiting possible.

Starr Ockenga
Garden Writer and Photographer
Livingston, New York

FROM THE CHAIRMAN

. . . .

The tenuous character of our times has all of us reevaluating our priorities. "Simpler" pleasures are again prevailing. We are finding solace and hope in our families, our friends, our homes—and, indeed, in nature. Our gardens, our homage to and stewardship of nature, must continue to be among these priorities. And it is the mission of the Garden Conservancy's successful Open Days Program to help lead the way.

Last year, thousands of appreciative visitors found fulfillment and enjoyment within the gates of our numerous and diverse gardens, welcomed by the talented garden owners who graciously and unstintingly shared the exquisite fruits of their talent and labor. We are also pleased that the Open Days Program has evolved into a unique forum for the valuable exchange of ideas and information among visitors and hosts, as well as a celebration of a mutual respect and love for nature and gardening.

The 2002 *Directory* represents the greatest expansion in the Open Days Program's eight-year history. This expansion stems from the selfless efforts of many dedicated individuals, foremost: the Garden Conservancy's generous founder, Frank Cabot; the invaluable Regional Representatives who so skillfully and diligently coordinate the activities within their respective regions and form the backbone of the organization; the glorious private and public gardens; and the indispensable staff. The revenues generated by the program are used to augment the critical preservation efforts of the Garden Conservancy and, in addition, support the endeavors of other nonprofit organizations designated by participating garden owners.

Our need to cultivate, create, protect, and enhance is a basic and powerful one. Gardening is true therapy. We revel in the unfurling leaves and swelling buds of spring, the magical burst of brilliant color in summer, the golden glow of autumn, and winter's bold defining of the garden's "bones." Assembling nature's bounties to create glorious, inspiring settings that exude joy and encourage serenity has become more of a necessity than ever. Through our links to the earth, we renew our faith, refresh our souls, revitalize our spirits, and replenish our sense of wonder.

Janet Meakin Poor
Chairman, Open Days Program

Welcome to the Open Days Program

· ·

The Garden Conservancy's Open Days Program is the only national program that invites the public to visit America's very best private gardens. Modeled after similar programs abroad, including England's popular *Yellow Book* and Australia's Open Garden Scheme, the Open Days Program began in 1995 with 110 gardens in New York and Connecticut. Since then the program has grown to include more than 450 private gardens nationwide in 2002.

The Garden Conservancy's Open Days Program is designed to introduce the public to gardens, provide easy access to outstanding examples of design and horticultural practice, and prove that extraordinary American gardens are still being created. By inviting people into America's private gardens, the Garden Conservancy emphasizes the importance of pre-serving fine gardens for future generations and building a constituency of committed individuals willing to act on behalf of gardens.

How is the Program Organized?

Each Open Day area has at least one Regional Representative who recruits private gardens in his or her area and assists with the promotion and advancement of the program. Over the years, this roster of volunteers has grown to include more than 150 men and women. You'll find a list of Regional Representatives in the Acknowledgments, beginning on page 9.

If you are interested in learning more about the organization of Open Days throughout the United States, please contact The Garden Conservancy, Open Days Program, P.O. Box 219, Cold Spring, NY 10516. You can call us at (845) 265-5384, fax us at (845) 265-5392, or email us at opendays@gardenconservancy.org.

Admission

A $5 admission fee is collected at each garden. Cash may be paid at the gate or visitors may purchase admission coupons through the Garden Conservancy at a discounted price (see the order form on the last page of the *Directory*). By purchasing a copy of the *Directory*, you receive a free coupon offer, good for entrance to one private garden. Admission coupons remain valid from year to year. Proceeds from the Open Days Program support the national preservation work of the Garden Conservancy, as well as local not-for-profit organizations designated by individual garden hosts.

Admission to the public gardens listed in the *Directory* is set by each public garden. Please see the individual listings for their admission fees. Open Days coupons may not be used at public gardens.

How to Use the Directory

. . . .

To make the *Directory* user-friendly, to minimize page flipping, and to maximize its use as a travel planner, we've arranged the garden listings as follows:

- Alphabetically by state (see the table of contents for page numbers)
- Within each state, chronologically by Open Day
- For each Open Day, by county, then alphabetically by town
- Within each town, alphabetically by garden name.

At the end of each chapter, after the private gardens, there is a listing and description of public gardens in that state to add to your garden-visiting itinerary, organized alphabetically by county and town.

Also, on page 25, you will find the Open Days by Date index, which lists every Open Day chronologically and every garden across the country that is open that day. That's followed by the Open Days by Location index, which lists all the gardens alphabetically by state, then by county, then town, with the dates they are open.

To help you locate a specific garden, we've also indexed them by garden name in the back of the *Directory*. For quick reference, at the beginning of each state chapter there is a listing of the Open Days in that state.

An area map is provided for each Open Day, with the locations of the towns that will have gardens open that day. Where appropriate, you will find a note under a particular Open Day referring to other nearby gardens just across state lines that are also open on that day.

The Garden Entries

Each private garden listing includes the name of the garden and its location, the garden host's description of his or her garden, the hours the garden is open, and driving instructions. The instructions assume you will be traveling from the nearest major highway. Please travel with a local map. For information about wheelchair accessibility and the difficulty of the terrain, please contact the Open Days Program.

Public garden listings include the garden name, street address, a telephone number and website, a brief description of the garden, hours of operation, admission fee, and driving instructions. We encourage you to contact the site directly for more information.

The information that appears in this *Directory* was, to the best of our knowledge, correct at the time the *Directory* went to press. Since its publication, however, some changes may have occurred. When possible, the Garden Conservancy will notify you of changes in advance; otherwise, please take note of the schedule changes posted at admissions tables or check the Garden Conservancy's website prior to your visit at www.gardenconservancy.org.

Etiquette in the Garden

The Garden Conservancy's Open Days Program is made possible only through our Garden Hosts hospitality. We ask you to please reward their generosity by following these simple guidelines:

- Do not pick any plant or remove any part of a plant from the garden. If you require help identifying a plant, please ask the Garden Host.
- Do not leave litter in the garden.
- Stay on the paths.
- Follow any signs or directions provided at the garden.
- Respect the privacy of the owners.
- Please leave all pets at home.
- Children must be supervised at all times.
- Park your car so that others can enter and leave the parking area.
- Please remember to check with the owner before taking photographs; tripods are not permitted.
- Respect the dates and times each garden is open as listed in the *Directory. Do not contact the garden host directly.* Please contact the Open Days Program office at (845) 265-5384 to pursue special visiting arrangements or to bring a group to a garden.

Our Counterparts Around the Globe

While the Garden Conservancy's Open Days Program is the only national garden-visiting program of its kind in the United States, it joins similar programs around the world encouraging people to garden and visits gardens every day.

England's National Gardens Scheme

Certainly the most well known is England's National Gardens Scheme and its publication *Gardens of England and Wales Open for Charity*, more familiarly known as the Yellow Book. The National Gardens Scheme, a registered charity, was founded in 1927. Around 3,500 gardens of quality and interest will open for the Scheme 2002. Proceeds from the entry fees support ten nursing, caring, and educational charities. For more information you may contact Miss Beryl Evans, Chief Executive, Hatchlands Park, East Clandon, Guildford, Surrey GU4 7RT ENGLAND, 44-0-1483-211535, fax 44-0-1483-211537, www.ngs.org.uk.

Australia's Open Garden Scheme

Originating in 1987 to promote the knowledge and pleasures of gardens and gardening across Australia, the Open Garden Scheme began with 63 gardens in one state. Today the program includes more than 700 private gardens in all states of Australia and welcomes more than one quarter of a million visitors per year. For more information contact: Neil Robertson, National Executive Officer, Australia's Open Garden Scheme, Westport, New Gisborne, Victoria 3438 AUSTRALIA, 61-3-5428-4557, fax 61-3-5428-4558, www.opengarden.abc.net.au.

The information presented in the *Open Days Directory* is collected by Garden Conservancy staff and Regional Representatives around the country. We rely on Garden Hosts to provide information for their listings. Information for public garden listings is likewise gathered from the site's staff. The Garden Conservancy is not responsible for the accuracy of the information published within these listings.

Nominations to include gardens in *The Garden Conservancy's Open Days Directory* are accepted. Please call or write for a survey form and nomination criteria. For these and any other inquiries regarding the *Open Days Directory*, please contact:

> Open Days Program
> The Garden Conservancy
> P.O. Box 219
> Cold Spring, NY 10516
> Telephone: (845) 265-5384
> FAX: (845) 265-5392
> Email: opendays@gardenconservancy.org

WHAT IS THE GARDEN CONSERVANCY?

. . . .

The Garden Conservancy is a national nonprofit organization founded in 1989 to preserve exceptional American gardens for the public's education and enjoyment.

In 1988, Ruth Bancroft's garden, a magnificent collection of cacti, succulents, and native California plants, first captivated the imagination of Frank Cabot. His keen interest in the prospects for the future of this important garden prompted swift action, and history was made on two fronts: he established the Garden Conservancy, the first national organization dedicated to the preservation of exceptional gardens; and the Garden Conservancy obtained the first conservation easement for a garden, thereby ensuring its preservation. Not long after legal custodianship was guaranteed for the Bancroft Garden, the Conservancy began mapping out the steps involved in transforming this garden, which had thrived under the constant care and vision of its creator, into a vital public facility. A dedicated group of area residents and garden lovers was enlisted to help oversee the preservation and operation of the garden and, with the continued assistance and support of the Conservancy, a strong master plan was developed. Today, Ruth Bancroft, at 92, can be found working in her garden every day. Meanwhile, the Ruth Bancroft Garden supports a full calendar of tours and educational outreach programs that welcome the public throughout the season.

Anyone who gardens knows the fragile nature of the gardener's creation: subject to the ravages of climate, weeds, erosion, pests, and other problems, even the most carefully designed gardens can vanish within just a few years when untended. When we lose an exceptional garden we lose its beauty, but we also lose the lessons it can teach us about the gardener's era—its values, horticultural science, and aesthetic standards. We conserve gardens because they are a vital part of our nation's cultural heritage.

Over the past twelve years, the Garden Conservancy has worked in partnership with garden owners, community groups, and public agencies to advocate the preservation of hundreds of gardens.

Saving a fine garden requires expertise, funding, and community support—resources the Garden Conservancy brings to bear in preserving great American gardens and opening them to the public. Our work is greatly facilitated by a network of committed volunteers—from our Open Days Garden Hosts and Regional Representatives to neighborhood advocates to the many professionals who offer invaluable advice and expertise. But perhaps the Conservancy's most important preservation resource is a growing membership consisting of thousands of individuals, corporations, and foundations nationwide who provide generous financial support. We thank all who have made the success of the Garden Conservancy possible.

Antonia F. Adezio
President, The Garden Conservancy

THE PRESERVATION PROJECTS
OF THE GARDEN CONSERVANCY

· ·

The Garden Conservancy takes a lead role in the preservation of a garden by helping it make the transition from private to nonprofit ownership and guiding the development of a sound financial and organizational plan. In addition to their regular visiting schedule, the Preservation Projects of the Garden Conservancy are all open this year through our Open Days Program (see page numbers below) and include:

> The Chase Garden, Orting, WA *(page 475)*
> The Fells at the John Hay National Wildlife Refuge, Newbury, NH *(page 258)*
> The John P. Humes Japanese Stroll Garden, Mill Neck, NY *(page 346)*
> Peckerwood Garden, Hempstead, TX *(page 456)*
> Rocky Hills—The Gardens of Henriette Suhr, Mount Kisco, NY *(page 296)*
> The Ruth Bancroft Garden, Walnut Creek, CA *(page 116)*

Among the many other gardens the Conservancy has assisted through its various preservation programs are:

Abkhazi Garden, Victoria, BC, Canada

Ashintully, Tyringham, MA

Aullwood Garden, Dayton, OH *(page 385)*

Bellamy-Ferriday Garden, Bethlehem, CT *(page 165)*

Blithewold, Bristol, RI

Bonnet House, Fort Lauderdale, FL

Cohen-Bray House and Garden, Oakland, CA

Dumbarton Oaks Park, Washington, DC *(page 175)*

Eudora Welty Garden, Jackson, MS

Gibraltar, Wilmington, DE

Hakone Gardens, Saratoga, CA

Harland Hand Garden, El Cerrito, CA *(page 110)*

Historic Deepwood, Salem, OR *(page 405)*

Historic Morven, Princeton, NJ *(page 279)*

The James Rose Center, Ridgewood, NJ *(page 276)*

Justin Smith Morrill Homestead, Strafford, VT

The Madoo Conservancy, Sagaponack, NY *(page 352)*

Makani Gardens, Ha'iku, HI

Maudslay State Park, Newburyport, MA

McKee Botanical Garden, Vero Beach, FL *(page 182)*

The McLaughlin Garden & Horticultural Center, South Paris, ME *(page 216)*

Mukai Farm and Garden, Vashon Island, WA

Palm Cottage Gardens, Gotha, FL

Pavilion Gardens at the University of Virginia, Charlottesville, VA

Sonnenberg Gardens, Canandaigua, NY

Springside Landscape Restoration, Poughkeepsie, NY *(page 344)*

Val Verde, Montecito, CA

Van Vleck House & Gardens, Montclair, NJ *(page 278)*

Yew Dell Farm, Crestwood, KY

Please note: If the garden is located in a state that is hosting Open Days events, you will find its description and visiting information in that chapter.

The Preservation Assistance Center

· ·

The Garden Conservancy's Newest Preservation Program

The Preservation Assistance Center was established in 1999 to offer short-term assistance to the growing number of garden enthusiasts interested in preserving gardens in their communities. From lending Garden Conservancy endorsement to helping garden advocates better assess the feasibility of their project to rethinking the strategic plan of a garden already in the public domain, the Preservation Assistance Center is making a difference. A Garden Survey form, part of a packet about the Conservancy's preservation work, is now available by calling the Preservation Projects Department at (845) 265-9396, or by logging on to our web site, www.gardenconservancy.org.

Following are some of the gardens the Preservation Assistance Center has helped.

WILLIAM NOBLE

Abkhazi Garden, Victoria, British Columbia

Known as "the garden that love built," this wonderful example of the Pacific Northwest style, created by war-torn lovers Nicholas and Peggy Abkhazi, was threatened when developers decided it was the perfect spot for 24 townhouses. Local activists rallied and, with the support of a provincial land trust and the Garden Conservancy's endorsement, quickly raised funds to buy the garden. Acknowledging the need to open Abkhazi Garden only weeks after its purchase, the Preservation Assistance Center outlined steps needed to adapt the garden to public access.

MICK HALES

Sonnenberg Gardens, Canandaigua, New York

This eclectic collection of Victorian-era gardens and Lord & Burnham conservatory complex in the Finger Lakes region of Upstate New York has enjoyed public support since the 1960s, when citizens of Canandaigua first began a campaign to restore this historic property. The task of restoring and maintaining such an inventory of gardens was beginning to prove unwieldy. Following a visit and review by Preservation Assistance Center specialists, Sonnenberg has recast its preservation plan to concentrate on improvements to the gardens' most notable features, such as the intricate Italian parterre shown here.

LAURA PALMER

Historic Deepwood, Salem, Oregon

Designed in 1929 by Elizabeth Lord and Edith Schryver, the gardens of Historic Deepwood are noted for luxurious plant combinations and relaxed formality. Deepwood is now owned and operated as a city park, and while its future as a public resource seems secure, the garden's aura of privacy, integrity of style, and need for expert plant maintenance present unique challenges. Recently, the Friends of Deepwood called on the Preservation Assistance Center. Director of Preservation Projects, Bill Noble, met with the group and looks forward to the opportunity to help them find horticultural expertise and a sympathetic approach to the restoration of this garden gem.

What's New at the Garden Conservancy

· ·

The Garden Conservancy is pleased to offer a range of new programs and tools designed to help the garden enthusiast become more closely connected with preservation efforts taking place across the country.

NEW CAREER OPPORTUNITY

One of the biggest challenges facing garden preservation projects across the country is finding appropriately skilled staff. **The Marco Polo Stufano Garden Conservancy Fellowship** was established to introduce experienced horticulturists and landscape designers to the rewards of this new field, and to identify and place such talent in a nine-month assignment at one of our Preservation Projects. Over the past few years, fellows have made lasting contributions at Peckerwood Garden in Hempstead, Texas; The Fells in Newbury, New Hampshire; and The Chase Garden in Orting, Washington. Applications for the 2003 fellowship will be available in September 2002.

NEW BOOK SERIES

Is there a garden in your life? Is it in danger of being lost—to developers, dwindling care, or lack of proper leadership? *Taking a Garden Public: First in a Series of Issues and Case Studies in Garden Preservation*, is designed to introduce you to the steps involved in saving America's gardens—steps that you can take to determine whether it is feasible for your project to become a public garden and, if so, how to proceed. Experts in the field of garden preservation have contributed more than 100 pages of advice and a wide selection of case studies of Conservancy Preservation Projects tell the stories of successful grassroots efforts. The second volume of *Taking a Garden Public* will illuminate the ins and outs of fund raising.

Taking a Garden Public is in loose-leaf format and is available at $20 (plus shipping and handling). Look for sample chapters and a printable order form on our web site or contact the Preservation Projects Department of the Garden Conservancy at (845) 265-9396.

NEW A VIDEO PRESENTATION

Preserving an American Legacy: An Introduction to the Garden Conservancy is a fifteen-minute video about how the Garden Conservancy came to be and where we are going, as told by the garden conservators helping to fulfill our mission. Since the video's premiere at our 10th Anniversary Celebration in Charleston, South Carolina, Conservancy members have asked how they could share *Preserving an American Legacy* with their own garden clubs and organizations. We are now pleased to offer a presentation kit that includes the video, an introductory script, and Garden Conservancy materials, all for a special price of $15.

For information on these programs or any of our Preservation Projects, please contact the Garden Conservancy at (845) 265-2029 or log on to our web site at www.gardenconservancy.org.

Open Days by Date

Saturday, March 23

ARIZONA

Maricopa County

    Glendale   Virginia Glasco's Garden, 10 a.m. to 4 p.m.

    Phoenix   Desert Oasis, 10 a.m. to 4 p.m.

                    Glendale Family Garden, 10 a.m. to 4 p.m.

Saturday, April 13

CALIFORNIA

San Mateo County

    Atherton   Suzanne's Garden, 10 a.m. to 4 p.m.

NORTH CAROLINA

Orange County

    Chapel Hill   Boyd-Martin Garden, 10 a.m. to 4 p.m.

                    The Robertson Garden, 10 a.m. to 4 p.m.

                    Tenney Farmhouse Garden—Elizabeth Pringle, 10 a.m. to 4 p.m.

TEXAS

Harris County

    Houston   1411 North Boulevard, 10 a.m. to 2 p.m.

                    Benton Residence, 2 p.m. to 6 p.m.

                    Brennan Residence, 10 a.m. to 2 p.m.

                    Casey Residence, 10 a.m. to 2 p.m.

                    Corn-Parker Garden, 2 p.m. to 6 p.m.

                    DeGeurin Garden, 2 p.m. to 6 p.m.

                    Kainer Residence, 10 a.m. to 2 p.m.

                    Garden of Karen & John Kelsey, 2 p.m. to 6 p.m.

                    Pinson Residence, 2 p.m. to 6 p.m.

                    Simon Residence, 10 a.m. to 2 p.m.

Waller County

    Hempstead   Peckerwood Garden, 9 a.m. to 1 p.m. *(public garden)*

Sunday, April 14

TEXAS

Harris County

    Carmine   Jacomini 5J Farm, 10 a.m. to 2 p.m.

    Houston   Rocking "S" Ranch & Garden, 10 a.m. to 2 p.m.

    Washington   Peaceable Kingdom Farm, 10 a.m. to 2 p.m.

Waller County

    Hempstead   Peckerwood Garden, 9 a.m. to 1 p.m. *(public garden)*

Saturday, April 20

CALIFORNIA
Marin County

Corte Madera	Keohane Garden, 10 a.m. to 4 p.m.
Ross	Tom Jackson & Kathy Grant's Garden, 10 a.m. to 4 p.m.
	Waltz Gardens—Juliet & Ashford Wood, 10 a.m. to 4 p.m.
Tiburon	Thompson Brooks, 10 a.m. to 4 p.m.
	Varda's Garden, 10 a.m. to 4 p.m.

FLORIDA
Indian River County

Vero Beach	Garden of Patricia & Robert Hubner, 10 a.m. to 4 p.m.
	Isolay, 10 a.m. to 4 p.m.
	Mangrove Gardens at Carwill Oaks, 10 a.m. to 2 p.m.
	Sandy's Garden, 10 a.m. to 4 p.m.
	Dr. & Mrs. William King Stubbs Garden, 10 a.m. to 4 p.m.

NEW YORK
Westchester County

Lewisboro	The White Garden, 10 a.m. to 4 p.m.

Sunday, April 21

OHIO
Hamilton County

Cincinnati	Judy Brandenburg's Garden, 10 a.m. to 4 p.m.
	The Robertson-Conway Garden, 10 a.m. to 4 p.m.
	Nancy & Ed Rosenthal's Garden, 10 a.m. to 4 p.m.

Saturday, April 27

OREGON
Washington County

Aurora	Huntington Garden at the Case House, 2 p.m. to 6 p.m.
Saint Paul	Cecil & Molly Smith Garden (*public garden*)
Sherwood	Bella Madrona, 2 p.m. to 6 p.m.
	Cavender Garden, 10 a.m. to 4 p.m.
Tualatin	Kaiser Permanente's Tualatin Poison Prevention Garden, 10 a.m. to 2 p.m. (*public garden*)

Sunday, April 28

CALIFORNIA
Los Angeles County

Beverly Hills	Goldstine Garden, 10 a.m. to 4 p.m.
	The House of Seven Gardens, 10 a.m. to 2 p.m.
Los Angeles	The Allee Garden, 10 a.m. to 4 p.m.
	Ronnie Allumbaugh Gardens at Getty House, the Official Residence of the Mayor of Los Angeles, 9:30 a.m. to 3 p.m.

Ruth Bracken Garden, 2 p.m. to 6 p.m.
Bungalow Estrada Gardens, 10 a.m. to 4 p.m.
El Chaparro California Native Garden, 10 a.m. to 2 p.m.
East Meets West, 10 a.m. to 2 p.m.
Helene Henderson Garden, 10 a.m. to 4 p.m.
Horton Garden, 10 a.m. to 2 p.m.
Kew West, 10 a.m. to 2 p.m.
Ozeta House, 10 a.m. to 4 p.m.
Sandra Taylor Garden, 2 p.m. to 6 p.m.
Yusts' Garden, 10 a.m. to 4 p.m.

NEW YORK
Putnam County
   Cold Spring   Stonecrop Gardens, 10 a.m. to 4 p.m. *(public garden)*
Westchester County
   Bedford Hills   Phillis Warden, 10 a.m. to 4 p.m.

Saturday, May 4
ALABAMA
Jefferson County
   Birmingham   Butrus Garden, 1 p.m. to 5 p.m.
Crowe Garden, 1 p.m. to 5 p.m.
HIS Garden, 1 p.m. to 5 p.m.
Philip Morris, 1 p.m. to 5 p.m.
The Gardens of Mountain Brook Park, 1 p.m. to 5 p.m.
Southern Living Magazine's Experimental/Demonstration
  Garden, 1 p.m. to 5 p.m.
Louise & John Wrinkle, 1 p.m. to 5 p.m.

NEW YORK
Suffolk County
   East Hampton   Irving & Dianne Benson's Garden, 10 a.m. to 2 p.m.
Mrs. Donald Bruckmann, 10 a.m. to 2 p.m.
Margaret Kerr & Robert Richenburg, 10 a.m. to 2 p.m.

Sunday, May 5
ALABAMA
Jefferson County
   Birmingham   Butrus Garden, 1 p.m. to 5 p.m.
Crowe Garden, 1 p.m. to 5 p.m.
HIS Garden, 1 p.m. to 5 p.m.
Philip Morris, 1 p.m. to 5 p.m.
The Gardens of Mountain Brook Park, 1 p.m. to 5 p.m.
Southern Living Magazine's Experimental/Demonstration `
Garden, 1 p.m. to 5 p.m.
Louise & John Wrinkle, 1 p.m. to 5 p.m.

CALIFORNIA
San Francisco County
    San Francisco   Kay Hamilton Estey, 10 a.m. to 4 p.m.
                          The Garden at 537 Chenery Street, 10 a.m. to 4 p.m.
                          Matt Gil Sculpture Garden, 10 a.m. to 4 p.m.
                          Mary's Rock Garden, 10 a.m. to 4 p.m.

NEW YORK
Westchester County
    Mount Kisco   Judy & Michael Steinhardt, 10 a.m. to 4 p.m.

PENNSYLVANIA
Centre County
    Boalsburg   Darlene & Paul's Gardens, noon to 4 p.m.
    Centre Hall   Rhoneymeade Arboretum, Sculpture Garden & Labyrinth,
                          12:30 p.m. to 4:30 p.m. *(public garden)*
    State College   Deno's Garden, 10 a.m. to 4 p.m.
                          Gabriel & Jill Welsch Garden, 10 a.m. to 4 p.m.

Saturday, May 11

CALIFORNIA
San Mateo County
    Atherton   Susan Fox & Jim Gafke, 10 a.m. to 2 p.m.
                          Peggy & Harvey Hinman, 10 a.m. to 2 p.m.
                          Gene & Chuck Pratt, 10 a.m. to 2 p.m.
    Menlo Park   The Woodruff Garden, 10 a.m. to 4 p.m.

NEW JERSEY
Bergen County
    Englewood   Peggy & Walter Jones, 10 a.m. to 4 p.m.
                          Mercer & Peter O'Hara, 10 a.m. to 4 p.m.

Essex County
    Livingston   Howard P. Fertig, 10 a.m. to 4 p.m.
    Short Hills   Winter's Garden, 10 a.m. to 4 p.m.
Hunterdon County
    Califon   Frog Pond Farm, 10 a.m. to 4 p.m.
    Stanton   Kallas Garden, 10 a.m. to 4 p.m.
Morris County
    Morris Plains   Watnong Gardens, 10 a.m. to 4 p.m.

NEW YORK
Dutchess County
    Amenia   Broccoli Hall—Maxine Paetro, 10 a.m. to 4 p.m.

OREGON
Clark County
    Vancouver   Kaiser Permanente's Salmon Creek Poison Prevention
                          Garden, 10 a.m. to 2 p.m. *(public garden)*

Saturday, May 18

DISTRICT OF COLUMBIA

Washington	The Dice/Sumner Garden, 10 a.m. to 4 p.m.
	Elizabeth's Haven, 10 a.m. to 2 p.m.
	Harriet & Eric Fraunfelter Garden, 10 a.m. to 2 p.m.
	Jane MacLeish's Garden, 10 a.m. to 2 p.m.
	Philip L. McClain Garden, 10 a.m. to 2 p.m.
	The Corinna Posner Garden, 10 a.m. to 4 p.m.
	The Gardens of Charles Read & Eileen White Read, 10 a.m. to 4 p.m.

MASSACHUSETTS

Essex County

Hamilton	Stormfield, 10 a.m. to 4 p.m.
Manchester	Appletrees, 10 a.m. to 4 p.m.
	Southgate Garden II, 10 a.m. to 4 p.m.

NORTH CAROLINA

Orange County

Hillsborough	Chatwood Garden, 10 a.m. to 4 p.m.
	Fairmount, 10 a.m. to 4 p.m.
	Pleasant Green Farm, 10 a.m. to 4 p.m.

Wake County

Apex	The Gardens At Rosecroft, 10 a.m. to 4 p.m.

OKLAHOMA

Tulsa County

Tulsa	The Gardens of Bonnie & Joe Klein, 10 a.m. to 4 p.m.
	The Gardens of Breniss & Daniel O'Neal, 10 a.m. to 4 p.m.
	The Burke Reynolds Garden, 10 a.m. to 4 p.m.

TENNESSEE

Hamilton County

Lookout	The Garden of Connie & John Higgason, 10 a.m. to 4 p.m.
Mountain	Reilly Garden, 10 a.m. to 2 p.m.
	Yates Garden, 10 a.m. to 4 p.m.

Marion County

Chattanooga	The Garden at Skillet Gap, 10 a.m. to 2 p.m.
	Reflection Riding Arboretum & Botanical Garden, 10 a.m. to 5 p.m. *(public garden)*

TEXAS

Dallas County

Dallas	Tony Cerbone's Exotic Dallas Garden, 10 a.m. to 4 p.m.
	Michael Cheever's Garden, 10 a.m. to 4 p.m.
	Einspruch Garden, 10 a.m. to 4 p.m.
	Judy Fender's Garden, 10 a.m. to 4 p.m.
	Rolston/Cohn Garden, 10 a.m. to 4 p.m.
	Peter & Julie Schaar, 10 a.m. to 4 p.m.
	Southbrook Gardens, 10 a.m. to 4 p.m.
	Terry Garden, 10 a.m. to 4 p.m.

Sunday, May 19

CALIFORNIA
Alameda County

Berkeley	Garden of Julie Chen & David Turner, 10 a.m. to 4 p.m.
	Il Giardino Fatato, 2 p.m. to 6 p.m.
	Masala Gardens, 10 a.m. to 4 p.m.
	Maybeck Cottage—Garden of Roger Raiche & David McCrory, 2 p.m. to 6 p.m.
El Cerrito	Harland Hand Garden, 10 a.m. to 4 p.m.
	Bob & Kay Riddell's Garden, noon to 4 p.m.

Contra Costa County

Walnut Creek	Ruth Bancroft Garden, 1 p.m. to 5 p.m. *(public garden)*

Los Angeles County

Arcadia	Merrill & Donivee Nash, 10 a.m. to 4 p.m.
Brentwood	Rosen Landscape, 2 p.m. to 6 p.m.
La Canada	Nakaki Landscape, 10 a.m. to 2 p.m.
Pasadena	Sally & Harlan Bixby Garden, 10 a.m. to 4 p.m.
	La Folie, 10 a.m. to 2 p.m.
Sierra Madre	Louise & Paul Neiby, 10 a.m. to 4 p.m.

CONNECTICUT
Fairfield County

Redding	Highstead Arboretum, guided walks at 10 a.m., noon, and 2 p.m.
Riverside	Susan Cohen, noon to 4 p.m.
Wilton	Jane Bescherer, 10 a.m. to 4 p.m.

Hartford County

Bloomfield	Dr. Ben Thaw, 10 a.m. to 2 p.m.

Middlesex County

Middetown	Shoyoan Teien—The Freeman Family Garden, 10 a.m. to noon *(public garden)*

New Haven County

Branford	Nickolas Nickou, guided tour at 10 a.m.
Guilford	Mary Anne & Dale Athanas, 10 a.m. to 4 p.m.
	G & G Garden, 10 a.m. to 4 p.m.

NEW YORK
Orange County

Mountainville	Cedar House—Garden of Margaret Johns & Peter Stern, 10 a.m. to 6 p.m.

Putnam County

Cold Spring	Stonecrop Gardens, 10 a.m. to 4 p.m. *(public garden)*

Westchester County

Armonk	Cobamong Pond, 10 a.m. to 4 p.m.
Bedford	Penelope & John Maynard, 10 a.m. to 6 p.m.
Bedford Hills	Phillis Warden, 10 a.m. to 4 p.m.
Hastings-on-Hudson	Midge & Dave Riggs, 10 a.m. to 4 p.m.
Ossining	Teatown Lake Reservation, 10 a.m. to 2 p.m. *(public garden)*

TENNESSEE
Davidson County

Nashville	Fletcher-Chapman Garden, 1 p.m. to 4 p.m.
	Follin Garden, 1 p.m. to 4 p.m.
	Martin Garden, 1 p.m. to 4 p.m.
	Simons Garden, 1 p.m. to 4 p.m.

Saturday, May 25
MASSACHUSETTS
Worcester County

Boylston	Maple Grove, 10 a.m. to 6 p.m.
Grafton	Mapel & Libuda Garden, 10 a.m. to 4 p.m.
North Grafton	Brigham Hill Farm, 10 a.m. to 6 p.m.

NEW YORK
Westchester County

Bedford	Lulu Farm, 10 a.m. to 4 p.m.
Mount Kisco	Rocky Hills—The Gardens of Henriette Suhr, 2 p.m. to 6 p.m.

Saturday, June 1
NEW YORK
Westchester County

Irvington	Mary Morrisett, 10 a.m. to 2 p.m.
Ossining	Paul & Sarah Matlock, 10 a.m. to 4 p.m.
Croton-on-Hudson	Gardens of Dianna & Howard Smith, 10 a.m. to 4 p.m.

WASHINGTON
King County

Seattle	Noel Angell & Emory Bundy, 10 a.m. to 3 p.m.
	Geller-Irvine Garden, 10 a.m. to 3 p.m.
	Carol Henderson, 10 a.m. to 3 p.m.
	Carol Isaacson-Rawn, 10 a.m. to 3 p.m.
	Carlo & Lalie Scandiuzzi, 10 a.m. to 3 p.m.

Sunday, June 2
CONNECTICUT
Fairfield County

Redding	Highstead Arboretum, guided walks at 10 a.m., noon and 2 p.m.

MASSACHUSETTS
Barnstable County

East Sandwich	Shalisan East, 10 a.m. to 4 p.m.
Sandwich	Whitesway, 10 a.m. to 4 p.m.

PENNSYLVANIA
Montgomery County

Gladwyne	Fernside Cottage, 11 a.m. to 4 p.m.
	Mr. & Mrs. John W. Powell II, 11 a.m. to 4 p.m.
Gulph Mills	Gulph Mills, 11 a.m. to 4 p.m.
Haverford	Baruch Garden, 11 a.m. to 4 p.m.
Wayne	Frogsleap—Mr. & Mrs. John D. Borne, 11 a.m. to 4 p.m.
Wynnewood	Gillean's Wood, 11 a.m. to 4 p.m.

Friday, June 7

NEW YORK
Saratoga County

Saratoga Springs	Brackett House Gardens, 11 a.m. to 4 p.m.
	Georgiana Ducas Garden, 11 a.m. to 4 p.m.
	Bruce Solenski, 11 a.m. to 4 p.m.

Saturday, June 8

CONNECTICUT
Litchfield County

Falls Village	Martha & Robert Rubin, noon to 4 p.m.
West Cornwall	Julia & John Scott, noon to 4 p.m.

MASSACHUSETTS
Middlesex County

Brookline	Lucy Aptekar & Gerry Leader, 10 a.m. to 4 p.m.
Cambridge	165 Brattle Street, 10 a.m. to 4 p.m.

Norfolk County

Dedham	The Lilacs, 10 a.m. to 4 p.m.
	Dan & Polly Pierce, 10 a.m. to 2 p.m.
Dover	Kevin J. Doyle & Michael Radoslovich—Cairn Croft, 10 a.m. to 4 p.m.
Wellesley	Hunnewell Garden, 10 a.m. to 4 p.m.
Westwood	Joseph Hudak & Kenn Stephens, 10 a.m. to 4 p.m.

NEW JERSEY
Essex County

Short Hills	Ursula & Andreas Enderlin, 10 a.m. to 4 p.m.
	George Sternlieb, 10 a.m. to 2 p.m.
	Winter's Garden, 10 a.m. to 4 p.m.

Summit County

Summit	Abbey's Acre, 10 a.m. to 4 p.m.
	Allen Garden, 10 a.m. to 4 p.m.

VERMONT
Bennington County
Dorset	Westerly, 10 a.m. to 4 p.m.
Manchester	Glebelands, 10 a.m. to 2 p.m.
	White Tree Farm, 10 a.m. to 4 p.m.
Manchester Center	Edwards' Garden, 10 a.m. to 4 p.m.
	Joan & Lee Fegelman's Garden, 10 a.m. to 4 p.m.
Manchester Village	The Sunken Garden, 10 a.m. to 2 p.m.

Sunday, June 9
CONNECTICUT
Tolland County
Coventry	David & Julia Hayes, 10 a.m. to 4 p.m.

Windham County
Canterbury	Westminster Gardens—Eleanor B. Cote & Adrian P. Hart, noon to 4 p.m.

NEW JERSEY
Essex County
Montclair	Emer Featherstone's Garden, 10 a.m. to 4 p.m.

Hunterdon County
Califon	Frog Pond Farm, 10 a.m. to 4 p.m.

Monmouth County
Rumson	Beliza Ann Furman, 10 a.m. to 4 p.m.

Morris County
Chatham	Jack Lagos, 10 a.m. to 4 p.m.
Morris Plains	Watnong Gardens, 10 a.m. to 4 p.m.

Somerset County
Far Hills	The Hay Honey Farm, 10 a.m. to 4 p.m.

NEW YORK
Columbia County
Copake Falls	Margaret Roach, 10 a.m. to 4 p.m.

Rockland County
Palisades	The Captain John House Garden, 10 a.m. to 4 p.m.
	Judy Tomkins Gardens, 10 a.m. to 4 p.m.

Westchester County
Bedford	Ann Catchpole-Howell, 10 a.m. to 4 p.m.

PENNSYLVANIA
Centre County
Centre Hall	Rhoneymeade Arboretum, Sculpture Garden & Labyrinth, 12:30 p.m. to 4:30 p.m. (*public garden*)
State College	Deno's Garden, 10 a.m. to 4 p.m.
	Olgi Draper's Garden, 10 a.m. to 4 p.m.
	Rae's Garden, 10 a.m. to 4 p.m.
	Gabriel & Jill Welsch Garden, 10 a.m. to 4 p.m.

Saturday, June 15

CONNECTICUT
Hartford County

East Windsor Hill	Pat & George Porter, 10 a.m. to 4 p.m.
Manchester	Diana & Roy Behlke's Gardens, 10 a.m. to 4 p.m.
	Lindland's Garden, 10 a.m. to 4 p.m.
	Watersong, 10 a.m. to 4 p.m.

ILLINOIS
Cook County

Evanston	Zerega Garden, 10 a.m. to 4 p.m.
Winnetka	Beauty without Boundaries, 10 a.m. to 4 p.m.
	Liz & Bob Crowe, 10 a.m. to 4 p.m.

Lake County

Highland Park	Cathy & Gene Rothert Garden, 10 a.m. to 4 p.m.

MARYLAND
Arlington County

Bethesda	The Jacobs Garden, 10 a.m. to 4 p.m.

NEW JERSEY
Monmouth County

Rumson	Linden Hill, 10 a.m. to 4 p.m.

NEW YORK
Dutchess County

Amenia	Broccoli Hall—Maxine Paetro, 10 a.m. to 4 p.m.

Westchester County

Katonah	Cross River House, 10 a.m. to 2 p.m.
	Roxana Robinson—Willow Green Farm, 10 a.m. to 4 p.m.
North Salem	Artemis Farm—Carol & Jesse Goldberg, 10 a.m. to 4 p.m.
	Jane & Bill Bird, 10 a.m. to 4 p.m.
	Lucy Hart Close, 10 a.m. to 4 p.m.
	Page Dickey & Francis Schell, 10 a.m. to 4 p.m.
	Keeler Hill Farm, 10 a.m. to 4 p.m.

OHIO
Montgomery County

Dayton	The Larkins Garden, 10 a.m. to 4 p.m.
	The Patterson Homestead, 10 a.m. to 4 p.m.
	Gloria B. Richardson Garden, 10 a.m. to 4 p.m.
	Ellie Shulman's Rose Terrace, 10 a.m. to 4 p.m.
	Wessex, 10 a.m. to 4 p.m.

OREGON
Marion County

Salem	Garry Oaks, 10 a.m. to 4 p.m.
	Lord and Schryver, 10 a.m. to 4 p.m.
	Villa Bacca Collina Estate Garden, 10 a.m. to 4 p.m.

VIRGINIA
Arlington County
   Arlington   Burnet-Deutsch Garden, 10 a.m. to 4 p.m.
                       Cozy Shack, 10 a.m. to 4 p.m.
                       Garden of William A. Grillo, 10 a.m. to 4 p.m.
                       Garden of Linda Scott & Mary Dufour, 10 a.m. to 4 p.m.
Fairfax County
   Fairfax   Dorothy & Art Phinney, 10 a.m. to 4 p.m.
   McLean   Hilltop Cottage, 10 a.m. to 4 p.m.
                       Ridder Garden, 10 a.m. to 4 p.m.

Sunday, June 16

CONNECTICUT
New London County
   Old Lyme   Ruth Perry, 10 a.m. to 2 p.m.
   Stonington   Mr. & Mrs. James L. Coker, 10 a.m. to 2 p.m.
                       Merry Meeting Farm, 10 a.m. to 4 p.m.
                       Mr. & Mrs. Juan O'Callahan, 10 a.m. to 2 p.m.
                       Mrs. Frederic C. Paffard, Jr., 10 a.m. to 2 p.m.

NEW YORK
Putnam County
   Cold Spring   Stonecrop Gardens, 10 a.m. to 4 p.m. *(public garden)*

OREGON
Multnomah County
   Portland   Russell Archer Garden, 10 a.m. to 2 p.m.
                       June Collins' Garden, 2 p.m. to 6 p.m.
                       Sara Mauritz Garden, 2 p.m. to 6 p.m.
                       The Jane Platt Garden, 10 a.m. to 4 p.m.
                       The Schatz/Spendelow Garden, 10 a.m. to 4 p.m.

Saturday, June 22

COLORADO
El Paso County
   Colorado Springs   Crossland Gardens, 10 a.m. to 4 p.m.
                       Dorothy's Garden, 10 a.m. to 3 p.m.
                       El Mardon, 10 a.m. to 4 p.m.
                       The Macon Rose Garden, 10 a.m. to 4 p.m.
                       Rose & Dave Robbins, 10 a.m. to 4 p.m.

ILLINOIS
Ogle County
   Oregon   Heuer's Hosta Garden, 10 a.m. to 4 p.m.
Winnebago County
   Chana   The Garden of Kurt & Ellen Laurent—Ancient Oaks,
                       10 a.m. to 4 p.m.

Rockford	The Garden of Pauline & Paul Clausen, 10 a.m. to 4 p.m.
	The Ewaldz Garden, 10 a.m. to 4 p.m.
	Gunn Garden, 10 a.m. to 4 p.m.
	River View Garden, 10 a.m. to 2 p.m.
	Sheila's English Cottage Garden, 10 a.m. to 4 p.m.
Stillman Valley	Bittersweet Acres, 10 a.m. to 4 p.m.

MASSACHUSETTS
Essex County

Manchester	Pauline & Joe Runkle, 10 a.m. to 4 p.m.
Manchester-by-the-Sea	The Garden at 9 Friend Street, 10 a.m. to 4 p.m.
Marblehead	Grey Gulls—Larry Simpson, 10 a.m. to 4 p.m.
	The Parable—Ellen Cool's Garden, 10 a.m. to 4 p.m.
Swampscott	Wilkinson Garden—Blythswood, 10 a.m. to 4 p.m.

NEW JERSEY
Bergen County

Maywood	Dail & Tony's Garden, 10 a.m. to 4 p.m.
Ridgewood	The Handley Garden, 10 a.m. to 4 p.m.
	The Zusy/Ortiz Garden, 10 a.m. to 4 p.m.
River Edge	Anthony "Bud" & Virginia Korteweg, 10 a.m. to 4 p.m.
River Vale	Cupid's Garden—Audrey Linstrom Maihack, 10 a.m. to 4 p.m.
Tenafly	Richard & Ronnie Klein, 10 a.m. to 4 p.m.
	Linda Singer, 10 a.m. to 4 p.m.
Wyckoff	Tall Trees—Garden of Janet Schulz, 10 a.m. to 4 p.m.

Middlesex County

Colonia	Babbling Brook, 10 a.m. to 2 p.m.

NEW YORK
Columbia County

Craryville	Susan Anthony & Richard Galef, 10 a.m. to 4 p.m.
	Marion & Irwin Kaplan—White Birch Farm, 10 a.m. to 4 p.m.
East Taghkanic	Grant & Alice Platt, 10 a.m. to 4 p.m.

Suffolk County

East Hampton	Irving & Dianne Benson's Garden, 10 a.m. to 2 p.m.
	Margaret Kerr & Robert Richenburg, 10 a.m. to 2 p.m.
	LongHouse Reserve, 10 a.m. to 2 p.m. *(public garden)*
Southampton	Brodsky Garden, 10 a.m. to 2 p.m.
	Kim White & Kurt Wolfgruber—Secret Garden, 10 a.m. to 4 p.m.

Sunday, June 23
CONNECTICUT
Fairfield County

Fairfield	Nancy & Tom Grant, 10 a.m. to 4 p.m.
	On the Harbor, 10 a.m. to 4 p.m.
Greenwich	Mr. & Mrs. Philip McCaull, noon to 4 p.m.
Redding	Gardens at Horsefeathers, noon to 4 p.m
Westport	Susan Lloyd, 10 a.m. to 4 p.m.
West Redding	Hughes-Sonnenfroh Gardens, 10 a.m. to 4 p.m.

Litchfield County

Bridgewater	Maywood Gardens, 10 a.m. to 2 p.m.
Litchfield	Dan & Joyce Lake, 2 p.m. to 6 p.m.
	Mr. & Mrs. David Stoner, noon to 4 p.m.
Roxbury	Martine & Richard Copeland, 10 a.m. to 4 p.m.
Washington	Linda Allard, 10 a.m. to 4 p.m.
	Charles Raskob Robinson & Barbara Paul Robinson, noon to 4 p.m.
	George Schoellkopf, 2 p.m. to 6 p.m.
Washington Depot	Gael Hammer, 10 a.m. to 4 p.m.

ILLINOIS
Cook County

Evanston	A Lakeside Garden, 10 a.m. to 4 p.m.
Wilmette	Craig Bergmann & James Grigsby, 10 a.m. to 4 p.m.
Winnetka	Helen & Dick Thomas, 10 a.m. to 4 p.m.

Lake County

Lake Bluff	Crabtree Farm, 10 a.m. to 4 p.m.

NEW YORK
Columbia County

Ancram	Adams-Westlake, 10 a.m. to 4 p.m.
Ancramdale	Cricket Hill Farm, 10 a.m. to 4 p.m.

Thursday, June 27
MASSACHUSETTS
Nantucket County

Nantucket	Beach Plum, 10 a.m. to 4 p.m.
	Blueberry Hill, 10 a.m. to 4 p.m.
	Dr. & Mrs. John W. Espy, 10 a.m. to 4 p.m.
	Inishfree—Coleman & Susan Burke, 10 a.m. to 4 p.m.
	Susan & Karl Ottison, 10 a.m. to 2 p.m.
	Eleanor & Arthur Reade, 10 a.m. to 4 p.m.
	Constance Umberger, 10 a.m. to 2 p.m.
Siasconset	Hedged About, 10 a.m. to 4 p.m.

Saturday, June 29

CONNECTICUT

Litchfield County

Falls Village	Bunny Williams, 10 a.m. to 4 p.m.
Kent	Skiff Mountain Farm, 2 p.m. to 6 p.m.
Sharon	Lee Link, noon to 4 p.m.
	Plum Creek Farm, 2 p.m. to 6 p.m.
West Cornwall	Jurutungo Viejo, 10 a.m. to 4 p.m.
	Michael Trapp, 10 a.m. to 4 p.m.

ILLINOIS

Cook County

Barrington	The Gardens at Wandering Tree—The "Glorée & Tryumphant" Railway Garden, 10 a.m. to 4 p.m.
Barrington Hills	Peggy & Eric Olsen, 10 a.m. to 4 p.m.
Hinsdale	The Gardens of Kellie & Barry O'Brien, 10 a.m. to 4 p.m.
Oak Brook	Susan & Ken Beard, 10 a.m. to 4 p.m.
	Tom Keck, 10 a.m. to 4 p.m.

Du Page County

Burr Ridge	Suzy & Sam Stout, 10 a.m. to 4 p.m.

MAINE

York County

Cape Neddick	Bochert Garden, 10 a.m. to 4 p.m.
	Home of Jonathan King & Jim Stott, 10 a.m. to 4 p.m.
	Sea Meadows, 10 a.m. to 4 p.m.
	Thurston Garden, 10 a.m. to 4 p.m.
York Harbor	Mr. & Mrs. H.V. Richard, 10 a.m. to 4 p.m.
	Victoria & Christopher Vasillopulos, 10 a.m. to 4 p.m.

MASSACHUSETTS

Bristol County

Dartmouth	Jan & Toby Hall, 10 a.m. to 4 p.m.
Fairhaven	Allen C. Haskell Farm, 10 a.m. to 4 p.m.
New Bedford	Allen C. Haskell Horticulturists, Inc., 10 a.m. to 4 p.m.
North Dartmouth	Fran & Clint Levin's Garden, 10 a.m. to 2 p.m.
South Dartmouth	Betsy & Greer McBratney, 10 a.m. to 4 p.m.
	Sea Thrift—Apponagansett Watch, 10 a.m. to 4 p.m.

NEW YORK

Otsego County

Cooperstown	Fynmere, 2 p.m. to 6 p.m.
	Heathcote, 2 p.m. to 6 p.m.
	Frank Kubis, 10 a.m. to 2 p.m.
	Garden of Loris & Jim Orthwein, 10 a.m. to 4 p.m.
	Garden of J. Mason & Rhea Reynolds, 2 p.m. to 6 p.m.
	Riverbrink—Garden of Gail Reid Freehafer & Dr. John Freehafer, 10 a.m. to 2 p.m.

PENNSYLVANIA
Bucks County

Doylestown	Fordhook Farm of the W. Atlee Burpee Co.,
	10 a.m. to 4 p.m.
New Hope	Jericho Mountain Orchards, 10 a.m. to 4 p.m.
Silverdale	Carol A. Pierce, 2 p.m. to 6 p.m.
Wrightstown	Hortulus Farm, 10 a.m. to 4 p.m.

WEST VIRGINA
Kanawha County

Charleston	Laughinghouse—the Giltinans' Garden, 10 a.m. to 4 p.m.
	Garden of Bill Mills & Thomas Gillooly, 10 a.m. to 4 p.m.
	Governor's Mansion, 10 a.m. to 4 p.m.
	Dr. & Mrs. George E. Toma, 10 a.m. to 4 p.m.
	Zeb & Sara Sue Wright's Garden, 10 a.m. to 4 p.m.
Malden	Kanawha Salines—Garden of Mrs. Turner Ratrie,
	10 a.m. to 4 p.m.

Sunday, June 30

NEW YORK
Dutchess County

Amenia	Jade Hill—Paul Arcario & Don Walker, 10 a.m. to 4 p.m.
Millbrook	Far A-Field, 10 a.m. to 4 p.m.
	Belinda & Stephen Kaye, 10 a.m. to 4 p.m.
	Hamilton & Edith Kean, noon to 4 p.m

Otsego County

Andes	Cynthia & Charles Bonnes, 10 a.m. to 4 p.m.
	Henry & Judy Jobmann, 10 a.m. to 4 p.m.
Oneonta	Freckelton Beal Gardens, 10 a.m. to 4 p.m.
Roscoe	Berry Brook Farm—Mermer Blakeslee & Eric Hamerstrom,
	10 a.m. to 4 p.m.

Saturday, July 6

ILLINOIS
Kane County

Saint Charles	Charles & Patricia Bell, 10 a.m. to 4 p.m.
	Jon & Missy Butcher, 10 a.m. to 4 p.m.
Wayne	Dove Cottage, 10 a.m. to 4 p.m.

PENNSYLVANIA
Centre County

Centre Hall	Rhoneymeade Arboretum, Sculpture Garden & Labyrinth,
	12:30 p.m. to 4:30 p.m. *(public garden)*
State College	Olgi Draper's Garden, 10 a.m. to 4 p.m.
	Rae's Garden, 10 a.m. to 4 p.m.

Sunday, July 7

CONNECTICUT

Litchfield County

Colebrook — Marveen & Michael Pakalik, 10 a.m. to 4 p.m.

Steepleview Gardens—Kathy Loomis, 10 a.m. to 4 p.m.

New Haven County

Meriden — George Trecina, 1 p.m. to 5 p.m.

OHIO

Hamilton County

Cincinnati — Beechwood Gardens, 10 a.m. to 4 p.m.

Judy Brandenburg's Garden, 10 a.m. to 4 p.m.

The Gardens of Brenda & John Demetriou,
    10 a.m. to 4 p.m.

Amy & John Duke's Daylily Gardens, 10 a.m. to 4 p.m.

J. Louis & Beth Karp's Garden, 10 a.m. to 2 p.m.

Julie Mahlin's Garden, 10 a.m. to 4 p.m.

Nancy & Ed Rosenthal's Garden, 10 a.m. to 4 p.m.

Hamilton — Joan Day's Garden, 10 a.m. to 4 p.m.

Indian Hill — Kurtz's Garden, 10 a.m. to 4 p.m.

Saturday, July 13

NEW HAMPSHIRE

Rockingham County

New Castle — Prince-Bergh Garden, 10 a.m. to 4 p.m.

Reynolds Garden, 10 a.m. to 4 p.m.

North Hampton — Bell-Manning House Garden, 10 a.m. to 4 p.m.

Shulman Garden, 10 a.m. to 4 p.m.

Portsmouth — Jameson & Priscilla French, 10 a.m. to 4 p.m.

Barbara Renner's Garden, 10 a.m. to 4 p.m.

NEW YORK

Dutchess County

Salt Point — Ely Garden, 10 a.m. to 4 p.m.

Stanfordville — Ellen & Eric Petersen, 10 a.m. to 4 p.m.

Zibby & Jim Tozer, 10 a.m. to 2 p.m.

Essex County

Keene Valley — Horse Farm Vegetable Garden, 2 p.m. to 6 p.m.

Woodland Gardens of Mr. & Mrs. Wynant D. Vanderpoel,
    2 p.m. to 6 p.m.

Westport — Kenjockety—Phelan-Shapiro, 2 p.m. to 6 p.m.

Putnam County

Cold Spring — Stonecrop Gardens, 10 a.m. to 4 p.m. (*public garden*)

Garrison — Manitoga, 10 a.m. to 2 p.m. (*public garden*)

Ross Gardens, 10 a.m. to 4 p.m.

Suffolk County

Cutchogue　　　　Manfred & Roberta Lee, 10 a.m. to 4 p.m.

　　　　　　　　　Alice & Charles Levien's Garden, 10 a.m. to 2 p.m.

East Hampton　　Ina Garten, noon to 4 p.m.

　　　　　　　　　Bob & Mimi Schwarz, noon to 4 p.m.

Mattituck　　　　Maurice Isaac & Ellen Coster Isaac, 10 a.m. to 4 p.m.

　　　　　　　　　Dennis Schrader & Bill Smith, 10 a.m. to 4 p.m.

NORTH CAROLINA

Buncombe County

Asheville　　　　Albemarle Inn, 10 a.m. to 4 p.m.

　　　　　　　　　John & Curry Jamison, 10 a.m. to 4 p.m.

　　　　　　　　　Kenilworth Gardens, 10 a.m. to 4 p.m.

　　　　　　　　　The Lake Garden, 10 a.m. to 4 p.m.

VERMONT

Bennington County

Dorset　　　　　　Westerly, 10 a.m. to 4 p.m.

Manchester　　　Glebelands, 10 a.m. to 2 p.m.

　　　　　　　　　White Tree Farm, 10 a.m. to 4 p.m.

Manchester Center　Edwards' Garden, 10 a.m. to 4 p.m.

　　　　　　　　　Joan & Lee Fegelman's Garden, 10 a.m. to 4 p.m.

Manchester Village　The Sunken Garden, 10 a.m. to 2 p.m.

Sunday, July 14

CONNECTICUT

Fairfield County

Newtown　　　　Sydney Eddison, noon to 4 p.m.

Windham County

Canterbury　　　Westminster Gardens—Eleanor B. Cote & Adrian P. Hart,

　　　　　　　　　noon to 4 p.m.

ILLINOIS

Cook County

Evanston　　　　A Walled Retreat, 10 a.m. to 4 p.m.

Glenview　　　　Windmill, 10 a.m. to 4 p.m.

Lake County

Lake Forest　　　A Garden on Old Meadow Lane, 9 a.m. to 4 p.m.

　　　　　　　　　Prairie Doc, 10 a.m. to 4 p.m.

MICHIGAN

Oakland County

Beverly Hills　　Toni & Joe Grinnan, 10 a.m. to 4 p.m.

　　　　　　　　　Suzanne's Garden—Suzanne Krueger & Dave Rider,

　　　　　　　　　　10 a.m. to 4 p.m.

　　　　　　　　　Denise & Bruce Wayne, 10 a.m. to 4 p.m.

Bloomfield Hills　Aerie Gardens, 10 a.m. to 4 p.m.

　　　　　　　　　Judy's Garden, 10 a.m. to 4 p.m.

　　　　　　　　　Larry & Sandy Mackle, 10 a.m. to 4 p.m.

Southfield　　　　Tom & Beth McMahon, 10 a.m. to 4 p.m.

NEW HAMPSHIRE
Rockingham County
   Hampton Falls   Carole & Bert Chanasyk, 10 a.m. to 4 p.m.
   Rye   Jim & Ellen Labrie's Seaside Garden, 10 a.m. to 4 p.m.
   Rye Beach   Sal Allocco's Garden, 10 a.m. to 2 p.m.
       Hochschwender Garden, 10 a.m. to 4 p.m.

NEW YORK
Columbia County
   Millerton   Helen Bodian's Garden, noon to 4 p.m.
Dutchess County
   Rhinebeck   Cedar Heights Orchard—William & Arvia Morris,
         10 a.m. to 4 p.m.
       Amy Goldman, 10 a.m. to 2 p.m.

Sunday, July 21
CONNECTICUT
Fairfield County
   Weston   Birgit Rasmussen Diforio, 10 a.m. to 4 p.m.
   West Redding   Hughes-Sonnenfroh Gardens, 10 a.m. to 4 p.m.
Hartford County
   Avon   Green Dreams—Garden of Jan Nickel, 10 a.m. to 4 p.m.
   Manchester   Watersong, 10 a.m. to 4 p.m.
   Simsbury   The Garden of Betty & Dick Holden, 10 a.m. to 4 p.m.
Litchfield County
   New Hartford   Nancy Zimbalist, noon to 4 p.m.
   Washington   Georgia Middlebrook, 2 p.m. to 6 p.m.
   Washington Depot   Gael Hammer, 10 a.m. to 4 p.m.

NEW YORK
Dutchess County
   Salt Point   Ely Garden, 10 a.m. to 4 p.m.
Westchester County
   Bedford Hills   Laura Fisher—Wildflower Farm, 10 a.m. to 2 p.m.
       Phillis Warden, 10 a.m. to 4 p.m.
   Cortlandt Manor   Vivian & Ed Merrin, 10 a.m. to 2 p.m.
   North Salem   Jane & Bill Bird, 10 a.m. to 4 p.m.

OREGON
Multnomah County
   Portland   Jeffrey Bale, 10 a.m. to 4 p.m.
       The Berry Botanical Garden, dawn to dusk (*public garden*)
       Catswalk Cottage—JoAnn & Roger Thomas,
        2 p.m. to 6 p.m.
       Nancy Goldman Garden, 10 a.m. to 4 p.m.
       Goodman-Schultz Garden, 10 a.m. to 2 p.m.
       Hogan/Sanderson, 10 a.m. to 4 p.m.

WISCONSIN
Milwaukee County
Bayside — Coffman-Morrison Gardens, 10 a.m. to 4 p.m.
River Hills — David Knox's Garden, 10 a.m. to 4 p.m.
The LaBahn Garden, 2 p.m. to 6 p.m.
Russell Garden, 10 a.m. to 4 p.m.

Saturday, July 27
ILLINOIS
Du Page County
Naperville — Flora, the Flower Fairy's Eclectic Garden, 10 a.m. to 4 p.m.
Kay & John Stephens, 10 a.m. to 4 p.m.

Will County
Naperville — Ron & Linda Henry, 10 a.m. to 4 p.m.

NEW HAMPSHIRE
Cheshire County
Dublin — Robertson Garden, 10 a.m. to 2 p.m.
Tiadnock, 10 a.m. to 2 p.m.
Harrisville — Sky Hill, 10 a.m. to 4 p.m.
Hillsborough County
Peterborough — Gardens of Stan & Cheri Fry, 10 a.m. to 4 p.m.

NEW YORK
Greene County
Ashland — Frog Pond Gardens, 10:30 a.m. to 4 p.m.
East Jewett — Daisy & Tom Wenzell's Valley Farm, 10:30 a.m. to 4 p.m.
Haines Falls — Dunn's Moss Garden, 10:30 a.m. to 4 p.m.
Santa Cruz—Skip & Anne Pratt's Garden, 10:30 a.m. to 4 p.m.
Tannersville — McCaffrey Garden, 10:30 a.m. to 4 p.m.
Minnehaha, 10:30 a.m. to 4 p.m.
Tony & Rosalyn Smith's Bittersweet Cottage, 10:30 a.m. to 4 p.m.

Sunday, July 28
ILLINOIS
Du Page County
West Chicago — The Ball Horticultural Trial Garden, 10 a.m. to 4 p.m.
Lake County
Highland Park — Magic Garden, 10 a.m. to 2 p.m.
Lake Forest — Camp Rosemary, 10 a.m. to 4 p.m.
The Gardens of John & Carol Walter, 10 a.m. to 4 p.m.
Mettawa — Mettawa Manor, 10 a.m. to 4 p.m.

PENNSYLVANIA
Centre County
    Boalsburg   Darlene & Paul's Gardens, noon to 4 p.m.
    State College   Gabriel & Jill Welsch Garden, 10 a.m. to 4 p.m.

Sunday, August 4
OREGON
Multonomah County
    Portland   The Berry Botanic Garden, dawn to dusk *(public garden)*
Washington County
    Sherwood   Bella Madrona, 2 p.m. to 6 p.m.
                             Cavender Garden, 10 a.m. to 4 p.m.

Sunday, August 11
CONNECTICUT
Fairfield County
    Redding   Highstead Arboretum, guided walks at 10 a.m.,
                                noon and 2 p.m.
Hartford County
    Plantsville   The Kaminski Garden, 10 a.m. to 4 p.m.
New Haven County
    Meriden   George Trecina, 1 p.m. to 5 p.m.

Sunday, September 8
CONNECTICUT
Fairfield County
    Cos Cob   Florence & John Boogaerts—Mianus Dawn,
                                1 p.m. to 5 p.m.
    Ridgefield   Garden of Ideas, 10 a.m. to 4 p.m.
Hartford County
    Avon   Green Dreams—Garden of Jan Nickel, 10 a.m. to 4 p.m.
    Farmington   Kate Emery & Steve Silk, noon to 4 p.m.
New Haven County
    Meriden   George Trecina, 1 p.m. to 5 p.m.

NEW YORK
Columbia County
    Ancram   Adams-Westlake, 10 a.m. to 4 p.m.
    Ancramdale   Cricket Hill Farm, 10 a.m. to 4 p.m.
Putnam County
    Patterson   The Farmstead Garden, noon to 4 p.m.
Westchester County
    Lewisboro   The White Garden, 10 a.m. to 4 p.m.
    North Salem   Dick Button—Ice Pond Farm, 10 a.m. to 4 p.m.
    Waccabuc   James & Susan Henry, 10 a.m. to 5 p.m.

Saturday, September 14
NORTH CAROLINA
Mecklenburg County

Charlotte	The Cooper Gardens, 10 a.m. to 4 p.m.
	Duncan Garden, 10 a.m. to 4 p.m.
	Hampton Gardens, 10 a.m. to 4 p.m.
	Minor Manor, 10 a.m. to 4 p.m.
	Gardens on Valleybrook, 10 a.m. to 4 p.m.
	UNC-Charlotte Botanical Gardens, 10 a.m. to 3 p.m. *(public garden)*
	Garden of Genie & Jim White, 10 a.m. to 4 p.m.
	The Garden of Lindie Wilson, 10 a.m. to 4 p.m.

Sunday, September 15
NEW YORK
Putnam County

Cold Spring	Stonecrop Gardens, 10 a.m. to 4 p.m. *(public garden)*

Rockland County

Palisades	The Captain John House Garden, 10 a.m. to 4 p.m.
	Judy Tomkins Gardens, 10 a.m. to 4 p.m.

NORTH CAROLINA
Mecklenburg County

Charlotte	The Cooper Gardens, 10 a.m. to 4 p.m.
	Duncan Garden, 10 a.m. to 4 p.m.
	Hampton Gardens, 10 a.m. to 4 p.m.
	Minor Manor, 10 a.m. to 4 p.m.
	Gardens on Valleybrook, 10 a.m. to 4 p.m.
	UNC-Charlotte Botanical Gardens, 10 a.m. to 3 p.m. *(public garden)*
	Garden of Genie & Jim White, 10 a.m. to 4 p.m.
	The Garden of Lindie Wilson, 10 a.m. to 4 p.m.

Saturday, September 28
TEXAS
Travis County

Austin	James deGrey David & Gary Peese, 10 a.m. to 6 p.m.
	Deborah Hornickel, 10 a.m. to 6 p.m.
	Old Ziller House Garden, 10 a.m. to 6 p.m.
	Possumhaw Hollow—The Spencer-Martinez Garden, 10 a.m. to 6 p.m.
	Bill & Anna Prothro, 10 a.m. to 6 p.m.
	Webber Garden, 10 a.m. to 6 p.m.

Sunday, October 13
NEW YORK
Westchester County

Armonk	Cobamong Pond, 10 a.m. to 4 p.m.

Open Days by Location

. . . .

ALABAMA
Jefferson County
  Birmingham
  Butrus Garden, May 4 & 5
  Crowe Garden, May 4 & 5
  HIS Garden, May 4 & 5
  Philip Morris, May 4 & 5
  The Gardens of Mountain Brook Park, May 4 & 5
  Southern Living Magazine's Experimental/Demonstration Garden, May 4 & 5
  Louise & John Wrinkle, May 4 & 5

ARIZONA
Maricopa County
  Glendale
  Virginia Glasco's Garden, March 23
  Phoenix
  Desert Oasis, March 23
  Glendale Family Garden, March 23

CALIFORNIA
Alameda County
  Berkeley
  Garden of Julie Chen & David Turner, May 19
  Il Giardino Fatato, May 19
  Masala Gardens, May 19
  Maybeck Cottage—Garden of Roger Raiche & David McCrory, May 19
  El Cerrito
  Harland Hand Garden, May 19
  Bob & Kay Riddell's Garden, May 19
Contra Costa County
  Walnut Creek
  Ruth Bancroft Garden, May 19 *(public garden)*
Los Angeles County
  Arcadia
  Merrill & Donivee Nash, May 19
  Beverly Hills
  Goldstine Garden, April 28
  The House of Seven Gardens, April 28

La Canada
Nakaki Landscape, May 19
Los Angeles
The Allee Garden, April 28
Ronnie Allumbaugh Gardens at Getty House, the Official Residence of the
    Mayor of Los Angeles, April 28
Ruth Bracken Garden, April 28
Bungalow Estrada Gardens, April 28
East Meets West, April 28
El Chaparro California Native Garden, April 28
Helene Henderson Garden, April 28
Horton Garden, April 28
Kew West, April 28
Ozeta House, April 28
Rosen Landscape, May 19
Sandra Taylor Garden, April 28
Yusts' Garden, April 28
Pasadena
Sally & Harlan Bixby Garden, May 19
La Folie, May 19
Sierra Madre
Louise & Paul Neiby, May 19
Marin County
Corte Madera
Keohane Garden, April 20
Ross
Tom Jackson & Kathy Grant's Garden, April 20
Waltz Gardens—Juliet & Ashford Wood, April 20
Tiburon
Thompson Brooks, April 20
Varda's Garden, April 20
San Francisco County
San Francisco
The Garden at 537 Chenery Street, May 5
Kay Hamilton Estey, May 5
Matt Gil Sculpture Garden, May 5
Mary's Rock Garden, May 5
San Mateo County
Atherton
Susan Fox & Jim Gafke, May 11
Peggy & Harvey Hinman, May 11
Gene & Chuck Pratt, May 11
Suzanne's Garden, April 13
Menlo Park
The Woodruff Garden, May 11

COLORADO
El Paso County
    Colorado Springs
    Crossland Gardens, June 22
    Dorothy's Garden, June 22
    El Mardon, June 22
    The Macon Rose Garden, June 22
    Rose & Dave Robbins, June 22

CONNECTICUT
Fairfield County
    Cos Cob
    Florence & John Boogaerts—Mianus Dawn, September 8
    Fairfield
    Nancy & Tom Grant, June 23
    On the Harbor, June 23
    Greenwich
    Mr. & Mrs. Philip McCaull, June 23
    Newtown
    Sydney Eddison, July 14
    Redding
    Highstead Arboretum, May 19, June 2, August 11
    Gardens at Horsefeathers, June 23
    Ridgefield
    Garden of Ideas, September 8
    Riverside
    Susan Cohen, May 19
    Westport
    Susan Lloyd, June 23
    Weston
    Birgit Rasmussen Diforio, July 21
    West Redding
    Hughes-Sonnenfroh Gardens, June 23, July 21
    Wilton
    Jane Bescherer, May 19
Hartford County
    Avon
    Green Dreams—Garden of Jan Nickel, July 21, September 8
    Bloomfield
    Dr. Ben Thaw, May 19
    East Windsor Hill
    Pat & George Porter, June 15
    Farmington
    Kate Emery & Steve Silk, September 8

Manchester
Diana & Roy Behlke's Gardens, June 15
Lindland's Garden, June 15
Watersong, June 15, July 21
Plantsville
The Kaminski Garden, August 11
Simsbury
The Garden of Betty & Dick Holden, July 21
Litchfield County
Bridgewater
Maywood Gardens, June 23
Colebrook
Marveen & Michael Pakalik, July 7
Steepleview Gardens—Kathy Loomis, July 7
Falls Village
Martha & Robert Rubin, June 8
Bunny Williams, June 29
Kent
Skiff Mountain Farm, June 29
Litchfield
Dan & Joyce Lake, June 23
Mr. & Mrs. David Stoner, June 23
New Hartford
Nancy Zimbalist, July 21
Roxbury
Martine & Richard Copeland, June 23
Sharon
Lee Link, June 29
Plum Creek Farm, June 29
Washington
Linda Allard, June 23
Georgia Middlebrook, July 21
Charles Raskob Robinson & Barbara Paul Robinson, June 23
George Schoellkopf, June 23
Washington Depot
Gael Hammer, June 23, July 21
West Cornwall
Jurutungo Viejo, June 29
Julia & John Scott, June 8
Michael Trapp, June 29
Middlesex County
Middletown
Shoyoan Teien—The Freeman Family Garden, May 19 *(public garden)*
New Haven County
Branford
Nickolas Nickou, May 19

Guilford
Mary Anne & Dale Athanas, May 19
G & G Garden, May 19
Meriden
George Trecina, July 7, August 11, September 8
New London County
Old Lyme
Ruth Perry, June 16
Stonington
Mr. & Mrs. James L. Coker, June 16
Merry Meeting Farm, June 16
Mr. & Mrs. Juan O'Callahan, June 16
Mrs. Frederic C. Paffard, Jr., June 16
Tolland County
Coventry
David & Julia Hayes, June 9
Windham County
Canterbury
Westminster Gardens—Eleanor B. Cote & Adrian P. Hart, June 9, July 14

DISTRICT OF COLUMBIA
District of Columbia
Washington
The Dice/Sumner Garden, May 18
Elizabeth's Haven, May 18
Harriet & Eric Fraunfelter Garden, May 18
Jane MacLeish's Garden, May 18
Philip L. McClain Garden, May 18
The Corinna Posner Garden, May 18
The Gardens of Charles Read & Eileen White Read, May 18

FLORIDA
Indian River County
Vero Beach
Garden of Patricia & Robert Hubner, April 20
Isolay, April 20
Mangrove Gardens at Carwill Oaks, April 20
Sandy's Garden, April 20
The Dr. & Mrs. William King Stubbs Garden, April 20

ILLINOIS
Cook County
Barrington
The Gardens at Wandering Tree—The "Glorée & Tryumphant" Garden Railway,
    June 29

Barrington Hills
Peggy & Eric Olsen, June 29
Evanston
A Lakeside Garden, June 23
A Walled Retreat, July 14
Zerega Garden, June 15
Glenview
Windmill, July 14
Hinsdale
The Gardens of Kellie & Barry O'Brien, June 29
Oak Brook
Susan & Ken Beard, June 29
Tom Keck, June 29
Wilmette
Craig Bergmann & James Grigsby, June 23
Winnetka
Beauty without Boundaries, June 15
Liz & Bob Crowe, June 15
Helen & Dick Thomas, June 23
Du Page County
Burr Ridge
Suzy & Sam Stout, June 29
Naperville
Flora, the Flower Fairy's Eclectic Garden, July 27
Kay & John Stephens, July 27
West Chicago
The Ball Horticultural Trial Garden, July 28
Kane County
Saint Charles
Charles & Patricia Bell, July 6
Jon & Missy Butcher, July 6
Wayne
Dove Cottage, July 6
Lake County
Highland Park
Magic Garden, July 28
Cathy & Gene Rothert Garden, June 15
Lake Bluff
Crabtree Farm, June 23
Lake Forest
Camp Rosemary, July 28
A Garden on Old Meadow Lane, July 14
Prairie Doc, July 14
The Gardens of John & Carol Walter, July 28
Mettawa
Mettawa Manor, July 28

Ogle County
  Oregon
  Heuer's Hosta Garden, June 22
Will County
  Naperville
  Ron & Linda Henry, July 27
Winnebago County
  Chana
  The Garden of Kurt & Ellen Laurent—Ancient Oaks, June 22
  Rockford
  The Garden of Pauline & Paul Clausen, June 22
  The Ewaldz Garden, June 22
  Gunn Garden, June 22
  River View Garden, June 22
  Sheila's English Cottage Garden, June 22
  Stillman Valley
  Bittersweet Acres, June 22

MAINE
York County
  Cape Neddick
  Bochert Garden, June 29
  Home of Jonathan King & Jim Stott, June 29
  Sea Meadows, June 29
  Thurston Garden, June 29
  York Harbor
  Mr. & Mrs. H.V. Richard, June 29
  Victoria & Christopher Vasillopulos, June 29

MARYLAND
Arlington County
  Bethesda
  The Jacobs Garden, June 15

MASSACHUSETTS
Barnstable County
  East Sandwich
  Shalisan East, June 2
  Sandwich
  Whitesway, June 2
Bristol County
  Dartmouth
  Jan & Toby Hall, June 29
  Fairhaven
  Allen C. Haskell Farm, June 29

New Bedford
Allen C. Haskell Horticulturists, Inc., June 29
North Dartmouth
Fran & Clint Levin's Garden, June 29
South Dartmouth
Betsy & Greer McBratney, June 29
Sea Thrift—Apponagansett Watch, June 29
Essex County
Hamilton
Stormfield, May 18
Manchester
Appletrees, May 18
Pauline & Joe Runkle, June 22
Southgate Garden II, May 18
Manchester-by-the-Sea
The Garden at 9 Friend Street, June 22
Marblehead
Grey Gulls—Larry Simpson, June 22
The Parable—Ellen Cool's Garden, June 22
Swampscott
Wilkinson Garden—Blythswood, June 22
Middlesex County
Brookline
Lucy Aptekar & Gerry Leader, June 8
Cambridge
165 Brattle Street, June 8
Nantucket County
Nantucket
Beach Plum, June 27
Blueberry Hill, June 27
Dr. & Mrs. John W. Espy, June 27
Inishfree—Coleman & Susan Burke, June 27
Susan & Karl Ottison, June 27
Eleanor & Arthur Reade, June 27
Constance Umberger, June 27
Siasconset
Hedged About, June 27
Norfolk County
Dedham
The Lilacs, June 8
Dan & Polly Pierce, June 8
Dover
Kevin J. Doyle & Michael Radoslovich—Cairn Croft, June 8
Wellesley
Hunnewell Garden, June 8

Westwood
Joseph Hudak & Kenn Stephens, June 8
Worcester County
Boylston
Maple Grove, May 25
Grafton
Mapel & Libuda Garden, May 25
North Grafton
Brigham Hill Farm, May 25

MICHIGAN
Oakland County
Beverly Hills
Toni & Joe Grinnan, July 14
Suzanne's Garden—Suzanne Krueger & Dave Rider, July 14
Denise & Bruce Wayne, July 14
Bloomfield Hills
Aerie Gardens, July 14
Judy's Garden, July 14
Larry & Sandy Mackle, July 14
Southfield
Tom & Beth McMahon, July 14

NEW HAMPSHIRE
Cheshire County
Dublin
Robertson Garden, July 27
Tiadnock, July 27
Harrisville
Sky Hill, July 27
Hillsborough County
Peterborough
Gardens of Stan & Cheri Fry, July 27
Rockingham County
Hampton Falls
Carole & Bert Chanasyk, July 14
New Castle
Prince-Bergh Garden, July 13
Reynolds Garden, July 13
North Hampton
Bell-Manning House Garden, July 13
Shulman Garden, July 13
Portsmouth
Jameson & Priscilla French, July 13
Barbara Renner's Garden, July 13

Rye
Jim & Ellen Labrie's Seaside Garden, July 14
Rye Beach
Sal Allocco's Garden, July 14
Hochschwender Garden, July 14

NEW JERSEY
Bergen County
Englewood
Peggy & Walter Jones, May 11
Mercer & Peter O'Hara, May 11
Maywood
Dail & Tony's Garden, June 22
Ridgewood
The Handley Garden, June 22
The Zusy/Ortiz Garden, June 22
River Edge
Anthony "Bud" & Virginia Korteweg, June 22
River Vale
Cupid's Garden—Audrey Linstrom Maihack, June 22
Tenafly
Richard & Ronnie Klein, June 22
Linda Singer, June 22
Wyckoff
Tall Trees—Garden of Janet Schulz, June 22
Essex County
Livingston
Howard P. Fertig, May 11
Montclair
Emer Featherstone's Garden, June 9
Short Hills
Ursula & Andreas Enderlin, June 8
George Sternlieb, June 8
Winter's Garden, May 11, June 8
Hunterdon County
Califon
Frog Pond Farm, May 11, June 9
Stanton
Kallas Garden, May 11
Middlesex County
Colonia
Babbling Brook, June 22
Monmouth County
Rumson
Beliza Ann Furman, June 9
Linden Hill, June 15

Morris County
> **Chatham**
> Jack Lagos, June 9
> **Morris Plains**
> Watnong Gardens, May 11, June 9

Somerset County
> **Far Hills**
> The Hay Honey Farm, June 9

Summit County
> **Summit**
> Abbey's Acre, June 8
> Allen Garden, June 8

NEW YORK

Columbia County
> **Ancram**
> Adams-Westlake, June 23, September 8
> **Ancramdale**
> Cricket Hill Farm, June 23, September 8
> **Copake Falls**
> Margaret Roach, June 9
> **Craryville**
> Susan Anthony & Richard Galef, June 22
> Marion & Irwin Kaplan—White Birch Farm, June 22
> **East Taghkanic**
> Grant & Alice Platt, June 22
> **Millerton**
> Helen Bodian's Garden, July 14

Dutchess County
> **Amenia**
> Broccoli Hall—Maxine Paetro, May 11, June 15
> Jade Hill—Paul Arcario & Don Walker, June 30
> **Millbrook**
> Far A-Field, June 30
> Belinda & Stephen Kaye, June 30
> Hamilton & Edith Kean, June 30
> **Rhinebeck**
> Cedar Heights Orchard—William & Arvia Morris, July 14
> Amy Goldman, July 14
> **Salt Point**
> Ely Garden, July 13, July 21
> **Stanfordville**
> Ellen & Eric Petersen, July 13
> Zibby & Jim Tozer, July 13

Essex County
 Keene Valley
 Horse Farm Vegetable Garden, July 13
 Woodland Gardens of Mr. & Mrs. Wynant D. Vanderpoel, July 13
 Westport
 Kenjockety—Phelan-Shapiro, July 13
Greene County
 Ashland
 Frog Pond Gardens, July 27
 East Jewett
 Daisy & Tom Wenzell's Valley Farm, July 27
 Haines Falls
 Dunn's Moss Garden, July 27
 Santa Cruz—Skip & Anne Pratt's Garden, July 27
 Tannersville
 McCaffrey Garden, July 27
 Minnehaha, July 27
 Tony & Rosalyn Smith's Bittersweet Cottage, July 27
Orange County
 Mountainville
 Cedar House—Garden of Margaret Johns & Peter Stern, May 19
Otsego County
 Andes
 Cynthia & Charles Bonnes, June 30
 Henry & Judy Jobmann, June 30
 Cooperstown
 Fynmere, June 29
 Heathcote, June 29
 Frank Kubis, June 29
 Garden of Loris & Jim Orthwein, June 29
 Garden of J. Mason & Rhea Reynolds, June 29
 Riverbrink—Garden of Gail Reid Freehafer & Dr. John Freehafer, June 29
 Oneonta
 Freckelton Beal Gardens, June 30
 Roscoe
 Berry Brook Farm—Mermer Blakeslee & Eric Hamerstrom, June 30
Putnam County
 Cold Spring
 Stonecrop Gardens, April 28, May 19, June 16, July 13, September 19 *(public garden)*
 Garrison
 Manitoga, July 13 *(public garden)*
 Ross Gardens, July 13
 Patterson
 The Farmstead Garden, September 8

Rockland County
  Palisades
  The Captain John House Garden, June 9, September 15
  Judy Tomkins Gardens, June 9, September 15
Saratoga County
  Saratoga Springs
  Brackett House Gardens, June 7
  Georgiana Ducas Garden, June 7
  Bruce Solenski, June 7
Suffolk County
  Cutchogue
  Manfred & Roberta Lee, July 13
  Alice & Charles Levien's Garden, July 13
  East Hampton
  Irving & Dianne Benson's Garden, May 4, June 22
  Mrs. Donald Bruckmann, May 4
  Ina Garten, July 13
  LongHouse Reserve, June 23 *(public garden)*
  Margaret Kerr & Robert Richenburg, May 4, June 22
  Bob & Mimi Schwarz, July 13
  Mattituck
  Maurice Isaac & Ellen Coster Isaac, July 13
  Dennis Schrader & Bill Smith, July 13
  Southampton
  Brodsky Garden, June 22
  Kim White & Kurt Wolfgruber—Secret Garden, June 22
Westchester County
  Armonk
  Cobamong Pond, May 19, October 13
  Bedford
  Ann Catchpole-Howell, June 9
  Lulu Farm, May 25
  Penelope & John Maynard, May 19
  Bedford Hills
  Laura Fisher—Wildflower Farm, July 21
  Phillis Warden, April 28, May 19, July 21
  Cortlandt Manor
  Vivian & Ed Merrin, July 21
  Croton-on-Hudson
  The Gardens of Dianna & Howard Smith, June 1
  Hastings-on-Hudson
  Midge & Dave Riggs, May 19
  Irvington
  Mary Morrisett, June 1
  Katonah
  Cross River House, June 15

Roxana Robinson—Willow Green Farm, June 15
Lewisboro
The White Garden, April 20, September 8
Mount Kisco
Judy & Michael Steinhardt, May 5
Rocky Hills—The Gardens of Henriette Suhr, May 25
North Salem
Artemis Farm—Carol & Jesse Goldberg, June 15
Jane & Bill Bird, June 15, July 21
Dick Button—Ice Pond Farm, September 8
Lucy Hart Close, June 15
Page Dickey & Francis Schell, June 15
Keeler Hill Farm, June 15
Ossining
Paul & Sarah Matlock, June 1
Teatown Lake Reservation on Wildflower Island, May 19 *(public garden)*
Waccabuc
James & Susan Henry, September 8

NORTH CAROLINA
Buncombe County
   Asheville
   Albemarle Inn, July 13
   John & Curry Jamison, July 13
   Kenilworth Gardens, July 13
   The Lake Garden, July 13
   The Richmond Hill Inn, July 13 *(public garden)*
Mecklenburg County
   Charlotte
   The Cooper Gardens, September 14 & 15
   Duncan Garden, September 14 & 15
   Hampton Gardens, September 14 & 15
   Minor Manor, September 14 & 15
   Gardens on Valleybrook, September 14 & 15
   UNC-Charlotte Botanical Gardens, September 14 & 15 *(public garden)*
   Garden of Genie & Jim White, September 14 & 15
   The Garden of Lindie Wilson, September 14 & 15
Orange County
   Chapel Hill
   Boyd-Martin Garden, April 13
   The Robertson Garden, April 13
   Tenney Farmhouse Garden—Elizabeth Pringle, April 13
   Hillsborough
   Chatwood Garden, May 18
   Fairmount, May 18
   Pleasant Green Farm, May 18

Wake County
> **Apex**
> The Gardens At Rosecroft, May 18

OHIO
Hamilton County
> **Cincinnati**
> Beechwood Gardens, July 7
> Judy Brandenburg's Garden, April 21, July 7
> Joan Day's Garden, July 7
> The Gardens of Brenda & John Demetriou, July 7
> Amy & John Duke's Daylily Gardens, July 7
> J. Louis & Beth Karp's Garden, July 7
> Julie Mahlin's Garden, July 7
> The Robertson-Conway Garden, April 21
> Nancy & Ed Rosenthal's Garden, April 21, July 7
> **Indian Hill**
> Kurtz's Garden, July 7

Montgomery County
> **Dayton**
> The Larkins Garden, June 15
> The Patterson Homestead, June 15
> Gloria B. Richardson Garden, June 15
> Ellie Shulman's Rose Terrace, June 15
> Wessex, June 15

OKLAHOMA
Tulsa County
> **Tulsa**
> The Gardens of Bonnie & Joe Klein, May 18
> The Gardens of Breniss & Daniel O'Neal, May 18
> The Burke Reynolds Garden, May 18

OREGON
Marion County
> **Aurora**
> Huntington Garden at the Case House, April 27
> **Salem**
> Garry Oaks, June 15
> Lord and Schryver, June 15
> Villa Bacca Collina Estate Garden, June 15

Multnomah County
> **Portland**
> Russell Archer Garden, June 16
> Jeffrey Bale, July 21
> The Berry Botanical Garden, July 21, August 4 (*public garden*)

Catswalk Cottage—JoAnn & Roger Thomas, July 21
June Collins' Garden, June 16
Nancy Goldman Garden, July 21
Goodman-Schultz Garden, July 21
Hogan/Sanderson, July 21
Sara Mauritz Garden, June 16
The Jane Platt Garden, June 16
The Schatz/Spendelow Garden, June 16
Washington County
Saint Paul
Cecil & Molly Smith Garden, April 27 *(public garden)*
Sherwood
Bella Madrona, April 27, August 4
Cavender Garden, April 27, August 4
Tualatin
Kaiser Permanente's Tualatin Poison Prevention Garden, April 27 *(public garden)*

PENNSYLVANIA
Bucks County
Doylestown
Fordhook Farm of the W. Atlee Burpee Co., June 29
New Hope
Jericho Mountain Orchards, June 29
Silverdale
Carol A. Pierce, June 29
Wrightstown
Hortulus Farm, June 29
Centre County
Boalsburg
Darlene & Paul's Gardens, May 5, July 28
Centre Hall
Rhoneymeade Arboretum, Sculpture Garden & Labyrinth, May 5, June 9, July 6
    (public garden)
State College
Deno's Garden, May 5, June 9
Olgi Draper's Garden, June 9, July 6
Rae's Garden, June 9, July 6
Gabriel & Jill Welsch Garden, May 5, June 9, July 28
Montgomery County
Gladwyne
Fernside Cottage, June 2
Mr. & Mrs. John W. Powell II, June 2
Gulph Mills
Gulph Mills, June 2
Haverford
Baruch Garden, June 2

Wayne
Frogsleap—Mr. & Mrs. John D. Borne, June 2
Wynnewood
Gillean's Wood, June 2

TENNESSEE
Davidson County
Nashville
Fletcher-Chapman Garden, May 19
Follin Garden, May 19
Martin Garden, May 19
Simons Garden, May 19
Hamilton County
Lookout Mountain
The Garden of Connie & John Higgason, May 18
Reilly Garden, May 18
Yates Garden, May 18
Marion County
Chattanooga
The Garden at Skillet Gap, May 18
Reflection Riding Arboretum & Botanical Garden, May 18 *(public garden)*

TEXAS
Dallas County
Dallas
Tony Cerbone's Exotic Dallas Garden, May 18
Michael Cheever's Garden, May 18
Einspruch Garden, May 18
Judy Fender's Garden, May 18
Rolston/Cohn Garden, May 18
Peter & Julie Schaar, May 18
Southbrook Gardens, May 18
Terry Garden, May 18
Harris County
Burton
Jacomini 5J Farm, April 14
Houston
1411 North Boulevard, April 13
Benton Residence, April 13
Brennan Residence, April 13
Casey Residence, April 13
Corn-Parker Garden, April 13
DeGeurin Garden, April 13
Kainer Residence, April 13
Garden of Karen & John Kelsey, April 13

Pinson Residence, April 13
Rocking "S" Ranch & Garden, April 14
Simon Residence, April 13
Washington
Peaceable Kingdom Farm, April 14
Travis County
Austin
James deGrey David & Gary Peese, September 28
Deborah Hornickel, September 28
Old Ziller House Garden, September 28
Possumhaw Hollow—The Spencer-Martinez Garden, September 28
Bill & Anna Prothro, September 28
Webber Garden, September 28
Waller County
Hempstead
Peckerwood Garden, April 13 & 14 *(public garden)*

VERMONT
Bennington County
Dorset
Westerly, June 8, July 13
Manchester
Glebelands, June 8, July 13
White Tree Farm, June 8, July 13
Manchester Center
Edwards' Garden, June 8, July 13
Joan & Lee Fegelman's Garden, June 8, July 13
Manchester Village
The Sunken Garden, June 8, July 13

VIRGINIA
Arlington County
Arlington
Burnet-Deutsch Garden, June 15
Cozy Shack, June 15
Garden of William A. Grillo, June 15
Garden of Linda Scott & Mary Dufour, June 15
Fairfax County
Fairfax
Dorothy & Art Phinney, June 15
McLean
Hilltop Cottage, June 15
Ridder Garden, June 15

WASHINGTON
Clark County
>
> Vancouver
> Kaiser Permanente's Salmon Creek Poison Prevention Garden, May 11

King County
>
> Seattle
> Noel Angell & Emory Bundy, June 1
> Geller-Irvine Garden, June 1
> Carol Henderson, June 1
> Carol Isaacson-Rawn, June 1
> Carlo & Lalie Scandiuzzi, June 1

WEST VIRGINIA
Kanawha County
>
> Charleston
> Laughinghouse—the Giltinans' Garden, June 29
> The Garden of Bill Mills & Thomas Gillooly, June 29
> Governor's Mansion—State of West Virginia, June 29
> Dr. & Mrs. George E. Toma, June 29
> Zeb & Sara Sue Wright's Garden, June 29
> Malden
> Kanawha Salines—Garden of Mrs. Turner Ratrie, June 29

WISCONSIN
Milwaukee County
>
> River Hills
> Coffman-Morrison Gardens, July 21
> David Knox's Garden, July 21
> The LaBahn Garden, July 21
> Russell Garden, July 21

Goodman-Schultz Garden, Portland, Oregon.

Open Days

Private garden visiting through the Open Days Program

There is no better way to learn about gardens than spending time in them. Within the pages of the *Open Days Directory*, you will find hundreds of private gardens welcoming your visit. We know that some of them may not be within your scope of travel this season, so we've decided to bring them to you. Enjoy these pages of colorful garden images and celebrate with us the diversity of America's gardens.

The Northwest

Panoramic views of snow-capped mountains, towering firs, a mild climate, and gardening opportunities that range from shady woodlands to the sunny Mediterranean style define this horticultural destination. Nurseries galore are an additional enticement. Visit in April, June, July, and August, and be sure to schedule time to see the outstanding public gardens of this region.

The Geller-Irvine Garden, Seattle, Washington. Photo by Keith Geller.

Jeffrey Bale's garden, Portland, Oregon.

Cavender Garden, Sherwood, Oregon. Photo by Dick Cavender.

Russell Archer Garden, Portland, Oregon.

The Northeast

Explore the diversity of old and new gardens in the Northeast where we launched our Open Days Program in 1995. From Maine through Pennsylvania, enjoy gardens on this region's varied seacoast, farmlands, and mountain tops. Kitchen gardens, rock gardens, city gardens, and meadows abound. Visit gardens in New York destinations such as the Hamptons, historic Cooperstown, Saratoga Springs, the Catskills, and the Adirondacks. Lake, river, ocean, and mountain views are everywhere throughout the glorious change of seasons. You can visit from the first spring blooms in April through the dazzling fall colors of October.

Linda Allard's garden, Washington, Connecticut. Photo by Laura Palmer.

Gulph Mills, Gulph Mills, Pennsylvania. Photo by Ralph Schumacher.

Mapel & Libuda Garden,
Grafton, Massachusetts.

Jim & Ellen Labrie's Seaside Garden,
Rye, New Hampshire.

Berry Brook Farm, Roscoe, New York.

California

Visit California's gardens and experience the imagination and diversity of this remarkable gardening state. Vegetable gardens and orchards contrast with tropical displays and dry gardens. Art in the garden is abundant in California and outdoor living spaces dominate. Drought-tolerant creations reinforce the water-conservation considerations of this region. Visit Open Days gardens in April and May.

The Matt Gil Sculpture Garden, San Francisco. Photo by Dan Carlson.

Rosen Landscape, Los Angeles.

Horton Garden, Los Angeles. Photo by R. G. Turner, Jr.

Midwest

The gardens of the Midwest
entice visitors to their
magnificent lake views, screne
woodland walks shaded by the
dominant towering oaks, petite
courtyard gardens, and country
estates. April, June, and July
are the times to visit.

*The Gardens at Wandering Tree,
Barrington, Illinois. Below, The Butcher
Garden, Saint Charles, Illinois.*

Cathy & Gene Rothert Garden. Highland Park, Illinois. Photo by Gene Rothert.

Beechwood Gardens, Cincinnati, Ohio.

Toni & Joe Grinnan's garden, Beverly Hills, Michigan. Photo by Maureen Electa Monte.

The South

Florida offers lush jungle ferns, orchids, palms, citrus, mangroves, and tropical retreats. Alabama's lush greenery and woodland displays are a delight in May. The wildflowers of North Carolina and Tennessee are on view throughout the spring, and the gardens of the Washington, D.C. area welcome visitors in May and June.

The Dr. & Mrs. William King Stubbs Garden, Vero Beach, Florida. Below, Jane MacLeish's Garden, Washington, D.C. Photo by Ping Amranand.

The Butrus Garden, Birmingham, Alabama. Photo by Mary Zahl.

The Ridder Garden, McLean, Virginia.

The West and Southwest

Colorado, Texas, and Arizona are showcases for native plants. A visit to this region will prove what determination and inspiration can accomplish. Cottage gardens and water gardens exist next to native desert flora and xeriscapes. Visit Texas to see live oaks, camellias, Mexican and Texan natives. Oklahoma boasts park-like settings with dogwoods, yews, and hollies. Visiting opportunities begin in March in Arizona and end in Austin in September.

Gardens of Breniss & Daniel O'Neal, Tulsa, Oklahoma.

Tony Cerbone's Exotic Dallas Garden, Dallas, Texas.

Peaceable Kingdom Farm, Washington, Texas. Photo by E. Winston-Mize.

Preservation Projects

The Garden Conservancy is currently involved in preserving more than two dozen outstanding private gardens. Our Sponsored Gardens are featured in photographs on the following pages. From Ruth Bancroft's bold and dramatic California garden, to the symbolic and contemplative Humes Japanese Stroll garden on Long Island's north shore, to the showplace New Hampshire country estate that is The Fells, the Garden Conservancy is committed to the conservation of these remarkable places for you. You will find descriptions and visiting information for these gardens within their corresponding Open Days area.

Peckerwood Garden, Hempstead, Texas. Photo by Elsie Kersten.

This is a partnership. Your participation in the Garden Conservancy's Open Days Program, from purchasing this *Directory* to visiting the private gardens listed in it, supports our preservation work. Revenue, from book sales to gate admissions, helps us provide the resources necessary to preserve many of America's finest gardens. We encourage you to join us with a Garden Conservancy membership. Complete information is included on the last page of the *Directory*. We are grateful for your support.

The Fells, at theohn Hay National Wildlife Refuge, Newbury, New Hampshire.

The Ruth Bancroft Garden, Walnut Creek, California. Photo by Mick Hales.

The John P. Humes Japanese Stroll Garden, Mill Neck, New York. Photo by Mick Hales.

The Chase Garden, Orting, Washington.

Public Garden Visiting through the Open Days Program

Hundreds of public gardens across the country play a vital role in enriching and educating Americans every year. The Open Days Program is pleased to include information on many of these important institutions and we encourage you to visit them. Check the local listings for information on such gardens in your area. The Open Days Program provides additional opportunities to visit public gardens across the country that have limited visiting hours or are open by appointment only. Some have arranged special open hours or events to coincide with area Open Days. These gardens are included in the Open Days by Date and Open Days by Location indexes beginning on page 24.

Two exceptional American gardens that are among the most popular destinations for Open Days visitors have become public only in the past ten years: Madoo Conservancy in Sagaponack, New York, and Stonecrop Gardens, in Cold Spring, New York. Open Days visitors can enjoy many additional visiting opportunities throughout the 2002 season.

The Garden Conservancy worked with artist Robert Dash to establish the Madoo Conservancy to preserve his garden for future generations. (See page 352 for details.) Photo by Mick Hales.

Stonecrop Gardens is the former garden of Frank and Anne Cabot, now a public garden under the direction of Caroline Burgess and affiliated with the Garden Conservancy. (See page 349 for details.)

Alabama

Louise & John Wrinkle's garden, Birmingham.

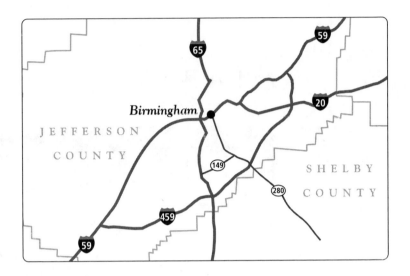

Saturday & Sunday, May 4 & 5

JEFFERSON COUNTY

Birmingham

Butrus Garden

2724 Old Mill Lane, Birmingham

A four-acre mature woodland in old Mountain Brook surrounds the grand house built in 1931 of soft gray limestone. Several years ago, visionary new owners revived it and created a new Italianate garden that has settled comfortably around the house. The emphasis is on greenery, stone, and water. Color is limited to white blooming plants incorporated into the landscape plan and into a few substantial pots filled with seasonal color. Visitors approach via a long driveway and cross a stone terrace in front, then glimpse the first of several outdoor rooms. In the first, the lawn is encircled with low boxwood, tall arborvitae, and pots of colorful annuals. In the next garden, an antique fountain and its pool stand at the center. An antique copper female figure, subtly tucked into one side, overlooks this space, which terminates in a stone pavilion, repeating the architecture of the side porch on the main house. Stepping down from the gardens, we move along stone paths featuring flowering spring perennials and annuals to a lower grass level surrounded by a woodland garden with large stone statuary focal points. There are many private nooks, including a lower terrace off the side of the house. A sense of complete privacy and peace permeates the place.

Hours: 1 p.m. to 5 p.m.

From Highway 280, take the Highway 149/Lakeshore Drive exit and go east. The road becomes Mountain Brook Parkway. Go about .3 mile on Mountain Brook Parkway to the intersection of Guilford Road and turn left. *Please park on Guilford Road and Mountain Brook Parkway. Look for People Movers to give visitors a ride.*

Proceeds shared with the Birmingham Botanical Society

Crowe Garden

2848 Balmoral Road, Birmingham

The gardens that surround this 1920s' landmark house appear to be original. They have, however, undergone extensive alterations. Three walls, five buildings, and seven gates—plus everything underfoot, except the driveway—date from 1989. The swimming pool has been retiled, two fountains reconfigured, and the servants quarters transformed into a pool house. There have also been some unplanned changes. More than a dozen major trees were lost to age or storms. Despite the trauma, the garden now boasts a fine, though young, collection of specimen hardwoods, evergreens, and conifers. The layout of this garden borrows, unabashedly, from English precedents. The park-like lawn and haha recall the eighteenth-century style; the entrance walk, with its urns, clipped box, the upright arborvitae, and the brick-walled formal garden are pure Edwardian. The Tudor folly is just for fun. The richly planted kitchen courts, mixed border, and planted pavement off the porch reflect the inspiration of Gertrude Jekyll; the cottage garden's exuberance of old-fashioned flowers pretends a bit of Sissinghurst. The raised-bed vegetable plot, however, is Victory-Garden American. Plants in this garden were chosen, first, for their structure. Box is a special favorite; pruned, free-grown or potted, it appears in almost every garden space. Upright plants like holly, conifers, and crape myrtle are also prized as living architecture. Container plants combine the best of structure and ornament. Benches, sculpture, finials, urns, and architectural fragments provide important focal points as well as decoration. Change, of course, is the only constant of any garden. Plans are currently afoot to rework the front lawn's shrubbery borders and to extend the woodland's walks. Whatever their form, however, these changes will always reflect Mary Catherine's not-too-subtle dictum of understatement: "Don't new it up!"

Hours: 1 p.m. to 5 p.m.

From Highway 280, take the Mountain Brook Village exit. Then take Canterbury Road or Montevallo Road to Overhill Road. Turn right onto Overhill, which becomes Balmoral Road at a large grass triangle. The Crowe house is dark brick on the upper side. *Please park on Balmoral Road.*

Proceeds shared with the Birmingham Botanical Society

HIS Garden

4910 Windwood Circle, Birmingham

Landscaping the view from the kitchen window is not unusual, but the garden that unfolded on this wooded lot is remarkable for its charm and individuality. Where once the view stopped on the far side of the pool, an arched arbor and fence clothed with crossvine now frame a vista. In the distance is the object of delight, a granite sphere that revolves and appears to float from a low pressure water source in its basin. The sphere is reflected in a circular mirror, thoughtfully placed to reflect the garden but never the visitor. Between the garden's gateway and its focal point is a gently stepped pathway that loops through the shelter of native trees underplanted with a masterful study of foliage texture. Even ordinary ground covers become features here, but there is plenty that goes beyond ordinary, including needle palms, cephalotaxus, rohdea, hellebores, and 'Dr. Merrill' magnolias. Each season has its flowers, but the interest is sustained by the restrained colors of gray, brown, and green that comprise the compositions of foliage, bark, natural and cut stone, metal, glass, and wood. The trickle of water from fountains and rill adds to the tranquility. Watch for Rocket and Sprocket, the rooster and chicken who strayed and stayed. Landscape architect Sam Hogue says, "The residence and its original walled enclosure around the swimming pool were heavily influenced by the villa style of design, a design style that reached its zenith in Italy during the late fifteenth and sixteenth centuries. Ultimately, this space is intended to 'massage' all of one's senses at one time, while being a place for introspection."

Hours: 1 p.m. to 5 p.m.

From Highway 280, turn south onto Valleydale Road/Highway 17. Go 3.7 miles on Valleydale to the traffic light at the intersection of Caldwell Mill Road. Turn left and go .5 mile on Caldwell Mill to the light at the top of the hill. Turn left onto Windwood Circle. Ours is the second house on the left. *Please park on Windwood Circle.*

Proceeds shared with the Birmingham Botanical Society

Philip Morris

2415 Park Lane, Birmingham

An editor's garden—after a long career with *Southern Living* magazine, I see the world in before and after terms, and my garden is that. When I bought the house (built circa 1928) in 1990, the fifty-foot-wide property had never even been fenced. The key to design has been to make the best of limited space. Shade-loving plants are used under the large southern red oak in front; a side lawn gets sun and serves to extend a small deck/porch; a rear loop under dogwoods features plant textures and a revived water feature. Foliage, texture, and white flowers set the theme throughout.

Hours: 1 p.m. to 5 p.m.

From Vulcan, take 21st Avenue South east to English Village at Cahaba Road. Turn right at the traffic light, then make an immediate left onto Park Lane just past Armand's restaurant. There are a few public parking spaces beside the restaurant. *Parking along the street (dead end) is limited and restricted to the right side. The best option may be to park anywhere in English Village and walk past Armand's and down charming Park Lane to the fourth house on the right.*

Proceeds shared with the Birmingham Botanical Society

The Gardens of Mountain Brook Park
190 Mountain Brook Park, Birmingham

Small gardens surround several houses in this new cluster community. Each reflects its owner's preferences, from borders overflowing with color to an outdoor living room with a lap pool. For passionate gardeners, every inch is filled. For those who prefer to enjoy the gardens from the comfort of their homes, serenity beckons. Come enjoy the opportunities for beauty in small spaces.

Hours: 1 p.m. to 5 p.m.

Look for a walled community off Montclair Road nearly opposite Crestline Post Office.

Proceeds shared with the Birmingham Botanical Society

Southern Living Magazine's Experimental/ Demonstration Garden
2100 Lakeshore Parkway, Birmingham

The small garden hidden behind the Southern Progress headquarters is an experimental garden where new plants are tried and stories are generated. Several gardening plants or ideas have been published in *Southern Living* magazine. Soil was first turned about five years ago when the test kitchens needed fresh herbs. Each year the *Southern Living* garden staff and Southern Progress gardeners add a little more to the garden. Today, you can see a vegetable garden, flower border, water feature, and bog.

Hours: 1 p.m. to 5 p.m.

From Highway 280, take the Highway 149/Lakeshore Drive exit. Head west past Brookwood Mall. Go under the Highway 31 bridge and turn right at the next traffic light at the Lakeshore Rehabilitation sign. Go up the hill, take the first left into Lakeshore Rehabilitation Center, and follow the signs. The garden is accessed via the Lakeshore parking lot.

Proceeds shared with the Birmingham Botanical Society

Louise & John Wrinkle
2 Beechwood Road, Birmingham

The original house and property were developed in 1938 by Louise's parents. Fourteen years ago, she and her husband moved back to her childhood home and extensively remodeled the house and grounds. A two-acre mature woodland garden features collections of hollies and vacciniums, as well as the ranunculus family. Southeastern natives and their Asian counterparts, many planted side by side for easy comparison, are subjects of equal interest. Guests may circulate freely among the upper gardens: a small boxwood parterre defined by a Belgian fence of native crab apple, a cutting garden, and an herb garden. A network of gravel paths leads visitors from these upper gardens to a wooded valley, where a brook flows year round.

Hours: 1 p.m. to 5 p.m.

From Highway 280, take the Highway 149/Lakeshore Drive exit. Turn right and go through the traffic light. The road becomes Mountain Brook Parkway. Go 1.1 miles to the light: turn right onto Overbrook Road, then go 16 miles and turn left onto Beechwood Road. The house is on the corner of Beechwood and Woodhill. *Please park on Woodhill and walk up the driveway.*

Proceeds shared with the Birmingham Botanical Society

Public Gardens

JEFFERSON COUNTY

BIRMINGHAM

Birmingham Botanical Gardens

2612 Lane Park Road, Birmingham (205) 414-3900 www.bbgardens.org

Birmingham Botanical Gardens features 67 acres of native and exotic plants. Major collections include camellia, cactus and succulent, rhododendron, iris, fern, lily, orchid, old-fashioned and modern roses, and sculpture. There is also a conservatory, plus vegetable and herb gardens. There is a renowned Japanese garden with an authentic teahouse and cultural performance pavilion. A horticultural library and ongoing horticultural programs are available. An attractive gift shop offers unusual garden items and flower-arranging supplies. Most areas are handicapped accessible.

Hours: Year round, daily, dawn to dusk

Admission: free

From I-20/I-59, exit onto Highway 280 east. Take the Mountain Brook/Zoo/Gardens exit. Turn left at the traffic light onto Lane Park Road. The gardens are on the left.

From I-65 south, take I-20 to I-59 east. Go 1 mile, turn right onto Highway 280 east and proceed as directed above.

From I-65 north, take Exit 250 onto I-459 east. Take Exit 19 and go 3.5 miles on Highway 280 west to the Zoo exit. Turn left at the light onto Lane Park Road. The gardens are on the left.

Birmingham Museum of Art/The Charles W. Ireland Sculpture Garden

2000 8th Avenue North, Birmingham (205) 254-2565

This multilevel sculpture garden is a unique space for the display of outdoor art. Welcoming you to this urban oasis is a lushly planted area shaded by towering water oaks. Beneath the oaks' central canopy is the striking installation, *Blue Pools Courtyard*, by Valerie Jaudon. Sculptures by Rodin, Botero, and others lie directly ahead as you continue your way through this extraordinary space. The final focal point is the magnificent *Lithos II* waterfall by Elyn Zimmerman. Within the sculpture garden is the Red Mountain Garden Area, created in 1956.

Hours: Year round, Tuesday through Saturday, 10 a.m. to 5 p.m. and Sunday, noon to 5 p.m.; closed Thanksgiving, Christmas, and New Year's Day.

Admission: free

From I-20/I-59, take the 22nd Street exit. Turn left onto 22nd Street, go 1 block, and turn right onto 8th Avenue North; go 1 block to 21st Street. The museum is on the corner of 21st Street and 8th Avenue North.

Arizona

Virginia Glasco's garden, Glendale.

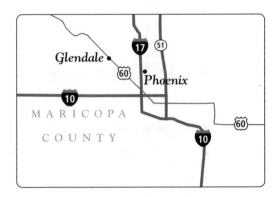

Saturday, March 23
MARICOPA COUNTY

GLENDALE
Virginia Glasco's Garden
5910 West Kathleen Road, Glendale

My small garden started in a barren backyard. Over the years, I have planted numerous trees, with many perennial flower beds among the brick pathways. The garden shed is decorated with a pretend window, lace curtains, and a window box. Vignettes of statuary and birdbaths mingle with the many old-fashioned blossoms to create an inviting cottage garden.

Hours: 10 a.m. to 4 p.m.

Take I-17 to Greenway Road. Travel west on Greenway to 59th Avenue. The American Graduate School is located on the southeast corner of this intersection. Turn north onto 59th Avenue to Nancy Road. Turn west onto Nancy and immediately north onto 59th Circle to Kathleen Road. Go to the second house on the north side of the street.

Proceeds shared with the Desert Botanical Garden

PHOENIX
Desert Oasis
Shadow Road, Phoenix

This is a little oasis. With native desert landscaping in the front and back, from the street this house does not stand out, but by the time you enter the front courtyard you realize this is not another xeriscape. With climbing roses cascading over the courtyard wall, wisteria on the entry pergola, and bougainvillea, honeysuckle, jasmine, hardenburgia, and bower vine climbing the walls of the house, you cannot help but wonder what is in the backyard. Natural stone planters, built from rocks found on site, contain a large iris and annual flower bed and a quaint rose garden. All the roses were carefully selected based on their heat tolerance and fragrance. It is truly a hidden garden within.

Hours: 10 a.m. to 4 p.m.

Turn west from Tatum onto Sunset/Mockingbird. Turn right at the "T." Follow the road to Starling and turn right. Follow to Shadow Road and turn left. The garden is on the right.

Proceeds shared with the Christian Family Care Agency

Glendale Family Garden
Thunderbird Road, Phoenix

This garden has something for everyone, especially small children. With a sandbox, a playground the size of most backyards, and long meandering pathways wide enough for bicycles, tricycles, and roller blades, children are never bored in this garden. Parents and grandparents will also find something of interest: the koi pond with two waterfalls and a wide variety of aquatic plants, the rose garden with arbors reminiscent of Monet's Grande Allée, several secluded areas, and three formal reflecting pools and fountains. With more than 700 ranunculus and other bulbs in the annual flower beds, tour buses often pass by in the winter to gaze at this amazing house and garden located in a cul-de-sac. The pathways are wide and easily wheelchair accessible.

Hours: 10 a.m. to 4 p.m.

Enter and park in the pasture off Thunderbird Road east of 67th Avenue at 65th Place. Located on the south side of Thunderbird Road between the medical office and Thunderbird Ranch.

Proceeds shared with the West Valley Child Crisis Center

Public Gardens
MARICOPA COUNTY

Phoenix
Desert Botanical Garden
1201 North Galvin Parkway, Phoenix (480) 941-1225 www.dbg.org

Surrounded by rugged red buttes, the Desert Botanical Garden's 145 acres comprise one of the most complete collections of desert flora in the world. The garden is home to more than 20,000 plants and is a renowned research facility. The exhibition "Plants and People of the Sonoran Desert" captures the life of the area's first inhabitants. Spring is an especially beautiful time to visit the Harriet K. Maxwell Desert Wildflower Trail, when hundreds of varieties of wildflowers burst into bloom.

Hours: October through April, daily, 8 a.m. to 8 p.m.; May through September, 7 a.m. to 8 p.m.; closed Christmas and Independence Day

Admission: $7.50 adults, $6.50 senior citizens, $1.50 children 5-12, children under 5 free

Take McDowell Road east to Galvin Parkway and turn south. The garden is on Galvin Parkway/64th Street just south of McDowell Road. The entrance is clearly marked on the east side of Galvin Parkway and is just north of the Phoenix Zoo, in Papago Park.

SCOTTSDALE
The Cactus Garden at The Phoenician

6000 East Camelback Road, Scottsdale (480) 423-2657 www.thephoenician.com

Up the steps, across from the main entrance to The Phoenician resort, the Cactus Garden is a small gem nestled against the base of Camelback Mountain. Flagstone pathways wind through a wide variety of well-marked cacti and succulents, punctuated by several pieces of bronze statuary.

Hours: Year round, daily, dawn to dusk

Admission: free

The entrance to The Phoenician is north off Camelback Road, between 56th and 64th Streets. Drive into the main entrance to the resort. The garden is directly across and up the steps.

SUPERIOR
Boyce Thompson Arboretum State Park

37615 Highway 60, Superior (520) 689-2811 http:\\arboretum.ag.arizona.edu

Boyce Thompson Arboretum is Arizona's oldest and largest botanical garden, featuring plants of the world's deserts. Nestled at the base of Picketpost Mountain, the arboretum was founded in the 1920s by mining magnate William Boyce Thompson. Encompassing 323 acres are several miles of nature paths through the gardens—including the Cactus Garden, the Taylor Family Desert Legume Garden, and the Curandero Trail of Medicinal Plants. Ayer Lake is home to a variety of waterfowl, as well as two species of endangered fish—the desert pupfish and gila topminnow. Other specialty gardens include the Wing Memorial Herb Garden, the Demonstration Garden, and the Hummingbird/Butterfly Garden. There are surprises around every bend, from a streamside forest to towering trees. The arboretum is a National Historic District and an Arizona state park. Monthly special events are held September through May.

Hours: Year round, daily, 8 a.m. to 5 p.m.; closed Christmas Day

Admission: $6 adults, $3 children 5-12, children under 5 free

Take Route 60/Superstition Freeway east from Phoenix. The entrance is located on the south side of the highway, just west of Superior.

CALIFORNIA

OPEN DAYS:

April 13
April 20
April 28
May 5
May 11
May 19

The Garden at 537 Chenery Street, San Francisco.

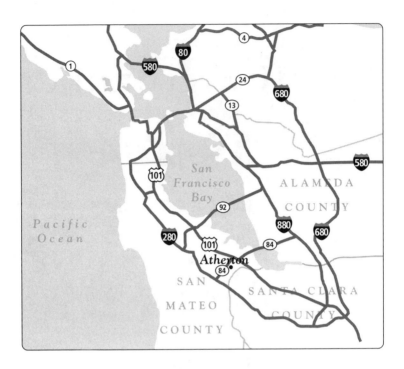

Saturday, April 13

SAN MATEO COUNTY

ATHERTON

Suzanne's Garden

88 Selby Lane, Atherton

Take a stroll through this gardener's garden, with paths continually inviting you to explore the entertainment areas, quiet rooms, places to sit, hidden nooks, and little surprises. The garden, filled with a good variety of plant material for seasonal color, display, cutting, and collecting, as well as favorites from Filoli, exhibits Suzanne's enthusiasm for plants and gardening. Designed by Bruce Chan and Suzanne in 1983, emphasis was placed on areas for entertaining, flexibility for gardening and plant material, and variations in proportions and space. The mounds in the garden add depth, interest, and visual focal points; the dry stone walls add texture and color. This garden was the cover article in *Better Homes & Gardens* magazine last June.

Hours: 10 a.m. to 4 p.m.

From Highway 101, take the Woodside Road/Route 84 west/Redwood City exit; from Route 280 take Route 84 east. Take El Camino Real south for .7 mile, turn right, and go west on Selby Lane, which is the first right turn in Atherton. The cul-de-sac, also called Selby Lane, is at the cross street Austin (stop sign), .4 mile from El Camino Real. Turn at the sign #88. *Please park along the street or in the cul-de-sac (on the west side only).*

Proceeds shared with Filoli

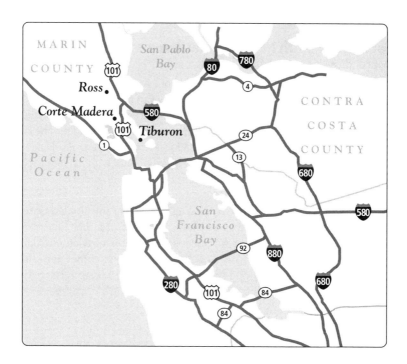

Saturday, April 20

MARIN COUNTY

CORTE MADERA

Keohane Garden

5164 Paradise Drive, Corte Madera

Enter our gates into a peaceful paradise away from the bustle of the world outside. Follow the meandering paths on a discovery of our varied garden areas. Start with the redwoods, pines, and cedars and take the path to the meadow flanked by apple and pear trees. A handmade rock patio overlooks a cottage garden and a bamboo grove. Choose a path that leads under the rose arbor to our beach area of billowy ornamental grasses by the bay. Continue on to find a cobbled walkway that leads to our vegetable and herb garden tucked in next to our home.

Hours: 10 a.m. to 4 p.m.

From Highway 101, take the Paradise Drive exit. Follow Paradise Drive for about 1.75 miles going east towards Tiburon. Marin Montessori School will be on the left after you go under a pedestrian overpass. We are next door to Marin Montessori School and directly across from Robin Drive. *Please park on the street or at the school.*

Proceeds shared with the Grail Movement of America

Ross

Tom Jackson & Kathy Grant's Garden

16 Brookwood, Ross

Twenty years ago, this shady, sloping site in the lee of Mount Tamalpais with winter rain, warm days, and cool nights seemed perfect for a Himalayan foothill garden. Now there is a canopy of *Trachycarpus* and other palms, magnolias, and camphor, with a middle story of rhododendron and bamboo. A spring forms the focus of the Zen rock garden. The art collection has grown with the garden. It has works by Viola Frey, Magdalena Abakamowitz, and others under the arbor and in the brick courtyard. The glass house, with its granite spa, potted palms, and sculpture, forms the jewel in this complex but intimate garden.

Hours: 10 a.m. to 4 p.m.

From San Francisco, take Highway 101 for 7 miles north of the Golden Gate Bridge. Take the Sir Francis Drake Boulevard exit west for 2.5 miles, past the College of Marin. At the traffic light, opposite the Marin Art and Garden Center, turn left onto Lagunitas. Cross the bridge and turn left onto Ross Common. At the next corner, turn right onto Redwood. Then take the first right onto Brookwood. The last house on the right, at the intersection with Bridge Road, is #16.

Waltz Gardens—Juliet & Ashford Wood

71 Shady Lane, Ross

In 1906, San Francisco was in shambles. The earthquake and fire forced the builders of Waltz Gardens to camp in Golden Gate Park. Double lots in Ross were purchased for $20 in gold and an Arts and Crafts style home was built. In the 1920s, the namesake Waltz family took residence. The daughter, Muriel, became a Bay area presence by hybridizing and growing fuchsias on the site. Although no greenhouses remain, the house and gardens for birds, butterflies, bees, and grandchildren maintain the soulful presence of Waltz Gardens nursery. Mature rhododendrons, azaleas, camellias, and roses, plus flowering trees, vegetables, and gates add to the charm of the garden.

Hours: 10 a.m. to 4 p.m.

From Highway 101, take the San Anselmo/Richmond Bridge exit to Sir Francis Drake Boulevard going west under the freeway. Go 2.5 miles from Highway 101 and pass the College of Marin. Turn left onto Lagunitas at the traffic light by Marin Art and Garden Center and the town hall. Turn right onto Shady Lane at Ross School and St. John's Church. Proceed past 2 stop signs to #71, located on the left, 2 driveways before the bridge.

From the East Bay, take I-580 over the Richmond/San Rafael Bridge. Take the Sir Francis Drake Boulevard/San Anselmo/Kentfield exit shortly after exiting the bridge. Follow Sir Francis Drake Boulevard east past the Larkspur Ferry Terminal to West Sir Francis Drake Boulevard. Go under the train trestle/freeway. Proceed as directed above. *Please park along Shady Lane on the shoulder opposite Waltz Gardens.*

Proceeds shared with the American Red Cross

TIBURON
Thompson Brooks
35 Hacienda Drive, Tiburon

The magnificent natural site of this north-facing garden coupled with the forms and rich textures of the architecture sets the stage for a seemingly simple and elegant garden. A collection of mature *Magnolia soulangianas* flanks a broad entry terrace of granite setts within which can be deciphered, "if you know the code," a love poem by Christopher Marlow. A series of asphalt discs, embedded with phrases cast in plastic letters, dots and dashes across the lawn, leading to a child's playroom with a view. Wide swaths of ornamental grasses follow the grand curves of the sculptural grass planes.

Hours: 10 a.m. to 4 p.m.

From Highway 101, take the Tiburon Boulevard/East Blithedale exit. Go east on Tiburon Boulevard. Drive 1.6 miles and turn left at the fourth traffic light onto Trestle Glen. Turn right at the first stop sign onto Hacienda Drive. Go .2 mile up the hill. As you curve to the left, you will see a pointed-roofed glass building on the right. Pull into the parking lot. You will see 3 mailboxes. Drive down the drive to the left of the mailboxes to the very end and drive through the wooden gate.

Proceeds shared with the Marin Horizon School

Varda's Garden
3825 Paradise Drive, Tiburon

Set like a jewel on a thirty-acre hilltop estate is one of the Bay Area's most stunning private gardens. Several crescent-shaped terraces curve around a natural bowl in the land and gently draw the eye down towards a water garden and the wide Bay view beyond. The garden overflows with ornamental grasses and perennials, and contains a rose arbor, mini-orchard, a circular organic vegetable garden, and more. Among the many mature trees on the estate stands a grove of torrey pines, rarely seen outside of San Diego County.

Hours: 10 a.m. to 4 p.m.

From Highway 101, take the Tiburon Boulevard exit towards Tiburon. After 3 or 4 traffic lights is "Blackie's Pasture." As the road narrows and veers right, turn left at Trestle Glen and follow to the end. Turn right onto Paradise Drive and proceed 1 mile to #3825, marked by a stone cairn on the right. Follow the steep driveway to the top.

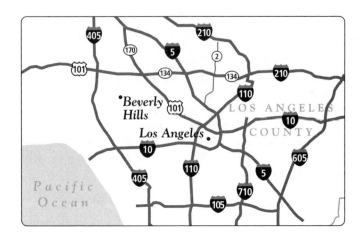

Sunday, April 28

Maps, one-day passes to all gardens, and information about the Garden Conservancy will be available at the Ronnie Allumbaugh Gardens at Getty House from 9:30 a.m. to 3 p.m.

LOS ANGELES COUNTY

BEVERLY HILLS

Goldstine Garden

601 North Arden Drive, Beverly Hills

The Goldstine house sits behind a small forest of "Liquidambars." Inside the entry courtyard, the transparent house opens itself to us. Alongside the walkway, reflecting pools mirror the sky and echo the lap pool in the rear garden visible beyond. This house by Frank Austin and Doug Greene views the outdoors from every room. While extending its Modernist lines into the hardscape, Katherine Glascock designed the planting to flow through the boundaries as though transplanted whole from a larger context. Ornamental grasses carpet the meadow areas with perennial and seasonal interest plantings at transitional areas.

Hours: 10 a.m. to 4 p.m.

From Highway 101, exit at Sunset Boulevard, heading west. Take a left at the traffic light onto Doheny Drive, then make a right onto Elevado Avenue (drive 4 blocks) and turn left onto Arden Drive. The house is at the corner of Arden Drive and Carmelita Avenue.

From I-10, take the La Cienega Boulevard exit, head north, and make a left onto Beverly Boulevard. Turn right onto Doheny Drive, after crossing Santa Monica Boulevard, and turn left onto Carmelita Avenue (drive 4 blocks) to Arden Drive. The house is on the northwest corner. *Please park on the street.*

Proceeds shared with the Jewish Family Service — Save-a-Family

The House of Seven Gardens
613 North Arden Drive, Beverly Hills

Fantabulous transitions characterize this magical series of usable living spaces. English architecture melds with the Bathing Buddha Turquoise Waterfall Garden sheltered by a living canopy of Spanish moss. Fragrant *Michelia alba*, *Agapetes*, and orchids enrobe the Sunken Italian Villa under a vine-embellished natural pergola with custom tile seating, a pizza oven, and fountain. Tree jasmine (*Schrebera*), cobaea vine, allspice, and coffee trees are a smidgen of what lurks here. More lies through another door, and another.

Hours: 10 a.m. to 2 p.m.

From Highway 101, take the Sunset Boulevard exit. Head west and turn left onto Doheny Drive. Turn right onto Elevado Avenue. Drive 4 blocks and turn left onto Arden Drive.

From I-10, take the La Cienega Boulevard exit. Head north. Turn left onto Beverly Boulevard. Turn right onto Doheny Drive after crossing Santa Monica Boulevard. Turn left onto Carmelita Avenue. Drive 4 blocks to Arden Drive and turn right. *Please park on the street.*

Los Angeles

The Allee Garden
822 South Longwood Avenue, Los Angeles

This park-like setting in urban Los Angeles features a natural spring-fed stream and lily pond. The naturalistic setting attracts all species of birds, white cranes, blue herons, mallard ducks, and a frequent guest, the giant kingfisher, who delights in swooping down to feed in the pond. A seamless integration of house, terrace, and garden includes a lap pool surrounded by bouquet canyon stone, a rose garden, succulents, and ferns. Surprising and unique.

Hours: 10 a.m. to 4 p.m.

From Highway 101, take the Highland Avenue/Hollywood Bowl exit and travel south on Highland. After crossing Wilshire Boulevard, turn left onto Eighth Street, then take the first right onto South Longwood Avenue.

From I-10, take the La Brea exit north to Olympic Boulevard. Turn right, go 1 block after crossing Highland, and turn left onto South Longwood Avenue.

From I-110, take I-10 and proceed as directed above.

Ronnie Allumbaugh Gardens at Getty House, the Official Residence of the Mayor of Los Angeles

605 South Irving Boulevard, Los Angeles

This historic Windsor Square garden was sensitively restored in 1995 by Kennedy Landscape Design Associates. The original Tudor Revival-style garden was designed in 1928 by the renowned garden maker A.E. Hanson, but, over the years, the garden had deteriorated. The garden today is interpreted creatively for use as the official mayor's residence, including a large rear lawn that can be fully tented. Paths lead visitors to the wisteria-covered pergola, the ivy house, and the sunken garden with fountain and tennis court. Historic features that were lost over the years have been restored, including the flagstone walk, sunken garden, and several interior walls.

Hours: 9:30 a.m. to 3 p.m.

From I-10, exit at La Brea Avenue north and proceed to Sixth Street. Turn right onto Sixth Street; Irving Boulevard is about 1 mile east of La Brea Avenue.

From I-110, exit at Sixth Street and proceed west about 4 miles to Irving Boulevard. Getty House is on the southwest corner of Irving and Sixth. *Please park on the street.*

Ruth Bracken Garden

379 North Bronson Avenue, Los Angeles

My garden is less than two years old, a dry, inherited land without a single tree or shrub. The front areas, a combination of white, green, and gray plantings, provide a cooling feeling, which is continued with *Eucalyptus polyanthemos*. Blood orange trees and roses, mixed with perennials, line the driveway. The backyard and my design office both begin with Saltillo tiles that spread to a vine-shaded patio. My color theme of blues and greens continues with the fences, plants, and furniture. A raised bed provides fresh herbs and vegetables; dwarf citrus and roses shade the deck, and two fountains cool. On the north side, a private deck with Japanese maples completes the garden.

Hours: 2 p.m. to 6 p.m.

From I-10, take the La Brea Avenue exit (north). Proceed on La Brea north to Beverly Boulevard (about 3 miles) and turn right (east) onto Beverly. Proceed to Bronson Avenue, about 2 miles. Bronson is 6 blocks east of the traffic light at Larchmont. Turn left (north) onto Bronson and proceed to the intersection of Bronson and Elmwood. My house is on the west side of the street.

Bungalow Estrada Gardens

379 North Wilton Place, Los Angeles

This urban cottage garden was created with loving care and an eye to distract us from the stressful pace of Wilton Place. The frontyard's rescued picket fence encloses this garden from the street. Our jacaranda tree, with fern-like leaves and blue flowers, shades our front yard. Perennials provide enough flowers for outside and inside our home most of the year. The large brick columns flanking our porch are covered with drooping purple/red fuchsia, reminding us of ballerinas. The rear yard is our sanctuary. The twisted willow tree, large ficus hedge, and charming garden accessories make our garden intimate. The willow tree was propagated from floral bouquet leftovers. The hand-painted door and the old wood ladder arbor are worth the price of admission. Our proudest accomplishment: the pond/waterfall brings the whole garden together. The rushing water, over 100 roses, and our large plant variety make our garden paradise complete.

Hours: 10 a.m. to 4 p.m.

From Highway 101, exit onto Gower Street and proceed south to Santa Monica Boulevard. Go east (left) to Wilton Place. Proceed south (right) onto Wilton Place. Pass Melrose Avenue to #379 North Wilton Place. Our home is 2 houses south of Elmwood on the west side of the street.

From I-10, exit onto La Brea Avenue north and proceed north to Beverly Boulevard. Go east (right) to Wilton Place. Proceed north (left) onto Wilton Place and continue to #379, on the west side of the street. You will pass Highland, Rossmore, and Larchmont Boulevard.

From I-110, exit onto Third Street and proceed west to Wilton Place. (Wilton Place is west of Western Avenue.) Proceed north (left) onto Wilton Place and continue to #379, on the west side of the street. *Please park on the street.*

Proceeds shared with Pet Pride

East Meets West

112 North Edinburgh, Los Angeles

A yoga and meditation center enjoys a surprising dichotomy from front to back. Rare perennials, roses, and an unusual variety of flowering shrubs create a veiled and private yet immediately warm and welcoming atmosphere. A surprising container garden resplendent in amazing color combinations complements the entry patio. Walk into the back and enter the lushness of Bali, featuring a traveller's tree, a spindle palm, orchids, and a splashing wall fountain feeding an unusual bog/streamside planting. It is peace and tranquility.

Hours: 10 a.m. to 2 p.m.

Take I-10 to Fairfax and go north. Turn left onto Third Street, then turn right onto Edinburgh.

From Highway 101, exit at Sunset Boulevard going west. Turn left onto Fairfax Boulevard, then right onto Third Street. Turn right onto Edinburgh.

El Chaparro California Native Garden

111 South Van Ness Avenue, Los Angeles

El Chaparro was created to bring the botanical wilds of Southern California into an urban setting and by so doing recreate the palette and scents of the nearby foothills and mountains. The garden is loosely organized by plant community, including chaparral, desert, island, and meadow. Within these groups, primary plants are grown alongside their native companions, essentially surviving on rainfall alone, just as they would in nature. Structure is provided by the distinctive personalities of three native oaks, two of which were moved from the wild in an effort to save them from destruction by the proverbial bulldozer. Added interest is provided by an arrangement of rustic pergola seats made from hickory branches, which adds to the sense of old California that is ever present in this garden.

Hours: 10 a.m. to 2 p.m.

From I-10, exit at La Brea Avenue. Go north on La Brea Avenue to Third Street. Turn right (east) onto Third Street, go about 1 mile, and turn left onto Van Ness Avenue. Van Ness Avenue is the first block east of the traffic light at Norton Avenue. Go north 2 blocks.

From Highway 101, take the Sunset Boulevard exit. Turn south onto Van Ness Avenue and go about 2 miles to First Street.

From I-110, take the Third Street exit. Go west for 4 miles and turn right onto Van Ness Avenue, which is the first right after the light at Wilton Place. Go north 2 blocks. Number 111 South Van Ness Avenue is on the southwest corner of South Van Ness and First Street. *Please park on the street.*

Proceeds shared with the Windsor Square Home Owners Association

Helene Henderson Garden

344 South Rossmore Avenue, Los Angeles

Our English-style garden welcomes you through a rose-covered pergola. The front garden features boxwood hedges, rosebushes, lavender, and a large urn. The backyard is centered around a magnificent California sycamore where, in its shade, a patio features a beautiful stacked-stone outdoor fireplace, five-foot-high hydrangeas, camellias, azaleas, and a water fountain. The pool is enclosed by hedges and has its own wisteria-covered pergola and an extensive English rose garden. The garden also includes an organic vegetable garden, with boxwood hedges and a rose-covered chicken coop.

Hours: 10 a.m. to 4 p.m.

From Highway 101, take the Vine/Rossmore Avenue exit and head south. The house is located between Third and Fourth Streets on the east side of the street.

From I-10, exit onto La Brea Avenue north and proceed to Third Street. Go east on Third Street to Rossmore Avenue. Turn south onto Rossmore Avenue; the house is located between Third and Fourth Streets.

From I-110, exit onto Third Street and head west to Rossmore Avenue. Turn south onto Rossmore Avenue; the house is located between Third and Fourth Streets. *Please park on the street.*

Proceeds shared with the Saint James School

Horton Garden

256 South Van Ness Avenue, Los Angeles

A series of garden rooms surrounds this circa 1910 Craftsman house located four miles west of downtown Los Angeles. The back garden was designed in 1989 by landscape architect Frances Knight. Garden designer and plantswoman Judy Horton has treated the garden as a work in progress ever since. The garden rooms or spaces consist of an intimate terrace planted with white flowering, fragrant vines; a large Craftsman-style pergola; mixed borders around a rectangular lawn; a dry garden; potting shed and naturalistic garden; various pot gardens; and a front garden that relies primarily on foliage for color. Fruit trees are used to create a theme and a feeling of abundance throughout the garden. The planting reflects the owner's interest in seasonal change in the garden.

Hours: 10 a.m. to 4 p.m.

From I-110, take the Third Street exit. Go west for 4 miles and take the first right after Wilton Place.

From Highway 101, take the Sunset Boulevard exit. Turn south onto Van Ness Avenue and go about 3 miles.

From I-10, take the Western Avenue exit. Go north about 3 miles to Third Street and turn left. The first traffic light is Wilton Place; turn right after Wilton Place. *Please park on the street.*

Kew West

112 South Edinburgh, Los Angeles

Extensive collections of tropicalia highlight this garden, living proof of what can be achieved in California horticulture. Thirty species of bamboo, twenty species of palms and cycads, over thirty varieties of ginger, banana, and heliconia, and many rare shrubs and trees create a mystic series of vignettes. One transits the jungle past a gurgling fern grotto into a profusion of bromeliads, orchids, and esoterica celebrating the abundance of the tropics. Litchi, mango, rose apple, jaboticaba, and more fruits complete this fantasy.

Hours: 10 a.m. to 2 p.m.

Take I-10 to Fairfax, and go north. Turn left onto Third Street, then right onto Edinburgh.

From Highway 101, exit onto Sunset Boulevard going west, turn left onto Fairfax Boulevard, and right onto Third Street. Turn right onto Edinburgh.

Ozeta House

1291 Ozeta Terrace, Los Angeles

Jewelry designer/garden artist Laura Morton redesigned the gardens and pool area of this 1921 blue-and-white concrete house to create the look and feel of a Mediterranean oasis and incorporate some "garden jewelry" concepts. Lavender rises out of the cream-colored flagstones surrounding the pool. The "jeweled" grout gleams as light reflects the inlaid sea treasures of glass, tile, shell, and crystal. Roses, jasmine, and mint perfume a tiled Moroccan seating area at one end, while at the other, a beaded dragonfly hovers over a fountain amidst citrus, figs, and herbs. A wisteria-covered "wall" partitions the east garden. Here a collection of bamboo and purple-black foliaged plants creates a cool and shady environment for a nineteenth-century opium bed.

Hours: 10 a.m. to 4 p.m.

From Highway 101, exit onto Highland Avenue and proceed south to Sunset Boulevard. Go west on Sunset Boulevard to Larrabee Street (at Tower Records in West Hollywood). Take Larrabee Street north of Sunset Boulevard. Turn left onto the first street (Ozeta Terrace). We are the first house on the right

From I-10, exit north onto La Cienega Boulevard. Proceed to Sunset Boulevard. Proceed west on Sunset Boulevard for 3 traffic lights to Larrabee Street. Proceed as directed above. *Parking passes are are available; please park on Larrabee Street, Saint Ives Drive, or Ozeta Terrace.*

Sandra Taylor Garden

516 South Norton Avenue, Los Angeles

I had always wanted an English cottage garden and Judy Horton made this dream come true! This is a small English-style garden of roses, iris, and perennials in front, with a back patio garden surrounded by scented vines and morning glories and accented by the sound of water. On a lower level is hidden Molly's Secret Garden, which is a totally secluded, meditative space where you are lost from its urban surroundings.

Hours: 2 p.m. to 6 p.m.

From I-110, take the Third Street exit. Go west for 4 miles, turn left onto Norton Avenue, and go 2 blocks.

From Highway 101, take the Highland Avenue exit, and continue south to Third Street. Turn left, go to Norton Avenue, and turn right 2 blocks.

From I-10, take the Western Avenue exit. Go north about 3 miles to Third Street and turn left. Go to Norton Avenue and turn left 2 blocks.

Yusts' Garden

500 South Rossmore Boulevard, Los Angeles

This garden is designed in the Italian style, divided into four sections—the formal garden, the hidden garden, the woods, and the orchard.

Hours: 10 a.m. to 4 p.m.

The garden is located at 500 South Rossmore Boulevard, 3 miles south of Hollywood and Vine at the southeast corner of Rossmore Boulevard and Fifth Street. Please note that Vine becomes Rossmore south of Melrose Avenue.

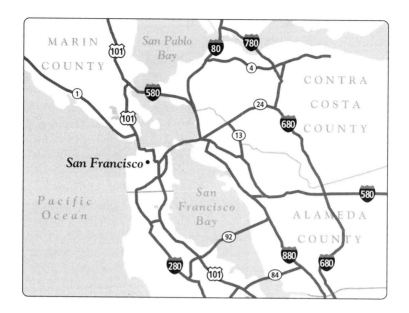

Sunday, May 5

SAN FRANCISCO COUNTY

SAN FRANCISCO

The Garden at 537 Chenery Street

537 Chenery Street, San Francisco

The garden has been created taking advantage of its inherent strengths—excellent soil, sunny position, gentle slope, and mild climate. Our love of English gardens is reflected in the design and choice of plants. A central flagstone path is flanked by broad borders of new and old roses, flowering shrubs, and as many different and unusual perennials as we could pack in. The color and fragrance in May and June is overwhelming. The path terminates onto a broad patio with a small pond on one side stocked with water plants and fish. We've also integrated a kitchen garden into the design and have tried to combine foliage and flower colors uniquely while creating a harmonious overall effect.

Hours: 10 a.m. to 4 p.m.

From San Francisco, take Dolores Street south to 30th Street. Turn right onto 30th Street, then immediately turn left onto Chenery Street. Go 5 blocks to #537.

From Marin or the East Bay, take I-280 towards Daly City. Exit at Monterey Boulevard. Turn right at the end of the exit ramp, then take the first left at the traffic light onto Diamond Street. Pass the BART station on the right, go through the light, and turn right at the first stop sign onto Chenery Street. Go 2 blocks to #537.

From I-280 north, take the San Jose Avenue exit. Turn left onto Dolores Street. Turn left again onto 30th Street and left once more onto Chenery Street. Go 5 blocks to #537. *Please park on the street.*

Proceeds shared with the Glen Park Garden Club

Kay Hamilton Estey

123 Conrad Street, San Francisco

Carved fourteen years ago from a concrete-covered hillside lot, the slope of this garden is softened by two small flagstone patios connected by a gentle sweep of rustic steps. A flowering cherry tree arches at center stage as the triangular lot falls away, playing with one's perspective. Experimental yet calming, this garden designer's plot is home to many unusual plants. The beds are crowded with plants that vary with season and whim, offering a mélange of colors, shapes, and sizes. Vines, perennials, grasses, succulents, and bulbs vie for attention. Tall fences and arbors provide a quiet haven. Bordered by one of the last unpaved lanes in San Francisco, the garden spills out through the gate and down the hill.

Hours: 10 a.m. to 4 p.m.

From San Francisco, take I-280 south. Take the Monterey Boulevard exit and make a sharp right at the first traffic light. Cross through the next light at Bosworth Street and continue on Diamond Street to the third stop sign. Turn left onto Sussex Street, then take the first right onto Conrad Street. Number 123 is the first white house on the right, just past Poppy Lane. Walk down the lane to the first garden gate on your left.

Proceeds shared with Strybing Arboretum

Matt Gil Sculpture Garden

75 Elmira Street, San Francisco

Husband and wife team, artist Matt Gil and writer Lesa Porché, envisioned their garden to be an open air gallery for Gil's original metal sculptures. It is a space unlike any other in San Francisco, a horticultural haven situated at the base of a steep, twenty-foot, native rock "mountain" and surrounded by walls of corrugated steel. Landscape designers Melanie Olstad and Dan Carlson of Wigglestem Gardens saw the rugged and exposed setting was ideal for South African natives, succulents, flowering perennials, and grasses. A specimen *Leucadendron* 'Safari Sunset,' bright yellow *Anigozanthos*, and variegated yucca add to the dynamic play of texture, form, and color.

Hours: 10 a.m. to 4 p.m.

From the north, take Highway 101 south to the Cesar Chavez Street exit. Follow the sign for Bayshore Boulevard. Take Bayshore to Industrial Street. Turn left onto Industrial Street. Drive 3 blocks and turn right onto Elmira Street.

From the south, take Highway 101 north to the Alemany exit. Follow the signs for Industrial Street. At the intersection, cross Bayshore Boulevard (you are now on Industrial Street). Drive 3 blocks and turn right onto Elmira Street.

Mary's Rock Garden

2530 Diamond Street, San Francisco

Jim Dixon designed my garden to be a peaceful woodland retreat in the urban environment. At the back of my small house, a winding gravel path meanders through raised rock beds containing a profusion of small trees, flowering shrubs, and perennials that attract numerous butterflies and birds. The path leads to stone steps up to a rock grotto and a series of rock terraces that proceed up the hillside. A large old silver maple toward the back right side of the garden provides a shady umbrella for rhododendrons, Japanese maples, hydrangeas, Pacific Coast irises, violets, and other shade-loving plants in the terraces. There are various little seating nooks throughout the garden from which to enjoy different views and the overall feeling of peace and tranquility.

Hours: 10 a.m. to 4 p.m.

From I-280 south, take the Monterey Boulevard exit and turn sharply right off the exit ramp. Proceed 2 blocks to a blinking traffic light and turn left onto Diamond Street. The BART station is on your right. Proceed 1 block through a light and continue about 6 blocks through Glen Park village and up the hill. The house is located on the steepest section of Diamond Street, on the corner of Arbor and Diamond.

From I-280 north, take the San Jose exit and merge onto San Jose Avenue. Turn right at Rousseau Street and right again onto Bosworth Street. Follow Bosworth under the freeway and turn right onto Diamond Street at the light. Proceed as directed above.

From the Glen Park BART station, turn right out of the BART station and walk 6 blocks on Diamond Street.

Proceeds shared with the Golden Gate Audubon Society

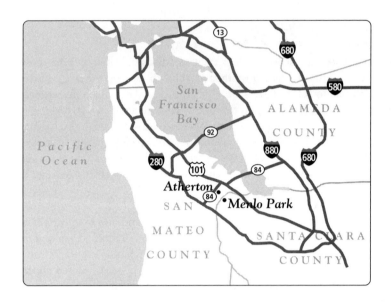

Saturday, May 11

SAN MATEO COUNTY

ATHERTON
Susan Fox & Jim Gafke
185 Stockbridge Avenue, Atherton

Roses, lavenders, rudbeckias, lavateras, clematis, and more surround this charming English-style, rolled shingle-roofed home placed in an acre of mature trees. Such features as perennial beds filled with roses, vine-laden arbors, antique garden urns brimming with color, a dry-stacked stone wall, an antique water feature, and more may be found as you wander. Shade and sun gardens can be found throughout.

Hours: 10 a.m. to 2 p.m.

From I-280, take the Woodside Road exit east. Turn right onto Alameda de las Pulgas. Turn left onto Stockbridge Avenue to #185. *Please park on the street.*

Peggy & Harvey Hinman
97 Selby Lane, Atherton

This garden has been owned by the same family since 1970 and has undergone many changes. Mary Gordon did the original design in 1978 and the owner designed many of the subsequent changes. The driveway has evolved from the original circular shape to its present configuration, now bordered by roses, lavender, and perennials. A formal rose garden now blooms where a sport court was and bricks cover the original concrete decking around the pool. A guest house looks out on a fountain centerpiece surrounded by a formal garden overflowing with dahlias, roses, and other perennials. A garden with year-round interest, it abounds with perennials, camellias, roses, and Japanese maples.

Hours: 10 a.m. to 2 p.m.

From Highway 101, proceed to Woodside Road/Route 84. Go west to El Camino Real. Take El Camino Real south for .7 mile. Turn right onto Selby Lane. Number 97 is the last house on the left before the first stop sign. *Please park along the street.*

Gene & Chuck Pratt
166 Encinal Avenue, Atherton

For over fifteen years, since first moving to this one-acre property, the owners have worked to integrate the garden with the interior living space it surrounds. The result is an extensive series of garden rooms, designed for living, relaxing, and reaping the rewards that a fully landscaped acre provides. As you travel through the garden, you will discover water features, occasional seating areas, arbors, dining areas, and meandering garden walks nestled amongst lush and fragrant plantings, all combined to invite you to stay a while and enjoy.

Hours: 10 a.m. to 2 p.m.

From Highway 101, take the Marsh Road/Atherton exit west. Marsh Road ends at Middlefield Road. Turn left onto Middlefield Road and continue to the elementary school on the corner of Encinal Avenue. Turn right onto Encinal and proceed to #166. *Please note that parking is prohibited on the south side of the street.*

MENLO PARK
The Woodruff Garden
1911 Oakdell Drive, Menlo Park

Azaleas, species geraniums, Japanese maples, *sasanqua* camellias, and other shade-loving plants surround the house in raised brick planters. Step through a gate and delight in a feast for the senses! A brightly colored butterfly garden, raised rock beds, fountains, a small rose garden, arbors and trellises, a small pond, and a gazebo nestled in flowering shrubs await you in this magical garden. See if you can find the slowly dripping fountain for butterflies.

Hours: 10 a.m. to 4 p.m.

From I-280, take the Sand Hill East/Menlo Park exit. At the major intersection of Sand Hill and Santa Cruz Avenue, turn left. At the first traffic light, bear right at the fork, continuing on Santa Cruz Avenue. Take the first right at Oakdell Drive. The garden is on the far right corner at #1911. *Please park on Oakdell Drive or Stanford Avenue.*

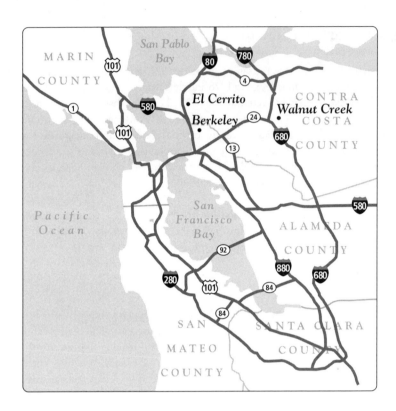

Sunday, May 19

ALAMEDA COUNTY

BERKELEY

Garden of Julie Chen & David Turner

490 Colusa Avenue, Berkeley

This garden, which has been in progress for the past eight years, is a testing ground for various garden notions I've had. One continuing theme is my use of drought tolerant plants juxtaposed with stone features and the occasional sculptural object. *Euphorbia, Agave, Salvia,* and *Phormium* figure largely in this picture but *Cordyline* and *Kniphofia,* even the *Restio* seem indispensable at this juncture. The built features—stone walls and paths, wood gates and benches—speak of a human element; they form a stage. But the real show, I'd say, is in the colors and forms, the comings and goings of the plants themselves.

Hours: 10 a.m. to 4 p.m.

From I-80, take the Central Avenue exit. Turn right onto Central. Turn right onto Carlson Boulevard. Turn left onto Fairmont. Stay on Fairmont for about .5 mile until the cemetery, where you take the easy right turn onto Colusa Avenue. Continue on Colusa for 1 block past the traffic circle. The house is on the right.

Proceeds shared with Strybing Arboretum

Il Giardino Fatato

2388 Vine Street, Berkeley

This garden was built on a lot next to our house, a lot that was left empty by the destruction of the big Berkeley fire of 1923 (part of a wall and stairs of the house that once stood there are still visible). It's a very young garden, completed in October of 2001. The design is by Ralph Barnes, the landscaping is by Bob Clark, and innumerable skilled people have contributed to it. We wanted a hidden retreat of beauty and of Italian memories, Italy being our other country. The lot was steep, so we built many rock walls and several patios at different levels. The central patio has an Italian fountain in the middle, another has a marble table and is covered by a pergola, yet another is surrounded by thujas and is the ideal place to read. Several levels of terraces allow easy access to the garden and extensive views. In the garden are roses, citrus, cypress, bay, bougainvillea, clematis, wisteria, dogwood, and a glorious, big old olive tree.

Hours: 2 p.m. to 6 p.m.

From I-80, take the University Avenue exit towards Berkeley. Keep left at the fork in the exit ramp and turn right onto University Avenue. Arriving near the Berkeley campus, turn left onto Shattuck Avenue, then right onto Vine Street. Climb the hill and find the garden at the end of Vine. It is surrounded by a pink wall and the entry is a light blue gate. *Please park on the street.*

Masala Gardens

620 Spruce Street, Berkeley

We wanted to transform the three major areas around our home into a *masala* (a pleasing mixture) of gardens that would impart a tremendous sense of peace and serenity. We often see a family of deer take refuge under an old apple tree in the large park-like front garden, which was planted thirty years ago. Landscape architect Josh Chandler built a garden of cascading rectangular pools, which complements the architectural simplicity of our home and blends beautifully with the panoramic view of San Francisco to the southwest. Grasses of different textures, colors, and heights surround the pools, with falling water creating delightful sounds. Landscape architect Lisa Ray transformed the third area into a tropical garden with plants ranging in colors of deep maroon, chartreuse, orange, magenta, and black. The exotic colors and shapes in this garden form a peaceful vista harmonious with the living room, filled with art from our visits to India.

Hours: 10 a.m. to 4 p.m.

From I-80 east, take the Buchanan Street exit. Buchanan becomes Marin Avenue after San Pablo Avenue. Keep on Marin Avenue until you get to a fountain at a roundabout. Take Marin Avenue up the Berkeley Hills (the third fork on the roundabout). Turn left onto Spruce Street and #620 is on your left. *Please park along the street and walk down the steep driveway.*

Maybeck Cottage—Garden of Roger Raiche & David McCrory

1 Maybeck Twin Drive, Berkeley

The historic Maybeck Cottage, once home of architect Bernard Maybeck, is surrounded by thousands of plants, many rarely seen. Roger and David have created a lush, horticulturally rich, hyper-naturalistic, fantasy setting to surround the cottage. This style, which they call "Planet Horticulture," combines plants, sculpture, and objects in a remarkable way. Take a unique journey to another world.

Hours: 2 p.m. to 6 p.m.

From Cedar Street (4 blocks north of University Avenue or 4 blocks south of Gilman Street; both are exits off I-80), proceed east uphill until Cedar Street ends at La Loma. Turn left onto La Loma. The second street on the right is Buena Vista at a 4-way stop sign. Turn right onto Buena Vista and *park along the road on Buena Vista.* Maybeck Twin Drive is the first left on Buena Vista. The first house up from the corner (not the corner house) is #1.

Proceeds shared with the UC Berkeley Botanical Garden

El Cerrito
Harland Hand Memorial Garden

825 Shevlin Drive, El Cerrito

Harland Hand designed and built his nearly half-acre garden on a hillside with breathtaking views of San Francisco Bay, the Bay Bridge, and Golden Gate Bridge. Inspired by the principles of fine art and the rock formations in the High Sierra, he sculpted concrete steps, paths, pools, and benches to create an emotionally evocative space. His plantings were known for dramatic color combinations of foliage and flowers. The garden has been featured in various books, magazines, newspapers, and television programs. After Mr. Hand died in September 1998, his sister took care of the garden for two years until the present owner, Marjory Harris, moved there in October 2000. Before she met him in early 1982, Ms. Harris had read Mr. Hand's "The Color Garden" (*Pacific Horticulture*, Spring 1978) many times, seeking guidance and inspiration as she developed her first garden on a steep hillside in San Francisco. In 1988, Mr. Hand designed Ms. Harris's second garden. She is honored to have as her third garden the horticultural masterpiece of her dear friend and mentor. Ms. Harris has added some new areas to the garden, including small private woods, screes, and waterfalls. Unusual plants will be available for purchase.

Hours: 10 a.m. to 4 p.m.

From I-80, take the Central Avenue/El Cerrito exit. Turn right onto Central Avenue. Turn left onto San Pablo Avenue. Turn right onto Moeser Lane. Go up the hill, turn right on Shevlin Drive, and proceed 1.5 blocks to the garden, #825 Shevlin Drive.

Proceeds shared with the California Horticultural Society

Bob & Kay Riddell's Garden

1095 Arlington Boulevard, El Cerrito

This garden, high in the El Cerrito hills overlooking the San Francisco Bay, was originally planted in the 1930s. The towering pines and a few old and interesting shrubs date to that period. We bought the house and the 1.25-acre property in 1973, at which time a long-range plan for the garden was developed by landscape architect Ernest Wertheim. The plantings in the shade of the pines are dominated by over 100 varieties of rhododendrons, many of which have attained mature size. There are rock gardens and a varied selection of magnolias, dogwoods, and maples, along with many unusual trees and shrubs. The sunny, south-facing slope at the back of the house was developed about eight years ago and planted with a variety of South African and Australian proteas, grevilleas, and other exotics. Developing and maintaining this garden has been a delightful, educational, and interesting hobby for us and continues to give us much pleasure.

Hours: noon to 4 p.m.

From I-80 or I-580, take the Central Avenue/El Cerrito exit. Drive east on Central Avenue. At the second traffic light, turn left onto San Pablo Avenue. Going north on San Pablo, turn right at the second light, Moeser Lane. Follow Moeser Lane almost to the skyline. Turn left at the stop sign onto Arlington Boulevard. Go north about 2.5 blocks to #1095, on the west side of the street. *Please park farther up on Arlington by the park and on several side streets.*

CONTRA COSTA COUNTY

The Ruth Bancroft Garden

1500 Bancroft Road, Walnut Creek

Please see public garden section for garden description, hours, and directions.

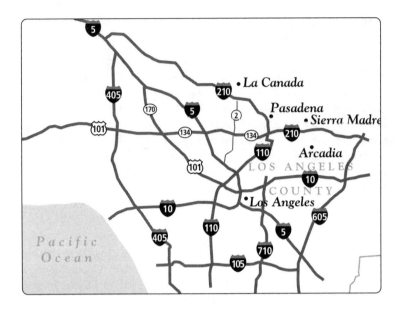

LOS ANGELES COUNTY

ARCADIA
Merrill & Donivee Nash
1014 Hampton Road, Arcadia

The home and garden are located in the Upper Rancho area of the historic Rancho Santa Anita, a neighborhood famous for its 200- to 300-year-old oak trees. The garden is a constantly evolving entity whose backbone is several hundred roses—Austins, hybrid teas, and old English. A formal pool, tennis court, and Dumbarton Oaks-inspired summerhouse provide a framework for perennials, climbing roses, clematis, and many varieties of trees. This garden is designed with the opportunity of almost year-round outdoor living in mind, but is at its most beautiful during the roses' first bloom.

Hours: 10 a.m. to 4 p.m.

From the west, proceed east on I-210. Exit at Rosemead North/Michillinda. Proceed north on Michillinda, cross Foothill Boulevard, and turn right onto Hampton Road. Continue to the intersection of Hampton and Dexter Roads. The house is #1014 Hampton, on the southwest corner of the intersection.

From the east, proceed west on I-210. Exit at Baldwin Avenue. Proceed north on Baldwin, cross Foothill Boulevard, and turn left at the second street, Hampton Road. Follow Hampton to the intersection of Dexter and Hampton Roads. Proceed as directed above.

Proceeds shared with the California Arboretum Foundation

La Canada
Nakaki Landscape
1021 Green Lane, La Canada

The property is about one third of an acre, which dictated our primary design goal—find a way to cozy-up this large yard. We utilized design features and focal points that would maximize the usefulness and aesthetic qualities of the entire outdoor space. We created three diverse outdoor living areas, two near the house and one in the upper level of the garden. We connected the three areas with rustic paths, walkways, lawns, and plantings and included a small greenhouse for heirloom orchids, a Craftsman-style arbor, a dog run, an herb and cut flower garden, and a vegetable garden. We installed two custom Rim Rock stone water features, one by each patio, to provide the serene look and sound of running water. The main feature that unifies the yard is a nearly 100-foot-long rock wall, which connects the lower and upper gardens. We were able to take advantage of the expanse of the space and produce a peaceful, beautiful, and usable outdoor environment.

Hours: 10 a.m. to 2 p.m.

From I-210, take the Angeles Crest Highway exit. Travel north off the freeway, proceed uphill about .5 mile, and turn left onto Green Lane. Number 1021 is on the right. *Please park on the street.*

Los Angeles
Rosen Landscape
1968 Westridge Road, Los Angeles

Designing and installing a landscape for this property presented many challenges. With a very strong commitment to environmental issues, the house was remodeled and rebuilt using non-toxic, ecological, and environmental techniques and materials. The landscape needed to reflect the same environmental concern, including the use of drought-tolerant, native (or similar) plants wherever possible. Second, the site itself was difficult to work with. The property is large, but much of it is very steep. The available level planting areas were limited. Some of the most important sight lines from the house were over areas with sharp drop-offs, making it appear that the yard ends abruptly. Third, for security reasons and to protect the landscape from deer and other wildlife, decisions had to be made about the type of fence materials and the locations of fence lines. Other challenges included dealing with the small amount of topsoil (average of twelve inches over bedrock), erosion control, and the desire to attract birds, butterflies, and bees. Our design goal was to create a landscape with as much colorful planting and usable space as possible and to give the illusion of a larger, flatter yard that stretches toward infinity and merges with the view, while using attractive, drought-tolerant, erosion-control plants suited to our Mediterranean climate. The end result is a beautiful, unified garden with creative outdoor niches to enjoy.

Hours: 2 p.m. to 6 p.m.

From I-405, take the Sunset Boulevard exit. Travel west on Sunset and turn right onto Mandeville Cyn. Take the first left at the 4-way stop sign onto Westridge Road. Follow this windy road about 1 mile up, pass #1968 driveway, and *park on Westridge Road or Westridge Terrace* and walk back down to #1968. The house is at the base of the driveway.

PASADENA
Sally & Harlan Bixby Garden
5 Oak Knoll Terrace, Pasadena

The Bixby garden in historic Pasadena hides behind adobe walls embedded with diverse original tiles from local and exotic artists. The southwestern landscape includes unusual cacti, agaves, and yucca, which are mixed with tropical palms, ferns, bamboo, bromeliads, decorative grasses, nasturtiums, lilies, and, of course, roses. Informal pathways of decomposed granite invite guests to wander among the timber bamboo, sycamore, live oak, citrus, king palm, and aloe trees. More tiles border a pool nestled among three large wisteria and rose-covered pergolas.

Hours: 10 a.m. to 4 p.m.

From I-210 in Pasadena, exit south onto Lake Avenue. Lake Avenue ends as the road curves to the right and becomes Oak Knoll. After two stop signs, take the first (Ridge) or second (Wentworth) road to the right where they join at Oak Knoll Terrace, a private road ending in a cul-de-sac. The Ritz-Charlton Hotel is just south of Wentworth Avenue; if you pass it, you have gone too far.

Proceeds shared with Descanso Gardens

La Folie
400 South San Rafael Avenue, Pasadena

This is a twentieth-century interpretation of an eighteenth-century Italian/French garden, with a top note of English naturalism. Several vignettes of roses, as well as perennials and woodlands, are set on the banks of historic San Rafael on the arroyo sew, with bowers and niches to contemplate life's wonder. Fountains splash to accent the scent of jasmine.

Hours: 10 a.m. to 2 p.m.

From Highway 134, take the San Rafael Avenue exit. Turn right onto Colorado Boulevard. Turn right onto San Rafael Avenue; #400 is on the left. *Park on the street.*

SIERRA MADRE
Louise & Paul Neiby
205 West Orange Grove Avenue, Sierra Madre

Paul's garden reflects the eclectic nature of Sierra Madre, a small village in the San Gabriel Mountain foothills. Tropical and desert specimen plants, mature trees, and compost piles are intermingled in the 1.3 acres. A stand of timber bamboo is almost 100 years old. Palm and oak trees enclose a pond-like pool. Hidden beneath tall magnolia trees is a rustic guest house in which Gutzon Borglum, the sculptor of Mount Rushmore fame, constructed a granite barbecue fireplace when he lived on the property as a young man. Paul has maintained the garden for 26 years to preserve the legacy of its former owners.

Hours: 10 a.m. to 4 p.m.

From I-210, exit at Baldwin Avenue/Santa Anita racetrack. Proceed north on Baldwin, cross Foothill Boulevard, and turn left at the stop sign onto Orange Grove Avenue. Follow Orange Grove Avenue to the second street on the right, Hermosa Avenue. The address is 205 West Orange Grove, on the northwest corner of Orange Grove and Hermosa. A high fence covered with ivy surrounds the property. *Please park on Hermosa Avenue and enter the property through the side walkway gate on Hermosa.*

Proceeds shared with the Sierra Madre Playhouse

Public Gardens

ALAMEDA COUNTY

BERKELEY

University of California Botanical Garden

200 Centennial Drive, Berkeley (510) 643-2755 www.mip.berkeley.edu/garden

One of the world's richest collections of living plants, virtually all of which were collected from the wild or can be traced to wild origins. In our 35 acres, there are more than 13,000 plant species from five continents, all arranged geographically. In addition, there is an Herb Garden, Chinese Medicinal Herb Garden, Redwood Grove, and areas dedicated to plants groups such as the Garden of Old Roses. Glasshouses are home to ferns and carnivorous plants, epiphytic orchids, cacti, succulents, and a tropical rainforest exhibit.

Hours: Labor Day through Memorial Day, daily, 9 a.m. to 4:45 p.m.; Memorial Day through Labor Day, daily, 9 a.m. to 7 p.m.; closed Christmas Day

Admission: $3 adults, $2 senior citizens, $1 children 3-18, children under 3 free

From San Jose, San Francisco, or Sacramento, take I-80 to Berkeley. Exit at University Avenue. Follow Unversity east to Oxford Street. Turn left. Go to Hearst. Turn right onto Hearst (east) to Gayley Road (second traffic light). Turn right. Go to the first stop sign. Turn left onto Stadium Rim Way. Go to the first stop sign. Turn left onto Centennial Drive. The garden is .75 mile up the hill on the right. The parking lot is 100 yards further up the hill.

OAKLAND

Dunsmuir Historic Estate

2960 Peralta Oaks Court, Oakland (510) 615-5555 www.dunsmuir.org

John McLaren, designer of Golden Gate Park in San Francisco, is said to have assisted in designing the gardens at the Dunsmuir Estate for the Hellman family, who owned the estate from 1906 until the late 1950s. Today, the fifty acres of meadows and gardens are still graced with a wide variety of trees, including Camperdown elms, bunya-bunya, and hornbeam, that surround the turn-of-the-century Neoclassical Revival-style mansion.

Hours: February through October, Tuesday through Friday, 10 a.m. to 4 p.m., also open the first Sunday of each month, May through September, 10 a.m. to 4 p.m.

Admission: grounds are free

From I-580 east, take the 106th Avenue exit. Make 3 quick left turns to cross the freeway, then turn right onto Peralta Oaks Drive. Follow signs to Dunsmuir.

From I-580 west, exit at Foothill/MacArthur Boulevard and veer to the right onto Foothill Boulevard. Turn right onto 106th Avenue and turn right again onto Peralta Oaks Drive.

Kaiser Center Roof Garden

300 Lakeside Drive, Oakland (510) 271-6197

The Kaiser Center Roof Garden is a 3.5-acre park located four floors above street level on top of the Kaiser Center garage. The garden, designed by the San Francisco firm of Osmundson and Staley, was installed in 1960. Despite a busy urban setting, boundary hedges, winding paths, bermed plantings, and a reflecting pond give the garden a quiet, oasis-like quality. A large variety of specimen trees, shrubs, perennials, and annuals provides year-round horticultural interest.

Hours: Year round, weekdays, 7 a.m. to 7 p.m.

Admission: free

From San Francisco, take the Bay Bridge to I-580 south (towards Hayward). One mile past the bridge, take the Harrison Street exit and turn right onto Harrison Street. Go straight through 3 traffic lights. Lake Merritt is on your left and the Kaiser Building is ahead to the right. Continue straight on Harrison Street and get into the right lane. Turn right onto 20th Street and make an immediate right into the parking garage. There is also street parking in the neighborhood. Take the garage elevator to the Roof Garden level.

CONTRA COSTA COUNTY

KENSINGTON

The Blake Garden of the University of California

2 Norwood Place, Kensington (510) 524-2449

This 10.5-acre garden was given to the university in the early 1960s by the Blake family. The garden was established when the house was designed and built in the 1920s. It has a large display of plants ranging from drought-tolerant to more moisture-loving plants from places such as Asia. The garden is divided into the formal area, the drought-tolerant section, the Australian Hollow, the cut-flower section, and the redwood canyon.

Hours: Year round, weekdays, 8 a.m. to 4:30 p.m.; closed on university holidays

Admission: free

From I-80, take the Buchanan Street off-ramp east to Buchanan Street. Follow Buchanan, which turns into Marin Avenue, until you arrive at a traffic circle with a fountain. Take the fourth exit off the circle onto Arlington Avenue. Travel 1.8 miles to Rincon Road on the left.

WALNUT CREEK

The Ruth Bancroft Garden

1500 Bancroft Road, Walnut Creek (925) 210-9663
www.ruthbancroftgarden.org

A PROJECT OF
THE GARDEN
CONSERVANCY

The Ruth Bancroft Garden rises above the status of a collection to an exceptional demonstration of the art of garden design. Working primarily with the dramatic forms of her beloved succulents, Mrs. Bancroft has created bold and varied compositions in which the colors, textures, and patterns of foliage provide a setting for the sparkle of floral color.

Hours: Open Day event May 19, 1 p.m. to 5 p.m.; otherwise, by appointment only.

Admission: $5

Located just north of Highway 24, exit I-680 onto Ygnacio Valley Road. Follow Ygnacio Valley Road 1.5 miles to Bancroft Road. Turn left and pass Stratton. At the end of the wooden fence, turn right into #1500 Bancroft Road.

ARCADIA

The Arboretum of Los Angeles County

301 North Baldwin Avenue, Arcadia (626) 821-3222 www.arboretum.org

The arboretum is a 127-acre horticultural and botanical museum jointly operated by the county of Los Angeles and the California Arboretum Foundation. The arboretum has plants from around the world blooming in every season. It is a wildlife refuge, complete with fish, turtles, ducks, geese, and other native and migrating birds that enjoy the sanctuary of Baldwin Lake and the Tropical Forest. It is Old California with historic buildings dating from 1840 that show early California lifestyles. The Hugo Reid Adobe is a California state landmark and the century-old Queen Anne Cottage is a national landmark. The arboretum staff has introduced more than 100 flowering plants to the California landscape and boast tree collections from many countries. A tram runs through the grounds every 30 minutes from 11 a.m. to 3 p.m. The arboretum is constantly adding horticultural classes, culture, and beauty to its acreage.

Hours: Year round, daily, 9 a.m. to 4:30 p.m.

Admission: $5 adults, $3 senior citizens and students, $1 children 5-12, children under 5 free

Off the 210 Freeway exit on Baldwin Avenue. The arboretum is in the San Gabriel Valley, freeway close to downtown Los Angeles, and right next door to Pasadena.

LA CAÑADA FLINTRIDGE

Descanso Gardens

1418 Descanso Drive, La Cañada Flintridge (818) 949-7979 www.descansogardens.org

Descanso Garden is a rare find—a woodland garden in the midst of California chaparral and Los Angeles urban sprawl. Here, in 160 acres, is an oasis of peace, beauty, and tranquility. Visitors stroll through the 35-acre California live-oak forest containing 50,000 camellia shrubs, the largest camellia forest in North America. They can admire the beauty of the five-acre International Rosarium filled with more than 4,000 antique and modern roses, or relax beside flowing streams containing shimmering koi. Each spring, thousands of tulips and other bulbs highlight the month-long Spring Festival of Flowers. Descanso also contains a one-acre lilac grove where lilacs for warm-winter climates originated. Visitors also enjoy viewing the California Native Plant Garden and hiking the chaparral trail surrounding the garden perimeter.

Hours: Year round, daily, 9:30 a.m. to 4:30 p.m., gates close at 5 p.m.; closed Christmas Day

Admission: $5 adults, $3 seniors/students, $1 children ages 5-10, children under 5 free

From I-210, exit onto Angeles Crest Highway. Turn south. Turn right onto Foothill Boulevard and left onto Descanso Drive.

SAN MARINO

The Huntington Library, Art Collections, and Botanical Gardens

1151 Oxford Road, San Marino www.huntington.org

The former estate of railroad magnate Henry Huntington showcases over 14,000 species of plants in 150 acres of gardens. Highlights include a twelve-acre desert garden, a rose garden, Japanese garden, jungle garden, and ten acres of camellias. Art and literary treasures are displayed in historic buildings on the grounds. English tea is served in the Rose Garden Tea Room.

Hours: September through May, Tuesday through Friday, noon to 4:30 p.m.; weekends, 10:30 a.m. to 4:30 p.m.; June through August, Tuesday through Sunday, 10:30 a.m. to 4:30 p.m.

Admission: $10 adults, $8.50 senior citizens, $7 students, children under 12 free

Located near the city of Pasadena, approximately 12 miles northeast of downtown Los Angeles. From downtown Los Angeles, take I-110 until it ends and becomes Arroyo Parkway. Continue north on Arroyo for 2 blocks to California Boulevard, turn right, and continue on California Boulevard for 2 miles. Turn right onto Allen Avenue and go straight for 2 short blocks to the Huntington gates. For recorded directions from other area freeways, call (626) 405-2274.

ORANGE COUNTY

LAGUNA BEACH

The Hortense Miller Garden

Laguna Beach (949) 497-3311

The Hortense Miller Garden, established in 1959, covers 2.5 acres in Laguna Beach. Over 1,500 species of plants are represented, including exotics from around the world, old-fashioned favorites, and native coastal sage scrub. In her well-designed, sustainable garden, Mrs. Miller uses little fertilizer, almost no pesticides, and a minimum of irrigation.

Hours: Year round, Tuesday through Saturday. Closed on major holidays. Visits booked in advance by Laguna Beach Recreation Department.

Admission: free

The garden is located at a private residence in a gated community. Guests are met by docents at Riddle Field on Hillcrest Drive and escorted to the garden.

SAN FRANCISCO COUNTY

SAN FRANCISCO

The Japanese Tea Garden

Golden Gate Park, San Francisco (415) 831-2700

The Japanese Tea Garden in Golden Gate Park, the oldest public Japanese garden in the United States, dates from 1894. Created for the California Mid-Winter Exposition to represent a Japanese village, the five-acre stroll garden includes a drum bridge, teahouse, pagoda, gift shop, two gates built for the 1915 Panama Pacific Exposition, and a Temple Belfry Gate, or *shoronomon*. The garden also has a notable collection of beautiful stone lanterns and a large bronze Buddha cast in 1790.

Hours: October 1 through February 29, daily, 8:30 a.m. to 5 p.m.; March 1 through September 30, daily, 8:30 a.m. to 6 p.m.

Admission: $3.50 general, $1.75 children 6-12, $1.25 seniors, children under 6 free

Located in the center of Golden Gate Park near the DeYoung Museum and Academy of Sciences on Hagiwara Drive.

Strybing Arboretum & Botanical Gardens
Ninth Avenue at Lincoln Way, San Francisco (415) 584-5815 www.strybing.org

Strybing Arboretum & Botanical Gardens sprawls over 55 acres and features 7,000 plant varieties from all over the world: Chile, Australia, South Africa, and New Zealand, to name a few. Specialty gardens include the Primitive Plant Garden, Moon-Viewing Garden, Asian Discovery Garden, California Natives Garden, and Fragrance Garden. You can stroll on your own or take a free guided tour offered by the Strybing Arboretum Society. If you are still not sated, visit the Helen Crocker Russell Library of Horticulture, a free reference library, open daily, 10 a.m. to 4 p.m. (except major holidays).

Hours: Year round, weekdays, 8 a.m. to 4:30 p.m., weekends and holidays, 10 a.m. to 5 p.m.

Admission: free, but donations are appreciated

Located in Golden Gate Park, at the corner of Ninth Avenue and Lincoln Way.

SAN MATEO COUNTY

MENLO PARK

Allied Arts Guild
75 Arbor Road, Menlo Park (650) 322-2405 www.alliedartsguild.com

One of the San Francisco Peninsula's most enduring institutions is Allied Arts Guild, with its shop and arts and crafts studios nestled in a California landmark setting of mission-style buildings and Spanish gardens. The gardens, reminiscent of those of Granada, provide an oasis of graciousness and serenity to those who come to shop, lunch, or simply bathe in their charm. The Guild benefits Packard Children's Hospital at Stanford.

Hours: Year round, Monday through Saturday, 10 a.m. to 5 p.m.

Admission: free

From Highway 101, take the University Avenue turn-off in Palo Alto and drive west on University Avenue to El Camino Real. Travel north for 1 mile to Menlo Park's Cambridge Avenue. Turn west onto Cambridge and follow to the end, which is the Allied Arts Guild parking lot.

PALO ALTO

The Elizabeth F. Gamble Garden
1431 Waverley Street, Palo Alto (650) 329-1356 www.gamblegarden.org

This 2.3-acre urban garden, located forty miles south of San Francisco, surrounds a turn-of-the-century house and carriage house. The formal gardens have been restored from the original plans. The working gardens include experimental demonstrations and displays. The formal gardens and buildings may be rented to private parties on weekends.

Hours: Year round, daily, dawn to dusk; access to certain areas may be restricted on weekend afternoons

Admission: free

From Highway 101, exit onto Embarcadero West. Turn left onto Waverley Street. The parking lot is on the left.

From I-280, exit onto Page Mill Road East, cross El Camino Real, and continue on Oregon Expressway. Turn left onto Waverley Street. The house is on the corner of Waverly Street and Churchill. The parking lot is north of the house.

WOODSIDE
Filoli

Canada Road, Woodside (650) 364-8300 www.filoli.org

Filoli is a 654-acre estate. It is a registered State Historical Landmark and is listed on the National Register of Historic Places. Sixteen acres of formal gardens are divided into a number of separate garden rooms.

Hours: Mid-February through October, Tuesday through Saturday, 10 a.m. to 2 p.m. Docent-led and self-guided tours every Tuesday and Wednesday; call for information.

Admission: $10

From I-280, take the Edgewood Road exit and follow the signs.

SANTA CLARA COUNTY

SAN JOSE
Emma Prusch Farm Park

647 South King Road, San Jose (408) 926-5555 www.sanjoseparks.org

Emma Prusch Farm Park offers visitors opportunities for recreation and to learn about San Jose's agricultural past. The park's 47 acres features San Jose's largest barn; more than 100 community and school garden plots; acres of open grass perfect for picnicking, kite flying, games, and relaxing; a rare fruit orchard featuring a strawberry tree, wild pear tree, and a raisin tree; a grove of international trees; close encounters with farm animals—everything from sheep, pigs, and steer to ducks, chickens, geese, and rabbits; and an old farm equipment display. In addition, there are school tours, environmental education classes, and summer camps, as well as year-round special events.

Hours: Year round, daily, 8:30 a.m. to dusk; closed Thanksgiving, Christmas, and New Year's Day.

Admission: free

From Highway 101, take the Story Road east exit. Turn left at King Road and left at the next light into the driveway.

From I-680, take the King Road exit and turn left onto King Road. Turn right at the second traffic light into the driveway.

From I-280, take the King Road exit and turn right. Proceed to the next light and turn right into the driveway.

COLORADO

Photo by Fawn Hayes Bell.

Saturday, June 22

EL PASO COUNTY

COLORADO SPRINGS

Crossland Gardens

13 Crossland Road, Colorado Springs

The Shepards' garden is a plethora of flora that captivates the visitor's eye with colors and textures. This formal garden setting combines traditional and modern styles of planting. A floral tour takes us through areas of shaded foliage, wispy pastel classics, and vibrant xerics, creating a variety of expressions. Overflowing planters complement the garden with a bounty of annual colors. The Shepards' progressive garden invites the visitor to join in their celebration of nature's beauty.

Hours: 10 a.m. to 3 p.m.

From I-25 south, take Exit 138/Circle Drive/Lake Avenue west towards the Broadmoor Hotel. Circle Drive becomes Lake Avenue. Turn left at the first roundabout onto Old Broadmoor Road and continue for 1 mile until you see the Broadmoor Elementary School on the right. At the school there is a 3-way intersection from which you turn left onto Marland Road. Go .25 mile to Crossland Road, turn right, and continue to #13 on the left side of the street. *Please park on the street.*

Dorothy's Garden

52 Marland Road, Colorado Springs

Perennial and dry landscape beds border the entry drive approaching a 1927 California mission-style Spanish Colonial home. Casual and natural beds frame the house. A stone path meanders past an old granite fountain, recently restored to reveal its original use as a watering trough for horses and dogs. The path journeys through additional gardens and areas for future planting. Most of the garden beds are young, while a host of mature and stately conifers graces the upper part of this nine-acre property. The owner's desire has been to incorporate native plants and those adaptable to varying soil and western mountain foothill conditions. The quest has been for a water-wise arrangement of color, texture, and trans-seasonal interest.

Hours: 10 a.m. to 3 p.m.

From I-25, take Exit 138/Circle Drive/Lake Avenue towards the Broadmoor Hotel. Circle Drive becomes Lake Avenue. Turn left at the first roundabout onto Old Broadmoor

Road, which curves to the right and goes past an elementary school. Take a soft left turn onto Cheyenne Mountain Boulevard, just past the school, and an immediate left onto Marland Road. Follow Marland straight ahead until it curves to the right. Follow the board fence and horse pasture on your left straight ahead to the gravel road. Continue following the gravel road (green mailbox, #52) past 2 houses on the left. This gravel drive curves into the third and last property. *Please park in the open field and grassy area on either side of the gravel drive up to but not beyond the 2 planted beds at the entrance area to the property. The area will be marked for parking.*

Proceeds shared with the Cheyenne Mountain Zoo

El Mardon

50 Marland Road, Colorado Springs

This magnificent garden sits on top of a high bluff with sweeping views of the city on one side and the tall peaks of Cheyenne Mountain to the west. The gardens are a perfect extension of the house, a 1927 Spanish Colonial designed by Chicago architect David Adler. The gardens comprise a series of outdoor patio rooms, each with a unique character and impressive plant palette. A large automobile courtyard greets the visitor and is marked by an eccentric statuary garden of dwarf conifers and woodland shade perennials. To the west, a high desert patio garden is a weave of color and texture, displaying the alluring possibilities even in the hottest garden area. The fine silvery hues of sage, lavender, and yarrow are combined with the showy colors of penstemon, agastache, and mass groupings of ornamental grasses. The heart of this landscape is a Tuscan-style orchard patio that includes weeping mulberry, bird's-nest spruce, and the contorted branches of Harry Lauder's walking stick. The unusual specimen plants provide balanced structure for a walled perennial garden containing rich color and textural combinations. At the center of the courtyard, a water garden carries soothing sounds of moving water throughout the patio and pool area. The final passage on the east side is a soothing walk through a whispering pine forest with an understory planting of azaleas, hosta, and woodland astilbe.

Hours: 10 a.m. to 3 p.m.

Proceeding west from Nevada Avenue on Lake Avenue (traveling towards the Broadmoor Hotel), at the first roundabout proceed around the turn onto Old Broadmoor Road (heading south), traveling through 3 residential "S" curves. Pass the elementary school, bear left at the first fork, and turn immediately left at the second fork onto Marland Road. Go .4 mile on Marland Road and follow the horse pasture lined with green fencing up to the driveway. *Please follow signs and park along Marland Road.*

The Macon Rose Garden

115 Glencrest Court, Colorado Springs

Our garden is a rose demonstration garden, often toured by rose societies and American Rose Society members. In its three quarters of an acre, you will find more than 300 varieties of roses, from the tiniest micro-miniatures to the strongest climbers, many of them rare. The hybrid tea and floribunda garden was installed during the completion of our home in 1993. In the following years, we added foundation plantings using old garden roses, a perennial border incorporating shrub roses, flagstone walks, water features, Monet-style arches, and a "wild" corner. Our roses give us five months of bloom, from mid-May to mid-October. Other flowering shrubs, bulbs, iris, clematis, peonies, phlox, and daylilies contribute color in season, making our garden a haven for hummingbirds, ladybugs, moths, and butterflies.

Hours: 10 a.m. to 3 p.m.

From I-25, exit west onto Exit 138/Circle Drive/Lake Avenue. Proceed west to Route 115/Nevada Avenue, exit to the left onto Route 115, and remain in the far right lane. At the first traffic light, turn right onto Cheyenne Mountain Boulevard. Proceed 1 block west, then turn left onto Broadmoor Valley Road. Proceed 2 blocks south to Glencrest Court. Turn right and go to #115 at the end of the street.

Rose & Dave Robbins

410 Brandywine Drive, Colorado Springs

Our garden is five years old. It has huge boulders and a creek. As a garden designer, I have tried to add interest and focal points on a difficult site by using color, texture, and form. Each garden has plant material for the amount of sun and water they need: an English garden by the entry in a soft palette, a "hell strip" of wild blooming plants by the curb, a boulder shade garden with ferns and Japanese maple, a Mediterranean garden with plants from that region, a xeric garden path with plants in gray and lavender, a stone terraced wall garden, and an Italian garden sprinkled with arbors, trellises, two water features, and an outdoor room. A truly private space.

Hours: 10 a.m. to 3 p.m.

Take Route 115 south, past Cheyenne Mountain Resort. Turn right onto Star Ranch Road. Stay left as Star Ranch splits into 2 streets. Do not go up Star Ranch; instead, you will be on Broadmoor Bluffs Drive. The third street on the right will be Thames. Turn right. Then turn right again onto Brandywine Drive. The garden is at #410.

Proceeds shared with the Horticultural Art Society of Colorado Springs

Public Gardens

EL PASO COUNTY

COLORADO SPRINGS

Cheyenne Mountain Zoo

4250 Cheyenne Mountain Zoo Road, Colorado Springs (719) 633-9925 www.cmzoo.org

The Cheyenne Mountain Zoo is located at 7,000 feet on the side of Cheyenne Mountain. The horticultural efforts are focused on native plants, theme gardens, and naturalized exhibits. Two favorite gardens are the Hummingbird Garden and the Butterfly Garden. The Hummingbird Garden was featured in the book *Hummingbird Gardens* and supplies many opportunities to see these wonders up close. In Asian Highlands, Siberian tigers are featured in a large naturalistic exhibit. The area is also home to some unusual trees and shrubs. Primate World, with a large outdoor gorilla exhibit, has been used in an experimental prescribed fire. Lion's Lair was landscaped using a combination of grasses and perennials to give the feeling of the open savanna. Your trip to the zoo will feel like a trip to the Great Rocky Mountains.

Hours: Year round, Labor Day through Memorial Day, 9 a.m. to 5 p.m.; Memorial Day through Labor Day, 9 a.m. to 6 p.m.

Admission: $10 adults, $8 senior citizens, $5 children 3-11, children under 3 free

From I-25, take Exit 138/Circle Drive/Lake Avenue and drive west for 2.8 miles to the Broadmoor Hotel. Turn right at the hotel and follow signs from there.

Colorado Springs Fine Arts Center Gardens
30 West Dale, Colorado Springs (719) 634-5581

Two gardens grace the grounds around the Southwest Deco building, both filled with sculptures. Plantings have been designed by the Broadmoor Garden Club and include many indigenous grasses, shrubs, and trees, all labeled. One garden is a pocket park on a main thoroughfare. The other garden is an enclosed sculpture courtyard within the museum, offering a different, more protected climate.

Hours: Year round, Monday through Saturday, 9 a.m. to 5 p.m. and Sunday, 1 p.m. to 5 p.m.

Admission: free on Saturday

From I-25, take Exit 143/Uintah Street east. Go east on Uintah Street about 3 blocks and turn right (south) onto Cascade Avenue. Drive through the campus of Colorado College and turn right (west) onto Dale. The corner garden at Cascade Avenue and Dale is the entrance to the Fine Arts Center property. Please park in the lot across from the building's entrance.

The Colorado Springs Xeriscape Demonstration Garden
2855 Mesa Road, Colorado Springs (719) 448-4555

The Xeriscape Demonstration Garden was designed in response to the need to conserve water. Since half of all water used annually is applied to lawns and gardens, planting with water conservation in mind was a goal. We are a demonstration garden where everyone is welcome to come see that xeriscape is a beautiful, low-water-use addition to their yards. The view from the garden is also quite an attraction, as we overlook the Garden of the Gods and Pikes Peak.

Hours: Year round, daily, 9 a.m. to 5 p.m.

Admission: free

From I-25, take the Fillmore exit. Turn west, pass Coronado High School, and proceed to the next traffic light. Turn right onto Mesa Road and go about .5 mile to the entrance.

The Demonstration Garden at the Horticultural Art Society of Colorado Springs
4403 Lyle Circle, Colorado Springs (719) 596-4901

The garden was a project of the local Nurserymen's Association, which banded together with a group of citizen gardeners in 1962 to form the Horticultural Art Society of Colorado Springs, Inc. It was designed to demonstrate, sometimes by trial and error, plants and shrubs that will thrive in a sheltered, semi-shaded city garden. Featured areas are perennial beds, rose beds, a fragrance garden for the handicapped, a children's garden, a regional native plant berm, a rock garden with a stream and wilding area, a ground-cover display, and the All-American Selections display garden. The Demo Garden has evolved through the years as a living entity; it will continue to change, but the basic design remains much as the founders envisioned it.

Hours: Year round, daily, dawn to dusk

Admission: free

From I-25, take Exit 143/Uintah Street east, then make the next right onto Glen Avenue. Proceed past Willow Pond and the city greenhouses to the garden, at the corner of Glen Avenue and Mesa Road in Monument Valley Park.

From the east, turn west off Cascade Avenue onto Cache la Poudre (at Colorado College). Cross the bridge west over Monument Creek and the garden is on the immediate right with a parking lot to the left.

Garden of the Gods Visitor Center

1805 North 30th Street, Colorado Springs (719) 634-6666

Imagine towering sandstone rock formations against a backdrop of snow-capped Pikes Peak and brilliant blue skies: that's the view from the beautiful Garden of the Gods Visitor Center. The Garden of the Gods is a unique biological melting pot where several life zones converge. The grasslands of the Great Plains meet the pinyon-juniper woodlands characteristic of the American Southwest, and merge with the mountain forests skirting 14,100-foot Pikes Peak. Around the visitor center can be found the various native gardens that naturally blend with this park, which has been designated as a National Natural Landmark.

Hours: June 1 through August 31, daily, 8 a.m. to 8 p.m.; September 1 through May 31, daily, 9 a.m. to 5 p.m.

Admission: free

From Denver, go south on I-25. Take Exit 146 onto Garden of the Gods Road. Turn left onto 30th Street and go .25 mile. The visitor center will be on your left.

Starsmore Hummingbird Garden

2120 South Cheyenne Canon Road, Colorado Springs (719) 578-6146

The Hummingbird Garden at Starsmore Discovery Center is full of native perennials that attract hummers. Penstemon, columbine, bee balm, agastache, Indian paintbrush, and fireweed are but a few. A new scree garden has been added to recreate the hot, dry, lean conditions loved by many of the penstemons, scarlet gilia, and others. The center sits at the mouth of the North Cheyenne Canon, which is a natural magnet for broadtail and rufous hummingbirds every summer. The garden is a project of the Friends of Cheyenne Canon volunteers.

Hours: June through August, daily, 9 a.m. to 5 p.m.

Admission: free

Take I-25 to Exit 140B/South Tejon and turn right onto Tejon. Tejon becomes Cheyenne Boulevard. Travel 3 miles west on Cheyenne Boulevard. Follow "Seven Falls" signs and "Starsmore Discovery" signs to South Cheyenne Canon Road. Please park in the lot.

CONNECTICUT

Georgia Middlebrook's garden, Washington.
Photo by Laura Palmer.

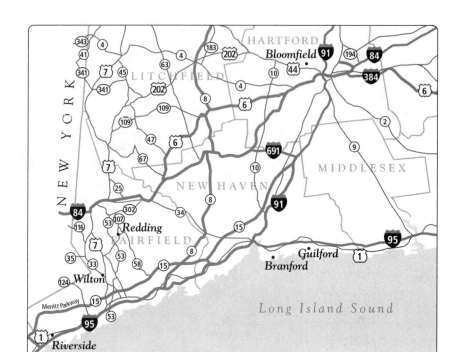

Sunday, May 19

Please also see listings for this date in New York

FAIRFIELD COUNTY

REDDING

Highstead Arboretum

127 Lonetown Road, Redding

The dappled shade provided by five native species of oak on a terrain of wet and dry soil proved perfect shelter and habitat for a collection of deciduous azaleas. Fourteen East Coast native species are now represented at a site where pinxterbloom azalea alone was originally found. This naturalistic setting in the heart of the woodland is also home to ericaceous companion plants and has been fenced for protection from deer. Mid- to late May should find several in bloom, a perfect opportunity to be spoiled by the color and fragrance during a ninety-minute guided tour of the arboretum. Set on fifty acres of geographic extremes, the arboretum is also open weekdays by appointment, and offering two other distinct seasonal walks on June 2 and August 11.

Hours: Guided walks 10 a.m., noon, and 2 p.m. Please call weekdays, 8:30 a.m. to 4:30 p.m., for more information (203) 938-8809.

From I-95 or Merritt Parkway/Route 15, take Route 7 north. Turn right onto Route 107 for 6 miles (be sure to follow signs for 107 as it crosses Route 53). Pass the police station, Redding Elementary School, and Redding Country Club. Take the second driveway on the left after the country club, 127 Lonetown Road. Follow signs into the arboretum; the driveway is .5 mile long.

RIVERSIDE
Susan Cohen
7 Perkely Lane, Riverside

Overlooking a tidal inlet, this small, sloping property has been shaped over the past twenty years by its current owners, who first removed overgrown shrubs and vines to create a garden in harmony with its waterfront setting. Susan Cohen, a landscape architect, created a fountain grotto from the old foundation walls of a derelict boathouse, regraded parts of the land, and designed flowering borders to surround the house. Four raised beds provide growing space for vegetables, herbs, and roses.

Hours: noon to 4 p.m.

From I-95, take Exit 5. Turn right onto Post Road/Route 1. Turn right again at the first intersection onto Sound Beach Avenue. Continue into Old Greenwich. Turn right at the traffic light onto West End Avenue. A Mobil gas station will be on the right. At the traffic circle, go left onto Riverside Avenue; there is a boatyard on the left. Turn left onto Marks Road, then take the first left onto Perkely Lane. The house, #7, is the second on the left. *Please park on Marks Road, beyond Perkely Lane.*

WILTON
Jane Bescherer
38 English Drive, Wilton

My small corner of paradise is a two-acre garden that starts at the top of a hill and gradually works its way down through stone steps, rose arbors, new stone walls, irises, sundials, herbs, old stone walls, peonies, bird baths, old roses, crab apple trees, and lilacs. It is a work in progress on an unfinished canvas.

Hours: 10 a.m. to 4 p.m.

From the intersection of Routes 33 and 7 in Wilton, take Route 33 north towards Ridgefield. From the traffic light at the white Congregational church, continue just over 2 miles and turn right onto Nod Hill. Take the next right onto Olmstead Hill and right again onto English Drive. The house, #38, is the second driveway on the left. *Please park along English Drive.*

HARTFORD COUNTY

BLOOMFIELD
Dr. Ben Thaw
11 Overbrook Farms, Bloomfield

This garden is a third-of-an-acre woodland with paths and an unusual "secret garden." It includes a three-acre collection of dwarf and slow-growing conifers, azaleas, and rhododendrons, as well as a collection of Richard Jaynes *Kalmia* hybrids.

Hours: 10 a.m. to 2 p.m.

From the junction of I-91 and I-84, take I-84 west to Exit 41/South Main Street. Follow it north 5.1 miles (South Main becomes North Main). Turn left onto Route 185 west/Simsbury Road. Go .5 mile. Overbrook Farms is on the left, opposite the Tumble Brook Country Club. *Please park in the wide circular driveway.*

NEW HAVEN COUNTY

BRANFORD
Nickolas Nickou
107 Sunset Hill Drive, Branford

This garden features many species and varieties of mature rhododendrons and azaleas. In addition, there are many rare trees and shrubs from China and Japan, coupled with woodland flowering plants and ferns.

Hours: guided tour at 10 a.m.; no wandering alone

From I-95, take Exit 55 to Route 1. Go east .4 mile and turn right onto Featherbed Lane; continue to the end. Turn left, go 200 feet, then turn right onto Griffing Road, which runs into Sunset Hill Drive. (Ignore the first right onto Sunset Hill Drive.) The yellow hydrant on the left marks the driveway. *Please park along the road.*

GUILFORD
Mary Anne & Dale Athanas
66 Christopher Lane, Guilford

A secret garden—from the front of this well-landscaped southern Colonial you would not realize that we have 35 gardens, garden rooms, and water features awaiting your enjoyment. Observe from the multi-level deck the amphitheater of plantings and streams surrounded by woodland. Highlights of the garden include a circular garden with its two-tiered fountain, formal perennial gardens, rock garden, ponds, daylily borders, and much more. We designed and planted all of the gardens over a period of nine years.

Hours: 10 a.m. to 4 p.m.

From the Hartford area, take I-91 south to Exit 15/Route 68/Durham. At the end of the exit ramp, turn left onto Route 68. Follow Route 68 until it ends in Durham. Turn right onto Route 17. Follow Route 17 about 1.5 miles (past Route 79, which will be on the left) to Route 77. Turn left onto Route 77. Follow Route 77 for several miles until you reach a traffic light at a major intersection. Turn right onto Route 80 and travel 1 mile to the light. Turn left onto Long Hill Road. Travel 1.3 miles and look for Christopher Lane on the left (two stone entrance walls). Turn left onto Christopher Lane and look for #66 on the left just before a cul-de-sac. It is a large white Colonial with a formal front porch (columns) set back from the road.

From the New York area, take I-95 north to Exit 57. Turn right at the light off the exit ramp and go 1 mile (past Bishop's Orchards on the left) to the first light. Turn left onto Long Hill Road. Go about 3 miles to Christopher Lane on the right. Turn right onto Christopher Lane and look for #66 on the left just before a cul-de-sac.

Proceeds shared with the Gillette Center

G & G Garden
411 Mulberry Point Road, Guilford

Our house is on a hill overlooking Long Island Sound. The four-acre premises are rocky and about half is woods with shade-loving plants. The entrance to the house is from a small Japanese garden with a pond, with mostly evergreens. There is a small rock garden. The remaining land is crossed by paths and surrounded by beds, mostly containing perennials and shrubs. There is a rather large waterfall created from a natural setting of rocks. The garden is informally planted but well maintained.

Hours: 10 a.m. to 4 p.m.

From New Haven, take I-95 east to Exit 57. Turn right off the exit ramp onto Route 1/ Boston Post Road. Continue past Bishop's Orchards. At the second traffic light (Mobil gas station on the right), turn right onto River Street. At the end of River Street, turn right onto Route 146/Water Street. Continue on Route 146 for .5 mile and turn left onto Mulberry Point Road, crossing the ridge over the railroad. Travel .75 mile on Mulberry Point Road and look for a black mailbox on the right, #411. Turn right into the paved driveway to the left of the mailbox. Bear left at the fork in the driveway and *follow instructions for parking.*

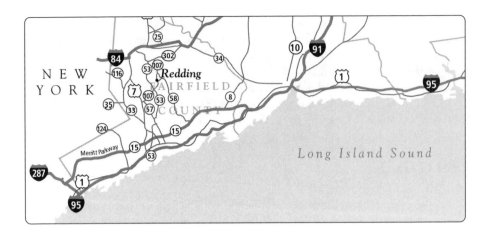

Sunday, June 2

FAIRFIELD COUNTY

Redding

Highstead Arboretum

127 Lonetown Road, Redding

A guided tour of Highstead's *Kalmia* collection in bloom presents the opportunity to compare the characteristics of mountain laurel found in the wild with plants that have been cultivated. A part of the North American Plant Collection Consortium, this collection has over sixty cultivars to admire. This ninety-minute guided walk will also traverse more than 26 acres of native mountain laurel growing in a variety of soils and exposures. Set on fifty acres of geographic extremes, the arboretum is also open weekdays by appointment, and offering two other distinct seasonal walks on May 19 and August 11.

Hours: Guided walks at 10 a.m., noon, and 2 p.m. Please call weekdays, 8:30 a.m. to 4:30 p.m., for more information (203) 938-8809.

From I-95 or Merritt Parkway/Route 15, take Route 7 north. Turn right onto Route 107 for 6 miles (be sure to follow signs for 107 as it crosses Route 53). Pass the police station, Redding Elementary School, and Redding Country Club. Take the second driveway on the left after the country club, 127 Lonetown Road. Follow signs into the arboretum; the driveway is .5 mile long.

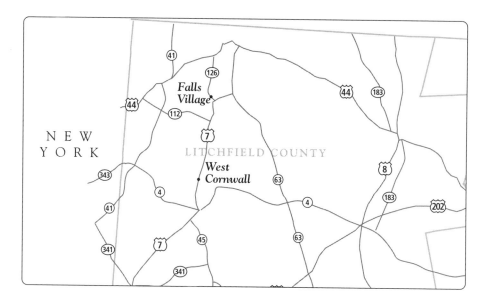

Saturday, June 8
LITCHFIELD COUNTY

FALLS VILLAGE

Martha & Robert Rubin
55 Hautboy Hill Road, Falls Village

This land must have been a settler's nightmare back in the eighteenth century, a steep north-facing hillside of glacial ledge, scattered stones, watery chasms, and bog. The woods of maple, oak, and ash were too dense to get a wagon through, but there was water in a fast-flowing stream, plenty of rock to build walls and foundations, and wood for a house, barn, icehouse, and shed. So it became a farm. Today, the land offsets its geological irregularities in more aesthetic ways. It bestows a glorious view and features winding, hidden footpaths through woodlands over streams to distant ponds and waterfalls. It has bowed to its human caretakers by allowing gardens of vegetables, shrubs, and flowers, an orchard, berry patches, and a contemplative garden surrounding a Japanese teahouse. But all that human hands have rendered accede to the natural aspect that made it possible. Martha Adams Rubin is the author of *Countryside Garden and Table.*

Hours: noon to 4 p.m.

Take Route 7 to Cornwall Bridge. At Cornwall Bridge, bear right onto Route 4 (or left, if you are coming from the north). Continue about 4 miles to a blinking traffic light, then continue straight ahead onto Route 43. Continue another 4 miles to a cemetery on the right and a Civil War monument on the left. Just beyond the monument, turn right onto Hautboy Hill Road. The Rubin garden is .6 mile on the left, #55.

From Route 63, drive 6 miles north of Goshen and turn left onto Hautboy Hill Road (or right, if you are coming from the north). The Rubin garden is .3 mile on the right.

WEST CORNWALL
Julia & John Scott
52 Cream Hill Road, West Cornwall

Over many years the owners have transformed this precipitous, rocky hillside terrain with a sixty-foot waterfall into a series of very different gardens. The upper garden adjoining the millpond has traditional shrubs, perennial beds, and a stone-edged cutting garden. This is linked by terraces, gardens, and an orchard to the lower pond and water garden. An early spring and wildflower garden borders the waterfall. It has magnificent views and is a garden full of surprises!

Hours: noon to 4 p.m.

Take Route 7 to Route 128 in West Cornwall. Turn east for 1 to 2 miles after the covered bridge. Take the first left, by Cornwall School (Cream Hill Road). Number 52 is on the right side (red board fence).

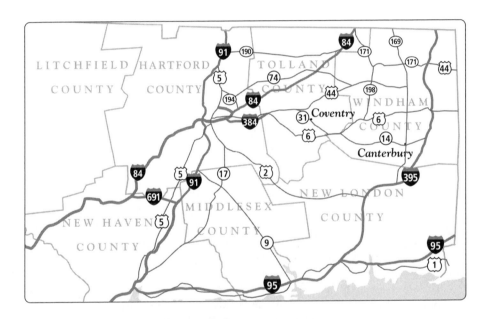

Sunday, June 9

Please also see listings for this date in New York

TOLLAND COUNTY

COVENTRY
David & Julia Hayes
905 South Street, Coventry

Sculptor David Hayes, whose work is found in many public and private collections in this country and in Europe, lives and works on this old farm. Hayes displays his completed works in an old orchard, by the pond, in a large hayfield, and behind the house. They are in or near informal gardens of herbs, wildflowers and ferns, roses (mostly old roses), annuals, and veg-etables. Wear comfortable shoes as the paths are not all smooth.

Hours: 10 a.m. to 4 p.m.

From I-84, take Exit 59/I-384. Follow I-384 to the end (about 8 miles). Take Route 44 about 3.5 miles, then turn right onto Silver Street (signs there for Caprilands and Hale Homestead). Follow about 2 miles to the end, turning left onto South Street (go to the right after Hale Homestead). Go 4.5 miles to #905. *Please park along the street. The drive-way is available for those with walking difficulties.*

WINDHAM COUNTY

CANTERBURY

Westminster Gardens—Eleanor B. Cote & Adrian P. Hart

26 Westminster Road, Canterbury

The area surrounding the house has border plantings of dwarf evergreens, rhododendrons, azaleas, other shrubs, and perennials. There is also a stone terrace with a waterfall. The back area is about three acres. It has nearly an acre of woodland gardens with crushed stone walk-ways, 650 different varieties of hosta, and many astilbes, pulmonarias, ferns, and other shade-loving plants. The remaining area has twenty gardens planted with various ornamental grasses, shrubs, perennials, and annuals, with tall bearded iris and peonies blooming in June, followed by Japanese iris and Siberian iris, with daylilies and Asiatic and Oriental lilies blooming in July. An Oriental garden with a goldfish pond is located next to the woods. Benches have been placed throughout the gardens so visitors may stop to rest. A new feature is a dry rock river complete with bridge.

Hours: noon to 4 p.m.

From I-395 south, take Exit 89. Turn right at the bottom of the exit ramp. Follow Route 14 about 6 miles to the stop sign at the bottom of the hill. Turn right. Go over the bridge to a 4-way stop at the intersection of Routes 169 and 14. Go straight on Route 14. Number 26 is the second house on the left after the Citgo gas station.

From I-395 north, take Exit 83A. Turn left at the bottom of the exit ramp. Follow Route 169 for about 10 miles to the intersection of Routes 169 and 14. Turn left onto Route 14/Westminster Road. Proceed as directed above. *Please park along the road. Handi-capped may park in the driveway.*

Proceeds shared with Pound Hounds, Inc.

Saturday, June 15

Please also see listings for this date in New York

HARTFORD COUNTY

EAST WINDSOR HILL

Pat & George Porter

1533 Main Street, East Windsor Hill

Surrounding an early nineteenth-century historic house in an historic district and on a scenic road, our gardens are both formal and English country. There are formal English rose beds, an herb garden, moon gardens, and perennial borders backed with yew or hemlock hedges. Plants and ferns swing on long hooks from old maple trees. A spectacular wall of climbing hydrangea backs a border of old roses that faces an espaliered apple tree allée. This leads to horse barns, an English glasshouse, a grape-covered pergola, swimming pool, ornamental grasses, and a rugosa rose border, all overlooking the Connecticut River meadows. In the south yard, a golden hops-covered pergola is surrounded by azaleas and rhododendron.

Hours: 10 a.m. to 4 p.m.

From I-91, turn east onto I-291. Cross the Connecticut River. Take Exit 4. Stay in the left lane. Turn left onto Route 5 north. Go 3 miles. Turn left at the traffic light onto

Sullivan Avenue. Turn left again onto Main Street and go 1 mile south. Number 1533 is on the right.

From I-84, take I-291 west. Turn right on the South Windsor exit. Turn left onto Route 5 north and proceed as directed above. *Please park on the street.*

MANCHESTER
Diana & Roy Behlke's Gardens
64 Bette Drive, Manchester

Enter our gardens through the rustic arbor to find a series of garden rooms featuring delightful vistas and focal points in shade gardens, perennial borders, and woodland gardens. Listen for the sound of a chugging steam engine in our latest endeavor, a miniature Victorian garden railroad. Watch the passenger train travel from "Carlisle Corners" through the tunnel to the farming village of "Daylily Gulch." The train then crosses over the bridge spanning a waterfall, past the operating watermill and fishpond. All the plantings in this garden are in scale to the railroad and miniature buildings. Climb up the stone steps for a panoramic last look at the railroad before visiting the mixed shrub and perennial border and hillside rock garden.

Hours: 10 a.m. to 4 p.m.

From I-84, head towards Boston. Pick up I-384 about 2 miles east of Hartford. Follow I-384 for 6 miles past the Manchester/Main Street exit, taking the Wyllys/Highland Street exit. Turn left off the exit ramp, crossing over the highway. Turn right at the first traffic light onto Highland Street. Follow Highland Street for 1 mile, crossing under the highway, and take the second right to Carter Street. Take the second right to Blue Ridge Drive. Take the first left to Bette Drive. Our house is the fourth on the right, a beige Colonial, #64.

Lindland's Garden
225 Timrod Road, Manchester

Welcome! My gardens have expanded on this one-acre property since 1976. In front, explore a shady perennial bed with a stone wall and wildflower garden that gives an early spring display. In the back, we had to remove the hemlock forest after a severe attack of woolly adelgid. This blank canvas is where I was challenged to create what is now two hillsides with vegetables, herbs, roses, and a small rockery. Stone walls, a trellis and an arbor add strong structure to the gardens that plants alone cannot.

Hours: 10 a.m. to 4 p.m.

From I-84 east, go to I-384 east for 5 miles to Exit 4/Highland Street. At the end of the exit ramp go right for .3 mile to the traffic light and turn right onto Spring Street. Travel .5 mile and turn left onto Tam Road. Go to the end and turn left onto Timrod Road. Number 225 is the third house on the left.

From I-384 *west towards Hartford*, take Exit 4/Highland Street. Proceed as directed above.

Watersong

85 Alton Street, Manchester

Although my yard is small, I've tried to use as many ideas as possible. The front walk and annual beds lead to a porch adorned with geraniums, vines, roses, and a puddle of a pond. Around the side, the path leads past a grass garden, through a perennial bed, small pond, and arbor, into a grassy courtyard. Perennial borders edge the backyard, in the middle of which lie a pond and waterfall. Entering the back courtyard, you're greeted by a locust tree in the center, a pagoda-style lath house, a pond with three streams running through, a garden of hostas and ferns, and a secluded screen porch, creating the perfect hideaway.

Hours: 10 a.m. to 4 p.m.

From I-84, take Exit 60/West Middle Turnpike. If you were travelling east, at the traffic light at the end of the exit ramp, turn right; if you were traveling west, turn left. Immediately get into the left lane. Follow the left lane to the second light (the third light if you are coming from I-84 west) and turn right onto West Middle Turnpike. Go through 4 lights and look for Vic's Restaurant. The second street on your left past Vic's is Alton Street. Turn left onto Alton Street and go to #85 (a light blue Colonial-style house on the right). *Please park along the street.*

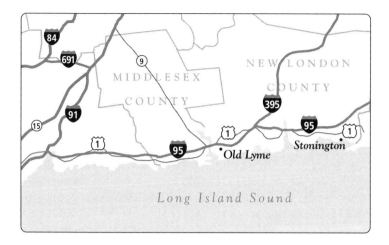

Sunday, June 16

NEW LONDON COUNTY

Old Lyme

Ruth Perry

Route 156, Old Lyme

Visit a cottage garden with a sense of humor. There is a rose garden, an herb garden, a bog garden, and lots of perennials. A developing formal garden is the most recent addition.

Hours: 10 a.m. to 2 p.m.

From I-95, take Exit 70/Old Lyme. Turn onto Route 156 north. Go about 5 miles to the intersection of Route 156 and Nehantic State Forest. The Perry garden is on the right. *Please park along Park Road.*

Stonington

Mr. & Mrs. James L. Coker

50 Church Street, Stonington

A variety of small gardens surrounding the residence feature old-fashioned plantings in a casual, contemporary setting. Perennial beds, a woodland garden, rock garden, and water garden are set among trees and shrubbery. Visitors are encouraged to discover secret places and to sit on terraces to view the Long Island Sound.

Hours: 10 a.m. to 2 p.m.

From I-95, take Exit 91/Stonington Borough Village. At the end of the exit ramp, if coming from the north, turn left; if coming from the south, turn right. Go .25 mile and turn left onto North Main Street. Go about 2 miles to a stop sign and turn right over the viaduct into the village. Follow Water Street to Church Street (Noah's Restaurant) and turn left. Go 2 blocks past the church to #50. *Please park on Church Street.*

Proceeds shared with the Calvary Nursery School

Merry Meeting Farm
264 Taugwonk Road, Stonington

Five acres of lawn and gardens surround a 1747 Georgian home. A 100-year-old lilac spreads 25 feet below a pink dogwood. The fifty-year-old euonymus hedge, towering weeping willow, honey locusts, gnarled cherry, aged maple trees, and eighteenth-century stone walls provide the setting for a sunny perennial border, shade gardens, kitchen garden, orchard, berry path, and formal rose garden containing more than 75 varieties planted over the past twenty years by owners Jack and Gracelyn Guyol.

Hours: 10 a.m. to 4 p.m.

From I-95, take Exit 91/Stonington Borough Village. At the end of the exit ramp, if coming from the north, turn right; if coming from the south, turn left. Go .8 mile on Taugwonk Road to Merry Meeting Farm on the right. *Please park in the driveway or, if full, in the field indicated on the right just past the Merry Meeting Farm sign.*

Mr. & Mrs. Juan O'Callahan
40 Salt Acres Road, Stonington

The four-acre seaside garden consists of grass with trees and border gardens along stone walls. There are six large cutting beds with a variety of flowers and bulbs, and four large rose beds enclosed in a yew hedge. A "secret garden" is built into the rock ledge next to the seawall. The greenhouse holds succulent plants in the summer. The view of Watch Hill, Sandy Point, and Fishers Island is spectacular.

Hours: 10 a.m. to 2 p.m.

From I-95, take Exit 91/Stonington Borough Village. At the end of the exit ramp, if coming from the north, turn left; from the south, turn right. Go .25 mile and turn left onto North Main Street. Continue for about 2 miles across Route 1 to a stop sign and turn left onto Trumbull Street. At the next stop sign, turn right over the bridge (railroad tracks) into the village. Follow Water Street to Church Street (Noah's Restaurant) and turn left. Go 2 blocks, then turn left onto Orchard Street. Turn right at the next block onto East Grand Street. Continue to the end of the causeway. *Please park under the trees.*

Proceeds shared with the Care Net Pregnancy Resource Center

Mrs. Frederic C. Paffard, Jr.
389 North Main Street, Stonington

A ninety-year-old boxwood hedge one-quarter mile long, a rose arbor, and an old-fashioned garden are highlights. There are also a formal perennial garden edged with boxwoods and a water garden. Interesting old outbuildings, a greenhouse, vegetable garden, natural pond with resident otters and blue herons, and meadow are adjacent. English boxwood and perennials will be available for sale, with ten percent of the proceeds to be donated to the Garden Conservancy.

Hours: 10 a.m. to 2 p.m.

From I-95, take Exit 91/Stonington Borough Village. Go south to North Main Street, then turn left towards Stonington Borough. Go about 1.5 miles to 389 North Main Street.

From Route 1, turn north onto North Main Street at the traffic light. Number 389 is the second driveway on the right. *Park anywhere.*

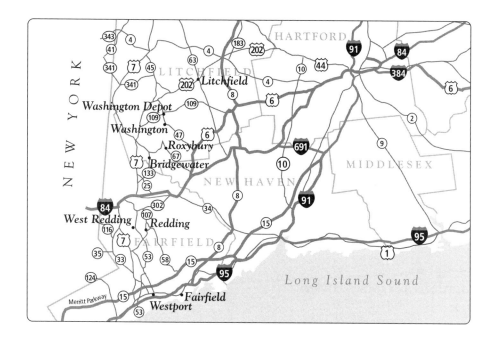

Sunday, June 23

Please also see listings for this date in New York

FAIRFIELD COUNTY

FAIRFIELD

Nancy & Tom Grant

4014 Redding Road, Fairfield

Our garden is an extension of an eighteenth-century reproduction Fairfield, Connecticut, Georgian-style house we built in 1972. Despite the fact that the house is new, it is listed in the historic and architectural survey of Fairfield by the Connecticut Historical Commission. We have tried to create an eighteenth-century feel to our garden to complement the house. What was once a vegetable garden has been taken over by more than 100 roses and peonies, perennials, shrubs, herbs, and annuals. We start many plants from seed and continually divide and change. We maintain the gardens ourselves.

Hours: 10 a.m. to 4 p.m.

From Merritt Parkway/Route 15, take Exit 44/Fairfield from New York. Turn left off the exit ramp, then left at the traffic light onto Route 58/Black Rock Turnpike.

From New Haven, turn left off the exit ramp and right at the light onto Route 58/Black Rock Turnpike. Go north towards the town of Redding for 1.9 miles to North Street/Division Street. Turn left onto North Street and proceed west past 2 stop signs for 1.5 miles. At the third stop sign, turn right onto Redding Road. Go north for .3 mile to #4014. The garden is on the southeast corner of Redding and Mile Common Roads. *Please park on Mile Common Road.*

On the Harbor
328 Sasco Hill Road, Fairfield

My gardens surround an 1894 Second Empire-style house overlooking Southport Harbor. They were begun in 1996 with the help of Mike Donnally. Boxwood, beech, and arborvitae provide structure and continuity throughout the various gardens. A garden room looks out onto a small parterre that is separated from the shade garden by antique garden gates. A small stone-and-brick terrace, designed by Agnes Clark in the 1950s, leads to the back terrace, overhung by a 75-year-old white wisteria. Below the terrace are raised beds containing peonies and iris and below the raised beds are parterres, whose structure provides year-round interest.

Hours: 10 a.m. to 4 p.m.

From I-95, take Exit 19 and turn onto Post Road travelling east towards Fairfield. At the first traffic light, turn left onto Sasco Hill Road. The house, #328, is on the right. *Please park along the road.*

REDDING
Gardens at Horsefeathers
313 Umpawaug Road, Redding

Horsefeathers is known in Redding as the Aaron Barlow house. Joel Barlow, after whom the Redding High School is named, one of Aaron's brothers, lived here after the French Revolution. Joel was a diplomat and a renowned poet. He was an attaché at the U. S. embassy in Paris at the time of Thomas Jefferson and was instrumental in the signing of the Purchase of Louisiana from France. While residing in the house, he composed *The Columbiad*, his most famous work. Circa 1723, the house is the oldest in Redding. The totally organic gardens are influenced by French and English period gardens and are structured around the "reflecting pool," with French curves of nepeta on the outer borders. Stone walls, boxwood, and a pergola give the garden architectural "bones" in all seasons.

Hours: noon to 4 p.m

From Route 7 north, take Route 107 at Georgetown for 1.7 miles to Umpawaug Road. Continue on Umpawaug Road for 3.5 miles to the Horsefeathers sign on the left. *Look for parking signs on the right.*

WESTPORT
Susan Lloyd
59 Center Street, Westport

A stone outcropping alongside the early nineteenth-century house hides the garden beyond. The long, narrow property ends at a brook with astilbe and hosta beds. This is a family garden with a treehouse and playground. The large perennial bed (124 by 16 to 20 feet) is a collection of purples, yellow, white, and some pink and illustrates a love of different foliage shapes and textures.

Hours: 10 a.m. to 4 p.m.

From I-95, take Exit 18. If heading north, turn left at the end of the exit ramp; if southbound, turn right. Turn right at the second traffic light onto Greens Farms Road. The first left is Center Street. Number 59 is the third house on the right, with a white picket fence.

From Merritt Parkway/Route 15, take Exit 42. If southbound, turn left at the end of the exit ramp; if northbound, turn right onto Weston Road; turn left at the second stop sign onto Cross Highway. Make the first right onto Roseville Road and cross Post Road (Route 1). Take the first left onto Hillandale. Turn right at the stop sign onto West Parish and turn right at the "T" in the road onto Center Street. Number 59 is on the left side. *Please park on the house side of the street.*

WEST REDDING
Hughes-Sonnenfroh Gardens
54 Chestnut Woods Road, West Redding

Our 22-year battle with the deer is, at last, over! We could no longer tolerate watching our beloved plants being eaten and last year we fenced in our entire five acres. What a difference a year makes. Our plants have recovered and are thriving in their protected environment. I am a landscape designer and my husband is an arborist, so we share a strong love, including plants. We have enjoyed watching the "children" grow and many of the conifers and shrubs have developed into mature specimens. I like big borders—the wider, the deeper, the better I like it. I also believe in placing the right plants in the right places, so they are content and work hard for me, smothering the weeds and blooming their heads off. Concentrating on the long view has always been important to me and I am finally pleased with the garden settings on our property. Our garden "rested" during the summer of 2001, but Tim and I did not. Our house, barn, and pool underwent facelifts this year. We hope you'll come visit us and enjoy our gardens. I would like to thank my mom for making the fence project financially possible, my beloved husband for all his hard work, and the plants for holding on until they were rescued by a six-foot fence. Now, if only we could rid the property of our resident woodchuck, mole families, and ticks, we'd be living in heaven!

Hours: 10 a.m. to 4 p.m.

From I-84, take Exit 3/Route 7 south. Go 3 miles to the traffic light at the junction of Route 35. Bear left through the light, continuing on Route 7 south. Go 1.5 miles. At the third light, turn left onto Topstone Road. Go .25 mile, downhill, cross the railroad tracks, and bear left uphill, continuing on Topstone Road for .5 mile. Take the second left onto Chestnut Woods Road. The house, #54, is the second on the right. *Please park along the driveway or on the north side of Chestnut Woods Road.*

Proceeds shared with the Redding Garden Club

LITCHFIELD COUNTY

BRIDGEWATER
Maywood Gardens
52 Cooper Road, Bridgewater

This private estate features a sunken perennial garden protected by ten-foot stone walls, a gazebo garden planted with butterfly- and hummingbird-attracting flowers and shrubs, a rose garden arranged in a French pattern design surrounded by a circle of hemlocks, a woodland path populated by mature beech and cherry trees as well as viburnums and rhododendrons, a ledge garden on an exposed hillside, a heather bed, a white garden, an herb garden, an ornamental kitchen garden, and a 4,000-square-foot greenhouse.

Hours: 10 a.m. to 2 p.m.

From I-84, take Exit 9 and travel north on Route 25 towards Brookfield Village. Turn right onto Route 133 east towards Bridgewater. Cross Lake Lillinonah Bridge and take the first right after the bridge onto Wewaka Brook Road. Go .75 mile and turn right onto Beach Hill Road to the end. Turn right onto Skyline Ridge. Go .5 mile and turn right onto Cooper Road. *Please park on the right across from the greenhouse complex.*

LITCHFIELD
Dan & Joyce Lake
258 Beach Street, Litchfield

Litchfield Horticultural Center is a 32-acre private residence with a retail landscape nursery and Christmas tree farm. Viewers can enjoy more than twenty perennial gardens, both sunny and shady, a large locust arbor, rustic pergola, ornamental grass garden, pond-side expressions, and woodland shade gardens. We have extensive amounts of native mountain laurel and many large boulders in our landscape. All areas are designed in harmony with nature and the naturalistic setting of ledges and several large ponds. We have fields of growing landscape trees and a landscaped container nursery with an allée and a formal design with tasteful accents. A new classic shade house and Zen gardens have been added this year.

Hours: 2 p.m. to 6 p.m.

In Litchfield, at the traffic light on Route 202 by Stop & Shop, turn onto Milton Road. After .25 mile, fork right onto Beach Street. Go 2 miles and the Horticultural Center is on the right. There are stone columns, stone walls, and large maple trees. We are 2 miles from Milton Road, 2.25 miles from Route 202.

Proceeds shared with Habitat for Humanity

Mr. & Mrs. David Stoner
183 Maple Street, Litchfield

The circa 1850 house and cottage-style garden overlook a pond and Prospect Mountain. In addition to perennial beds, there are more than sixty roses and fifty peonies, a variety of small trees and shrubs, and a cutting garden. The vegetable garden and grape arbor are large and beautiful.

Hours: noon to 4 p.m.

From the west, take Route 202 east through Bantam to the first left across from Ristorante. Follow to Maple Street and go north for .75 mile. The house, #183, is on the west side of the street. *Please park in the driveway or along street.*

Proceeds shared with the Bellamy-Ferriday House & Garden

ROXBURY
Martine & Richard Copeland
12 Eastwoods Road, Roxbury

This three-acre hillside garden, bordered by stone walls and staircases, which connect the multi-level terraces, incorporates the structures and features of the French and Italian traditions—vistas, parterres and hedges of yew and box, potted plants, water features, statues, and seats—with a variety of plant material. Exuberant plantings in the rose garden, the old-fashioned flower garden, and the shade garden are contained by the green architecture in this work in progress.

Hours: 10 a.m. to 4 p.m.

From the Roxbury Green, take Route 67 east towards, Southbury. About 2.5 miles from the green, after going down a hill, turn left onto Rucum Road. Cross Bacon Road, continue up the hill, and turn left onto Eastwoods Road (at the top of the hill). Number 12 is the second driveway on the right.

From I-84, take Exit 14 in the direction of New Britain (Route 172 north) for 4.5 miles, passing New Britain and continuing to the stop sign at the intersection with Route 67. Turn left onto Route 67 and continue about 2 miles, until you see Bacon Road on the right. Take Bacon Road to the stop sign. Turn right onto Rucum Road and follow as directed above. *Please park along the road.*

WASHINGTON
Linda Allard
156 Wykeham Road, Washington

High on a hillside, with a panoramic view of the Litchfield Hills, this garden has Old-World charm. Surrounded by stone walls covered with espaliered fruit trees and climbing roses and hydrangeas, the garden is partly formal and partly potager. A lush rose arbor filled with pale pink and white roses interwoven with clematis separates the two. Boxwood hedges define the white formal garden enhanced by a variety of green textures. Geometric beds overflowing with fruits, vegetables, herbs, and flowers are a true depiction of potager. This part of the garden changes yearly; plantings are worked by color and color combination.

Hours: 10 a.m. to 4 p.m.

From Washington Green, at Gunn Memorial Library, turn onto Wykeham Road. Follow for about 1.5 miles until Old Litchfield Road forks left. Stay right on Wykeham for about .25 mile. Go up a small hill to a red barn on the right side of the road. The entrance to the garden is opposite the red barn. Number 156 is on the stone wall; proceed through the gate to the garden.

Charles Raskob Robinson & Barbara Paul Robinson
88 Clark Road, Washington

Brush Hill, included in Rosemary Verey's book *The Secret Garden* and *House & Garden* magazine (October 1997), is set between an eighteenth-century Connecticut farmhouse and barn amidst old stone walls. The garden includes a rose walk featuring old roses and climbers, a fountain garden planted in yellows and purples, herbaceous borders, and a terraced garden planted in hot colors leading up to a garden folly and through a woodland arch to a developing woodland walk with a newly created series of cascading pools. There is an old Lord & Burnham greenhouse, along with a white wisteria-draped bridge over the pond with waterlilies and grass borders.

Hours: noon to 4 p.m.

From I-84, take Exit 15/Southbury. Take Route 6 north to Route 47 and turn left. Go 4 miles, passing Woodbury Ski Area on the left, and turn right onto Nettleton Hollow Road. Go 4.1 miles, past the intersection of Wykeman and Carmel Hill Roads, and take the next sharp left onto Clark Road (a dead end). The house, #88, is the first and only one on the left. *Please park along Clark Road before the driveway.*

George Schoellkopf
Nettleton Road, Washington

An old-fashioned, but unusual, rambling formal garden informally planted with an exuberant abundance of both common and exotic plants in subtle, and sometimes surprising, color combinations. High walls and hedges divide separate "rooms" and open to create interesting vistas out towards the landscape. New areas are currently under construction.

Hours: 2 p.m. to 6 p.m.

From I-84, take Exit 15/Southbury. Take Route 6 north through Southbury and Woodbury. Turn left onto Route 47 north. Go 4 miles, pass Woodbury Ski Area on the left, and turn right onto Nettleton Hollow Road. Go 1.7 miles. The house is on the right. *Please park along the road.*

WASHINGTON DEPOT
Gael Hammer
63 River Road, Washington Depot

This is a cottage garden designed to engulf the house with flowers and shrubs and provide different spaces for outdoor living. Special areas include oversized borders, a grass garden, a white moon garden, an enormous "step" garden, and container gardens on an old-fashioned porch and sunny deck. The garden has been featured in *Martha Stewart Living* and *House Beautiful* magazines.

Hours: 10 a.m. to 4 p.m.

From Route 109, travel to Washington Depot. Take River Road .5 mile from town. *Please park in front of the house.*

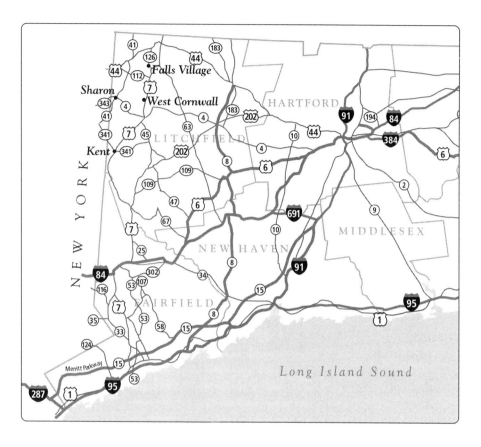

Saturday, June 29
LITCHFIELD COUNTY

FALLS VILLAGE

Bunny Williams

Point of Rocks Road, Falls Village

Interior designer and garden book author Bunny Williams' intensively planted fifteen-acre estate has a sunken garden with twin perennial borders surrounding a fishpond, a parterre garden, a year-round conservatory filled with tender plants, a large vegetable garden with flowers and herbs, and a woodland garden with meandering paths and a pond with a waterfall. There are also a working greenhouse and an aviary with unusual chickens and fantail doves. Recent additions include an apple orchard with mature trees, a rustic Greek Revival pool house folly, and a swimming pool with eighteenth-century French coping.

Hours: 10 a.m. to 4 p.m.

From Route 7 north, go to Falls Village. Turn left at the blinking traffic light onto Main Street/Route 126. Bear right (still on Route 126). Go to the stop sign at Point of Rocks Road. The driveway is directly ahead. *Please park in the field adjacent to the house.*

K<small>ENT</small>
Skiff Mountain Farm
3 West Woods Road, Kent

Set atop a mountain with breathtaking views, this garden was left unattended for several years. Four years ago, the new owners began to redefine the 120-foot sweeping border, which is filled with large plantings of herbaceous perennials. An eighteenth-century barn is a focal point, surrounded by an orchard of considerable age. A formal evergreen garden is the center of the lattice-enclosed entry. A fountain becomes the focal point of this garden room. An expansive stone terrace surrounding the house provides a spectacular vantage point for viewing the garden. A boxwood-framed white garden borders the terrace.

Hours: 2 p.m. to 6 p.m.

From the intersection of Routes 7 and 341 at the monument in Kent, take Route 341 west towards Macedonia State Park, over the Housatonic River bridge. Immediately after crossing the bridge, turn right onto Skiff Mountain Road (just opposite the entrance to the Kent School). Proceed up the mountain for 4.9 miles. The Marvelwood School will be on the right at the intersection of Skiff Mountain and West Woods Roads. Proceed on for 100 yards to the entrance to Skiff Mountain Farm on the left. *Please park along West Woods Road.*

S<small>HARON</small>
Lee Link
99 White Hollow Road, Sharon

Three stone walls cascade down a sunny hillside. The space between each is planted with perennial borders, which bloom with the flowering seasons of spring and summer. One level is set off by a water garden, which reflects a winter conservatory on the hill behind it.

Hours: noon to 4 p.m.

From the junction of Routes 7 and 112, turn onto Route 112. Go about 2 miles on Route 112 until you see the sign "Entrance to Lime Rock Race Track." Turn left onto White Hollow Road and travel 2.5 miles. The house, #99, is on the right, opposite a white fence.

From Route 41 in Sharon, turn right onto Calkinstown Road. Take the second left onto White Hollow Road. Our driveway is on the left, opposite a white fence.

Plum Creek Farm
498 Cornwall Bridge Road, Sharon

There is an over 100-foot-long perennial border planned for summer-long flowering as well as foliage texture and color interest. The grounds overlook a three-tiered formal garden with vistas to a pond with a geyser and a view of a folly in the woods. A walking path runs from the formal garden past a hillside planted with hostas, the upper pond with geyser, a waterfall to a lower pond, and a long shrub border. A woodland/fern walk crosses a bridge, passes the folly, and meanders along a stream before crossing a second bridge and returning to the house.

Hours: 2 p.m. to 6 p.m.

From Route 6, proceed to the intersection of Route 4 at Cornwall Bridge, cross the bridge, and take Route 4 toward Sharon (uphill) for 2 miles. The driveway is on the right with white gates and a small white bridge beyond. Follow the driveway to the top of the hill.

From the intersection of Routes 41 and 4 at the clocktower in Sharon, take Route 4 towards Cornwall Bridge for 5.8 miles. The driveway is on the left. Proceed as directed above.

West Cornwall
Jurutungo Viejo
20 Kirk Road, West Cornwall

On the banks of the Housatonic River the gardens of Jurutungo Viejo offer unmatched vistas that reflect the gardener's testament to nature and experimentation. Doug Mayhew and his firm, Mayhew Orion Inc., have been described as "an avant garde voice who creates his own natural wonders." Jurutungo Viejo is an exotic oasis from another world. Gourds and castors pervade the monumental cast-iron temple alongside *Cycas, Araucaria, Musa, Cryptomeria, Agave, Dicksonia, Cyathea, Melianthus,* et al. Whether exploring the arboretum or getting lost among the moods of painters and poets, visitors can share in the unusual ecosystem this four-acre garden offers.

Hours: 10 a.m. to 4 p.m.

From West Cornwall, take Route 7 north about 1.5 miles. Turn right onto Kirk Road. The garden is located at 20 Kirk Road. Follow signs.

From the intersection of Routes 112 and 7, go about 3.5 miles south on Route 7 and turn left onto Kirk Road. Proceed as directed above. *Please park along the street.*

Michael Trapp
7 River Road, West Cornwall

This Old World-style garden is intimate, with cobbled paths, terraced gardens, raised perennial beds, and reflecting pools. Overlooking the Housatonic River, the property has a distinct French/Italian flavor.

Hours: 10 a.m. to 4 p.m.

From Route 7, take Route 128 east through the covered bridge into West Cornwall. Continue on Route 128, taking the second left onto River Road. The house is yellow with gray trim. It is the first on the left and sits behind the Brookside Bistro. *Please park in front or along the road.*

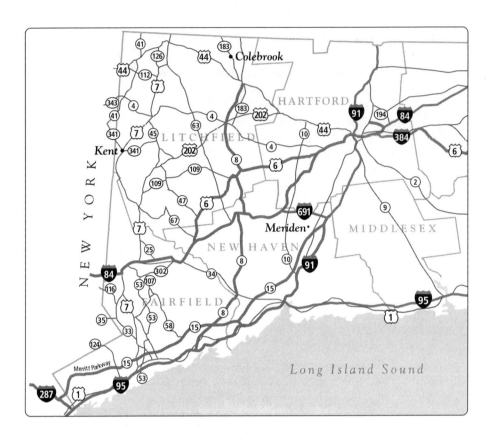

Sunday, July 7
LITCHFIELD COUNTY

COLEBROOK
Marveen & Michael Pakalik
46 Stillman Hill Road, Colebrook

One open, sunny acre with distant views of the Berkshires features three long herbaceous perennial/shrub borders, each devoted to the seasons, and a new evergreen shrub border that keeps mysteriously expanding. A lovely woodland garden blends with native flora. A stone patio features unusual container plantings and some of the funky garden ornaments were featured in the Time-Life book *Decorating Your Garden*.

Hours: 10 a.m. to 4 p.m.

From Route 8 north or Route 44 west, travel to Winsted, then take Route 183 north to Colebrook. At the intersection of Routes 182 and 183, turn left and go to the top of hill. The house, #46, is the first white house on the right.

From Route 44 east towards Norfolk, bear left at George's Norfolk Garage and take Route 182 about 4 miles (just past Route 182A) to the top of the hill. The house, #46, is a white house on the left. *Please park on the street.*

Steepleview Gardens—Kathy Loomis

25 Stillman Hill Road, Colebrook

The many gardens at Steepleview were created in a former cow pasture at the top of a sunny hill to showcase an ever-changing rainbow of floral colors that complement one another. Interesting plant habits and foliage textures are featured in the more than 25 cottage-style gardens displaying hundreds of different hybrid daylilies, stunning six-foot-tall spikes of delphinium, and a very large collection of familiar and unusual perennials. Butterflies and hummingbirds are frequent garden visitors, lured to the flowers planted specifically to attract them. Bright, beautiful colors are the main theme of the gardens at Steepleview.

Hours: 10 a.m. to 4 p.m.

From Winsted on Route 44, turn right onto Route 183/Colebrook Road. Continue for about 3 miles to the 4-way intersection with Route 182. There is a large barn on the left. Turn left onto Route 182. Steepleview Gardens will be at the third house on the left (a gray farmhouse at the top of the hill).

From Norfolk on Route 44, turn left onto Route 182 just before George's Norfolk Garage. Travel about 4 miles. Look for the Pinney Street sign on the right. Do not take this road, but begin counting houses after it. Steepleview Gardens will be the third house on the right. *Please park on the road.*

Proceeds shared with the Litchfield Hills Audubon Society

NEW HAVEN COUNTY

MERIDEN

George Trecina

341 Spring Street, Meriden

A professional landscape designer's display and trial gardens, with one-third of an acre of continuous mixed borders containing more than 300 varieties of woody plants and perennials, some unusual. The planting schemes are enhanced with an assortment of annuals, tender perennials, and container plantings with a decidedly tropical theme. The sloping front yard—structured with paths, walls, and stairways—features a white garden and a "wild" garden.

Hours: 1 p.m. to 5 p.m.

From I-91, take I-691 west to Exit 6/Lewis Avenue. Turn right to the end. Turn right onto Hanover Street to the first traffic light. Turn left onto Columbus Avenue and go to the second stop sign. Turn left onto Prospect Avenue, then turn at the first right onto Spring Street to the fourth house on the right, #341.

From I-84, take I-691 east to Exit 5/Chamberlain Highway. Go right to the end. Turn left onto West Main Street to the first light. Turn right onto Bradley Avenue and go to the first stop sign. Turn left onto Winthrop Terrace and past the light onto Columbus Avenue. Continue from Columbus Avenue as directed above. *Please park along Spring Street.*

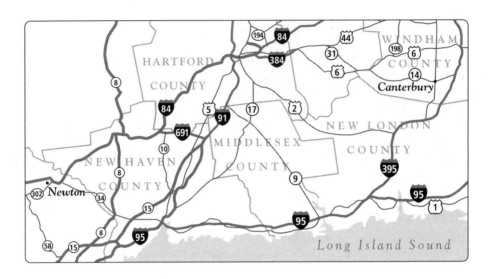

Sunday, July 14

Please also see listings for this date in New York

FAIRFIELD COUNTY

Newtown
Sydney Eddison
Echo Valley Road, Newtown

This garden includes a fine display of daylilies and other perennials in brilliant color combinations created by the owner, a self-taught gardener and garden author. Extensive shade plantings feature mature rhododendrons, hostas, ferns, and other plants tolerant of low-light situations.

Hours: noon to 4 p.m.

From I-84 east, take Exit 10. Turn left at the traffic light at the end of the exit ramp. Continue uphill through two lights and under the railroad bridge. Make the first right onto the Boulevard. Go past a 4-way stop. Continue over a railroad bridge and under I-84. Make the first right onto Echo Valley Road. Go .7 mile to a large brown sign that reads "Paugussett State Forest, Public Access." Go into the entrance of the state forest. The house is a tan Colonial on the left. *Please park in the public parking lot in the state forest. Additional parking is available at the foot of the hill at the brown-shingled Colonial house of Mae and Bob Schmidle.*

WINDHAM COUNTY

Canterbury
Westminster Gardens—Eleanor B. Cote & Adrian P. Hart
26 Westminster Road, Canterbury

Please see June 9 for garden description, hours, and directions.

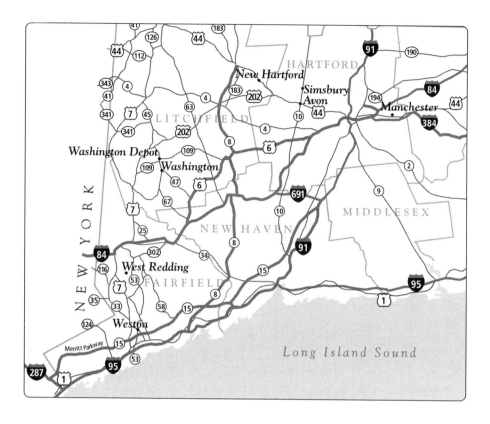

Sunday, July 21

Please also see listings for this date in New York

FAIRFIELD COUNTY

WESTON

Birgit Rasmussen Diforio

7 Indian Valley Road, Weston

A steep and dramatic 100-foot-long granite ledge, uncovered and terraced by the owner, dominates this hilly site. It culminates at the rear of the property with a recirculating waterfall and pond. Large, undulating mixed borders emphasize contrasts in the color and texture of foliage. A stone terrace, tucked away at the start of the woodland walk, offers a completely different atmosphere and is a favorite retreat for reading and relaxing.

Hours: 10 a.m. to 4 p.m.

From Merritt Parkway/Route 15, take Exit 42 and go north on Route 57. At the blinking traffic light past Weston Center, turn left over the river and continue on Route 57 for about 3 miles. Indian Valley Road is on the right.

From I-84, take Route 7 south. Turn left at the Exxon gas station at Route 107, then right onto Route 57/Georgetown Road. Indian Valley Road is less than 1 mile on the left.

WEST REDDING
Hughes-Sonnenfroh Gardens
54 Chestnut Woods Road, West Redding

Please see June 23 for garden description, hours, and directions.

HARTFORD COUNTY

AVON
Green Dreams—Garden of Jan Nickel
71 Country Club Road, Avon

Behind the iron gates of a twenty-year-old established garden, winding paths and secret rooms create a fantasy garden. Contrasting styles feature extravagant use of distinctive perennials, shrubs, and grasses. Vistas abound, offering contemporary and European ideas intertwined with elements of architectural interest. Iron, stone, wood, concrete, and pottery add dramatic flair to the Old World charm of the magnificent garden.

Hours: 10 a.m. to 4 p.m.

From I-84, take Exit 39/Farmington/Route 4. From the intersection of Routes 10 and 4, turn right onto Route 10 for 5.7 miles to Route 44. Turn left onto Route 44 and follow for .7 mile to the intersection of Route 10 and Old Farms Road. Turn left onto Old Farms Road and travel 1.3 miles to Country Club Road. Turn right onto Country Club Road and travel .3 mile to #71. *Please park across the street on Tamara Circle.*

Proceeds shared with the Animal Friends of Connecticut

MANCHESTER
Watersong
85 Alton Street, Manchester

Please see June 15 for garden description, hours, and directions.

SIMSBURY
The Garden of Betty & Dick Holden
7 Crane Place, Simsbury

This garden, begun in 1963, is an effort to establish an Americanized version of an English cottage garden. It is a diverse collection of perennials and vines vying for their place in the sun. A sincere effort has been made to have profuse bloom from early spring to late fall. The garden includes a small water garden, vegetable garden, mini-rose garden, and grape arbor. Emphasis is placed on unusual foliage plants. Beautiful fences, numerous rock walls, and arbors enhance the plantings. A variety of golf and baby shoes planted with sedum are tucked into corners. The birds, bees, and butterflies are ever-present visitors in this certified backyard habitat.

Hours: 10 a.m. to 4 p.m.

From I-84, take Exit 39/Farmington/Route 4 into downtown Farmington. Turn right onto Route 10 north through Avon into Simsbury. After passing the "Welcome to Simsbury" sign, turn left at the next traffic light onto Old Meadow Plain Road. Continue to the top of the hill. Turn left onto Woodcliff Drive. Bear left at the fork and take the next left onto Crane Place. The garden is on the right, #7.

LITCHFIELD COUNTY

NEW HARTFORD

Nancy Zimbalist

752 Town Hill Road, New Hartford

The layout of this garden was designed and installed by the Olmsted Brothers in the 1940s. Below the terrace is a formal perennial garden centered on a bird bath. There is also a rock garden with two ponds; a small herb garden; an eclectic garden by a pool house with peonies, heaths, heathers, ericas, and dwarf junipers; a bed of Russian sage, buddleia, and sedum in front of the pool house; and a cutting garden. Sweeping lawns. A breathtaking garden. The house has been in the same family since 1926.

Hours: noon to 4 p.m.

From Route 219, between Routes 202 and 44, proceed 3.5 miles to #752 (The Rafters), on the left.

From Route 202, proceed 1 mile to the house, on the right. *Please park in the parking area, in the circular part of the driveway to allow cars to pass by, or in the front of the far right garage door.*

WASHINGTON

Georgia Middlebrook

204 Nettleton Hollow Road, Washington

This property and its 1750 house boast a silver-foliage herb garden surrounding an old sundial, a crow's-foot-pattern Colonial garden, a salad garden under espaliered pear trees, a collection of old roses near a pond, and a large perennial border. A collection of Bill Heise metal sculptures sets off the gardens, as do five bridges over waterways. There is a pond trail and a developing wildflower garden.

Hours: 2 p.m. to 6 p.m.

From I-84, take Exit 15/Southbury. Go 5 miles through Southbury and Woodbury to Route 47. Turn left towards Washington. Go 4.5 miles to Nettleton Hollow Road. Bear right at the fork and continue 2.5 miles to #204.

From the north, take Route 109 through Washington Depot and follow to Nettleton Hollow Road, 2.3 miles from Depot. Turn right and continue 2 miles to #204. *Please park off the road or along the shoulder.*

WASHINGTON DEPOT

Gael Hammer

63 River Road, Washington Depot

Please see June 23 for garden description, hours, and directions.

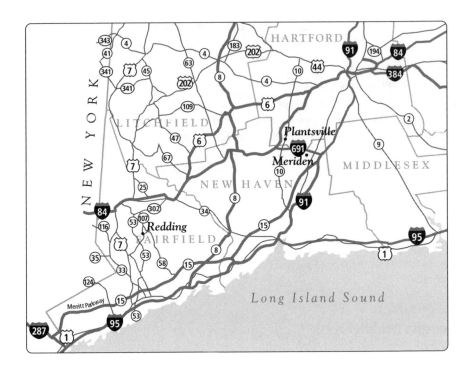

Sunday, August 11

FAIRFIELD COUNTY

REDDING

Highstead Arboretum

127 Lonetown Road, Redding

The sweet smell of swampland? A magnificent natural stand of sweet pepperbush fills the air with its summer scent. Nearly three acres of this unusually late native bloomer are made accessible by boardwalk for a dry-footed discovery of the swamp habitat at Highstead. This habitat is one of several at the arboretum maintained to allow the appreciation of the native plants, birds, and wildlife dwelling there. A one-hour guided walk will lead you to the pond and meadow, where selected cultivars of this shrub have been introduced for comparison. Set on fifty acres of geographic extremes, the arboretum is also open weekdays by appointment, and offering two other distinct seasonal walks on May 19 and June 2.

Hours: guided walks at 10 a.m., noon, and 2 p.m. Please call weekdays, 8:30 a.m. to 4:30 p.m., for more information (203) 938-8809.

From I-95 or Merritt Parkway/Route 15, take Route 7 north. Turn right onto Route 107 for 6 miles (be sure to follow signs for 107 as it crosses Route 53). Pass the police station, Redding Elementary School, and Redding Country Club. Take the second driveway on the left after the country club, 127 Lonetown Road. Follow signs into the arboretum; the driveway is .5 mile long.

HARTFORD COUNTY

PLANTSVILLE
The Kaminski Garden
513 Marion Avenue, Plantsville

I am always amazed as I pass from the front yard, where grass barely grows, through the gate into the three-year-old garden's hues of green punctuated with flowers. Mature trees anchor the yard; sweeping curves define garden beds where the emphasis is on foliage. The tumbled bluestone used for the patio, raised planting beds surrounding the deck, garden bed edgings, and the pathways to the free-form pool soothe the eye with its consistency. Shade predominates throughout, as do a wide variety of shade-tolerant perennials, shrubs, and Japanese maples. Sun abounds by the pool; specimen evergreens and sweeps of flowers thrive here.

Hours: 10 a.m. to 4 p.m.

From I-84, take Exit 30/Marion Avenue. From Hartford (I-84 west), turn right onto Marion Avenue; from Waterbury (I-84 east), turn left onto Marion Avenue. Once on Marion Avenue, travel about 1 mile, passing Frost Street. The next driveway on the right is our home, #513. The house is slate blue with a detached two-car garage. *Please park in the driveway.*

Proceeds shared with the Dana-Farber Cancer Institute

NEW HAVEN COUNTY

MERIDEN
George Trecina
341 Spring Street, Meriden

Please see July 7 for garden description, hours, and directions.

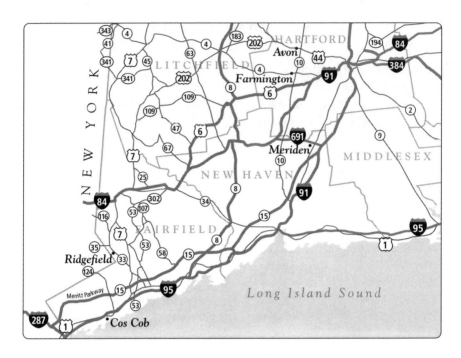

Sunday, September 8

Please also see listings for this date in New York

FAIRFIELD COUNTY

Cos Cob

Florence & John Boogaerts—Mianus Dawn

316 Valley Road, North Mianus, Cos Cob

This tiny, steep site overlooking the Mianus River is an American hybrid of the Italian Renaissance with British Arts and Crafts stonework planted in the "natural style" of William Robinson and Gertrude Jekyll with creepers, ramblers, roses, herbaceous plants, and bulbs. The garden is a sequence of terraces carved into the wooded hillside. The cross-axial patterns repeat, in miniature, the disciplined hillside gardens of Tuscany and the Veneto. The fern grotto and loggia are New England rustic interpretations of Edwin Lutyen's Hestarcombe. The boxwood parterre leads to the perennial garden, the grape arbor, the potager, and the espaliered apple trees. At the top of the ramp and trail is a stone belvedere covered by a wrought-iron trellis dome with an oculus after Palliado.

Hours: 1 p.m. to 5 p.m.

From I-95, take Exit 4 and turn onto Indian Field Road north, towards Greenwich. Travel .7 mile and turn right (there is a Mobil gas station) onto East Putnam Avenue. Travel .5 mile, turn left (there is a Gulf gas station) onto Orchard Street, bear right at the triangle, and turn right at the next intersection, Valley Road. Travel 1.6 miles after the second stop sign to the fourth house on the left, #316.

From Merritt Parkway/Route 15 east, take Exit 33. Bear right onto Den Road. At Roxbury

Road, turn left at the stop sign and go 1.7 miles to Westover Road. Go 1.7 miles to Mianus Road and turn right. Mianus Road becomes Valley Road. Go 1.7 miles to #316, on the right.

From Merritt Parkway/Route 15 west, turn right onto Den Road and go .5 mile to Bangall Road. Turn left and continue, passing a red barn and horse farm on the right, .5 mile to Riverbank Road. Turn left and cross over Merritt Parkway. Riverbank Road becomes Westover Road. Proceed as directed above. *Please park along the road.*

RIDGEFIELD
Garden of Ideas
647 North Salem Road, Ridgefield

Fourteen years ago, this spot was covered with Kentucky bluegrass and poison ivy-infested woods. Today a fine collection of both woody and herbaceous ornamental plants grows here, along a stunning natural marsh. A large raised-bed vegetable garden produces a bounty of delicious edibles from April through November. Stroll through shade and sun, ponder poetic verse displayed along the way, and relax in one of many secluded nooks. Other points of interest include hand-built cedar structures, whimsical statuary, water features, unusual annuals, and lots of birds and bugs. Recent completion of a plankway across the marsh allows exploration of heretofore uncharted garden territory.

Hours: 10 a.m. to 4 p.m.

From Route 35 in Ridgefield, take Route 116 for 2.9 miles. The garden is on the left.

From Route 121 in North Salem, take Route 116 into Connecticut. The house is on the right, 1.3 miles from the New York border. *Please park in the paved parking area.*

HARTFORD COUNTY

AVON
Green Dreams—Garden of Jan Nickel
71 Country Club Road, Avon

Please see July 21 for garden description, hours, and directions.

FARMINGTON
Kate Emery & Steve Silk
74 Prattling Pond Road, Farmington

Our evolving one-acre garden on a sloping site in the woods reflects a fascination with using colorful foliage to create season-long interest. Our many annuals should be at their best in early September. Numerous sun and shade mixed borders are connected by meandering paths and a dry, gravel stream bed. Features include a tulip walk, lilac garden, shrub border, a fall garden, and stone patio with unusual container plantings.

Hours: noon to 4 p.m.

From I-84, take Exit 39. Move to the right lane of the exit ramp. At the end, take the right turning lane towards UConn Health Center. Go about 100 yards, turn left onto Prattling Pond Road (across from the entrance to the commuter parking lot), and continue straight to #74, the last driveway on the right. *Please park in the driveway or on the road past the driveway.*

MERIDEN
George Trecina
341 Spring Street, Meriden

Please see July 7 for garden description, hours, and directions.

Public Gardens

FAIRFIELD COUNTY

BROOKFIELD
Brookfield Historical Society Museum Garden
165 Whisconier Road, Brookfield (203) 740-8140 www.brookfieldcthistory.org

Designed by Dr. Rudy J. Favretti, this nineteenth-century herb garden complements the 1876 museum it adjoins. The focal point is a sundial surrounded by coralbells and thyme. There is a brick walk throughout the property. The garden was created and is maintained by the Brookfield Garden Club.

Hours: Year round, daily, dawn to dusk
Admission: free
Located on the corner of Routes 25 and 133 in Brookfield.

DARIEN
Bates-Scofield House
45 Old King's Highway North, Darien (203) 655-9233 www.darien.lib.ct.us/historical

The herb garden, adjacent to the Bates-Scofield House Museum, was planted and is maintained by the Garden Club of Darien. It contains many varieties of culinary, medical, and strewing herbs known to have been used in Connecticut in the eighteenth century.

Hours: Year round, daily, dawn to dusk
Admission: grounds are free
From I-95, take Exit 13. Turn left onto Post Road. At the second traffic light, turn left onto Brookside Road. Bear right at the curve; the house and parking lot are on the left.

FAIRFIELD
Connecticut Audubon Birdcraft Museum
314 Unquowa Road, Fairfield (203) 259-0416 www.ctaudubon.org

America's oldest private songbird sanctuary was founded in 1914. The five-acre sanctuary (originally fourteen acres), planted to attract birds with trees and shrubs, was designed by Mabel Osgood Wright (1859-1934), a pioneering American conservationist, photographer, and author. Demonstration plantings to attract birds and butterfly meadow restoration are in progress.

Hours: Year round, Tuesday through Friday, 10 a.m. to 5 p.m. weekends, noon to 5 p.m.
Admission: suggested donation $2 adults, $1 children
From I-95, take Exit 21/Mill Plain Road. Go north on Mill Plain Road for .5 mile to stop sign. Turn right onto Unquowa Road and proceed for .5 mile to the parking entrance immediately on the left after the I-95 overpass.

NEW CANAAN
New Canaan Nature Center
144 Oenoke Ridge Road, New Canaan (203) 966-9577 www.newcanaannature.org

Two miles of trails crisscross natural areas of this forty-acre site, providing access to unusual habitat diversity—including wet and dry meadows, two ponds, wet and dry woodlands, dense thickets, an old orchard, and cattail marsh. Highlights include a bird and butterfly garden, a large herb garden, wildflower garden, naturalist's garden, small arboretum, and a 4,000-square-foot solar greenhouse.

Hours: Year round, Monday through Saturday, 9 a.m. to 4 p.m.

Admission: free

From Merritt Parkway/Route 15, take Exit 37 and follow Route 124 through town. Located on Route 124, 1 mile north of the New Canaan town center.

RIDGEFIELD
Ballard Park & Garden, Town of Ridgefield
Route 35, 400 Main Street, Ridgefield (203) 431-8156

This semiformal garden was donated in 1964 to the Town of Ridgefield by Mrs. Edward L. Ballard. It is maintained by the Ridgefield Garden Club. It is a garden of long bloom period perennials, compact shrubs, and easy-care annuals. The park has a Fletcher Steele-designed pergola.

Hours: Year round, daily, dawn to dusk

Admission: free

The entrance is in the middle of town on Route 35. Park at the former Grand Union. Entrance to the park is on the north end.

STAMFORD
The Bartlett Arboretum
151 Brookdale Road, Stamford (203) 322-6971

The arboretum is a 63-acre living museum embracing natural woodlands, perennial borders, meadows, display gardens, and an educational greenhouse. The site includes a trail system and a raised boardwalk through a seven-acre wetland. The arboretum offers a wide variety of educational programs and courses for children, enthusiasts, and serious horticulturists, plant sales, a plant information service, and guided tours and walks.

Hours: Year round, daily, dawn to dusk

Admission: free

From Merritt Parkway/Route 15, take Exit 35. Follow High Ridge Road/Route 137 north (left off north or southbound ramps) for 1.5 miles to Brookdale Road on the left.

Stamford Museum & Nature Center
39 Scofieldtown Road, Stamford (203) 322-1646 www.stamfordmuseum.org

The Stamford Museum & Nature Center's 118 acres include woodland trails and a 300-foot boardwalk winding along a stream to provide a trail walk experience for parents with strollers, the elderly, and people in wheelchairs. A garden with plants indigenous to Connecticut is at the boardwalk entrance. On the early New England farm, herbs and vegetables grow. The setting for the entire property includes flowering trees, shrubs, and ground covers, as well as a small lake, waterfall, marble fountain, and sculpture.

Hours: Year round, Monday through Saturday and holidays, 9 a.m. to 5 p.m., Sundays, 11 a.m. to 5 p.m.

Admission: $6 adults, $5 senior citizens and children 5-13, children under 5 free

From I-95, take Exit 7 to Washington Boulevard/Route 137 north to Merritt Parkway/Route 15. Located .75 mile north of Exit 35 on Merritt Parkway/Route 15 at the junction of High Ridge Road/Route 137 and Scofield Road.

STRATFORD

Boothe Memorial Park—Wedding Rose Garden
55 Wild Wood Drive, Stratford (203) 381-2046

A brick pathway lined with seasonal perennials, annuals, and shrubs leads to the exuberant Wedding Rose Garden. Separated into two garden rooms, the Wedding Garden has a restored fountain and displays 'Love,' 'Honor,' and 'Cherish' roses. The Rainbow Room features a colorful explosion of 34 varieties. Climbing roses on trellises and an arbor enclose the garden.

Hours: Year round, daily, dawn to dusk

Admission: free

From I-95 south, take Exit 38/Merritt Parkway. Continue to Exit 53. Go south on Route 110 to Main Street Putney, which forks to the right. Head south on Main Street for .25 mile to the park on the left.

From I-95 north, take Exit 33. Follow Ferry Boulevard, bear left at the fork, and go under the thruway. Bear right onto East Main Street/Route 110 to its end (Main Street Putney). Go .7 mile to the park on the right.

WESTPORT

The Bird & Butterfly Demonstration Garden at the Nature Center for Environmental Activities
10 Woodside Lane, Westport (203) 227-7253

The garden serves as an example of well-behaved plants that do not threaten the Connecticut environment. Both native and well-behaved non-native plants were selected for their function: to feed and protect birds and butterflies. The promise to promote the balance of nature has been kept. It is a pesticide-free garden. The garden was installed in 1995.

Hours: Year round, Monday through Saturday, 9 a.m. to 5 p.m., Sunday, 1 p.m. to 4 p.m.

Admission: suggested donation $2 adults, $1 children

From I-95, take Exit 17 and turn left at the end of the exit ramp onto Route 33 north. Go 1.5 miles to the intersection of Route 1. Turn left onto Route 1 and go .5 mile to the second traffic light. Turn right onto King's Highway north. Take the first left onto Woodside Avenue (which becomes Woodside Lane). Go .9 mile to the Nature Center.

WILTON

Weir Farm National Historic Site
735 Nod Hill Road, Wilton (203) 834-1896 www.nps.gov/wefa

From 1882 to 1919, Weir Farm was the summer home of the American Impressionist painter J. Alden Weir. Sixty acres have been preserved of the landscape that inspired Weir and his contemporaries Childe Hassam, John Twachtman, and Albert Pinkham Ryder. A self-guided tour allows visitors to explore the sites where some of their paintings were done. Guided tours are available of the art studios and the circa-1915 restored rustic enclosed garden. A Colonial Revival sunken garden, built by Weir's daughter in the 1930s, was rehabilitated in the spring of 1998 and is adjacent to the visitor center. Call for tour schedule.

Hours: Year round, daily, dawn to dusk.

Admission: free

From I-84, take Exit 3/Route 7 south. Follow for 10 miles into the Branchville section of Ridgefield and turn right at the traffic light onto Route 102 west. Take the second left onto Old Branchville Road. Turn left at the first stop sign onto Nod Hill Road. Follow for .7 mile; the site is on the right and parking is on the left.

HARTFORD COUNTY

BURLINGTON

Harriet Beecher Stowe Gardens

Beach Road, Burlington (860) 673-5782

Harriet Beecher Stowe Gardens at Nook Farm is a lovely example of overflowing, intimate cottage gardening on a domestic scale, created by historic landscape designers Stevenson, Fuoco, and Canning. The main feature of these gardens is the Blue Cottage Garden, which is ablaze with blue flowers mid-June. In these gardens, timed to be in bloom from May to September, one will also enjoy tulips in May, two deliciously scented long borders of antique roses in June, Harriet's meadow flower garden, and a shade wildflower garden. During July and beyond, the Pink and Red Garden, "High Victorian" Texture Garden, and Orange Yellow and White Garden take center stage.

Hours: Year round, daily, dawn to dusk

Admission: free

From I-84, take Exit 46/Sisson Avenue. Turn right onto Sisson Avenue, then turn right onto Farmington Avenue. Turn right onto Forest Street. The parking lot is on your right.

FARMINGTON

Hill-Stead Museum's Sunken Garden

35 Mountain Road, Farmington (860) 677-4787 www.hillstead.org

Designed circa 1920 by landscape designer Beatrix Jones Farrand, the Sunken Garden at Hill-Stead is a centerpiece of an exceptional 152-acre hilltop property. The one-acre garden is surrounded by original stone walls and includes 36 different flower beds, some containing as many as fifteen plant varieties. Nearly ninety varieties of perennials, in color combinations of pinks, blues, whites, purples, and grays, are represented. Farrand chose the textures and colors of plantings to complement the French Impressionist masterpieces that are displayed in situ in Hill-Stead's 1901 Colonial Revival mansion. In the 1980s, members of a local garden club restored the garden to Farrand's original plans. Today, expert volunteers continue to manage its care and propagation. University of Connecticut Master Gardeners provide tours, talks, and workshops to museum visitors and students. Since 1992, the Sunken Garden has been the site of a summer-long poetry and music festival

Hours: Year round, daily, 7 a.m. to dusk

Admission: free

From I-84, take Exit 39/Route 4 west. Go to the second traffic light and turn left onto Route 10 south/Main Street. At the next light, turn left onto Mountain Road. The museum entrance is .25 mile on the left.

Stanley-Whitman House

37 High Street, Farmington (860) 677-9222 www.stanleywhitman.org

Period herb garden. Public tours available.

Hours: May through October, Wednesday through Saturday noon to 4 p.m.; November through April, weekends, noon to 4 p.m.; or by appointment.

Admission: $5 adults, $4 seniors, $2 students

From I-84, take Exit 39/Route 4. Proceed straight on Route 4 west .8 mile to the traffic light at the intersection of Routes 4 and 10. Turn left at the light onto Route 10/ Main Street, proceed about .2 mile to the next light, turn left onto Mountain Road, and proceed .2 mile. Turn left onto High Street and go .1 mile. Look for the museum sign on the right.

HARTFORD

Elizabeth Park Rose & Perennial Garden

Asylum Avenue, Hartford (860) 242-0017 www.elizabethpark.org

This 15,000-specimen rose garden is the oldest municipal rose garden in the country. Also included are perennials, rock gardens, heritage roses, an herb garden, a wildflower garden, and annual displays. The Lord & Burnham greenhouses offer seasonal displays. The new cafe is open year round.

Hours: Year round, daily, dawn to dusk; greenhouses, weekdays, 8 a.m. to 3 p.m.

Admission: free

From I-84, take Exit 44/Prospect Avenue. Head north on Prospect Avenue. The park is on the corner of Prospect and Asylum Avenues.

WEST HARTFORD

Noah Webster House

227 South Main Street, West Hartford (203) 521-5362 www.ctstateu.edu/noahwebster.html

The Noah Webster House has a raised-bed teaching garden planted with herbs and other plants available to the Websters during the middle of the eighteenth century. A small demonstration plot of vegetables is also grown. Plants are labeled, so visitors may guide themselves through the garden.

Hours: Year round, daily, dawn to dusk

Admission: free

Located 1 mile south of I-84 at Exit 41. Follow signs at the end of the exit ramp and travel for 1 mile. The museum is on the left.

WETHERSFIELD
Webb House Colonial Revival Garden at the Webb-Deane-Stevens Museum
211 Main Street, Wethersfield (860) 529-0612 www.webb-deane-stevens.org

Designed by landscape architect Amy Cogswell in 1921 and restored in 1999-2000, the garden features stone-dust walkways leading to the handmade cedar arbors and Colonial Revival-style geometric beds filled with old-fashioned flowers such as Canterbury bells, larkspur, hollyhocks, perennial foxglove, and more than forty roses. Please call for information on tours and special events.

Hours: May through October, Wednesday through Monday, 10 a.m. to 4 p.m.; November through April, weekends only, 10 a.m. to 4 p.m.

Admission: free

From I-91, take Exit 26 and follow the signs to the Historic District and the Webb House and Deane House.

LITCHFIELD COUNTY

BETHLEHEM
Bellamy-Ferriday House & Garden
9 Main Street North, Bethlehem (203) 266-7596 www.hartnet.org/~als

The Ferriday Garden is a romantic, nine-acre landscape comprised of interesting woody and herbaceous plants. The garden was initially designed circa 1920 and developed through the early 1980s. Since 1992, the Antiquarian and Landmarks Society staff has been busy restoring the large collections of lilacs, old roses, peonies, and perennials. A formal yew and chamaecyparis parterre connects an orchard and meadow, creating a pleasing stroll through the garden.

Hours: May through October, Wednesday, Friday, and weekends, 11 a.m. to 4 p.m.

Admission: $3 garden, $5 house and garden

From I-84, take Exit 15/Southbury. At the end of the exit ramp, take Route 6 east for 13 miles to Route 61. Turn left onto Route 61 north. At the intersection of Routes 61 and 132, stay on Route 61 and take the first left into the driveway.

BRIDGEWATER
Beatrix Farrand Garden at Three Rivers Farm
694 Skyline Ridge Road, Bridgewater (860) 354-1788

The 1921 Beatrix Farrand Garden at Three Rivers Farm was rediscovered in 1993 and recreated adapting the original Farrand hardscape and design to the present environmental conditions. The garden is located within a beautiful 275-acre property, now mostly wooded, where the Shepaug and Housatonic Rivers converge. A 1931 magazine article described the entire property as a Chinese garden and "arboretum of rare charm," with 105 varieties of Chinese flora. These flora and many more were left to their own devices for nearly sixty years. Some were lost or cut unknowingly, some continue to struggle for light in the shade of the forest, some have greatly overstepped their bounds, and others are preserved to carry on their original charm.

Hours: By appointment only

Admission: $5

From I-84, take Exit 9 and travel north on Route 25 to Brookfield Center. Turn right onto Route 133 east towards Bridgewater. Cross Lake Lillinonah Bridge and take the first right onto Wewaka Brook Road. Go .75 mile and turn right onto Beach Hill Road to the end. Turn right onto Skyline Ridge Road. Go to the very end of this dead-end road and take a sharp left. Please park along the road between the buildings.

LITCHFIELD

Laurel Ridge Foundation
Wigwam Road, Litchfield

The display of the genus *Narcissus* was planted over about ten acres in 1941. The original 10,000 daffodils have naturalized for the past fifty years. The current owners have maintained the display and welcome visitors to drive by and share its splendor.

Hours: April through May, daily, dawn to dusk

Admission: free

Take Route 118 east from Litchfield to Route 254. Turn right onto Route 254 and go 3.5 miles. Turn right onto Wigwam Road. The planting is about 1 mile on the left.

White Flower Farm
Litchfield (860) 567-8789 www.whiteflowerfarm.com

White Flower Farm is best known as a mail-order nursery, but it's also a great place to visit. In addition to the working nursery, the grounds are home to an impressive collection of mature trees and shrubs. There are also numerous display gardens featuring perennials, tender perennials and annuals, bulbs, and roses. Tour maps are available at the visitor center or the store.

Hours: April through October, daily, 9 a.m. to 6 p.m.; November through March, daily, 10 a.m. to 5 p.m.

Admission: free

The garden is located on Route 63; it is .7 mile north of Route 109 and 3.5 miles south of Route 118. Watch for the sign and please park in the lot just north of the store.

THOMASTON

Cricket Hill Garden
670 Walnut Hill Road, Thomaston (860) 283-1042 www.treepeony.com

A visit to this garden/nursery has been likened to stepping into a scroll painting of Chinese tree peonies. See more than 200 named varieties of tree peonies in an array of colors, flower forms, and fragrances. Free catalog available.

Hours: May through June, Wednesday through Sunday, 10 a.m. to 4 p.m.; other times by appointment

Admission: free

From I-95 or I-84, take Route 8 north. Take Exit 38/Thomaston, turning left at the bottom of the exit ramp onto Main Street. Turn left at the third traffic light onto Route 254. Go .5 mile on Route 254 to a blinking yellow light. Turn left onto Walnut Hill Road. Go up the hill 1 mile and see our sign on the right.

WOODBURY

Gertrude Jekyll Garden at the Glebe House Museum

Woodbury (203) 263-2855

In 1926 the famed English horticultural designer and writer Gertrude Jekyll was commissioned to plan an "old-fashioned" garden to enhance the newly created museum dedicated to the election of America's first Episcopal bishop. Although small in comparison with other elaborate designs she completed in England and Europe, the Glebe House garden includes 600 feet of classic English-style mixed-border and foundation plantings, a small formal quadrant, and an intimate rose allée.

Hours: April, May, September and October, Wednesday through Sunday, 1 p.m. to 4 p.m.; June through August, Wednesday, Thursday, Friday, and Sunday, 1 to 4 p.m., Saturday, 10 a.m. to 4 p.m.; November, weekends only, 1 p.m. to 4 p.m.

Admission: free

From I-84, take Exit 15/Southbury. Continue on Route 6 east for 10 minute to Woodbury. Look for the junction of Route 317. Take Route 317 to the fork, bear left, and the Glebe House Museum is 100 yards ahead.

MIDDLESEX COUNTY

MIDDLETOWN

Shoyoan Teien—The Freeman Family Garden

343 Washington Terrace, Middletown (860) 685-2330 www.wesleyan.edu.east

Shoyoan Teien is a Japanese-style viewing garden designed and built by Stephen Morrell in 1995. Inspired by the "dry landscape" aesthetic, the garden's raked gravel riverbed evokes the prominent bend in the Connecticut River as it flows through wooded hills near Middletown. Japanese tea ceremonies are periodically performed in the adjacent tatami room. The special tour of the garden on May 19 will be hosted by Stephen Morrell, designer of our Japanese garden. Guests can ask questions and receive professional guidance from Mr. Morrell.

Hours: Open Day event May 19, 10 a.m. noon, otherwise open weekends during the academic year, noon to 4 p.m.; please call for specific open dates

Admission: free

From the north, take I-91 south to Exit 22 (left exit) to Exit 15/Route 9 and follow the signs to Wesleyan.

From the south, take I-95 to Exit 18/I-91 north or take Merritt/Wilbur Cross Parkway/Route 15 to Route 66 east and follow the signs to Wesleyan.

From the Northeast, take the Massachusetts Turnpike/I-90 west to I-84 west to Hartford, then I-91 south to Exit 22 south (left exit). Go south on Route 9 and follow the signs to Exit 15/Wesleyan.

Take I-95 south through Providence, to Exit 15/Route 9 north and follow the signs to Wesleyan.

NEW HAVEN COUNTY

HAMDEN
Pardee Rose Gardens
180 Park Road, Hamden (203) 946-8142

The Pardee Rose Garden covers about three acres in East Rock Park. The rose beds are laid out geometrically, leading to a three-tiered central brick rose garden, and are planted with 1,500 rosebushes. More than 400 named varieties are currently grown. There are two greenhouses, as well as annual and perennial flower plantings.

Hours: Year round, daily, dawn to dusk

Admission: free

From I-95, take I-91 to New Haven. Take Exit 5 and continue north on State Street for 2 miles. Turn left onto Farm Road. The garden is 1 block up the hill.

TOLLAND COUNTY

COVENTRY
Caprilands Herb Farm
534 Silver Street, Coventry (860) 742-7244 www.caprilands.com

More than thirty world-famous theme gardens designed by Adelma Grenier Simmons illustrate the use of herbaceous plants, shrubs, annuals, vegetables, and herbs in numerous creative and decorative arrangements and settings. Highlights include a silver garden, saints' garden, Shakespeare Garden, butterfly garden, large botanic garden, naturalist's garden, small arboretum, and large post-and-beam greenhouse built into a hillside and displaying many herbal varieties suitable for northern gardens. The gardens are framed by a sheep meadow with a flock of Scottish blackface sheep, complementing the dyer's and weaver's garden.

Hours: Year round, daily, except holidays, 9 a.m. to 5 p.m. (shops open 10 a.m.)

Admission: free

The farm is on Silver Street in North Coventry, south of Routes 44 and 31. Route 31 is accessed from I-84. Route 44 is accessed from I-384E.

ULSTER COUNTY

WOODSTOCK
Bowen House—Roseland Cottage
556 Route 169, Woodstock (860) 928-4074 www.spnea.org

The gardens were laid out in 1850 as part of the landscape of Henry Bowen's summer "cottage" built in 1846. Boxwoods border the 21 beds of annuals and perennials, forming a parterre garden. Landscape designer Andrew Jackson Downing's theories inspired the design of the ribbon and carpet-bedding plantings. Noteworthy trees and shrubs include a tulip tree, Japanese maple, Chinese wisteria, and old-fashioned roses.

Hours: Year round, daily, dawn to dusk

Admission: free

From I-395, take Exit 97/Route 44 west for 1 mile. Go west on Route 171 for 3 miles and north on Route 169 for 1 mile. The house is on the left.

DISTRICT
OF COLUMBIA

Jane MacLeish's Garden, Washington.
Photo by Ping Amranand.

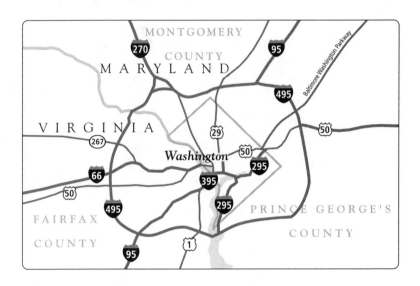

Saturday, May 18

WASHINGTON

The Dice/Sumner Garden

4870 Reservoir Road, N.W., Washington

This intimate urban garden was planned by landscape designer Tom Mannion and planted by Jim Dice. Many hostas, ferns, astilbes, liriope, and other plants offer their myriad forms, textures, and shades of green. Color is supplied by annuals in containers and ceramic pots. A subtle Oriental influence is noted in the unadorned stone walls and native stone steps. The garden was seen in the April 1994 issue of *Southern Living* magazine and received a Grand Award in 1994 from the Landscape Contractors Association of MD, DC, and VA.

Hours: 10 a.m. to 4 p.m.

From downtown D.C., take the Whitehurst Freeway onto M Street in Georgetown. Turn left onto Canal Road turn right uphill onto Foxhall Road. Continue to Reservoir Road. On Foxhall, turn left; turn left downhill on Reservoir Road, before the Exxon gas station, onto MacArthur Boulevard (Reservoir and MacArthur Boulevard share 1 block) and *park on the north side of Reservoir Road opposite #4870.*

Elizabeth's Haven

1701 Poplar Lane, N.W., Washington

Our garden was created in 1999, following a major renovation of the house. The front yard has a new brick walk, which flows through a boldly curving lawn. The lawn is surrounded by masses of flowering shrubs, ornamental grasses, and perennials. One huge umbrella pine (*Sciadopitys*), transplanted from our old house, stands sentry by the front steps. Groves of heritage birch and crape myrtle provide vertical accents and privacy. In back, there is a rose garden by the swimming pool, a garden of moisture-loving plants, a fantastic natural-spring spa inspired by our visit to the Lady Bird Johnson Wildflower Center in Austin, Texas, and sweeps of goldenrod, mosquito grass, hellebores, and other flowering things. We enjoy an abundance of butterflies all summer. The gardens were designed by Tom Mannion. He promises to teach us the names of the more unusual plants before you come to visit.

Hours: 10 a.m. to 2 p.m.

From the Beltway/I-495, take the Georgia Avenue exit south towards Washington, D.C. Take Georgia Avenue to 16th Street south. Pass the "Welcome to Washington" sign on the left of the traffic circle (intersection/merging of Route 29 and 16th Street). Stay south on 16th Street for 3 to 4 blocks. Turn right onto Primrose and take an immediate left onto Orchid. Follow the curve of the road to the right. Number 1701 is the first house on the right on Poplar Lane where Orchid and Poplar meet. *Please park on the street.*

Harriet & Eric Fraunfelter Garden

3725 Upton Street, N.W., Washington

Renowned California landscape architect Thomas Church designed this city garden to surround the Georgian Revival house, remodeled in 1972. It was one of his few East Coast projects and among the last of his career. In 1991, under the guidance of landscape designer Sarah Broley and with gifts of plants from gardening friends far and wide, the owners began to restore Church's original design and to enhance his plans with colorful perennials in the various outdoor rooms by pulling up a brick terrace and planting herbaceous borders. A native plant garden was installed on a steep slope along the street entrance. Extensive ground cover areas were replanted with new butterfly and shady woodland gardens.

Hours: 10 a.m. to 2 p.m.

From the Beltway/I-495, take the Connecticut Avenue exit south towards Chevy Chase. Go 4.5 miles to Van Ness Street. Turn right and go through 1 traffic light; at the next corner (37th Street), turn left. Go 1 block to Upton Street and turn right. Number 3725 is the fifth house on the right.

Jane MacLeish's Garden
3743 Upton Street, N.W., Washington

This small garden was developed to provide a variety of inviting, seductive, and surprising spaces for an active family. There is a choice of places to eat, a lawn for croquet, and beds filled with a collection of plants. Shapes gently woven with plant material are so subtle that many miss them. An old limestone temple is tucked in the rear of the garden. The sound of water greets visitors in this ever-changing garden.

Hours: 10 a.m. to 2 p.m.

From the Beltway/I-495, take the Connecticut Avenue exit south towards Chevy Chase. Go 4.5 miles to Van Ness Street. Turn right and go through 1 traffic light; at the next corner (37th Street), turn left. Go 1 block to Upton Street and turn right. Number 3743 is the sixth house on the right. *Please park along the road.*

Philip L. McClain Garden
1728 Poplar Lane, N.W., Washington

The Philip L. McClain Garden surrounds a stone house built on a rising east slope up from Rock Creek Valley at the upper part of the District of Columbia. The third-of-an-acre lot contains several garden rooms created by the many varieties of plants used in restoring the garden over the last decade. Plants such as China fir, various kinds of southern magnolia, Serbian spruce, and purple-leaf weeping beech serve both to screen and enhance neighboring views. The pergola, pond, terrace, garden walls, and walks were installed by the owner, a garden designer.

Hours: 10 a.m. to 2 p.m.

From the Beltway/I-495, go south on Georgia Avenue towards Washington. After 2 traffic lights, veer right onto 16th Street. Travel about 1 mile, crossing East-West Highway (Maryland 210) and continuing toward the D.C. border (1 block). Go around the circle, continuing into the District on 16th Street, N.W. (1 short block). At the traffic light, take Portal Street to the right. (As one travels on Portal Street, there is a ravine of trees on the right and residences on the left.) Go 3 blocks and turn left onto Poplar Lane. The fourth house on the right is #1728.

From downtown Washington, travel north on 16th Street, N.W. After passing Walter Reed Hospital, begin looking for the last light in D.C., which is Portal Street. Proceed as directed above. *Please park on the street.*

The Corinna Posner Garden
1837 Plymouth Street, N.W., Washington

This romantic garden is located near the northern tip of Washington, D.C., close to Rock Creek Park. The sound of trickling water is audible from the street. The horseshoe-shaped entry walk leads you through the front garden. A beautiful wrought-iron gate, crafted by Daniel Boone, leads to a vertical stone waterfall, pebble pool, and two seats. Art is interspersed throughout. Follow the walk through trellised arches into the more private rear garden, which was designed by Corinna Posner and Nicolien van Schouwen of European Garden Design. There, the magnet is a larger "gently roaring" waterfall over horizontal rocks into a pond, with underwater night illumination, a stone bridge, and water plants. The whole rear garden is designed on a diagonal with an unusual stone retaining wall, protruding rocks, rare plants, and multi-level patios. This small sanctuary has become a truly "outdoor living space," integrated with the adjoining indoor living area through huge glass windows.

Hours: 10 a.m. to 4 p.m.

From the Beltway/I-495, take Exit 30. Go south towards Silver Spring on Colesville Road, crossing Georgia Avenue and East-West Highway to a small circle at 16th Street (about 2.2 miles). Continue past the circle on North Portal Drive to its end (about .4 mile). Turn left onto East Beach Drive and go to the bridge at Kalmia Road (about .1 mile). Turn right across the bridge and immediately left onto West Beach Drive. Go .1 mile to Plymouth Street. Turn right onto Plymouth Street (about .1 mile). The fourth house on the right is #1837. *Please park on the street.*

The Gardens of Charles Read & Eileen White Read
5175 Tilden Street, N.W., Washington

Nicolien van Schouwen of European Garden Design faced a formidable challenge in creating a garden for the Reads, newly arrived from California in 1999. Though the corner lot was a lovely terraced site surrounding a stone Colonial home, the outdoors were horribly neglected, with not a single flower, and the perimeter was surrounded by 35 tall, rangy hemlock trees that imparted a haunted look. Of Dutch ancestry, Ms. van Schouwen created a series of outdoor rooms, some formal and others cottage style, that recall nineteenth-century European gardens. The "rooms" are divided by rustic Pennsylvania bluestone walls, boxwood and holly hedges, lattice fences, and stone staircases. A gravel allée surrounds a tiny pond and continues under a pleached canopy of fourteen native shadblow trees (*Amelanchier* x *grandiflora* 'Autumn Brillances') to a mirror-backed arbor. A medieval knot garden encloses summer herbs and early spring bulbs. To conserve water, the design includes minimum amounts of turfgrass and not a single annual flower. Plant materials provide four seasons of display: fruit trees, camellias, and 3,000 bulbs bloom in early spring; heirloom roses, hollyhocks, iris, and lilies take the garden into summer. Fall is ablaze with ajania, asters, dendranthema, grasses, and sedum; winter color comes from bergenia, red-twig dogwood, witch hazel, hellebores, sweetbox, and the berries of callicarpa, holly, viburnum, and wintergreen.

Hours: 10 a.m. to 4 p.m.

From the Beltway/I-495, take the Connecticut Avenue exit and follow it south, turning right onto Nebraska Avenue. Just past American University, turn right at the second traffic light (Rockwood Parkway/Newark Street). Follow for 5 blocks to the corner with Tilden Street. *Please park on Rockwood Parkway and enter at the rear garden gate.*

Public Gardens

DISTRICT OF COLUMBIA

WASHINGTON

Dumbarton Oaks Gardens & Dumbarton Oaks Park

Gardens: 1703 32nd Street, N.W., Washington (202) 339-6401

Park: 9 Lovers Lane, R Street, N.W., Washington (202) 282-1063 www.nps.gov/rocr.cultural

The Dumbarton Oaks Gardens and Dumbarton Oaks Park were designed as one project by noted architect Beatrix Farrand in cooperation with her clients, Mr. & Mrs. Robert Woods Bliss, who purchased the property in 1920. The design, mostly completed in the 1920s and 1930s, progressed from formal terraced gardens near the house to an informal, naturalistic landscape in the stream valley below, with designed views between them. In 1940, the Blisses gave the house and related formal gardens to Harvard University as a research center and conveyed the 27-acre, naturalistic landscape to the National Park Service. Dumbarton Oaks Park is managed by the National Park Service, Rock Creek Park.

Hours: Gardens open April through October, daily, 2 p.m. to 6 p.m.; November through March, daily, 2 p.m. to 5 p.m. Park open year round, daily, dawn to dusk

Admission: $5 adults, $3 senior citizens and children. Park is free.

The gardens' entrance is at R and 31st Streets, N.W., 1.5 blocks east of Wisconsin Avenue. Please park along the street. *The park's entrance* is north on Lovers Lane from R Street, east of 31st Street; Lovers Lane runs between Dumbarton Oaks Garden's east wall and the west edge of Montrose Park. The entrance is on the left at the bottom of the hill.

Tudor Place Historic House & Garden

1605 32nd Street, N.W., Washington (202) 965-0400 www.tudorplace.org

Tudor Place was built in 1816 by Thomas Peter and his wife, Martha Curtis Peter, grand-daughter of Martha Washington. The house, designed by Dr. William Thornton, was the home of six generations of the Peter family. It is now a house museum and garden committed to protecting, preserving, maintaining, and interpreting the historic property and its collection, while instilling the value of the past in the public perception.

Hours: Year round, Monday through Saturday, 10 a.m. to 4 p.m., closed major holidays

Admission: $2 suggested donation

Located between Q and R Streets in Georgetown, a 20-minute walk from Dupont Circle or Foggy Bottom Metrorail stops. Metrobus stops are nearby at Q and 31st Streets and Wisconsin Avenue. Street parking only.

U.S. National Arboretum

3501 New York Avenue, N.E., Washington (202) 245-2726 www.usna.usda.gov

This is America's Arboretum, 446 acres of gardens and collections in the heart of the city. There are extensive collections of native and Asian plants in natural settings. The National Herb Garden and the National Bonsai and Penjing Museum are world renowned, as is the Gotelli Collection of Dwarf and Slow-Growing Conifers. Azalea, dogwood, magnolia, and native plant displays are spectacular in the spring. Perennials, flowering shrubs and trees, and an extensive aquatic plant display provide color throughout the summer months. A forty-minute tram tour is offered on weekends from mid-April through mid-October for a nominal fee.

Hours: Year round, daily, except Christmas Day, 8 a.m. to 5 p.m.; the National Bonsai and Penjing Museum is open daily, 10:30 a.m. to 3:30 p.m.

Admission: free

Located in northeast Washington, D.C., off New York Avenue (Route 50) and Bladenburg Road. The gates are located on the New York Avenue service road and on R Street, off Bladenburg Road. Bus service from Union Station is available on weekends. Parking is free.

Washington National Cathedral/ Bishop's Garden

Wisconsin & Massachusetts Avenue, N.W., Washington (202) 537-5521 www.cathedral.org/cathedral

The Bishop's Garden, often described as an "oasis in the city," includes a rose garden, two perennial borders, a yew walk, three herb gardens, the bishop's lawn, and the shadow house. Tours are offered by All Hollows Guild, founded in 1916 to maintain and beautify the gardens and grounds of the cathedral. Plants are based on Christian myths and legends, on historical interest, or are native to America. The gardens were designed by Frederick Law Olmsted, Jr. A self-guided garden tour brochure is available in the herb cottage gift shop nearby.

Hours: Year round, daily, dawn to dusk. Tours offered without reservations, April through October, Wednesdays, 10:30 a.m. Group tours offered by reservation only.

Admission: free

Take Massachusetts Avenue, N.W., to Cathedral Close (at the intersection of Wisconsin Avenue, N.W.). Turn onto Cathedral Grounds (close) at South Road. Gardens are entered through the arch (on foot) about 300 feet from Wisconsin Avenue on South Road.

FLORIDA

Mangrove Gardens at Carwill Oaks, Vero Beach.

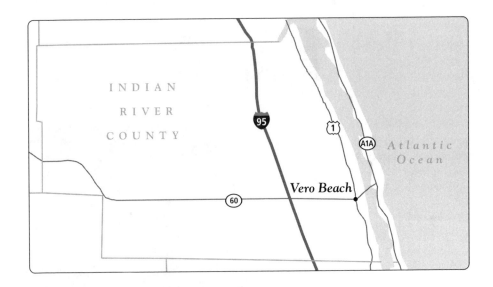

Saturday, April 20

INDIAN RIVER COUNTY

VERO BEACH

Garden of Patricia & Robert Hubner

911 Greenway Lane, Vero Beach

Experience the serenity of this glorious garden, designed by Janet Meakin Poor, embracing harmonious shades of green varying textures of leaves, fronds, and branches, all shaded by a canopy of majestic live oaks. Touches of pure white emerging from azaleas and gardenias enhance the cool, calm setting. A unique, bold, blue-green Bismark palm stands as a sentry at the front entry. Stroll around the path to the rear of the house to enjoy views of the verdant golf course in both directions. Enter the screened terrace, dominated by a handsome black rectangular pool and a fountain surrounded by Sago and fishtail palms, beautifully enhanced by the owners' expansive, magnificent collection of white orchids. The focal point of the entrance to this tranquil landscape is the replica of Claude Monet's famous Giverny bridge, which spans a trickling black stone pool and a myriad of lush jungle ferns. Even the artist himself would be inspired to paint in such surroundings.

Hours: 10 a.m. to 4 p.m.

From I-95, take Exit 68/Route 60. Proceed east on Route 60 to Indian River Boulevard (about 8 miles) and turn right. Proceed to the next traffic light and turn left onto the 17th Street Bridge (before power plant on left). Cross over Route A-I-A and take the first immediate left onto Club Drive. At the second stop sign, turn right onto Greenway Lane; the first driveway on the left is #911. After your visit to the Hubner garden, proceed east on Greenway Lane to Ocean Drive where you will find Sandy's Garden at the intersection of Ocean Drive and Ladybug Lane.

Isolay

225 Sago Palm Road, Vero Beach

Fanciful and fruitful, Isolay is guarded by great old live oaks, nourished by the Indian River, and involved in a complicated relationship with the mangrove world. The approach is over a moat whose banks protect the basic food chain of the area. Both beauty and function are demonstrated by a wide waterfall providing extra oxygen for all the water creatures. There are many destinations here: a large palapa; a citrus garden; an island, floored with bromeliads and decorated with naturally growing orchids; a bed of tall grasses; a kitchen garden shuddering with butterflies; and "Jere's Garden," which has become more Irish than tropical. In trying to save the land from eroding into the river, we have serendipitously created a beautiful stone wall, a lot of new usable yard, and a renewal of our beach. Many colors, patterns, and scents combine to form a tranquil place, sheltered by palm trees, bamboo, and our loving care.

Hours: 10 a.m. to 4 p.m.

From Route 60, proceed to Route A-1-A north and go about 2 miles. Turn left (west) onto Fred Tuerk Drive at Indian River Shores Town Hall. Follow the road to the rear gates of the community of John's Island. Register your vehicle with the guard, who will issue you a numbered Garden Conservancy sign, which must be prominently displayed on your windshield. Proceed as directed by the guard. (Visitors will be admitted at the gate only by showing a copy of *The Garden Conservancy's Open Days Directory: 2002 Edition,* an Open Days flyer, or a ticket of admission. No exceptions will be made.)

Mangrove Gardens at Carwill Oaks

455 Coconut Palm Road, Vero Beach

Located on the Indian River Lagoon, our garden encompasses mangroves, wetlands, lagoons, spoil islands, and upland grounds accessible by a series of walkways, bridges, and paths. Enter the mangroves from the drive court and be greeted by the soft gurgling of the freshwater stream as it trips its way through a mini-rainforest. Follow the forest paths north to Orchid Island and stop for a visit in the Thai Orchid House. Proceed along Dendrobium Walk to General's Island and meet our permanent visitor from Xian, China. Continue west along Evelyn's Walk toward the sound of Tibetan wind chimes and find the Kitchen Garden, which is located along the Indian River. Wander the paths through the Kitchen Garden and proceed directly south along River Walk, crossing the southern lawn to a path that leads you to Panther's Lair walkway and island. View a large lagoon containing creatures indigenous to our area. Possibly see various wading birds feeding in the shallows of the lagoon. Return to the southern lawn and proceed along the east side of the house to the lake terrace with its herb garden pots. The drive court where the tour started is a short walk away via a paver path through the potting/growing area used for propagation of some of the plants just seen. It is our hope that our gardens will demonstrate that mankind and mangroves are not mutually exclusive but can co-exist and flourish. Here the mangrove fringes and their tidal lakes provide a place for all marine life to begin—a nursery for the ocean's bounty. Take away with you the thought that, with careful planning, this precious ecosystem, so important to our rivers and oceans, can and should be preserved for the present and for all time.

Hours: 10 a.m. to 2 p.m.

From Route 60, proceed to Route A-1-A north and go about 2 miles. Turn left (west) onto Fred Tuerk Drive at the Indian River Shores Town Hall. Follow the road to the rear gate of the community of John's Island. Register your vehicle with the guard, who will issue you a numbered Garden Conservancy sign, which must be prominently displayed on your windshield. Proceed as directed by the guard. (Visitors will be admitted at the gate only by showing a copy of *The Garden Conservancy's Open Days Directory: 2002 Edition*, an Open Days flyer, or a ticket of admission. No exceptions will be made.)

Proceeds shared with the McKee Botanical Garden

Sandy's Garden
921 Ladybug Lane, Vero Beach

In creating our new environment, I knew I wanted to be in harmony with the rich history of our neighborhood, Old Riomar, famous for its historic homes and oak-canopied lanes. I had the luxury and challenge of creating something from a clean palette, so I started with a sense that it was more about the land than about a building. My architect, Peter Moor, said, "Riomar is its own landscape as a whole. This building takes some of its formal moves from the classic older homes in Riomar, for example, by using uneven gables to soften the meeting of the house into the landscape. In this project, I used the building simply to create the spaces. I used the auto as part of the landscape, inviting it to the front door, European style, as a coach once approached a country home." I wanted the garden as part of my life, not as a supplement to it. So, one enters the jasmine-covered arched garden space, by auto or on foot, wandering on Chicago brick paths around the south end through my orchid pagoda into the motor court, continuing on in between the main house and guest cottage to the north end of the property. This is where I have my own little citrus grove, which thrives on the warm winter salt air and moisture, providing my kitchen with fresh grapefruit, oranges, and limes and their hypnotic aroma during the spring blossom season. Several thunbergia vines run almost wild, adding a kind of riotous look to the north space. Facing the ocean side is my pool garden, bordered by birds of paradise, seagrape, plumbago, and cracker rosebushes. The outdoor loggia is filled with pots of seasonal plants and overlooks the southeast garden, where my little boy birdbath attracts local birds, bees, and butterflies. From this outdoor space one goes through a gate to my kitchen garden, which is filled with herbs, seasonal flowers, topiaries, and architectural garden pieces.

Hours: 10 a.m. to 4 p.m.

From Route 60, go south on Club Drive to Ladybug Lane. The house is located on the corner of Ladybug and Ocean Drive. *Please park on the street.*

Proceeds shared with the McKee Botanical Garden

The Dr. & Mrs. William King Stubbs Garden

135 Sago Palm Road, Vero Beach

Situated along the natural shoreline of an interior cove of the Indian River, our house siting and landscape planning incorporate and conserve existing natural features. See our majestic live oaks, which we relocated to the property. Sensitive native planting and site grading with the use of natural Florida fieldstone boulders yield an entrance through a meandering gravel way, which winds its way through the enhanced Florida hammock adjacent to the wetland estuary system. See how our conservation-minded planning protects the mangrove marsh area in a pleasing, useful natural setting. Blooms and fragrances of native flowering shrubs and trees attract lots of wildlife and birds. A fern glade exists at our lowest elevation. Ascend to the upper level of the south lawn to the circular garden swimming pool and sculpture to capture a dramatic, open, and sunny view of the Indian River. Transcend the gracious stone garden steps to the lower riverside elevation and dock beyond. Walk through our terraced, free-flowing rose garden, where some of our long-time favorites and award-winning bloomers await you! Meandering stone retaining walls and elevated planters were designed to create the desired higher elevation for the roses and to allow space for proper growing medium and soil mixes. Edible fruits and flowering plantings along the west garden path call us and lots of butterflies and hummingbirds to this part of the garden! The west garden path leads to our west side yard terrace and country flower garden.

Hours: 10 a.m. to 4 p.m.

From Route 60, proceed north on Route A-1-A into the town of Indian River Shores. Continue north 1.3 miles until you reach the main entrance/gatehouse at John's Island. Turn left (west) and stop at the gatehouse. Register your vehicle with the guard, who will issue you a numbered Garden Conservancy sign, which must be prominently displayed on your windshield. Proceed as directed by the guard. (Visitors will be admitted at the gate only by showing a copy of *The Garden Conservancy's Open Days Directory: 2002 Edition,* an Open Days flyer, or a ticket of admission. No exceptions will be made.)

Proceeds shared with the McKee Botanical Garden

Public Gardens

INDIAN RIVER COUNTY

Vero Beach

McKee Botanical Garden

350 U.S. Highway 1, Vero Beach (561) 794-0601 www.mckeegarden.org

The garden is now eighteen acres of what was originally an eighty-acre tropical hammock along the Indian River. McKee Botanical Garden was originally designed by landscape architect William Lyman Phillips in the early 1930s. Phillips created the basic infrastructure of streams, ponds, and trails. Native vegetation was augmented with ornamental plants and for years McKee Jungle Garden was one of Florida's most popular attractions. The garden went into decline during the 1970s due to competition from new large-scale attractions. All but the eighteen acres was sold to condominium developers, but fortunately the historic core of the garden remains. The garden has reopened as a public botanical garden, with visitor facilities—a library, café, gift shop, and rentable meeting space in the historic buildings.

Hours: Year round, Tuesday through Saturday, 9 a.m. to 4:30 p.m., Sunday, 9 a.m. to 4:30 p.m.

Admission: $6

The garden is located at 350 U.S. Highway 1, at the southern gateway to Vero Beach, on the mainland. It is 2 hours southeast of Orlando and 1 hour north of West Palm Beach.

ILLINOIS

The Gardens at Wandering Tree—
The "Glorée & Tryumphant Garden Railway," Barrington.
Photo © Huff & Puff Industries.

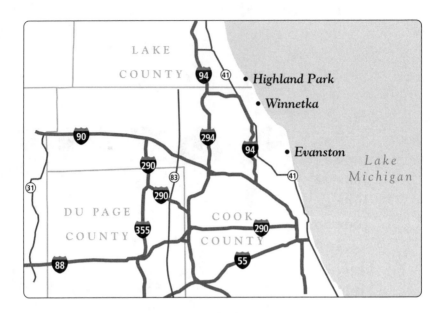

Saturday, June 15

COOK COUNTY

EVANSTON

Zerega Garden

821 Madison, Evanston

In this city garden, a walkway of brick steps leads towards the front porch of the 78-year-old Tudor style house. A Japanese maple 'Bloodgood' by the front entrance and a Chinese dogwood *Cornus kousa* on the opposite corner are surrounded by many perennials contained by flagstone walls and pachysandra. In the backyard, the pond with Japanese koi, waterlilies, lotus and a waterfall seems to slow down time. Plantings finishing this scene include ferns, wild ginger, a variety of hostas, and dwarf bamboo. A few large trees provide some shade, creating the perfect environment for a mix of Japanese maple, bamboo, variegated sedum, and many more perennials.

Hours: 10 a.m. to 4 p.m.

From Edens Expressway/I-94, take the Dempster east exit and follow about 2 miles to Ridge Road. Turn right (south) onto Ridge to Washington Avenue. Turn left (east) at Washington and go 2 blocks to Sherman Avenue. Turn right onto Sherman and follow to Madison (1 block). Turn right again at Madison and go to #821.

From Chicago, take Lake Shore Drive north to the Hollywood exit. Turn right onto Sheridan Road and follow Sheridan north to the Evanston city limits. There is a cemetery on the left; continue past the cemetery to the first traffic light. Turn right and follow Sheridan to Kedzie (about .5 mile). Turn left (west) on Kedzie and travel about 8 blocks to Chicago Avenue. Turn left onto Chicago Avenue, make an immediate right onto Madison, and go to #821. *Please park on the street.*

WINNETKA
Beauty without Boundaries
1001 Green Bay Road, Winnetka

"House in the Garden" is for visitors of any age or ability. The owner worked with Deborah Nevins to create a classical garden without barriers, yet with a sense of intimacy between people and the landscape. The Hicks yew garden rooms each create a different experience. From the terrace, hide away in the sixteenth-century topiary garden and pergola with Chinese roundels. Gaze at the dappled shade of the Haifa honey locust allée with tapestry-like plantings. See the sturdy, lowland plants which populate a dell and the amphitheater formed by billowy cushions of boxwood; the gracious ribbon-like garden path is wide enough for two people, one in a wheelchair, moving side by side. The accessible decomposed granite path drains quickly. Benches strategically punctuate the path (distance can also be a barrier). Note, behind the water spout, the evergreen path which gives the feel of a walk in the forest. The symmetrical, open lawn with water spout and beech tree is bordered by an eight-foot sandy subsurface that packs hard and is bump and barrier free. Yorkstone pavers are set with one-eighth inch joints in stone dust for fast drainage with enough roughness to grip soles and rubber tires, yet not so much to be bumpy. All house entrance courts slope slightly, avoiding the need for steps and adding access for all guests to the French-style manor house. If you are interested in learning more about gardens with this type of accessibility, please visit the Enabling Garden at Chicago Botanic Garden.

Hours: 10 a.m. to 4 p.m.

From Edens Expressway/I-94 south, take the Tower Road exit. Go east on Tower Road to Burr (1 block before Green Bay Road). Turn right onto Burr and go 2 blocks. *Park on the street and enter property through 2 pillars across from Hubbard Woods School*

From Edens Expressway/I-94 north, take the Willow Road East exit. Go east on Willow Road to Hibbard Road. Turn left onto Hibbard and go to Tower Road. Turn right and proceed as directed above.

Liz & Bob Crowe
1228 Westmoor Road, Winnetka

A vista from every window was the goal in the creation of our new small garden. The bones consist of a latticework fence, an arbor, a pergola, terraces, and a small shed. These design elements are used in various parts of the garden for interest, variety, and focal points with resting places for enjoyment throughout. Foliage color and texture are high on our list as we continue to select and refine choices of plant material. Two young yellowwood trees grace the front yard, whitebuds shield us from neighbors, a golden rain tree shadows the terrace, and a red chestnut tree is gaining in scale. The garden was designed and is completely maintained by its owners.

Hours: 10 a.m. to 4 p.m.

From the north, take Edens Expressway/I-94 south to the Tower Road exit. Go east on Tower Road (1.4 miles) to Hibbard Road (3-way stop). Turn right onto Hibbard Road. Take the second left onto Westmoor Road. The house is the third on the right.

From the south, take Edens Expressway/I-94 to the Willow Road east exit. Continue east on Willow Road (.75 mile) to Hibbard Road. Turn left onto Hibbard Road to Westmoor Road (.8 mile). Turn right onto Westmoor Road. The house is the third on the right. *Please park along Westmoor Road.*

HIGHLAND PARK
Cathy & Gene Rothert Garden
356 Russet Lane, Highland Park

The evolution of our garden and its care are a genuine team effort which we both enjoy for restoration of our physical, mental, and spiritual health. It is a naturalistic design with a good balance of sun, shade, wet, and dry areas that has enabled us to include quite a diversity of plants. We planned it fifteen years ago bearing in mind that, as a gardener with a disability, I would need special features and use adapted tools and techniques, as well as carefully choose and position plants so gardening would be a safe, comfortable, and fun experience. As a wheelchair user, I need easy access to areas that I frequently visit, so I have relied on firm, level pathways and a deck to get to key places in the garden. I have used large containers and a bed on or next to the paved areas to position high-maintenance annuals, vegetables, and herbs at an easy-to-reach height. The rest of the garden is dominated by well-mulched and densely planted lower maintenance mixed borders that are anchored with small trees, dwarf conifers, and shrubs offering year-round interest. Among these is a large collection of both native and exotic low-maintenance bulbs and perennials, including many wildflowers and grasses. Together, my wife and I take care of the in-ground beds. I use special long-handled tools that enable me to reach all but the most remote places. If you are interested in learning more about this type of gardening, please visit the Enabling Garden at the Chicago Botanic Garden.

Hours: 10 a.m. to 4 p.m.

Take Skokie Road to the Clavey Road exit. Drive west .25 mile to the stop sign at Ridge Road. Turn left (south) and go about 300 feet. Turn right (west) onto Balsam Road. Continue .1 mile to Russet Lane and turn right. The third ranch house on the left, painted in earth tones, is #356. *Please park along the road.*

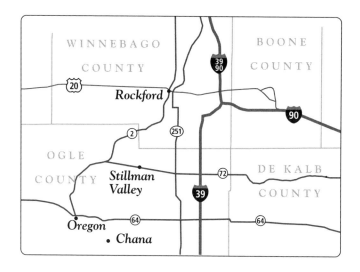

Saturday, June 22

OGLE COUNTY

OREGON
Heuer's Hosta Garden
589 South Harmony, Oregon

Hidden down a long driveway, shade and sunshine gardens weave through lawn and forest. Sunshine beds include perennial and annual herbs, grasses, and flowering perennials and shrubs, including many varieties of sedum, nepeta, verbascum, euphorbia, artemesia, and deciduous shrubs. Drifts of daylilies and Asiatic, Oriental, trumpet, and Orienpet lilies meander through our front acreage. Beckoning from the front-of-the-house hosta plantings are eight-foot-tall metal arbors covered with 'Henry Kelsey' and 'Polka' roses, which anchor the rugosa, shrub, English, and Explorer series rose collections. Proceeding through the arches, our visitors find the hosta beds beneath towering white pines, along the forest edge, and winding through the woods. An assortment of cherubs accents the deep woods hosta beds and all our other beds contain metal towers, "bugs," or various whimsies to mark unusual perennials. Interspersed throughout are the stars of the place. Over 200 varieties of hosta fill their own beds, mingle with other shade-loving plants, or peek out from under sun-loving annuals and perennials.

Hours: 10 a.m. to 4 p.m.

From Oregon, travel west on Route 64 from the city center and the junction of Routes 2 and 64. Continue 1 mile west to Oregon Trail Road. Turn left and go 3 miles to the "T" at Oregon Trail Road and Harmony Road. Turn left and go 1 mile south to the mailbox with #589 and hostas planted around it. Turn left and go down the long lane. *Please park on the north side of the lane leading to the house.*

Proceeds shared with the Mount Morris Public Library

WINNEBAGO COUNTY

CHANA

The Garden of Kurt & Ellen Laurent—Ancient Oaks

5550 East Canfield Road, Chana

Our home is set on three-plus acres with a southern exposure partially protected by ancient bur oaks that, in tandem with pines and other trees, provide dappled shade for shrubs and perennials. Korean lilac, hydrangea, rhododendrons, and various evergreens are nestled in rock terraced gardens, embellished by the varied textures of hosta, ferns, astilbes, and shade companions. I am the shady gardener while Ellen balances the gardening in the sun with the never-still grass and flowers that shade can't match. In addition to hundreds of square yards of plantings and a very secluded area with a small pool and a sittin' rock, we rely on a paving brick patio graced by a woodbine-entwined pergola beside a pond that adds another dimension to our gardening.

Hours: 10 a.m. to 4 p.m.

Located about 10 miles west of I-39 and 2.5 miles south of Route 64. Turn south onto Chana Road and proceed 2.5 miles to Canfield Road, which takes you west. We are the second residence on the right, a brick house about 150 feet from the road.

ROCKFORD

The Garden of Pauline & Paul Clausen

2715 Karen Drive, Rockford

Our 41-year-old garden is a passionate plant collector's dream of acquiring as many varieties and species of perennials that are available for our northern Illinois climate. An extensive and noteworthy collection of rare and unusual perennials displays an artfully woven tapestry of brilliant color combinations, abundance of bloom, diversity of foliage textures, and heady fragrances. The garden is augmented by trickling water flowing into the pond under a majestic old spruce tree. A leisurely stroll through the garden presents the visitor with spectacular scenery, plus an element of surprise in discovering only perennials comprise the garden proper. Special attention is given to the microclimates and niches. A number of perennials rated for a warmer plant hardiness zone are grown in the garden's southerly exposure, including *Cyclamen hederifolium, Arum italicum, Arisaema candidissimum, Begonia grandis, Deinanthe caerulea, Ligularia crispata,* and the terrestrial orchid *Bletilla striata.* Statuary and garden ornaments are strategically interspersed throughout the curved lines of the flower beds to enhance the plantings. Birds have an important place in the garden and are provided with many feeders, houses, and baths. Accenting annuals are arranged on the patio to create lush and unusual container plantings with a variety of colors and texture combinations. May you find enjoyment and inspiration in this plant collector's paradise!

Hours: 10 a.m. to 4 p.m.

From I-90, take Exit 64/Rockford/East Riverside Boulevard. Turn left onto Riverside Boulevard and go 6.5 miles, passing through Loves Park and crossing the Rock River and Route 2 to Rockton Avenue. Turn left onto Rockton Avenue and go 1 block. Turn right onto Karen Drive and go 1.5 blocks. The garden is on the right side of the street, #2715. *Please park on the street.*

Proceeds shared with the Northern Illinois Botanical Society

The Ewaldz Garden

2922 Carriage Lane, Rockford

The scent of 200 rosebushes reaches you as you enter our garden through a vine-covered pergola. We have chosen sixty varieties of hybrid tea and floribunda roses to fill our terraced beds. Bordering the entire garden are seventy shrub roses of diverse types: hardy Canadian, Austin English, heirloom, and modern varieties. We also have thirty rose cultivars hybridized by the late Dr. Griffith Buck of Ames, Iowa. The shrub roses were carefully selected for their delightful fragrance, repeat blooming pattern, and winter hardiness. As companion plants for our roses, we have delphinium, clematis, iris, lilies, and many other perennials and annuals. Our garden is at its peak for abundant blooms and fragrance in the third and fourth weeks of June.

Hours: 10 a.m. to 4 p.m.

From I-90, take Exit 64/Rockford/East Riverside Boulevard. Turn left onto Riverside Boulevard and go 6.5 miles, passing through Loves Park and crossing the Rock River and Route 2 to Rockton Avenue. Turn left onto Rockton Avenue and go 1 block. Turn right onto Karen Drive and go 2 blocks. Turn left onto Packard Parkway and go 1 block to Carriage Lane. Turn right and the garden is at #2922 in the middle of the block on the left. Please park on the street.

Proceeds shared with the Klehm Arboretum & Botanical Garden

Gunn Garden

22 Johns Woods Drive, Rockford

Six ancient oaks shade the garden, which contains many varieties of trillium, asarum, arisaema, and ferns. Other shade lovers such as pulmonaria, corydalis, epimedium, tiarella, and tricyrtis join hostas and ground covers under a large variety of azaleas and other shrubs. Concolor firs, Japanese white pines, and the dwarf Alberta spruce complement perennials with glaucous foliage. Spring finds the garden filled with color from 3,000 bulbs. Sculptures of the four seasons surround the slate patio, and statuary and birdhouses are found throughout the garden.

Hours: 10 a.m. to 4 p.m.

From I-90, take Exit 64/Rockford/East Riverside Boulevard and travel west across the Rock River on the Riverside Bridge. Continue west to North Main Street/Route 2 and turn right onto North Main. Travel 2 blocks to a white stone wall (The Oaks) and turn right onto Johns Woods Drive.

River View Garden

2503 Harlem Boulevard, Rockford

Our home and garden are located on the site of Harlem Park, which occupied the Rock River front from the present location of Auburn Street Bridge to near the Rockford Country Club from 1891 until the mid-1920s. When we purchased the home, woods had taken over the back and become overgrown and not very attractive. We decided that we needed to get control of the woods and yet try not to create more maintenance for ourselves than necessary. Ours is a shaded backyard with patches of sunshine throughout the day, so we knew that we would need to enhance the woodsy feel with plants, shrubs, and trees that would be at home in our shade. We created a grassy area near the house and added pathways to divide the plantings into beds through which we can stroll. The paths are lighted for night-time strolling and we added three water features to the paths for interest. We have lots of ferns, of course, as well as several varieties of hostas, bleeding hearts, lilies, foamflowers, coralbells, and azaleas. It was my wish to include a pond, but with all of the tree roots to contend with, we didn't think we'd have much success, so we had a deck built to accommodate a small lily and fishpond. Our garden is a new one and the summer of 2002 is only the second full season for most of the plantings. The perimeters of the backyard garden are still incomplete as I find new and different things I wish to add. The front yard has been established for five years and includes an entry garden with a flowering dogwood and hostas. The beds closer to the street are perennial beds that include plantings that do well in less than full sun. These beds get rearranged as my tastes and interests evolve and change.

Hours: 10 a.m. to 2 p.m.

From Wisconsin taking I-90, take Exit 64/Rockford/East Riverside Boulevard exit, go west on Riverside Boulevard, and cross the Rock River. After crossing the river, go to the third traffic light and turn south (left) onto North Main Street. Take North Main south to Fulton Avenue (about 1 mile). Turn left onto Fulton and go to the end, which curves to the right to turn into Harlem Boulevard. We are at the first cross intersection going south on Harlem Boulevard and are the house on the northeast corner.

From Chicago, take I-90 to the Business 20 exit onto East State Street. Take East State west to Perryville Road. Turn north (right) onto Perryville Road and take Perryville to Springcreek Road. Turn west (left) onto Springcreek and continue on Springcreek until you cross the Rock River. Springcreek becomes Auburn Street as you cross the river. Immediately at the end of the bridge after crossing the river, turn north (right) onto Harlem Boulevard and go north to the northeast corner of Harlem Boulevard and Willoughby Terrace. We are right on the northeast corner.

Sheila's English Cottage Garden
3501 Shirley Road, Rockford

As the garden is located on a busy corner, I decided to create a "little bit of England" to be enjoyed by both myself and those who pass on their way to and from work. Each year I feel I must add something new for this large audience. Consequently, as each successive season passes, more grassland gives way to flowers and shrubbery. Other natural changes continually occur; the loss of a large elm tree meant that a previously shaded area is now thrown into the sun. The frequent presence of visitors, many of a more mature age, caused me to consider the placement of stone steps on the hillside at the rear of the property. This has made the garden at the top of the hill more accessible; it has also added considerable aesthetic value. Window boxes, birdhouses, and garden whimsy abound.

Hours: 10 a.m. to 4 p.m.

From the intersection of East State Street and Fairview Avenue, go south on Fairview. The second street on the left (east) is Shirley Road. The garden is on the southeast corner of the Fairview/Shirley intersection. The house is about 350 yards from East State Street, 3501 Shirley Road. *Please park along the street.*

STILLMAN VALLEY
Bittersweet Acres
7908 Winding Oak Lane, Stillman Valley

Our garden is nestled on two and one half acres in rural Stillman Valley. Over the past ten years, we have created 200 feet of perennial borders with many spring bulbs and old and new varieties of perennials, as well as shrubs and evergreens. We also have a small pond, vegetable garden, rose and ornamental grass garden, and numerous shrubs and trees, all surrounded by a wild and wooded area that we have left natural for the wildlife to enjoy. There is a meandering path through the wooded area on which to stroll and explore. Our goal is to make the garden a place of beauty and enjoyment from the first bud of spring to the last flower of autumn. We hope you enjoy the garden and invite you to stay as long as you like.

Hours: 10 a.m. to 4 p.m.

From I-90, take the Route 20 Bypass west to Illinois 2/South Main Street. Go to the second traffic light (UPS on the left) and turn right onto Kishwaukee Road. At the barn with the image of a smiley face, turn right, go to the first crossroad, and turn left onto Crestview Road. Go to the third road and turn left onto Wildwood. Go to the bottom of the hill and turn right onto Winding Oak Lane.

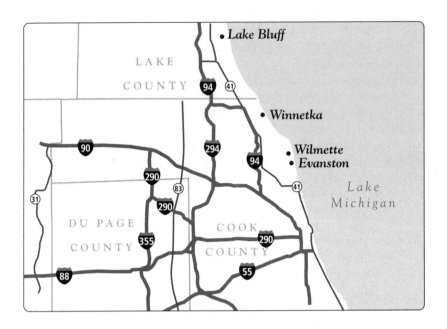

Sunday, June 23
COOK COUNTY

EVANSTON
A Lakeside Garden
706 Roslyn Terrace, Evanston

Having grown up on the coasts of Connecticut and Rhode Island and summering on Cape Cod, I tried to have our home and garden reflect that heritage. In 1994, our shingle-style house grew out of a 1950s' ranch and an acquired neighboring property. With the overwhelming visual and physical strength of Lake Michigan, landscape architect Douglas Hoerr wisely realized that we needed a great deal of strength in our landscape, consequently, the stone walls and naturally placed boulders. The garden was designed with several smaller areas to be enjoyed in various types of weather, summer days down on the lake, warm afternoons on the porch, and windy days in protected areas. Many spring bulbs, viburnums, Sargent crab apple trees, climbing roses, hydrangeas, cotoneasters, grasses, and the existing cracked willows combine to create the feeling of openness and protection needed when living on Lake Michigan.

Hours: 10 a.m. to 4 p.m.

From south Evanston, continue north on Sheridan Road to the last street in Evanston. Turn right onto Roslyn Place and follow it towards the lake, bearing right onto Roslyn Terrace (a private road) and following it to the last house.

From the north, take Lake Street east and go right on Sheridan Road to the third left after the Bahai Temple. Turn left onto Roslyn Place and proceed as directed above.

WILMETTE

Craig Bergmann & James Grigsby
1924 Lake Avenue, Wilmette

A very small "secret garden" at the office and home of two garden designers is all but concealed from the busy street. This intimate garden provides the setting for many unusual evergreen and woody plants—including a sixty-year-old *Magnolia soulangiana*—herbaceous perennials, and tender plantings. The old Lord & Burnham greenhouse (circa 1900) was the first greenhouse ever used by New Trier High School in nearby Winnetka. The garden has been featured in Rosemary Verey's book *The American Man's Garden* and *Horticulture* and *House & Garden* magazines.

Hours: 10 a.m. to 4 p.m.

From Edens Expressway/I-94, take the Lake Avenue exit if traveling north or the Skokie Road exit to Lake Avenue if traveling south. Continue east on Lake Avenue about 1.5 miles. The house is at Lake Avenue and Columbus Street (1924 Lake Avenue). *There is limited parking on Columbus Street. Additional parking is at the church parking lot east at Lake and Ridge Roads. Entry to the garden is at the rear of the house.*

WINNETKA

Helen & Dick Thomas
82 Indian Hill Road, Winnetka

We inherited the fine bones of this garden several years ago when we became the second owners of this lovely French-style house. The bluestone terrace as well as the hawthorn allée were all part of the original landscape plan in 1956. With the help of landscape designer Janet Meakin Poor, we have added a low entrance wall and inserted the two charming knot gardens in the front courtyard. The small standard lilacs (*Syringa patula* 'Miss Kim') anchor these petite gardens. Two more knot gardens were added in the south terrace, echoing those in the front of courtyard. Small crab apples (*Malus* 'Tina') are featured in these two gardens. With the addition of a sunroom, a brick terrace area was created to form an intimate kitchen garden where lush herbs, climbing roses, clematis, and colorful perennials spill over the pink brick borders. Six boxwood-edged gardens surround a vibrant display of our favorite roses and form the entrance of the pool area. The east-west perennial gardens enhance the south end overlooking the Brussels block pool deck. A lattice fence frames the productive vegetable garden at the rear. A unique pair of Chinese lions handsomely guards the Oriental-inspired pergola. On the shaded east perimeter of our property, a flagstone path leads one through our evolving woodland garden.

Hours: 10 a.m. to 4 p.m.

From the south, take Edens Expressway/I-94 to Lake Avenue east. Travel east on Lake Avenue to Ridge Road. Turn left (north) onto Ridge Road and continue to Indian Hill Road, which will be on your left. Follow Indian Hill Road to #82, about .5 mile.

From the north, take Edens Expressway/I-94 to the Skokie Road exit. Proceed to Lake Avenue. Turn left (east), proceed as directed above.

From Sheridan or Green Bay Road, turn west onto Lake Avenue. Proceed as directed above.

LAKE COUNTY

LAKE BLUFF

Crabtree Farm
Sheridan Road, Lake Bluff

These gardens surround estate buildings designed in 1926 by David Adler. They are located on Crabtree Farm, the only remaining farm in Illinois that overlooks Lake Michigan. The gardens include a cottage garden by Ellen Shipman, a Neoclassical folly house, and an original greenhouse and potting shed next to the cutting and vegetable garden. There is an indoor tennis court with espaliered ivy walls and an enclosed walled garden. The garden also has vistas, pathways, and a golfing area in its woodland and wildflower settings. A ravine walk and raised walkways lead to a private Lake Michigan beach.

Hours: 10 a.m. to 4 p.m.

From Route 41, take the Lake Bluff exit to Route 176. (Driving northbound, take the first exit past the underpass. Driving southbound on Route 41, take the exit to Route 176.) Go east on Route 176 to Sheridan Road. Go north on Sheridan Road .5 mile to Crabtree Farm. Drive between the ponds and *follow signs to park in the field.*

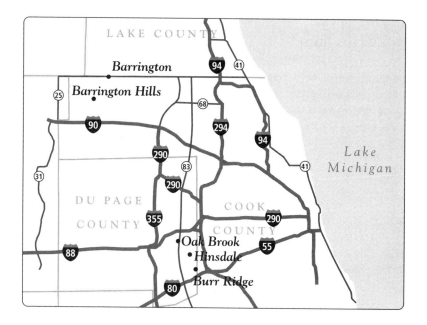

Saturday, June 29

COOK COUNTY

BARRINGTON

The Gardens at Wandering Tree—The "Glorée & Tryumphant" Garden Railway

125 Arrowhead Lane, Barrington

Thirty-five years ago, my husband, Harvey, and I purchased a ten-acre property known as Wandering Tree. Nestled beside a three-acre pond frequented by waterfowl, the gardens of Wandering Tree are varied. There are rose gardens, a woodland garden featuring a 400-year-old oak, a pleached arch of 24 crab apple trees, a Japanese garden with a bridge and stream, an herbaceous border, a sunken formal vegetable potager, dooryard gardens, and, perhaps most importantly, the "Glorée and Tryumphant" Garden Railway. This internationally recognized prototypical garden railway consists of 6,000 square feet of miniature waterfalls, bridges, trestles, streams, city and country vignettes, and miniature plant material of every description, as well as eleven different half-inch scale toy trains. Our company, Huff and Puff Industries Ltd., designs and installs garden railways nationwide.

Hours: 10 a.m. to 4 p.m.

From Chicago, take Kennedy Expressway to I-90. Follow signs to Rockford. Exit at Route 53 north and follow to the end, Lake Cook Road. Go west to Route 12, about .5 mile. Turn right and follow Route 12 north to Miller Road. Turn left (west) onto Arrowhead Lane. Turn right (north) into #125.

From the North Shore, take Lake Cook Road or Route 22 west to Route 12/Lake Zurich. Turn right (north) onto Miller Road. Turn left (west) onto Arrowhead Lane (1.1 mile). Turn right (north) into #125.

Barrington Hills
Peggy & Eric Olsen
237 Oak Knoll Road, Barrington Hills

Tucked away on fifteen acres graced with towering oaks and a natural pond is our 1922 country estate. Amid quaint arbors and fountains, our garden includes formal venues—a flagstone walled terrace, a cottage perennial pool garden, arborvitae hedges, a boxwood-defined English rose garden, and informal areas such as a two-acre woodland walk teaming with daffodil beds overplanted with shade perennials. Our garden has three peak color seasons. Throughout spring, masses of bulbs along with many azaleas, rhodies, magnolias, redbuds, dogwoods, and forsythias put on a show. Summer brings an explosion of roses, lilies, clematis, astilbes, phlox, tamaracks, spirea, hydrangeas, and hostas. At summer's end, cimicifuga, anemones, and sedums complement the turning colors of oaks, maples, and serviceberries.

Hours: 10 a.m. to 4 p.m.

From I-90, exit onto Barrington Road north (about 12 miles). In Barrington, turn left at the traffic light onto Main Street, also called County Line (1 mile). Go through the light on Hart Road and turn right onto Old Hart Road (.3 mile). Turn left onto Oak Knoll Road (.25 mile). Turn left into the fourth driveway on the left side (1 block). *Please park as directed.*

Oak Brook
Susan & Ken Beard
3711 Madison Street, Oak Brook

We have lived and gardened on these three acres in Oak Brook for 34 years. Each year we tackle a new project in the garden, trying to make a private oasis for our family and grandchildren. Three years ago we added a nineteen-foot bridge, which made the flow of the garden more interesting. An arbor with an eight-foot opening was also completed in an effort to keep the deer out. Most of the property is in various degrees of shade, which lends itself to hosta and many other woodland plants (ferns, epimedium, corydalis, etc.) that border paths lined with flagstone and wood chips. I am a hosta collector, with 280 plus varieties and climbing. The garden has been designed to play down the old swimming pool, which was here when we moved in, and to give views with focal points from every room in the house and during every season of the year.

Hours: 10 a.m. to 4 p.m.

Take I-294 to Ogden Avenue. Go west towards Hinsdale and pass York Road to the next traffic light, which is Madison Street. Go right about .6 mile, across from the far end of Brownswood Cemetery. The garden is at the rough cedar-and-stone two-story house on the right side of the street. *Please park on the east side of the road (the same side as the house).*

Tom Keck

3421 Spring Road, Oak Brook

This two-acre garden is oriented toward fall colors and the selection of trees and shrubs is slanted toward fall coloration. Grasses (approximately eighty different types) provide year-round attraction but complement the tree selection. The hostas show well through August, but my latest interest is in conifers, of which a small selection has been introduced.

Hours: 10 a.m. to 4 p.m.

Take Route 83 to Ogden Avenue. Travel east to Madison Street at the second traffic light. Travel north to the end of Madison and cross Spring Road. Continue into the driveway at the intersection of Spring Road and Madison.

Proceeds shared with Lexington College

DU PAGE COUNTY

BURR RIDGE

Suzy & Sam Stout

15W051 Sedgley Road, Burr Ridge

Our garden is a prairie, a pond, and a wood in the middle of which, incidentally, sits our four-year-old country French farmhouse. Our dream was to live immersed in the beauty and serenity of nature—a shelter from the complexities of modern life. Begin your visit down a meandering drive through a prairie ablaze with wildflowers and native grasses and get a glimpse of the pond and woods beyond. The drive continues into a small courtyard of the farmhouse surrounded by a low limestone wall against which grow roses, delphiniums, climbing hydrangeas, and lilies. An allée of immature dwarf apple trees completes the exit of the drive out to the road. You are invited to wander the property designed by architect Anthony Tyznik, who laid out drives, paths, bridges, prairie, and pond, then clothed them in beauty all year round in an unfolding array of ever-changing color and texture. Spring thrills with the bloom of native prairie wildflowers, crabs, lilacs, redbud, dogwood, and shadblow. The prairie sings in summer with the intensity of a sea of yellow coreopsis. In the fall, there is the brilliance of all the blues and purples of native asters. Old birdhouses, vintage garden ornaments, as well as the wonderful sounds of birdsong, the plunk of a bullfrog, splash of a bass, or the sighting of a stealthy great blue heron, or our red-shouldered hawk, will, we hope, add to the enjoyment of your visit.

Hours: 10 a.m. to 4 p.m.

From I-55/Stevenson Expressway south, exit onto County Line Road north. Cross Plainfield Road and continue north to Sedgley Road (60th Street), which runs west only and is opposite the entrance to Katherine Legge Park. Turn west (left) onto Sedgley and go to the second house from the corner on the left side. *Please park on the north side of the street only.*

HINSDALE
The Gardens of Kellie & Barry O'Brien
527 West Maple Street, Hinsdale

This three-quarter-acre garden reflects the lifestyle and personality of Kellie O'Brien and her husband, Barry. Fifteen years ago, they transformed their 1950s' ranch home into a stately Tudor, which created the background for the continuous perennial gardens weaving throughout their property. The front sunny borders are a combination of unusual evergreens and perennials. In the spring, thousands of daffodils and tulips announce the beginning of a new season. Hydrangeas, roses, and buddleias all add to the ongoing changes from early spring to late fall. Special attention to combining different textures is evident in the grouping of these plants. Walking through the hosta walk to the back 2,000-foot bluestone patio, you will pass an English fishpond, rose-covered balustrades, and many groupings of container gardens. This is where the O'Briens host many family celebrations and spend hours with their five grandchildren, introducing them to the world of plants. The back gardens are mainly shade gardens with huge mature hostas, astilbes, hydrangeas, and a variety of unusual shade plants. The shed and vegetable garden are a reflection of Kellie's farm background. The swing under the mulberry tree is where quiet moments are spent at the end of the day looking through the "magic window" created by an opening in the trees facing west. The garden has speakers throughout to further enhance this peacefulness that a garden brings.

Hours: 10 a.m. to 4 p.m.

The garden is between Madison and Monroe, 1 block north of Chicago Avenue or 4 blocks south of Ogden Avenue. The house is a red brick Tudor on the north side of Maple. *Please park on the street.*

Proceeds shared with the Illinois Citizens for Life

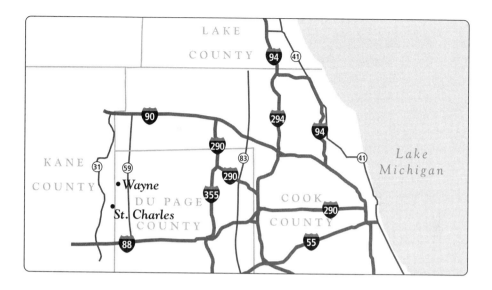

Saturday, July 6

DU PAGE COUNTY

WAYNE

Dove Cottage

35W074 Army Trail Road, Wayne

When we discovered our home nine years ago, it was calling to me. As a landscape designer, I had located the project of my dreams! Our 1853 farm cottage-style home had excellent "bones." Surrounded by mature trees, old stone walls, a slate patio with a trellis and an outdoor fireplace, and a pool, there was not a flower in sight within four acres of land. Overgrown shrubbery was quickly removed and flagstone paths added to create movement and intimacy. The front garden reflects my love of English cottage gardens with their profusion of heirloom roses and perennials. Over the years, we have created a moon garden, shade, cutting, and formal herb bed with espaliered apple trees, and a wildlife pond. My husband Steve's art is reflected in his contributions: the birdhouses, feeders, dovecote, trellising, pergola, and my favorite, our barn, lovingly crafted by hand in the manner of an East Coast heirloom. Ours is an organic and wildlife-encouraging environment, therefore not pristine, but shared by many.

Hours: 10 a.m. to 4 p.m.

From Route 59 (south of I-90 and north of Route 64), turn west at the intersection of Army Trail Road. Travel through the quaint village of Wayne, over the railroad tracks, and to the first traffic light at Dunham Road. Travel 1 mile to Dove Cottage on the north side of the road. The entrance to the barn will be posted with a pink-and-green sign reading "Scentimental Gardens."

Proceeds shared with the Garfield Farm Museum

KANE COUNTY

SAINT CHARLES
Charles & Patricia Bell
39W582 Deer Run Drive, Saint Charles

In a semi-rural area west of Chicago, amid the tall oak trees and open vistas, we have established a series of gardens on two acres featuring numerous sun- and shade-tolerant perennials. Colors and textures are combined to accent and highlight how our collection of more than 400 varieties of daylilies can interact with other sun-loving plants. Several hundred varieties of perennials, decorative grasses, and flowering shrubs provide a constantly changing view in the gardens during the growing season. In the shade gardens, spring brings Virginia bluebells, bleeding hearts, primroses, brunnera, epimedium, and other shade lovers, giving way to hostas, astilbe, and ferns to provide various shades of green and variegated leaf patterns throughout the summer and fall. Various annuals are used throughout the gardens and in containers for constant color. A garden is a personal expression that is meant to be shared with others—our gardening principle.

Hours: 10 a.m. to 4 p.m.

From I-90, take Randall Road to Bolcum Road (about 9 miles) and turn right. Continue to Denker Road and turn right. Turn left onto the first street, which is Deer Run Drive, and continue to the first house on the right.

From I-88, take the Farnsworth Road exit. Travel north onto Farnsworth Road about 5 miles to Fabyan Parkway and turn left. Travel about 3.5 miles and turn right onto Randall Road. Take Randall Road to Bolcum Road (about 3 miles north of Route 64) and turn left. Proceed as directed above. *Please park along the street.*

Proceeds shared with the Morton Arboretum

Butcher Garden
37W756 Woodgate Road, Saint Charles

The five-acre site began as an exhausted farm field. The garden, created just five years ago, has a contemporary Japanese style. Attention was paid to water management, views, plant compositions, pathways, secret gardens, stone/boulder selection and placement, moss garden development, private seating areas, tennis court, zigzag bridge, pavilions, waterfalls, reflecting ponds, and strolling gardens, as well as incorporating the wetlands. Significant aesthetic and functional goals had to be combined with environmental concerns. The bordering wetlands were a defining element that required engineering hydrology and geology studies, resulting in the construction of a sediment pond and creek to redirect water flow and improve water quality entering the greater wetlands. This is an exciting, dynamic garden, with something for everyone.

Hours: 10 a.m. to 4 p.m.

From the south, take I-88 to Route 31. Travel north on Route 31 for 1 mile to Oak Street. Take Oak Street west for 1.3 miles to Randall Road. Take Randall Road north for about 8 miles to St. Charles. Turn west onto Crane Road. Turn west again onto Gray Barn Road. Turn left at Woodgate. The Butcher garden is part of an old farm. The house is the contemporary stone home at the end of the main driveway. *Please park along the road.*

From the north, take I-90 west to Randall Road. Go south on Randall Road for about 11 miles to Crane Road and proceed as directed above.

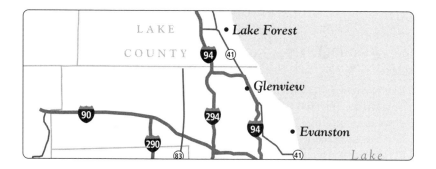

Sunday, July 14

COOK COUNTY

EVANSTON
A Walled Retreat

2738 Euclid Park Place, Evanston

A brick-walled garden from the twenties is the setting for Douglas Hoerr's interpretation of a lush pleasure garden. Gravel crunches, water splashes, and "oohs" and "aahs" are certain to escape your lips as you explore the many garden rooms of this little oasis. The garden features an orchid-filled screened dining enclosure, a loggia-edged Italianate garden, and a secret pattern garden.

Hours: 10 a.m. to 4 p.m.

From Wilmette, head south on Sheridan Road and follow Sheridan as it jogs east. Make an immediate right turn onto Euclid Park Place and proceed to #2738, located on the far northeast border between Evanston and Wilmette. *Please park on the street.*

Proceeds shared with the Chicago Botanic Garden

GLENVIEW
Windmill

2660 Pfingsten Road, Glenview

Windmill, our eight-acre estate, was originally a farm. Since we moved here 45 years ago, we have created four gardens: the perennial border, the cottage garden, the circular rose garden (planned to be as low maintenance as possible), and the vegetable garden, which has expanded over the years to satisfy our culinary interests. We also have the hobby greenhouses, where plants are started for the flower and vegetable gardens. In 2000, a mini-tornado destroyed the windmill and severely damaged many beautiful old trees, two of which we now fondly refer to as our Picasso Trees, because of their contorted forms.

Hours: 10 a.m. to 4 p.m.

From I-294 or Edens Expressway, exit at Willow Road and go east from the tollway; or west from Edens to Pfingsten Road. Travel south 100 yards to #2660 on the right (west side of the road; the southwest corner of Pfingsten and Willow Roads).

LAKE COUNTY

LAKE FOREST
A Garden on Old "Meadow Lane"
285 West Laurel Avenue, Lake Forest

In 1954, we moved into the big brick house on seven acres east of our present residence. It had been planted in the English manner with American elm, white pine, peonies, and iris. Some of these plants are still thriving after seventy years. Landscape architect Anthony Tyznik created our first landscape design. Our children grew up in the big house and moved away. We stayed put and in 1984 built our present passive solar house on 2.5 acres of the original site. We downsized in all respects except the garden. The key to our garden's success seems to be the way the lawn curves around the house and flows to the west like a slowly meandering river on barely sloping land, giving unity to the whole. There are many vistas to pause and examine. As plants matured and increased, borders expanded. Daylilies, hostas, celandine poppies, and other plants were divided and have found homes in other yards. We had to let out some seams for the garden's ample middle-aged curves, but she remains a shapely lady! Follow the river—oops, lawn—from east to west to see perennial borders, shade gardens, an old, but still in service, tennis court and swimming pool, espaliered fruit trees, a campfire where lightning struck spruces creating an opening, beehives, and, in the northwest corner, an ornamental pond with a gazebo, which beckons the wanderer like a beacon. Around the pond is a compost pile, a vegetable garden, and another perennial border before you return to the courtyard. For those who wish to stroll farther, a gate will be open through the stockade fence south of our house to Lake Forest Open Lands, a prairie preserve with beautiful pathways.

Hours: 9 a.m. to 4 p.m.

Take Route 41, an extension of Edens Expressway north, to Westleigh Road in Lake Forest; go east on Westleigh to Green Bay Road. Turn left onto Green Bay and go about .5 mile beyond the traffic light at Deerpath to Laurel Avenue. Turn west onto Laurel Avenue, where you must *park your car on the marked side of the road.* Our house is the last of 5 on a narrow cross street at the bottom of the hill where you turn left. *Visitors with disabilities may be driven to our house but cannot leave cars in our courtyard or along the drive.*

Proceeds shared with the Madoo Conservancy

Prairie Doc
1170 Hawkweed Lane, Lake Forest

Our garden is a celebration of the native Illinois landscape. Through restoration, recreation, and the use of eco-modeling, a variety of habitats has been developed for not only our enjoyment, but for all of the wildlife as well. Hawks and herons, butterflies and birds all find comfort in our sanctuary. At roadside you are greeted by a small hill covered with young oaks, hickories, and haws underplanted with native grasses and forbs. The rear of the house is a magnificent remnant prairie with wetlands and a pond, encompassing a total of five acres. A beautiful deck and boardwalk allow for full enjoyment of all of the environs back here.

Hours: 10 a.m. to 4 p.m.

Located .7 mile north of Deerpath on Green Bay Road. Go left on Laurel Avenue (west of Green Bay) to the end (.5 mile). Hawkweed Lane "T"s into Laurel on the right. Number 1170 is the last house on the left.

Proceeds shared with the Lake Forest Open Land Association

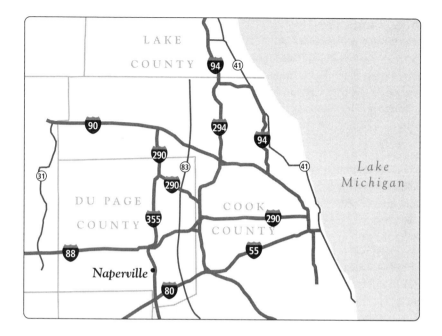

Saturday, July 27

DU PAGE COUNTY

NAPERVILLE

Flora, the Flower Fairy's Eclectic Garden

970 Sylvan Circle, Naperville

Carolyn Lauing-Finzer, artist, teacher, and member of the Illinois Storytellers Guild, has transformed her one-acre Oak Hills yard into a creative and colorful floral adventure course. This "no mow" environment is registered with the National Wildlife Federation's Backyard Habitat Program, the Wild Ones, and is an official Illinois Bird and Butterfly Sanctuary. Paver brick patios, stone walls, and whimsical sculptures join with wood chip trails that lead visitors to secret, remembrance, dreamcatcher, dwarf rose, herb, butterfly, moon, and water gardens. Antique planters, a Peace Pole, an "herbarium" greenhouse, two woodpecker "condominiums," ground arbor, benches, and visual treats abound in this textural, peaceful haven!

Hours: 10 a.m. to 4 p.m.

From Route 53 and Maple Avenue (also known as Chicago Avenue and 55th Street) in Lisle, go west on Maple about 7 miles to Julian Street. Turn left onto Julian Street, go 2 blocks, and turn left onto Porter Avenue. Follow Porter up a winding hill, where it merges with Sylvan Circle. The Finzer yard is the fourth on the outer rim of Sylvan from the junction of Porter and Sylvan. Look for the redwood ranch house, prairie-style garage door and lights, colorful banners, and Merrimac gravel driveway.

Ron & Linda Henry

28W700 Leverenz, Naperville

The garden, backed by open vistas, is an exuberant combination of flowering beds and borders full of vibrant and unusual annuals and perennials, two ponds, a variety of shrubs, vines, and grasses. Ablaze with color and awash in interesting shapes and textures, the garden is an outdoor extension of the house. Trellises and arbors hold roses, clematis, and many annual vines. In early September, the billowing, white sweet clematis running up the custom-made trellises at the side of the house holds center stage in the white garden. A bridge, spanning the faux lake of blue fescue, treats the visitor to one of the many elements of Linda's creativeness in the whimsical touches amidst the blue grass, while the various tender summer bulbs planted throughout the grounds add a feel of the tropics. The planting schemes are further enhanced by an assortment of container plantings. Many out-of-the-ordinary annuals, a bouquet waiting to be gathered, attest to this gardener's interest in the rare, new, and unusual.

Hours: 10 a.m. to 4 p.m.

From I-88, take the Naperville Road exit south to 75th Street (Naperville Road becomes Naper Boulevard about .5 mile south of I-88). Turn right onto 75th and proceed about 3.75 miles to Book Road. Turn left onto Book Road and proceed about 2 miles to Leverenz. Turn left onto Leverenz. The house is several houses down on the north side (left side) of the street. *Please park on the street.*

Kay & John Stephens

620 Berry Court, Naperville

In 1964, with four children and one dog, we moved to a bare, flat, sun-baked, windswept acre of clay on the outskirts of Naperville, population 14,000. Today we are blessed with nine Naperville grandchildren, three dogs, and a contoured, completely altered topography offering an ever-changing retreat from urban sprawl. Stands of evergreens insulating us from traffic's sights and sounds now provide protection for a developing conifer tapestry and a Dragon's Eye pine. Paths connect different vistas of woodsy shade and open sun; there are flowering trees and shrubs, decorative grasses, roses, perennials, and annuals. Fences provide support for climbers and safety for toddlers and puppies. Our artist daughter's sculpted copper sprinklers provide all-season visual interest as well as a great watering system. Our gardens continue to be an ever-changing source of education, pleasure, solace, and exercise.

Hours: 10 a.m. to 4 p.m.

From Route 59 (accessible from I-88), go east on Aurora Avenue (called New York Avenue on the west side of the street). This intersection has many commercial buildings and Fox Valley Center. Stay on Aurora Avenue past the intersection of Route 34. Shortly, you will come to the River Road intersection. One block past River, turn south onto Berry Court. Number 620 Berry Court is the second house on your left. Note: Do not take Berry Drive, which goes north.

Proceeds shared with Families Helping Families

Sunday, July 28
DU PAGE COUNTY

WEST CHICAGO
The Ball Horticultural Trial Garden
622 Town Road, West Chicago

The Ball Horticultural Trial Gardens have been the site for the evaluation and display of the newest annuals and perennials since the early 1930s. This is a unique opportunity for garden enthusiasts to stroll the colorful six-acre gardens usually reserved for the wholesale customers of the 97-year-old Ball Horticultural Company, world leader in the breeding, production, distribution, and marketing of floricultural products. As guests wander the grounds, they will see more than 3,000 varieties of flowering plants in the Parkway Garden and Anna's Garden, along with unique water features in the Circle Garden and the new Simply Beautiful Garden. Thousands of containers and baskets line the Sun Container Garden and the Shade House, while experimental varieties can be viewed in the All-America Selections Evaluation Garden. Guests may want to allow from one to two hours to visit these exceptional gardens.

Hours: 10 a.m. to 4 p.m.

Entrance to parking is just off Roosevelt Road/Route 38 in West Chicago. The driveway that enters the parking area is marked by a small green-and-blue-lettered sign that reads "My Favorite Company and Pan-American Seed." A small greenhouse and two flower beds are visible from the road. From the east, continue west on Roosevelt Road past Route 59. The entrance will be .2 mile beyond Town Road, the first driveway west of Town Road to the north. If you reach the railroad tracks, you have gone too far west.

From the west, continue east on Roosevelt Road past the intersections of Kirk Road and Washington/Fabyan Parkway. Railroad tracks cross the road .5 mile east of the Fabyan intersection and the entrance to the gardens is another .2 mile east of the tracks. Turn left into the drive. If you reach Town Road, you've gone too far east.

Proceeds shared with the University of Illinois Cooperative Extension

LAKE COUNTY

HIGHLAND PARK
Magic Garden
2219 Egandale Road, Highland Park

These tranquil three-acre grounds along Lake Michigan were originally designed by Jens Jensen in 1928 and updated in 2001 by Douglas Hoerr Landscape Architecture of Evanston, Illinois. The revised landscape features an informally planted "garden room" bursting with pinks, blues, and whites and framed by curvilinear boxwood parterres. Decorative wrought-iron arbors covered with climbing pink roses and mandevillas frame an inviting gravel path. The garden is anchored on one end by an antique bronze fountain and by a pair of rare myrtle topiaries on the other. Butterflies congregate by day, and family and friends come to dine by night.

Hours: 10 a.m. to 2 p.m.

From Route 41, take the Deerfield Road north. Go east on Linden Avenue and turn left. Go to Park Avenue which deadends at the lake. At the stop sign, turn left onto Egandale Road. Drive up the hill. The first house on the right at the top of the hill is #2219.

From Sheridan Road, turn north onto Linden Avenue and proceed as directed above.

LAKE FOREST
Camp Rosemary
930 Rosemary Road, Lake Forest

This garden was designed by Rose Standish Nichols in the 1920s and is made up of wonderful garden rooms partitioned by pines, yews, and boxwood hedges. A sweeping lawn and luscious container plantings at the front steps are the first hints of delightful discoveries inside: a charming box-edged parterre, a thyme garden, and an urn brimming with roses, perennials, and annuals set against an ancient yew hedge affectionately called "the couch." Other areas include a chapel-like white garden with two reflecting pools and a vine-and-rose entwined pergola garden with three exuberant borders surrounding a small pool. During the spring of 1998, work began in earnest on the walled garden, which now graces the area surrounding the pool house. Elegant wide grass steps, paired rose borders, a linden allée, intricately patterned knot gardens, and four well-planted perennial borders are all key elements of this new land-scape. In contrast to the softer colors of the perennial beds near the pergola, these borders reflect a stronger palette of red, orange, violet, and blue. Some wonderful burgundy and silver foliage plants complement the whole scheme. Beyond the walled garden is a lush wooded ravine. A meandering path traces the ravine's edge beginning at the grass labyrinth and ending in the small glade, which overlooks the ravine. From this vantage point, a statue of Diana, the huntress, watches over the whole garden.

Hours: 10 a.m. to 4 p.m.

From Route 41, take the Deerpath Road exit east (right). Proceed through town, over the railroad tracks, to the stop sign at Sheridan Road. Turn right. Go .5 mile, past Lake Forest College, past the blinking yellow light, and past Rosemary Road on the right. Go one-half block to Rosemary Road on the left. Turn left (east). Number 930 is in the middle of the block on the left. *Please park in the front driveway area and on the south side of Rosemary Road.*

The Gardens of John & Carol Walter
401 North Ahwahnee Road, Lake Forest

This 2.5-acre French country residence once consisted of a variety of undeveloped, disassociated garden features. Through the collaboration between client and the landscape architecture firm Rocco Fiore & Sons, the property was transformed into the sequence of stately garden rooms found today. A visit to the property begins through curved stone walls, columns, and wrought-iron gates that open to reveal the deceptively young landscape. Beneath the canopy of majestic 100-year-old oaks, the winding drive terminates at the house's gravel courtyard. Here the formal boxwood and rose garden "foyer" invites you to stroll through the first of many rooms. The trickling sound of a revitalized fountain calls from the nearby water garden where annual and perennial masses accent the seasonal changes seen throughout. Continuing through the garden, naturally planted borders of evergreen trees, flowering ornamentals, and shrubs create a subtle and private backdrop for the Walters' collection of unique sculptures. The main terrace, once overgrown and excessive in size, was reconfigured for the installation of boxwood, rose, and annual gardens. Remaining stone from the terrace was used within the lower cutting and knot gardens. Besides lending to the established appearance of the property, these beautiful garden rooms are also functional, providing an abundant source of cut flowers and fresh herbs for use within the house.

Hours: 10 a.m. to 4 p.m.

From the Tri-State Tollway/I-294 north, take the Route 60/Town Line Road exit east to Route 41 north. Turn left onto Route 41 and proceed .25 mile to Deerpath Road. Turn right on Deerpath Road and continue .25 mile to Ahwahnee Road (the second right). Turn right onto Ahwahnee Road (not Ahwahnee Lane) and continue to #401. Out of respect of neighboring property owners, *please park on Ahwahnee Road and walk along the entrance drive.*

METTAWA
Mettawa Manor
25779 Saint Mary's Road, Mettawa

The house and grounds were built in 1927 as a family compound. The current owners, only the second in the manor's rich history, have been working for the past ten years to refurbish some garden areas and create new ones. The centerpiece of the garden is a newly built walled English-style garden with forty-foot perennial borders on either side of a sunken lawn that leads to a spring walk and rose room centered on an old fountain. Outside the east gate is a golden garden and an orchard/meadow underplanted with 20,000 narcissi and bordered by a fenced potager/cutting garden and a circular herb garden. The eighty-acre property has two ponds, a woodland garden, an eight-acre prairie, and a parkland of specimen trees, and is surrounded by a newly reclaimed oak-hickory forest.

Hours: 10 a.m. to 4 p.m.

Take Edens Expressway/I-94 to Tri-State Tollway/I-294. Exit at Route 60 west/Town Line Road, follow 1 mile to Saint Mary's Road, and turn left just past the horse stables to the Open Days signs on the left side of Saint Mary's Road marking the driveway entrance.

Public Gardens

COOK COUNTY

CHICAGO

Garfield Park Conservatory

300 North Central Park Avenue, Chicago (312) 746-5100

Opened in 1908, the Garfield Park Conservatory is one of the largest gardens under glass in the world. This landmark building was the vision of celebrated landscape architect Jens Jensen, who based its form on the domed haystacks that dotted the Midwest. The conservatory's eight exhibit houses feature plants from around the world, as well as a new indoor Children's Garden. The conservatory produces four annual flower shows and offers a variety of education and community programs.

Hours: Year round, daily, 9 a.m. to 5 p.m.

Admission: free

From I-290, take the Eisenhower Expressway exit at Exit 26A/Independence and go north. Take Independence to Washington Boulevard and turn right. Take Washington Boulevard east to North Central Park Avenue and turn left.

Grandmother's Garden

Fullerton Avenue & Stockton Drive, Chicago (312) 747-0740

Wide, undulating, island beds of annuals, perennials, and grasses are set off by broad expanses of lawn weaving the gardens together. These lovely, free-form beds are a fine counterpoint for the formal plantings at the Lincoln Park Conservatory across the street.

Hours: Year round, daily, dawn to dusk

Admission: free

Take Fullerton Avenue to Stockton Drive. The garden is located on the west side of Stockton Drive, south of Fullerton, near the entrance to the Lincoln Park Zoo.

The Lincoln Garden

North State Parkway, Chicago (312) 747-0698

Set amid a broad expanse of lawn in Lincoln Park, these gardens are at the foot of a handsome sculpture of Abraham Lincoln (1897). The six raised beds were established in 1989 and measure 30 feet by 360 feet. There are eighty varieties of perennials. Annuals are added to provide seasonal color and interest. The six segments have alternating warm and cool color schemes. The gardens remain standing in winter, with the hardy perennials and ornmental grasses giving form and color to the landscape.

Hours: Year round, daily, dawn to dusk

Admission: free

North State Parkway at North Avenue (1600 North) just east of the Chicago Historical Society.

Lincoln Park Conservatory
2391 North Stockton Drive, Chicago (312) 742-7736

Lincoln Park Conservatory has provided a botanical haven in the city for over a century. It was designed by a well-known architect for the Victorian era, Joseph L. Silsbee, both to show-case exotic plants and to grow flowers for use in Chicago's parks. Today the conservatory houses palm, fern, and orchid collections, and produces four annual flower shows.

Hours: Year round, daily, 9 a.m. to 5 p.m.

Admission: free

From Lake Shore Drive, take the Fullerton Avenue exit and travel 2 blocks west.

From I-94, take the Fullerton Avenue exit and travel 2 miles east. The conservatory is located on the southeast corner of Fullerton Avenue and Stockton Drive.

EVANSTON

The Shakespeare Garden
Garrett Place, Evanston

Designed by Jens Jensen in 1915 and surrounded by the original hawthorn hedges planted in 1920, the garden is romantic, secluded, and especially beautiful in June and July when its eight flower beds are filled with roses, lilies, pansies, artemisia, herbs, campanula, forget-me-nots, and daisies, all evocative of Shakespeare's poetry. Nestled within Northwestern University's campus and listed on the National Register of Historic Places in 1988, this garden is said to have been "loved into existence" by the members of the Garden Club of Evanston, who continue to care for it 82 years later.

Hours: Year round, daily, dawn to dusk

Admission: free

From the north or south, enter Evanston along Sheridan Road and proceed to Garrett Place (2200 North). Park on Garrett Place, east of Sheridan Road. The garden is reached by a bluestone walk on the east side of the Howe Chapel (on the north side of the street). Enter along this walk; the garden is not visible from either Sheridan Road or Garrett Place.

Michigan Avenue Plantings
Michigan Avenue, Evanston (847) 733-0140

Stretching thirty city blocks, these island beds fill Michigan Avenue with big, bold, beautiful seasonal plantings designed by Douglas Hoerr Landscape Architecture. Tulips underplanted with violas herald spring. Masses of annuals, perennials, and grasses celebrate summer. Kale, pansies, and chrysanthemums, added to the fall-blooming perennials and grasses, announce fall, creating a stunning effect for miles along this stately avenue. These plantings are funded and maintained by the Michigan Avenue Streetscape Association, a nonprofit organization of Michigan Avenue property owners and merchants.

Hours: Year round, daily, dawn to dusk

Admission: free

From the north, take Lake Shore Drive south to the Michigan Avenue exit. The central median planters extend from Roosevelt Road north to Oak Street.

GLENCOE

Chicago Botanic Garden

1000 Lake Cook Road, Glencoe (847) 835-5440 www.chicagobotanic.org

The garden, a living museum, covers 385 acres and features 23 specialty gardens, including a rose garden, a waterfall garden, an English walled garden, a bulb garden, a three-island Japanese garden, a fruit and vegetable garden, prairies, lagoons, and the 100-acre Mary Mix McDonald Woods. *In July of 1999, the garden added the Enabling Garden which shows strategies like raised beds, containers, and verticle gardens as well as special tools and techniques that make gardening accessible to everyone.* Nine islands on 75 acres of waterways and six miles of shoreline are distinguishing features of this "garden on the water." The living collections include more than 1.7 million plants, representing more than 8,500 plant types. Demonstration gardens showcase plants best suited for the Midwest. Research trial gardens hold plants being evaluated for performance in Chicago's environment. Conservation areas feature native and endangered flora of Illinois. Facilities include classrooms, an exhibit hall, an auditorium, a museum, a library, production and education greenhouses, the Daniel F. & Ada L. Rice Plant Resource Center, an outdoor pavilion, a carillon, bell tower, food service, and gift shop. Services include adult education, programs for schoolchildren, tram tours of the garden, horticultural therapy, and plant information. Owned by the Forest Preserve District of Cook County and managed by the Chicago Horticultural Society.

Hours: Year round, daily, 8 a.m. to dusk; closed Christmas Day

Admission: $7.75 for parking

Lake Cook Road in Glencoe is located .5 mile east of Edens Expressway/Route 41 at Lake Cook Road.

DU PAGE COUNTY

LISLE

The Morton Arboretum

4100 Illinois Route 53, Lisle (630) 968-0074 www.mortonarb.org

The Morton Arboretum is a 1,700-acre nonprofit outdoor museum of woodlands, wetlands, gardens, and a restored native prairie. Established in 1922, the arboretum's mission is to collect and study trees, shrubs, and other plants from around the world, to display them in naturally beautiful landscapes for people to study and enjoy, and to teach people to grow them in ways that enhance our environment. The arboretum also offers year-round education opportunities for visitors of all ages. Families can enjoy the arboretum by driving its eleven miles of roads or hiking its extensive pathways. The arboretum also conducts annual special events throughout its four seasons of beauty.

Hours: Year round, daily, 7 a.m. to 5 p.m.

Admission: $7 per car

Located at I-88 and Road 53, 25 miles west of Chicago.

LAKE COUNTY

LAKE FOREST

Lake Forest Open Lands Association

350 Waukegan Road, Lake Forest (847) 234-3880 www.lfola.org

Mellody Farm Preserve is a fifty-acre nature preserve with restored prairies, savanna, and wetlands. The preserve is also the site of the Lockhart Family Nature Center, a restored historic gatehouse and surrounding landscape of the J. Ogden Armor estate circa 1909. Vestiges of the original estate landscape designed by Ossian Simmonds and Jens Jensen are still evident today.

Hours: Year round, daily, dawn to dusk

Admission: free

From the Tri-State Tollway/I-294 & I-94, exit at Route 60 and proceed east to Waukegan Road north to Deerpath Road west into the nature center parking lot. Located on the southwest corner of Waukegan and Deerpath Roads.

VERNON HILLS

Cuneo Museum & Gardens

1350 North Milwaukee Avenue, Vernon Hills (847) 362-3042

A crushed red granite roadway leads the visitor across a fieldstone bridge and into the 78 acres of gardens and grounds surrounding the Cuneo Museum. The property includes formal gardens originally designed by Jens Jensen in 1915, a conservatory, Deer Park, and a private nine-hole golf course. Display garden plantings change with the seasons and feature antique fountains and statuary and three lakes.

Hours: Year round, Tuesday through Sunday, 10 a.m. to 5 p.m.

Admission: $5 per car

Two miles west of I-94 at Route 60; museum and garden's entrance is on Milwaukee Avenue .5 mile north of Route 60 on the west side of the road.

ROCKFORD
Anderson Gardens
340 Spring Creek Road, Rockford (815) 229-9390 www.andersongardens.org

Anderson Gardens is located on an eight-acre site, which contains an authentic Japanese pond strolling garden, a guest house, teahouse, gazebo, and four waterfalls. Lanterns, bridges, a stone pagoda, water basins, and gates are also part of this award-winning garden. A Japanese garden provides a place for meditation and contemplation. Part of the original five acres and all of the new three acres are handicapped accessible.

Hours: May through October, weekdays, 10 a.m. to 5 p.m., Saturday, 10 a.m. to 4 p.m., Sunday, noon to 4 p.m.

Admission: $5 adults, $4 senior citizens, $3 students, children under 5 free

From the east, take I-90 west to Rockford. Exit at Business 20/East State Street. Go west (right) on Business 20 to Mulford Road. Turn north (right) onto Mulford Road and drive to Spring Creek Road. Turn west (left) onto Spring Creek Road and drive 3 miles to the garden entrance at Parkview Avenue and Spring Creek Road. Turn north (right) into the parking lot.

From the north, take I-90 east to Rockford. Exit at Riverside Boulevard. Go west (right) on Riverside Boulevard to Mulford Road. Turn south (left) onto Mulford Road and drive to Spring Creek Road. Turn west (left) onto Spring Creek Road and drive 3 miles to the gardens.

Klehm Arboretum & Botanic Garden
2701 Clifton Avenue, Rockford (815) 965-8146 www.klehm.org

Klehm Arboretum & Botanic Garden has over 150 acres of magnificent trees and plants. Explore this "living museum" every season—majestic colors of fall, hundreds of blooming crab apples in spring, butterfly gardens in summer, and snow-covered evergreens in winter. The Botanical Education Center has changing exhibits, a gift shop, and rooms available for rent for workshops, special events, and wedding receptions.

Hours: Memorial Day through Labor Day, daily, 9 a.m. to 8 p.m.; the rest of the year, 9 a.m. to 4 p.m. Call for special holiday hours, a schedule of special events, tours, and classes.

Admission: $2 adults, children under 16 free

Off I-90, State Road 20, exit west; to Main Street (State Road 2), exit north; 2 miles to Clifton Avenue, exit west; 1/2 block to 2701 Clifton Avenue.

Maine

Victoria & Christopher Vasillopulos's garden, York Harbor.

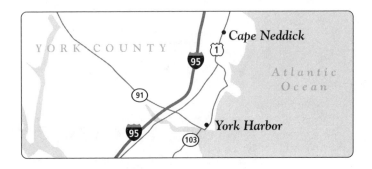

Saturday, June 29
YORK COUNTY

CAPE NEDDICK

Bochert Garden

538 Shore Road, Cape Neddick

Adjoining the garden at number 530 Shore Road (Thurston Garden, see next page) is the garden of Dr. Mark L. Bochert. A "study in green," this yard features hostas, native trees, shrubs, and a wonderful lawn that highlights the pond. Dr. Bochert and his brother have made an effort to integrate their properties. The focus was to provide pleasant walks for dogs, cats, and humans. Serene and cool, this property is a marvelous retreat on even the hottest summer days. Wear walking shoes!

Hours: 10 a.m. to 4 p.m.

From I-95, take Exit 4/The Yorks. Go east to the traffic light and turn left onto Route 1. Proceed 3.5 miles to River Road and turn right. Go to the stop sign and turn left (north) onto Shore Road. Proceed 2.1 miles, past rocky beaches, and look for the "Sea Meadows" sign on a mailbox on the right. Proceed to the next right, Fairborne Lane. Turn in and *follow signs for parking in field.* Visitors may turn left into the first of three featured gardens (Sea Meadows and the Thurston Garden are both at this location) for more detailed information.

Proceeds shared with Saint Peter's by the Sea

Home of Jonathan King & Jim Stott

Walt Kuhn Road, Cape Neddick

This one-year-old garden is constructed in a more formal style with raised cobblestone beds defined by peastone paths. Strong pergolas and arbors are covered with young heirloom roses and other climbers. The planting style is a loose cottage type with a combination of perennials, biennials, and annuals. It is a three-season garden that combines cutting flowers and a kitchen garden with both vegetables and herbs. The backyard shade garden is a study of native shade plants, including orchids.

Hours: 10 a.m. to 4 p.m.

From I-95, take Exit 4/ The Yorks. At the traffic light at Route 1, turn left onto Route 1 north. Go about 3 miles. Turn right onto River Road, just past the Pie in the Sky Bakery. Take the first left onto Walt Kuhn Road (about 500 yards down River Road).

Follow the newly paved road to the right and all the way to the end. The home is between two stone pillars. *Please park along the road.*

Proceeds shared with the AIDS Response Seacoast

Sea Meadows
511 Shore Road, Cape Neddick

This five-acre wooded area is located on a rocky Maine coastline overlooking the Atlantic Ocean. The rolling lawns and gardens include a small but old orchard, ponds, and marshy areas.

Hours: 10 a.m. to 4 p.m.

From I-95, take Exit 4/The Yorks. Go east to the traffic light and turn left onto Route 1. Proceed 3.5 miles to River Road and turn right. Go to the stop sign and turn left (north) onto Shore Road. Proceed 2.1 miles, past rocky beaches, and look for the "Sea Meadows" sign on a mailbox on the right. Proceed to the next right, Fairborne Lane. Turn in and *follow signs for parking in field.* Visitors may turn left into the first of three featured gardens for more detailed information.

Thurston Garden
530 Shore Road, Cape Neddick

We built our home on two-plus acres, much of it still wooded. In the past eleven years, we have planned and done all of the landscaping ourselves. Our goal was to establish neat gardens that could be enjoyed from inside as well as provide relaxing strolls. We have tried to provide pretty views from anyplace in the yard. We have attempted to use hardy, low-maintenance plants and to preserve the pre-existing bounty of native ferns and early spring wildflowers. The vegetable garden provides produce from late May to November. We garden organically, as the many nibbled leaves indicate. Wear walking shoes!

Hours: 10 a.m. to 4 p.m.

From I-95, take Exit 4/The Yorks. Go east to the traffic light and turn left onto Route 1. Proceed 3.5 miles to River Road and turn right. Go to the stop sign and turn left (north) onto Shore Road. Proceed 2.1 miles, past rocky beaches, and look for the "Sea Meadows" sign on a mailbox on the right. Proceed to the next right, Fairborne Lane. Turn in and *follow signs for parking in field.* Visitors may turn left into the first of three featured gardens for more detailed information.

Proceeds shared with Saint Peter's by the Sea

York Harbor
Mr. & Mrs. H.V. Richard
23 Aldis Lane, York Harbor

This is an ocean-side garden, with many roses and lots of flowers and color. Natural rocks divide our two houses like walls.

Hours: 10 a.m. to 4 p.m.

Turn off Route 1A onto a very small lane called Aldis Lane just south of Trinity Church. We are the last house down on the water to the right. *Please park on Route 1A and walk down Aldis Lane.*

Proceeds shared with the Great Works Regional Land Trust

Victoria & Christopher Vasillopulos
425 York Street, York Harbor

Our garden is the expression of three lifelong passions: love of art, love of animals, and a shared love of my husband's work as a professor and scholar of ancient Greece. Although we have completed only thirty percent of the plan, we have established a formal rose garden edged by boxwood and a bed of twenty peonies backed by 'Casablanca' lilies, which are flanked by rhododendrons planted in a walled Corinthian granite bed. Four five-foot-tall statues of the four seasons appear in the peony bed. Beds within the cobblestone driveway circle are filled with 'Hidcote' lavender, formal six-foot urns, juniper, and late-blooming tulips. Establishing a formal garden in a traditional New England village continues to be a challenge, one that provides incredible pleasure.

Hours: 10 a.m. to 4 p.m.

From the junction of Routes 1 and 1A in York, turn onto Route 1A north and follow for 1.6 miles, past Saint George's Episcopal Church and Harmon Park Road. Our home is the first driveway on the right past Harmon Park Road.

Public Gardens
OXFORD COUNTY

SOUTH PARIS

The McLaughlin Garden & Horticultural Center
97 Main Street, South Paris (207) 743-8820 www.mclaughlingarden.org

For sixty years, gardeners, garden lovers, and those in search of beauty and serenity in South Paris, Maine, have been welcome to enter the gate of the McLaughlin Garden. With the recent death of Bernard McLaughlin, the people of Maine are now challenged to preserve this horticultural treasure. Bernard began the garden in 1936, while working in a South Paris grocery store, and gardened in his spare time until retiring in 1967. From that point until his death, Bernard devoted his full energies to the garden, purposefully collecting plant material from everywhere so he and his wife would have something to enjoy. Encompassed by the lush wooded landscape we enjoy today, it is difficult to imagine that when Bernard acquired the property, the house and barn were surrounded by hayfields. With its opened gate, the horticultural talent and generosity of Bernard McLaughlin and his family have blessed visitors from Maine, other New England states, and other countries. Committed to keeping his collection open to all, Bernard was a quiet mentor to countless other gardeners, sharing his wisdom and promoting gardening at every opportunity.

Hours: April through September, daily, 8 a.m. to 8 p.m.

Admission: free

Located at the junction of Western Avenue and Route 26 in South Paris, .8 mile north of the Oxford Hills Comprehensive High School. Parking is available along Western Avenue.

Maryland

OPEN DAY:

June 15

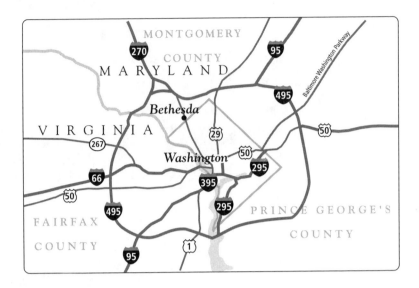

Saturday, June 15

Please also see listings for this date in Virginia

MONTGOMERY COUNTY

BETHESDA

The Jacobs Garden

6619 Elgin Lane, Bethesda

Our garden's evolution began almost 25 years ago with the purchase of a small home on an exquisite 2-acre woodland lot. Its early state included a beautiful woodland filled with mature trees, azaleas, wildflowers, rhododendrons, and more. Under the guidance of land-scape architect Lester Collins, the woodland area established the frame within which our garden grew. We built and planted some stone terraces which stepped down the gentle rear slope from the house to the pool area and pergola. Years later, with the invaluable assistance of Wolfgang Oehme and James van Sweden, we added a lily pond, masses of perennials, and grasses creating a unique setting which incorporates a natural garden in a structured form. Most recently, we have added a conservatory laced with plants, a covered trellis on the upper terrace, and with the help of the landscape architect firm Clinton and Associates expanded some of the perennial beds.

Hours: 10 a.m. to 4 p.m.

From I-495, take the River Road exit towards Washington, D.C., and turn right onto Wilson Lane. Take the first left onto Selkirk. Take the second left at the top of the hill onto Elgin Lane. Number 6619 is the second house on the left. *Please park on the gravel area along the fence.*

MASSACHUSETTS

OPEN DAYS:

May 18
May 25
June 2
June 8
June 22
June 27
June 29

The Garden at 9 Friend Street, Manchester-by-the-Sea.
Photo by Frederick L. Rice.

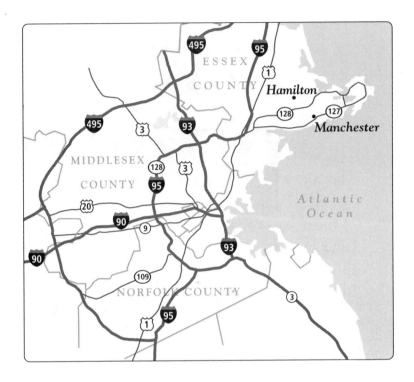

Saturday, May 18

ESSEX COUNTY

HAMILTON
Stormfield

375 Bridge Street, Hamilton

We sit in the middle of eighty acres, surrounded by fields, woods and marsh.

Hours: 10 a.m. to 4 p.m.

Located 1.25 miles from Route 1A on Bridge Street at the bottom of the hill. Willows on the right and an 1820 gatehouse mark 375 Bridge Street entrance. Route 128 picks up Route 1A in Beverly and goes through Wenham, then Hamilton, and Bridge Street is shortly after Myopia Hunt Club on the right. *Please park in the grass field on the right of the entrance.*

MANCHESTER
Appletrees

6 Jersey Lane, Manchester

The Appletrees estate was built in 1896 on an old apple orchard, and was thus named by it first owner. The garden was originally laid out in the early years of the twentieth century by William Ernestus Bowditch, a landscape architect from Milton, Massachusetts. While this park-like property has undergone some changes over the years, many of the original features remain. These include an allée of ironwood trees, ancient yew hedges, a sunken garden, and many old and beautiful specimen trees, such as ginkgo, albizia, catalpa, dogwood, and copper beech, among others. The formal, walled sunken garden was recently renovated and has a beautiful antique fountain in the center surrounded by lovely perennial beds and seating areas for rest and relaxation. The current owners have continued to enhance this 3.5-acre landscape, adding, among other things, a cottage garden set against a clipped privet hedge, a shade garden surrounding an old shed, and various garden benches set throughout upon which to enjoy the views.

Hours: 10 a.m. to 4 p.m.

From Route 128, take Exit 16/Manchester/Pine Street. Take Pine Street to the end at the center of Manchester. Turn right onto Route 127 for about .8 mile, just past a large open meadow. Turn right onto Jersey Lane. Appletrees is at #6, the third driveway on the left, about 100 yards up the lane. *Please park in the driveway, on the left side near the entrance.*

Southgate Garden II
22 School Street, Manchester

This is a small half-acre garden. The land sloped away from the house and ended in a spongy wet area, so wet, in fact, that the owner was mired in it and had to yell for help! The problem was solved by digging a pond, which has provided joy for frogs and grandchildren. The garden is maintained in loving memory of that owner. The entrance to the property is graveled; steps descend to the garden proper, which is guarded by a stone lion in the style of the fifteenth century, which has been bumped around and even stolen once.

Hours: 10 a.m. to 4 p.m.

From Route 128, take Exit 15/Manchester/School Street. Follow School Street to #22 on the right. *Please try to park in the town lot behind the Town Hall. Our little driveway will be totally inadequate.*

Proceeds shared with the Manchester Women's Club Scholarship Fund

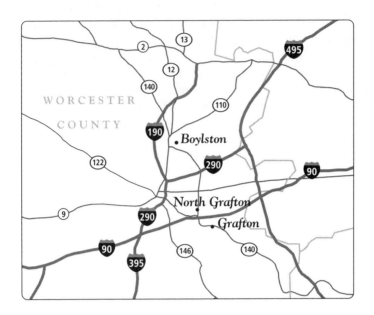

Saturday, May 25

WORCESTER COUNTY

BOYLSTON

Maple Grove

16 School Street, Boylston

Designed around a late eighteenth-century half-Cape-Cod style house, Maple Grove is framed by mature sugar maples. Located within the historic district of Boylston, the garden is adjacent to an eighteenth-century cemetery, giving it charming borrowed scenery. A true collector's garden, Maple Grove has a wide assortment of choice woody and herbaceous plants in a connected series of borders, beds, and islands, with sculpture and water features.

Hours: 10 a.m. to 6 p.m.

From I-290, take Exit 23A/Route 140 north. Go 1.8 miles to the first traffic light and turn right onto Route 70. Go 1 mile to historic Boylston Center. Make a sharp right, circling around the old cemetery, and turn onto School Street.

From I-290 west from Boston, take Exit 24. Turn right at the end of the exit ramp and go to the blinking light. Turn left onto Route 70. Travel .25 mile to the center of Boylston (gazebo on the left). At the fork in the road, bear left at the cemetery. Go to the first house on the right. *Please park along the street.*

Proceeds shared with the Worcester County Horticultural Society

GRAFTON
Mapel & Libuda Garden
95 Brigham Hill Road, Grafton

Our ten-year-old garden has begun to mature with an eclectic circa 1910 stone bungalow as a backdrop. A unique collector's garden has developed. Perennial gardens around the house anchor it to the surrounding site. Bluestone terraces lend ample space for sitting and displaying container plants. A vegetable garden with small fruits and woodland gardens blend into the mix. The water garden and meadow areas are enjoyed by wildlife. Also, a small greenhouse has opened new realms of gardening possibilities. Set back from an historic country road, our garden is truly peaceful and relaxing.

Hours: 10 a.m. to 4 p.m.

From Massachusetts Turnpike/I-90, take Exit 11/Route 122/Millbury/Worcester. Bear right after the tollbooth to Route 122 south. Travel .5 mile and turn right onto Brigham Hill Road. Travel .2 mile to an intersection and continue straight across on Brigham Hill Road. Travel 1.5 miles toward Grafton Center. Number 95 is on the right side after a sharp curve. Two mailboxes mark the driveway directly across from a fire hydrant. The garden is at the end of the 400-foot driveway.

From I-495, take Massachusetts Turnpike/I-90 west and proceed as directed above. *Please park along the road.*

Proceeds shared with the Tower Hill Botanic Garden

NORTH GRAFTON
Brigham Hill Farm
128 Brigham Hill Road, North Grafton

Brigham Hill Farm is on the crest of historic Brigham Hill. "Gentleman Johnny" Burgoyne marched his troops past the Georgian farmhouse in the Revolution. Complete with resident ghost and the "Irish Curse," the garden unfolds around the house and barn, each part different from the rest. Shaded by 100-year-old sugar maples, paths lead to a kitchen herb garden, then to a raised vegetable garden. An exuberant quarter-acre garden of perennials is surrounded by large stone walls. A hillside woodland garden of 1.5 acres includes pools, ledges, and woodland paths with many interesting native plants.

Hours: 10 a.m. to 6 p.m.

From Massachusetts Turnpike/I-90, take Exit 11/Route 122/Millbury/Worcester. Turn right onto Route 122, go .25 mile, then turn right onto Brigham Hill Road (across from the entrance to Wyman Gordan Co.). Go 1.5 miles to the top of the hill. We are the yellow house and barn on the left, #128. *Parking is in the field across from the drive.*

Proceeds shared with the Tower Hill Botanic Garden

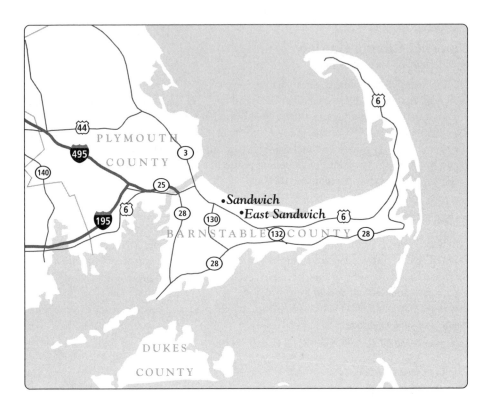

Sunday, June 2

BARNSTABLE COUNTY

East Sandwich

Shalisan East

43 Oak Ridge Road, East Sandwich

This is an informal garden on four acres. My husband was a collector for over thirty years. He collected specimens from all over the world. My job was placement. There are interesting trees, rhododendrons, azaleas, camellias, kalmias, magnolias, and so much more. This is a second home by the sea, with the challenge of Cape Cod, which doesn't provide the best soil, but we managed to get it going. We also have a monkey puzzle tree, which is of interest to many people. I show this garden in my husband's memory.

Hours: 10 a.m. to 4 p.m.

Located on Cape Cod, off Route 6A/Carleton Shores. Eight miles from the Bourne Bridge, take the second left off Carleton Drive to 43 Oak Ridge Road. *Please park along the property on the street.*

Proceeds shared with the American Rhododendron Society

SANDWICH
Whitesway
78 Boardley Road, Sandwich

My garden is being created on nine acres of gently sloping virgin woodland, a work in progress that began eleven years ago. I started collecting rare and unusual rhododendrons, azaleas, and kalmia, eventually expanding into an extensive array of companion plants, such as Japanese maples, magnolias, hostas, clematis, and holly. There are also many unusual trees, such as Japanese umbrella pine, fringe tree, paulownia, weeping beech, and mimosa. I am trying to establish a collection of hardy roses—if only the Cape Cod weather would cooperate. My companions in this endeavor are three cats, three peacocks, and a flock of bantam chickens. I use no chemicals, so my garden is a heaven to a great variety of bird life.

Hours: 10 a.m. to 4 p.m.

From Sagamore Bridge, take Mid-Cape Highway/Route 6 to Exit 2. Turn right off the exit ramp and follow Route 130 south for 1.5 miles. Turn left onto Cotuit Road and drive 2.5 miles. Turn left onto Boardley Road. Number 78 is .5 mile on the right. *Please park on the street.*

Proceeds shared with the American Rhododendron Society

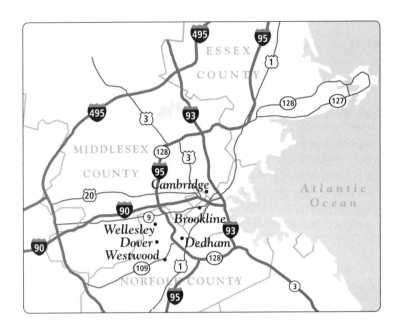

Saturday, June 8

MIDDLESEX COUNTY

BROOKLINE

Lucy Aptekar & Gerry Leader

38 Cumberland Avenue, Brookline

Recalling Japanese garden traditions and American modernism, there is a geometric stone path through stately pines, past an ancient boulder on the edge of a round lake, along an allée of *Cryptomeria*, across a dry pond and river, up a hillside to a contemplative teahouse—and all within a small urban/suburban yard!

Hours: 10 a.m. to 4 p.m.

From Route 128, take Route 9 east to Brookline Village, close to the Boston line. Turn right at the traffic light at Dunkin' Donuts and the fire station at High Street. Take the third left onto Cumberland Avenue. Look for #38.

From Boston, take Boylston Street/Route 9 west to Brookline Village. Turn left at the fire station onto High Street and proceed as directed above. *Please park anywhere on Cumberland Avenue.*

Proceeds shared with the Lincoln Public School

CAMBRIDGE

165 Brattle Street

165 Brattle Street, Cambridge

The gardens surrounding this historic Brattle Street house continue to expand. The five major planting areas are each different from the other, in formality and age. The front garden and the rear centerpiece are more formal. The beds at the front and along the driveway are over fifteen years old, while new beds are in their second and fifth years. Along the driveway a line of older existing trees has been extended with new hedges. A large diversity of herbaceous material—bordering on the chaotic—is tucked everywhere. The design is modeled after a British garden, with a few Oriental elements. It is designed and maintained by the architect/owner "with a bit of help from his friends." The garden is a two-time Massachusetts Horticultural Society Medalist.

Hours: 10 a.m. to 4 p.m.

From Harvard Square, take Brattle Street west. Number 165 is on the north side of Brattle Street, between Lowell and Channing Streets.

From Fresh Pond, take Brattle Street east. *Please park on the north side of Brattle Street.*

NORFOLK COUNTY

DEDHAM
The Lilacs
188 Village Avenue, Dedham

The old Colonial house, carriage house, and barn were built in the late eighteenth century. Our garden was started in 1962. Many trips to England and Europe were our inspiration and our friendship with Allen Haskell brought about a design for part of the backyard garden in 1981. The rest of the garden was designed by the owners. Over the years, we have added many garden rooms that have a distinct English flavor.

Hours: 10 a.m. to 4 p.m.

From Route 128, take Exit 16A/Dedham/Route 109. The house is about 5 streets down on the right, #188 Village Avenue, on the corner of Village and Allindale Road (gray house). *Please park along Allindale Road.*

Dan & Polly Pierce
354 Westfield Street, Dedham

Located at the edge of a pond, the gardens of this Georgian-style house complement a naturalistic oak woodland setting of towering trees and granite outcroppings. Rhododendrons and wildflowers predominate, and the discipline of shade is evident. Rock gardens, perennial borders, rose and herb gardens, as well as two vegetable gardens, attest to the broad horticultural interests of the owners. This is a gardener's garden, informal and graceful, full of unusual horticultural material.

Hours: 10 a.m. to 2 p.m.

From Route 128, take Exit 16A/Dedham/Route 109. Follow Route 109 east about .9 mile to Westfield Street. Turn left onto Westfield; bear left at the fork at the "Not a Through Street" sign. Continue up Westfield Street to #354 on the left at the stone wall. *Please park on the street.*

Proceeds shared with the New England Wildflower Society

DOVER
Kevin J. Doyle & Michael Radoslovich—Cairn Croft
81 Wilsondale Street, Dover

My garden is a personal garden. The cairns mark its location, and croft means "a special place within." My design intention for the garden is to have guests enter and quickly forget from where they have come. It is a place of unspeakable joy. Cairn Croft has been featured in _Fine Gardening_ magazine, _Horticulture_ magazine, and _The Victorian Garden_.

Hours: 10 a.m. to 4 p.m.

From Route 128, take Exit 16B/Dedham/Route 109. Travel 1 mile or less on Route 109 west and take the second right onto Summer Street. Travel 1 mile to the end. Turn left onto Westfield Street. Travel 300 yards; turn left onto Wilsondale Street. Travel .2 mile. Watch for cairns on the left at #81. _Please park beyond the house on the opposite side of the street._

WELLESLEY
Hunnewell Garden
845 Washington Street, Wellesley

Four generations of the Hunnewell family have had a hand in this estate garden, which includes a formal azalea garden and pinetum. Greenhouses produce delicate camellias, exotic orchids, flowers, and fruit. The highlight of your visit is bound to be the whimsical yet monumental clipped evergreens that adorn the sloping shores of Lake Waban.

Hours: 10 a.m. to 4 p.m.

From Massachusetts Turnpike/I-90 west, take Exit 16. Follow signs to Route 16 west/ Washington Street. Follow west for about 5 miles, passing through Wellesley Hills, to the center of Wellesley. Follow Route 16/South Natick/Holliston. The next traffic light marks the entrance to Wellesley College. Proceed 6 miles to #845. _Follow parking instructions._

WESTWOOD
Joseph Hudak & Kenn Stephens
64 Churchill Road, Westwood

Twenty-five years from its raw beginning, today this suburban acre presents a year-round collection of common and unique plants in an entirely secluded setting. Organized by the landscape architect Mr. Hudak and embellished with garden artifacts of distinction by Mr. Stephens, this collection blends trees, shrubs, perennials, and bulbs into seasonally interesting combinations rarely found elsewhere. The design is a "funnel" concept, which enlarges as you proceed from the front entrance to the rear of the lot. Grand sweeps of lawn connect the front yellow garden to the red garden and climax in the "Paisley Patch" in the lower garden.

Hours: 10 a.m. to 4 p.m.

From Route 128, take Exit 16B/Dedham/Route 109 west and go about 1 mile. Turn left onto Churchill Road, which dead ends. The garden is near the top of the hill on the left. _Please park only on the house side of Churchill Road._

Proceeds shared with the International Design Symposium

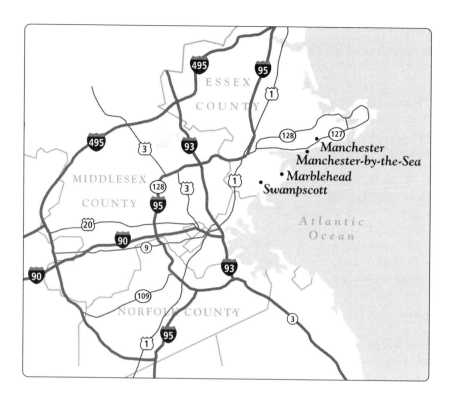

Saturday, June 22

ESSEX COUNTY

Manchester
Pauline & Joe Runkle
30 Plum Hill, Manchester

The property was purchased in 1984. It was an abandoned pig farm. On the four acres we built our house, one room deep for views in all directions. The gardens are planted among sculptured rock outcroppings. At the front are roses and perennials; to the side, a miniature fruit orchard and herb gardens; and to the rear, a large meadow garden.

Hours: 10 a.m. to 4 p.m.

From Route 128 north, take Exit 15/Manchester/School Street. Bear right off the exit ramp and go .5 mile. Turn left onto Lincoln Street (one way). Follow small signs for "Magnolia." At the end of Lincoln Street, turn left onto Summer Street (street is unmarked; look for a Texaco gas station on the left). One mile from this turn is the entrance to Hickory Hill on the left. If you come to Ocean Street on the right, you have gone too far. Bear left at the fork in the road and take your final left onto Ancient Country Way Extension. We are the second house on the right. The house is a tall gray contemporary with a sweeping open lawn. Look for #30 on the telephone pole and at the entrance to the drive.

MANCHESTER-BY-THE-SEA
The Garden at 9 Friend Street
9 Friend Street, Manchester-by-the-Sea

The first garden at 9 Friend Street was laid out in 1928 for the present owner's grandfather. Mr. Frederick Rice, a floral and garden designer and lecturer, has made major changes during the past eighteen years. The English cottage-style garden, ablaze with color and awash with texture, is laid out in a series of rooms furnished with an extraordinary variety of perennials, annuals, roses, vines, and deciduous and evergreen shrubs. Brick and stone patios have been constructed for outdoor living. There are two fishponds, a pavilion, and a teahouse. The garden was featured in the 1996 summer issue of *Country Home-Country Gardens* magazine and in Meredith Publishing's *Country Garden Planner*.

Hours: 10 a.m. to 4 p.m.

From Route 128 north, take Exit 15/Manchester/School Street. Turn right onto School Street at the end of the exit. Pass Essex County Club on the left and proceed through the blinking light. Friend Street is the second right beyond Sacred Heart Catholic Church. The house, #9, is gray with black shutters, on the right, the only house on the street with a white picket fence. *Please park on Friend Street or in the lot behind Sacred Heart Church.*

Proceeds shared with the Manchester Council on Aging

MARBLEHEAD
Grey Gulls—Larry Simpson
429 Ocean Avenue, Marblehead

This stretch of craggy coastline presents a challenging environment to the garden owner, not least because of winter winds so harsh that wattle fences are required to protect the plants. Nonetheless, hundreds of unusual annuals, perennials, and bulbs now thrive here. Moreover, the garden is continually changing as horticulturist/designer Larry Simpson experiments with new concepts and plant combinations. Each season perennials are added and a large garden of annuals redesigned around a different theme. A whimsical vegetable garden was installed recently, featuring heirloom varieties, vines climbing fancifully over wooden obelisks, and delectable small fruits. Perhaps the most ambitious innovation has been the creation of a salt marsh in a tidal pool that had formerly supported no plant life. Even the garden's design reflects a consciousness of its unique location, with sinuous beds mirroring the surrounding curves of shore and sea. A number of pools and fountains further complement the ocean's presence, with their waterlilies, lotus, giant koi, and bronze sculpture, while at the same time providing a harmonious mood.

Hours: 10 a.m. to 4 p.m.

From Route 128, take Exit 25/Route 114 east. At the traffic light in Marblehead, turn right onto Ocean Avenue. Cross the causeway and stay to the right for 1.5 miles to the traffic circle. Bear right at the traffic circle and go to 429 Ocean Avenue (number painted on rock). The house is on the right. *Please park on the street.*

The Parable—Ellen Cool's Garden

19 Circle Street, Marblehead

In the oldest part of Marblehead, alongside a 1720 house of historic interest, there is a garden gate, which leads into a highly developed and very personal landscape. Here there are examples of the buildings, structures, tools, materials, and books which, together with the gardens, comprise the setting for a landscape designer's life and work. Many unusual early-, late-, and long-blooming plants combine with artifacts of stone and wood to make satisfying compositions from April until November. Ellen has created landscapes for a number of adjoining and nearby properties and a map can be provided if you choose to do a walking tour of those that can be viewed from the street.

Hours: 10 a.m. to 4 p.m.

From the south, take Route 1A north to Route 129 east (becomes Atlantic Avenue in Marblehead); just past the Mobil gas station on the left, turn right onto Washington Street and follow it to the Old Town House, then turn right onto State Street, to the Marblehead Harbor, then turn left onto Front Street. Circle Street will be the third and fourth left.

From the north or west, take Route 114 east to the end at the Old Town House. Proceed as directed above. *Look for parking on Front Street, as the parking on Circle Street is very limited.* The walk by the water is, in any case, very pleasant. Number 19 is halfway up from the water on the right side.

Proceeds shared with the Long Hill Reservation

SWAMPSCOTT

Wilkinson Garden—Blythswood

29 Little's Point Road, Swampscott

Two families, Little and Proctor (now Wilkinson), have owned Blythswood from its inception in 1847 to the present. Arthur Little, a well known Boston architect, named and styled his summerhouse after an English country home and that aspect is still reflected in the gardens, lawns, shrubs, and trees contained within the 6.5 acres of grounds. The site rises from a rocky headland on Massachusetts Bay to a ridge dominated by the main house, and then slopes gently westward down a long tree-lined gravel driveway to the old stable and farm areas. Among the current plantings are a rose garden, a peony that came from China in 1829, and 52 species of trees. Simplicity reflects a change from many groundskeepers to one part-time head gardener and assistant, who care for the formal beds, lawns, and urns.

Hours: 10 a.m. to 4 p.m.

From the town of Swampscott, with the ocean on the right, take Puritan Road for 1 mile. Little's Point Road is on the right. Look for the "Marion Court Junior College and Blythswood" sign; it is a shared driveway.

From Marblehead, take Route 129/Atlantic Avenue and turn left onto Puritan Road. Little's Point Road is 3 blocks on your left. *Please do not park on the grass.*

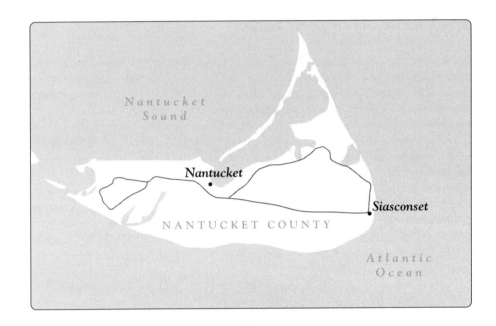

Thursday, June 27

NANTUCKET COUNTY

NANTUCKET

Beach Plum

1 Harborview Drive, Nantucket

Beach Plum garden is surrounded by 'Kwanzan' cherry and 'Bradford' pear trees and is entered down a driveway bordered by 'Bonica' roses, hydrangeas, and rhododendrons. The new garden created around the rose-covered cottage has large herbaceous borders, a hosta garden, and two long rose beds. A bed for peonies and lilies flanks the cottage. The old garden of thirty years surrounding the big house is a contrast in green tranquility. Herbaceous borders and lawn are surrounded by a hedge of althea, and the house itself is lined with hydrangeas.

Hours: 10 a.m. to 4 p.m.

From Nantucket, go to Milestone Circle, go two thirds of the way around the rotary, and take Siasconset Road. After .2 mile, take Quidnet-Wauwinet and Polpis Road on the left. After .7 mile, turn left onto Shimmo Pond Road (Moor's End Farm). It becomes a dirt road. Take the second left after .2 mile onto Harborview Drive. The garden is entered by foot, down the white pebble road on the right marked by a #1 on white stone.

Proceeds shared with the Nantucket Garden Club

Blueberry Hill

8 Quaise Pastures Road, Nantucket

An oak forest and tupelo grove protect the house and garden from ocean winds. The natural-istic landscape designed by Lucinda Young contrasts rolling serene meadow views of West Poplis Harbor with an enclosed garden set in a small building envelope on a conservation restriction, consisting of heaths, heathers, and a crab apple espalier. A vegetable garden and chicken yard are hidden from view.

Hours: 10 a.m. to 4 p.m.

Located 3.3 miles on Poplis Road from the Milestone Road turnoff. Turn left after the mailbox #209 onto Quaise Pastures Road. The hardtop road turns to gravel. *Please park at the circle before the gate (except wheelchairs).* We are #8. Walk through the gate and bear left up the hill.

Dr. & Mrs. John W. Espy

4 New Dollar Lane, Nantucket

This is an unusual "in-town" garden because of a large lawn with spreading elm trees. The house is 200 years old and has a converted stable in the garden. The formal terraced garden features a sixty-year-old *grandiflora* magnolia, a waterlily pond, roses, and perennials.

Hours: 10 a.m. to 4 p.m.

Located just off the monument on Main Street. At the monument, turn onto Milk Street, then take the first left. It is a white house with green door, the third on the left.

Proceeds shared with the Nantucket Historical Association

Inishfree—Coleman & Susan Burke

37 Gardner Road, Nantucket

The challenge for this garden was to preserve the panoramic view of Nantucket Harbor, while enjoying unusual plantings in the foreground. Native plants along the coastal dunes' horizon surround the haha filled with exotic plants and ornamental grasses. The effect allows one to enjoy many sight lines through the columns of the house's porch, over and through the gar-den to the freshness of blue water and sailboats beyond.

Hours: 10 a.m. to 4 p.m.

From Nantucket Town, proceed to the rotary; go left on Milestone Road toward Siasconset. Take the second left (Polpis Road). Go about 1 mile until you pass Moor's End Farm (on the left). Take the left at the end of the cornfield onto Gardner Road. Go .7 mile to the end and turn right onto the Burke property. It is the first house on the left past the gate.

Proceeds shared with the Nantucket Garden Club

Susan & Karl Ottison

170 Orange Street, Nantucket

Our property borders Nantucket Harbor and was used as a cow pasture back in the 1930s and 1940s. After the cows, the land was left unattended for many years and natural bushes and plants took over. In 1979 we started designing paths through the *Rosa rugosa* and poison ivy and planting rhododendrons, hollies, blueberries, and daylilies, all the time leaving the swamp rose mallows, blue flag, yellow flag, cattail, wild dogwood, pussy willows, and ferns that surround a small natural pond.

Hours: 10 a.m. to 2 p.m.

Located 1 mile from Main Street and Central Town. Take Main Street to Orange Street. Go 1 mile to the rotary and go around as if going back to town on Orange Street. We are on the right at the rotary, #170. Look for 2 large wooden posts with sign that reads "Susan and Karl Ottison." Look for a shell driveway with our house and shop on the right. *Please park in the yard and side lot.*

Eleanor & Arthur Reade

41 India Street, Nantucket

A small, elongated, in-town lot jigs and jags between two historic streets. Although very long in some places, it is only eight to ten feet and never more than thirty feet wide. It is in the shadow of the 1780-90 house and parts are in deep shade while others are in bright sun. We had to achieve interest, flow, unity, and color in this limited and irregular space. This is accomplished by a continuous serpentine line and the use of sinuous stone walls. Pre-existing plant material was retained to provide a backdrop and sense of maturity. The garden style is cottage. Although only completed in May of 2001, it was featured on the annual Nantucket Garden Club tour in August of the same year.

Hours: 10 a.m. to 4 p.m.

India Street is a one-way street, going from Liberty/Gardner towards town. Number 41 is the third house on the left going towards town. The garden gate has a tile number plaque. The garden runs between Hussey and India Streets.

Proceeds shared with the Nantucket Historical Association

Constance Umberger
Eel Point Road, Nantucket

This informal garden has evolved in stages over the years from a flat, treeless, grassless barn-yard surrounding a house—the former horse barn. The challenges of sun, wind, deer, and rabbits have resulted in a garden of six enclosed rooms within an overall enclosure of fencing, hedging, and stone walls. The rooms, which are planned to give year-round interest and to provide places for outdoor sitting and dining, include a cottage garden; a pool garden with massed spring-flowering bulbs, trees, and shrubs; the Green Room, with box globes and other topiary; and the New Garden, with long double perennial borders. There are two pergolas and a small pool with frogs, turtles, and fish.

Hours: 10 a.m. to 2 p.m.

From either Cliff Road or Madaket Road, turn onto Eel Point Road. Take the first sand road on the right off Eel Point Road, where there will be a stop sign on a bike path, 3 or 4 mailboxes, and several name signs. Turn into the second driveway on the right, a long, straight driveway with post-and-rail fencing. Turn into the lower house drive at the bottom of the hill on the right. *Please park in the field.*

Proceeds shared with the Royal Oak Foundation

SIASCONSET
Hedged About
Polpis Road, Siasconset

Hedged About is a 2.5-acre property with five different garden areas. First is the perennial flower border seen from the road, then an herb garden, a fenced area for holding plants and covered area for blueberries, a mainly hosta garden, and a completely invisible shrub garden of about .5 acre with gazebo, fountain, decorative garden shed, and curving grass paths. The flower border was much enlarged since 1976 when we bought the house. A path through it was added at that time and it was completely replanted with the help of horticulturist Geraldine Weinstein. The placement of plants in the border is the work of the owner. The flower border, herb garden, and hosta beds were put in and designed by me with some labor provided by family and one garden crew. The "Nook" or secret garden, was designed by Nantucket landscape designer Lucinda Young.

Hours: 10 a.m. to 4 p.m.

From the village of Siasconset, 6 miles from the rotary on Milestone Road, go towards Sankaty Head on Polpis Road (Sankaty Road) about .25 mile. Hedged About is on the left. The flower garden is easily seen from the hedge at the end of the driveway. The house has green trim and an upper enclosed porch. *Please park along the road by the front hedge.*

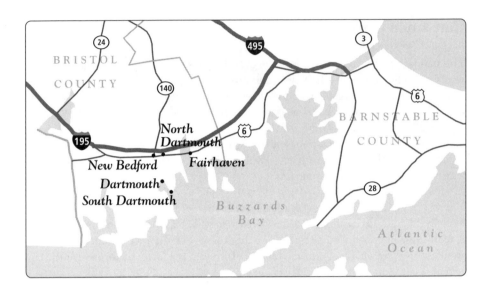

Saturday, June 29

BRISTOL COUNTY

DARTMOUTH

Jan & Toby Hall

167 Bakerville Road, Dartmouth

Most of our plant material has come from friends' gardens over the last thirty years, including box bushes, standardized bays, and fuchsia. Our favorite plants are fragrant, non-invasive, and low maintenance. Patterns of growth, acquisition of stone, and limitations of time determine the shape, size, and character of more than two dozen gardens surrounding our house and stone walls. We use stones to complement plants, raise the gardens above flooding, or serve as useful platforms.

Hours: 10 a.m. to 4 p.m.

From I-95, take Exit 12S onto Faunce Corner Road. Turn left onto Route 6, then make an immediate right onto Tucker Road. Continue 7.1 miles to #167 just beyond a vineyard on the left; the house is a gray-and-white Greek Revival style. Tucker Road becomes Bakerville Road.

Proceeds shared with the Rotch-Jones-Duff House & Garden Museum

FAIRHAVEN
Allen C. Haskell Farm
46 Charity Stevens Lane, Fairhaven

A facility for raising specimen nursery stock, also home of Allen's exotic animal collection, including Scottish Highland cattle, emu, camels, San Clemente goats, an extensive peafowl collection, swans, Canada geese, and various other breeds of birds.

Hours: 10 a.m. to 4 p.m.

From I-195 east, take Exit 18/Route 240 south/Fairhaven to the first traffic light. Get in the left lane and turn left onto Bridge Street. Proceed to the end and turn left at the stop sign onto New Boston Road. Go over the overpass to the first left, Charity Stevens Lane, to the end.

NEW BEDFORD
Allen C. Haskell Horticulturists, Inc.
787 Shawmut Avenue, New Bedford

An extensive nursery, immaculately cared for greenhouses, display gardens, rare and unusual plant material, plantings of distinction, extensive hosta collection, annuals, perennials, trees, shrubs, Italian pottery, statuary, and a bird collection make this a definite oasis for the serious gardener.

Hours: 10 a.m. to 4 p.m.

From I-195, take Exit 13B onto Route 140 north to Exit 3/Hathaway Road. Turn left off the exit ramp onto Hathaway. Proceed to the first traffic light, turn right, and proceed 4 blocks until you see a stone wall on the right. *Please park along Shawmut Avenue* and enter at the main entrance.

NORTH DARTMOUTH
Fran & Clint Levin's Garden
441 Slocum Road, North Dartmouth

The Gold Medal citation from the Massachusetts Horticultural Society in 1996 described the garden as "an estate of unusual design and horticultural features where surprises frequent every corner." An enclosed rose garden, shade garden, and serpentine lawns surround the house designed in the Frank Lloyd Wright tradition. Stone walls set off species of daylilies and lily cultivars. A natural pond area is a highlight.

Hours: 10 a.m. to 2 p.m.

From I-195, take Route 140 east. Turn right at the end of Route 140 onto Route 6 east. Turn left at the first traffic light onto Slocum Road. Continue for .25 mile to the first right, Patton Street. Turn right at the end of the block onto Truman Avenue and into the driveway of the Levins' home. This is the rear of the property, with ample parking and a view of the house and gardens.

Proceeds shared with the Rotch-Jones-Duff House & Garden Museum

SOUTH DARTMOUTH
Betsy & Greer McBratney
29 Grinnell Road, South Dartmouth

Our house, overlooking Buzzards Bay, was built in 1964 on four acres of dairy farm pasture. In 37 years, its fine trees and shrubs have matured. Vegetable gardens are surrounded by espaliered fruit trees. We have heath and heather gardens and a sunken garden featuring alpine troughs. Small raised perennial beds have an unusual color scheme of wine, yellow, and gray foliage. We also have a caged blueberry patch, a state-of-the-art compost area, and a large daffodil collection succeeded by ornamental grasses in the summer. New defenses against deer are being employed.

Hours: 10 a.m. to 4 p.m.

From I-195, take Route 140 east. Turn right at the end of Route 140 onto Route 6 east. Turn left at the first traffic light onto Slocum Road. Turn right onto Russells Mills Road. Go a short distance to the police station and turn left onto Elm. Take Elm to the village center and turn right onto Bridge Street to cross Padanaram Bridge. Turn left immediately onto Smith Neck Road. Go 1 mile and turn left at the sign for Birchfield Farm. Come to a slight rise and take the first right onto Grinnell Road. It's the second house on the left, with a red door, post-and-rail fence, and gray mailbox with our name on it.

Proceeds shared with the Rotch-Jones-Duff House & Garden Museum

Sea Thrift—Apponagansett Watch
288 Russells Mills Road, South Dartmouth

In Alfred Walker's garden, fine plantings of ornamental trees and shrubs blend harmoniously with an 1860 whaleship owner's house. The gardens, conceived thirteen years ago, are situated at the head of the Apponagansett River. A splendid view opens behind the Italianate-style house; hostas emerge beside and underneath shrubs and trees. Plantings around outbuildings reflect the historical nature of the property, as does an eighteenth-century burial ground in the undulating landscape between the house and the river. A woodland walk meanders back to the most dramatic feature of the garden, a great lawn surrounded by stone walls and boxwood hedges that features unusual trees and shrubs.

Hours: 10 a.m. to 4 p.m.

From the end of Route 140, turn right onto Route 6. Turn left at the first traffic light onto Slocum Road. Continue past the light at Allen Street. Slocum Road becomes Russells Mills Road at Friendly's Pizza. Keep straight, bearing right, and pass the Dartmouth police station on the right. Number 288 is the fifth house on the left after the police station. *Please park on the adjacent streets on the right (Utica Lane) just past the house.*

Proceeds shared with the Rotch-Jones-Duff House & Garden Museum

Public Gardens

BARNSTABLE COUNTY

SOUTH WELLFLEET

Wellfleet Bay Wildlife Sanctuary of the Massachusetts Audubon Society

291 State Highway, Route 6, South Wellfleet (508) 349-2615 www.wellfleetbay.org

Located on the "forearm" of Cape Cod, the 1,000-acre Wellfleet Bay Wildlife Sanctuary offers outstanding opportunities for exploration of the natural world. From forest to field, from sandy beach to tidal flats, five miles of trails traverse eight different habitats, which represent the diversity of Cape Cod. Designed and managed by Audubon volunteers, there is a sizable garden of shrubs, perennials, annuals, and herbs known to attract butterflies and humming-birds. This garden is animated in season by flights of winged visitors coming to their favorite nectar and larval food plants, of which more than 100 have been introduced. More than forty butterfly species have been counted. A section of meadow has also been set aside just for wildflowers.

Hours: Year round, daily, dawn to dusk

Admission: $3 adults, $2 children and seniors

From Route 6, turn west immediately north of the Eastham/Wellfleet town line.

BRISTOL COUNTY

NEW BEDFORD

Rotch-Jones-Duff House & Garden Museum

396 County Street, New Bedford (508) 997-1401 www.rjdmuseum.org

The property encompasses a full city block of urban gardens surrounded by a traditional board fence. The centerpiece of the gardens, a nineteenth-century wooden pergola, is surrounded by a formal cutting garden, a wildflower walk, a boxwood specimen garden, and a boxwood rose parterre garden. Restoration of the rose garden was initiated in 1996 under the direction of Stephen Scaniello, noted rosarian at the Brooklyn Botanic Garden, with the planting of more than 200 rosebushes. New rose beds were added in 1999. A replica of an historic wooden apiary with interior exhibit space serves as the Garden Educational Center.

Hours: January through May, Tuesday through Saturday, 10 a.m. to 4 p.m., Sunday, noon to 4 p.m.; June through December, Monday through Satuday, 10 a.m. to 4 p.m., Sunday, noon to 4 p.m.

Admission: $4 adults, $3 AAA and senior citizens, $2 children. Group tours are available for groups of ten or more; the group tour rate is $4 per person.

From Providence and points south, take I-195 east to Exit 15. Go straight through 1 set of traffic lights. At the next set of lights, turn right onto Union Street. Go through 3 lights; at the fourth light, turn left onto County Street. Go .25 mile and the Rotch-Jones-Duff House & Garden Museum (yellow house with green shutters) is on the left.

From Boston and points north, take Route 128 south to Route 24 south to Route 140 south to the end. Go straight through the light. You will pass Buttonwood Park on your left; go all the way to the next light. Turn left onto Hawthorn Street. Go straight through the next light. Travel on Hawthorn Street to end. Turn left onto County Street. The museum is the second building on the right.

ESSEX COUNTY

BEVERLY
The Sedgwick Gardens at Long Hill
572 Essex Street, Beverly (978) 921-1944 www.thetrustees.org

From 1916-1979, Long Hill was the country estate of the Sedgwick family. It was first purchased by noted author and editor (1909-1938) of *Atlantic Monthly* magazine, Ellery Sedgwick, and his first wife, Mabel Cabot Sedgwick, an accomplished horticulturist and author of *The Garden Month by Month*. The antebellum-style house was built in 1921 and contains original woodwork from the 1802 Issac Ball House in Charleston, South Carolina, on which the house is styled. The gardens were first designed and planted by Mrs. Sedgwick. After her death in 1937, Mr. Sedgwick's second wife, the former Marjorie Russell of England, a distinguished gardener and propagator of rare plants, added many plants to the gardens, including unusual species and varieties of trees and shrubs, many introduced by the Arnold Arboretum. Today, the Sedgwick Gardens reflects the collective interests and tastes of both women. Five acres of cultivated grounds are laid out in a series of separate garden areas surrounding the house, each distinct in its own way and accented by a tremendous diversity of garden ornaments, structures, and statuary. These areas are flanked on all sides by over 100 acres of woodland (containing two miles of trails and footpaths), as well as an apple orchard and meadow. More than 400 species of plants are grown, many very unusual. Long Hill serves as the Headquarters of the Trustees of Reservations, a member-supported Massachusetts nonprofit conservation organization.

Hours: Year round, daily, dawn to dusk, with occasional restricted access during weddings. Guided garden tours are offered seasonally; call for regular and group rates.

Admission: free

From Route 128, take Exit 18 onto Route 22 (Essex Street) north and proceed for 1.3 miles. Bear left at the fork in the road and continue for .2 mile to the brick gateposts and entrance drive on the left.

CAMBRIDGE

Mount Auburn Cemetery

580 Mount Auburn Street, Cambridge (617) 547-7105

Mount Auburn Cemetery, founded in 1831, is America's first landscaped cemetery, with 174 acres and more than 5,000 native and exotic trees identified and tagged. Many important and famous people are buried here. A fascinating place to visit and wonderful for bird watching. Audio tour available for rent or purchase.

> *Hours:* Year round, daily, 8 a.m. to 5 p.m. (7 p.m. during the summer)
> *Admission:* free
> *The entrance is on Mount Auburn Street near the boundary of Cambridge and Watertown,* approximately 1.5 miles west of Harvard Square, just west of Mount Auburn Hospital and Freshpond Parkway. The cemetery is easily reached by public transportation from Harvard Square (#71 or #73 bus).

FRAMINGHAM

Garden in the Woods of the New England Wildflower Society

180 Hemenway Road, Framingham (508) 877-7630 www.newfs.org

Garden in the Woods, New England's premier wildflower showcase, displays the largest landscaped collection of native plants in the Northeast. Forty-five acres with woodland trails offer vistas of wildflowers, shrubs, and trees. More than 1,700 varieties of plants, including more than 200 rare and endangered species, grow in protective cultivation. Garden in the Woods also has the largest wildflower nursery in New England.

> *Hours:* April 15 through June 15, daily, with extended hours in May to 7 p.m.; June 16 through October 31, Tuesday through Sunday, 9 a.m. to 5 p.m. Last admission to garden trails is 1 hour before closing.
> *Admission:* $6 adults, $5 seniors, $3 children 6.
> *From Route 128,* take Route 20 west; go 8 miles on Route 20 to Raymond Road (second left after traffic light in South Sudbury); 1.3 miles to Hemenway Road.
> *From Massachusetts Turnpike/I-90,* take Exit 12 to Route 9 east. Go 2.4 miles to Edgell Road (Route 9 overpass), then 2.1 miles to the light. Turn right onto Water Street and then turn left onto Hemenway Road. Follow the garden signs.

JAMAICA PLAIN

Arnold Arboretum of Harvard University

125 The Arborway, Jamaica Plain (617) 524-1718 www.arboretum.harvard.edu

The 265-acre Arnold Arboretum displays North America's premier collection of more than 13,000 hardy trees, shrubs, and vines. The grounds were planted and designed by the arboretum's first director, Charles Sprague Sargent, and America's first landscape architect, Frederick Law Olmsted. Highlights include crab apple, conifer, lilac, rhododendron, and bonsai collections.

> *Hours:* Year round, daily, dawn to dusk
> *Admission:* free
> *From Storrow Drive,* take the Fenway/Park Drive exit. Follow signs to the Riverway, which becomes the Jamaicaway and then the Arborway/Centre Street.

From I-95/Route 128, exit onto Route 9 east. Follow Route 9 for 7 miles to the Riverway/Centre Street.

From Southeast Expressway/I-93, take Exit 11/Granite Avenue/Ashmont onto Route 203. Follow it past Franklin Park. This site is also accessible by public transportation.

Waltham

Lyman Estate, The Vale

185 Lyman Street, Waltham (781) 891-4882

The Lyman Estate, known as The Vale, is one of the finest examples in the United States of a country property laid out according to the principles of eighteenth-century English naturalistic design. The greenhouses were built from 1800 to 1930 and contain century-old camellias and grapevines, as well as tropical and subtropical plants. Unusual plants are available for sale year round. Please call for the date of specialty sales. The Vale is a property of the Society for the Preservation of New England Antiquities.

Hours: Year round, daily, dawn to dusk. Greenhouses are open year round, Monday through Saturday, 9:30 a.m. to 4 p.m.

Admission: free

From Route 128, take Exit 26/Route 20 east to Waltham/Boston. Follow Route 20 (it becomes Main Street) through the center of Waltham about 1.7 miles. At the Kentucky Fried Chicken, turn left onto Lyman Street. Follow Lyman .5 mile to a rotary and bear immediately right into the estate driveway (check for a SPNEA sign).

WORCESTER COUNTY

Boylston

Tower Hill Botanic Garden

11 French Drive, Boylston (508) 869-6111 www.towerhillbg.org

Located on 132 rural acres, Tower Hill Botanic Garden features a spectacular spring bulb display, an orangerie filled with fragrant citrus trees and blooming nonhardy plants, a lawn garden of over 350 varieties of trees and shrubs, secret and cottage gardens with colorful perennials and unusual annuals, a seasonal vegetable garden, a wildlife garden, an orchard of heirloom apple cultivars, walking trails, and a panoramic view. New to the landscape is the .5-acre Systematic Garden. Laid out in the Italian style, it features sculpture, three water features, and an elaborate pergola. The Stoddard Education and Visitors' Center hosts lectures, workshops and demonstrations, flower shows and exhibits, an 8,000-volume library, garden shop, and weekend cafe.

Hours: Year round, Tuesday through Sunday and holiday Mondays, 10 a.m. to 5 p.m.; closed Thanksgiving, Christmas Eve and Day, and New Year's Day

Admission: $7 adults, $5 senior citizens, $3 children 6-18, children under 6 free

Located in central Massachusetts, 10 miles northeast of Worcester. From I-290, take Exit 24. Travel 3.25 miles towards Boylston to 11 French Drive; the entrance is on the right.

Michigan

Toni & Joe Grinnan's garden, Beverly Hills.
Photo by Maureen Electa Monte.

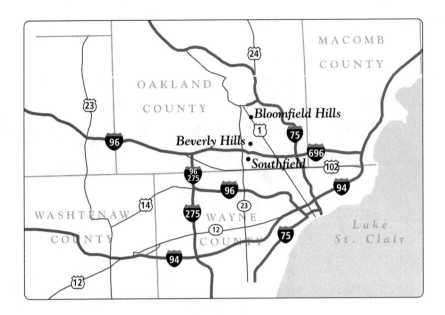

Sunday, July 14

OAKLAND COUNTY

BEVERLY HILLS

Toni & Joe Grinnan

1 Stone House Lane, Beverly Hills

The more formal front gardens and pond were designed to play off the symmetry of this circa 1935 stone Colonial home. Evergreens for structure and perennials for color are the mainstays of these gardens. The waterfall, pond, and plantings in the rear were designed in more natural shapes to blend with the woods and foliage along the Rouge River. Look into the charming but practical potting shed where the owners, who do most of the gardening themselves, like to putter on cold or rainy days.

Hours: 10 a.m. to 4 p.m.

Enter through the arbor from the adjoining garden of Bruce and Denise Wayne (see next page). *Please park along Riverbank Drive or in the parking lot of the office building on the southeast corner of Lahser and Thirteen Mile Roads.*

Proceeds shared with the Womens' National Farm & Garden Association—Franklin Branch

Suzanne's Garden—Suzanne Krueger & Dave Rider
21805 Fourteen Mile Road, Beverly Hills

Four years ago, we renovated a 1906 farmhouse and built the garden surrounding it. All grass was removed, walks were built, and over 5,000 perennials were planted. The front sun garden is a riot of blossoms and color, with all the old-fashioneds that you would expect: 'Blue Sky', 'Black Knight', and Mountain mix delphiniums, roses (including my favorite "first prize"), hollyhocks, and lilies. More roses adorn the white picket fence that leads to the kitchen herb garden. The backyard is a quiet, deeply shaded hosta garden with slate paths winding around five ponds and waterfalls.

Hours: 10 a.m. to 4 p.m.

Located just east of Lahser, on the south side of Fourteen Mile Road, between Lahser and Evergreen, 3 miles north of I-696.

Proceeds shared with the Franklin Garden Club

Denise & Bruce Wayne
25 Riverbank Drive, Beverly Hills

Our garden was designed four years ago to complement the turn-of-the-century architecture of our house. We wanted a mostly perennial garden that would be in constant bloom, changing every few weeks from early spring until late fall with a profusion of color and texture. The front yard is enclosed with a picket fence giving a courtyard effect, featuring a boxwood parterre, climbing roses, hosta, clematis, foxglove, daylilies, phlox, Shasta daisies, astilbe, spirea, sedum, honeysuckle, trumpet vines, ferns, and a pair of hydrangea trees on either side of a brick paver walk. The driveway is packed on both sides with deciduous shrubs, towering evergreens, assorted perennials, and annuals wrapping around the back of the house along a bluestone path with a three-tiered fountain, a deck and brick paver patio, offering year-round privacy. We believe we've achieved the feel of a much larger garden in a compact area that is always full of wonderful surprises.

Hours: 10 a.m. to 4 p.m.

Take Riverbank Drive east off Lahser Road. It is the first street off Lahser, south of Thirteen Mile Road. The garden is the first house on the right on Riverbank Drive. The rear garden leads into the adjoining Grinnan Garden. *Please park on the street or in the parking lot of the office building .12 mile north on the corner of Thirteen Mile and Lahser Roads.*

Proceeds shared with the Womens' National Farm & Garden Association—Franklin Branch

BLOOMFIELD HILLS
Aerie Gardens
703 Lone Pine Hill, Bloomfield Hills

Aerie Gardens is situated on a 5.5-acre hilltop vista, which includes 2.5 acres of woods and a small pond and stream. Wetland gardens and woodland gardens, waterfall gardens, hillside gardens, both sun and shade gardens are all connected by paths, trails, and stone stairways. Sculptures by Marshall Fredericks are incorporated into the gardens.

Hours: 10 a.m. to 4 p.m.

Lone Pine Hill runs north of Lone Pine Road midway between Woodward Avenue and Cranbrook Road in Bloomfield Hills. The entrance to Aerie Gardens is at the top of Lone Pine Hill. *Please park along one side only of Lone Pine Hill.*

Proceeds shared with the Cranbrook House & Gardens Auxiliary

Judy's Garden
3916 Cottontail Lane, Bloomfield Hills

This spectacularly diverse three-quarter-acre property contains a woodland garden, sun garden, and a two-tiered, 10,000-gallon water garden with streams and waterfalls. More than 300 varieties of hosta, New Zealand hostas, plants from other parts of the world, unusual and rare specimen evergreens and shrubs, wildflowers, numerous varieties of fragrant flowers, ferns, grasses, and an interesting integration of textures, shapes, and colors complement the curved lines of the beds. The visually stimulating garden rooms are augmented with garden art, sculpture, birdhouses, a unique children's playhouse and garden shed, and the constant sound of the waterfalls.

Hours: 10 a.m. to 4 p.m.

Located between Lahser and Telegraph Roads north of Maple Road/Fifteen Mile Road. Travel east on Maple Road from Telegraph Road to the second traffic light. Turn left onto Gilbert Lake Road. At the third street on the left, turn left onto Cottontail Lane. The garden is the first driveway on the right. *Please park on the street.*

Larry & Sandy Mackle

460 Goodhue Road, Bloomfield Hills

In 1972, we moved into our house built in 1929. The landscaping on the two acres was 1929 vintage, overgrown, and included what nature planted. Our garden displays more than 500 hostas, 1,000-plus daylilies, 140 conifers, and a large number of companion plants, perennials, and annuals. There are a pond and rock garden and garden statuary, most of which is in dappled sunlight.

Hours: 10 a.m. to 4 p.m.

Heading north out of Detroit, take Woodward Avenue to Lone Pine Road. Turn west and go past the Cranbrook Road traffic light to Goodhue Road. Turn south onto Goodhue to the first house on the left.

SOUTHFIELD

Tom & Beth McMahon

29734 Pleasant Trail, Southfield

A dramatic and intimate garden contained on a small city lot. Winding paths carry you through plantings of unusual conifers, over 150 varieties of hosta, hundreds of ornamental grasses, flowering perennials and annuals, and many rare Japanese maples and dogwoods. The only thing you will not find is any lawn. The main focal point is a 15,000-gallon koi pond set into the backyard with waterfalls and streams, blended into the setting with large boulder work.

Hours: 10 a.m. to 4 p.m.

From Evergreen Road South, proceed about .5 mile past Thirteen Mile Road to Hickory Leaf, turn left onto Hickory Leaf, and proceed to the end. Turn right onto Spring River and take to the end. Turn left onto Pleasant Trail and we are the second house on the right. *Please park on the street.*

Public Gardens

OAKLAND COUNTY

BLOOMFIELD HILLS

Congregational Church of Birmingham

1000 Cranbrook Road, Bloomfield Hills (248) 644-8065

Within a nine-acre property we have created the most interesting group of gardens, blooming from early spring with bulbs to asters in the fall. We have award-winning displays of tree and herbaceous peonies. Included are five kinds of irises, *Lilium* beds, several hosta beds, daylily beds, and a memorial garden. Rose beds complement specimen trees and shrubs.

Hours: Year round, daily, dawn to dusk

Admission: free

Take Woodward Avenue north to Cranbrook Road.

Cranbrook House & Gardens

Lone Pine Road, Bloomfield Hills (248) 645-3147

Stroll through the forty acres of gardens surrounding historic Cranbrook House, the 1908 Arts and Crafts-style manor house of founders, George and Ellen Scripps Booth. The formal gardens and terraces are enhanced by sculptures, fountains, paths, lakes, and streams. Tended by volunteers, the gardens are even more exquisite than when the Booths created them.

Hours: May through Labor Day, Monday through Saturday, 10 a.m. to 5 p.m., Sunday, 11 a.m. to 5 p.m.; September, daily, 11 a.m. to 3 p.m.; October, weekends only, 11 a.m. to 3 p.m.

Admission: $5 adults, $4 senior citizens, children under 5 free

Lone Pine Road is north of Quarton Road about 16 miles, east of Telegraph/Route 24, and west of Woodward Avenue/M-1.

New Hampshire

OPEN DAYS:

July 13
July 14
July 27

Jim & Ellen Labrie's Seaside Garden, Rye.

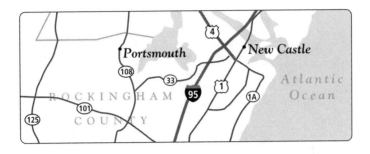

Saturday, July 13
ROCKINGHAM COUNTY

NEW CASTLE
Prince-Bergh Garden
183 Portsmouth Avenue, New Castle

Built on the grounds of a former nursery, this garden features hand-picked, large lichen-covered boulders, a whimsical stone bookshelf (complete with stone books), a Luniform urn water feature, and an open fire pit built with cut Stone Isle granite. The main garden is a sweeping three-tiered garden that separates an upper and lower yard. Plantings include an extensive array of perennials, as well as ferns, heathers, heaths, succulents, and even a few thriving cactus.

Hours: 10 a.m. to 4 p.m.

Follow Route 1B from the south end of Portsmouth. Cross over both bridges that bring you to New Castle. Once you cross the causeway, we are the first house on the right overlooking the historic New Castle Cemetery, as well as the harbor and Piscataqua River, #183. Please park on Portsmouth Avenue.

Proceeds shared with the Seacoast Land Trust

Reynolds Garden
167 Portsmouth Avenue, New Castle

The primary focus of this seaside garden is its collection of hostas. I first chose them for their low maintenance but have since become an enthusiastic collector. The garden itself owes its long, narrow shape to the foundations of the carnation greenhouse that existed here early in the previous century.

Hours: 10 a.m. to 4 p.m.

From I-95 north, take Exit 3/Route 33/formerly Route 101. Turn right off the exit ramp. Follow Middle Road/Route 33 through 2 traffic lights (.9 mile). Middle Road forms a "Y" with South Street. Stay right at "Y". Go a few hundred yards to a light at the junction of Route 1. Cross Route 1 and go straight on South Street. Follow South Street to a light at Sagamore Road and Route 1A (.6 mile at big cemetery). Go straight through the light, up over a hill past a tiny store on the left, and, at .4 mile, turn right onto Newcastle Avenue (at the lavender-colored house). Follow Newcastle Avenue out onto Newcastle Island (1.3 miles). As you come onto the island, Riverside Cemetery will be on your right and the Naval Prison on your left across the river. Turn right at the second driveway at the sign for 167 Portsmouth Avenue.

From I-95 south, take Exit 3B/Route 101 and proceed as directed above. *Please park on Portsmouth Avenue.*

Proceeds shared with the Seacoast Land Trust

PORTSMOUTH

Jameson & Priscilla French
45 Driftwood Lane, Portsmouth

At the end of Driftwood Lane is the site of the last working farm in the south end of Portsmouth. The land around the circa 1860 farmhouse has been transformed into a variety of gardens and recreational spaces for a growing young family. Formal beds edge the driveway as you approach the house. As you enter the pool area, the pergola, covered with two colors of wisteria and a *tangutica* clematis, is a focal point. Stairs lead down to a formal English-style vegetable and flower garden, divided by an obelisk covered with passiflora and other flowering vines. I take pride in mixing flowers and vegetables for food production and aesthetic values and in growing 90% of my annuals from seed. You'll notice my weakness for dahlias and pelargoniums. My wife and children tolerate my gardening passion but love the fresh produce!

Hours: 10 a.m. to 4 p.m.

From I-95, take Exit 7/Market Street into downtown Portsmouth. Keep the Piscataqua River on your left. Follow Market Street/Bow Street/State Street/Mercy Street past Prescott Park and Strawbery Banke Museum. At the end of Mercy Street (fish market on left), go straight on Route 1B/New Castle Avenue after the 3-way stop. Driftwood Lane is the third right. *Do not park on New Castle Avenue; follow signs to designated spots on Driftwood Lane.*

Proceeds shared with the Seacoast Land Trust

Barbara Renner's Garden
30A Franklin Street, Portsmouth

As you stroll down Franklin Street towards the South Mill Pond, on the left is the circa 1790 Colonial double house of Barbara Renner. Terraces of fieldstone have been used in my garden to create a multi-layered effect. Successive dry stone walls step down over fifteen feet towards the pond. I built a small parterre of used bricks around a weeping cherry. You will notice my passion for clematis and other flowering vines. I have the perfect spot for the 'Duchess of Albany', which thrives next to the purple hues of 'General Sikorski'! Several seating areas offer different views of the garden, birds, and vistas of Portsmouth and Mill Pond. Another delight is my hamamelis ('Arnold's Promise'), a joy to see when it blooms yellow in late February surrounded by deep snow. My garden is a constant learning labor of love.

Hours: 10 a.m. to 4 p.m.

From I-95 north, take Exit 7/Market Street to the historic district into Portsmouth. Turn left, passing the Sheraton Hotel on your right. There you will find a large parking house. With Market Square behind you, proceed down Pleasant Street. After the Mark Wentworth home, Franklin Street is the second street on the right, a 10-minute walk. *There is very little parking on Franklin Street.*

Proceeds shared with the Seacoast Land Trust

Sunday, July 14
ROCKINGHAM COUNTY

Hampton Falls
Carole & Bert Chanasyk
15 Evergreen Road, Hampton Falls

Our large informal style garden is located in a two-acre wooded country setting. Various evergreens and deciduous trees surround and provide a natural backdrop for the garden. Multiple stone walls carve throughout the garden to provide a traditional New England feeling. Classic and unusual perennials and annuals spill over the many curved stone wall beds. The garden displays a variety of textured foliage and continually pleasing and vibrant accent colors throughout the season. Many footpaths among the flowers invite visitors for a closer view. Overall, the garden provides a pleasing and visually exciting experience.

Hours: 10 a.m. to 4 p.m.

From I-95 north, take Exit 1 (the first New Hampshire exit) and turn right at the end of the exit ramp onto Route 107. Turn left onto Route 1 north and follow for several miles to the Hampton Falls Commons (2 traffic lights). Turn left onto Route 88, travel 2.5 miles, then turn left onto Sanborn Road. Take the first left onto Evergreen Road. Our house is the third one on the right.

From I-95 south, take Exit 1, turn left at the end of the exit ramp, and proceed as directed above. Our house is the third on the right. *Please park along the road.*

NORTH HAMPTON
Bell-Manning House Garden
48 Ocean Boulevard, North Hampton

The house and garden have been owned by one family for the past 84 years and face the ocean. During that time, the gardens have remained essentially unchanged. The flower beds include a small rose garden, adjoining an 1890s' barn, and a very pretty cutting garden complete with an old stone well covered with climbing hydrangea. There is also an extensive walled roadside annual border with climbing pink roses and clematis.

Hours: 10 a.m. to 4 p.m.

From I-95, take Exit 13. Take Route 27 to Route 1A and turn left at the ocean. Go about 1.5 miles to the intersection of Route 111, also known as Atlantic Avenue. Go down 3 houses; ours is a large white house with green shutters. *Parking is available at the Fuller Gardens on Willow Avenue. To get there, go past the house, take an immediate left onto Willow, and go about 200 yards. The parking lot is on the left.*

Proceeds shared with the North Hampton Public Library

Shulman Garden
29 Old Locke Road, North Hampton

Our traditional New England perennial garden was sited in the same place as a formal garden had been when the house was built in 1938. There are many old specimen trees on the property, including the largest Carolina silverbell tree in New England and an unusually large North American cherry. This property, with the sound and view of the ocean, feels like the farm country west of here.

Hours: 10 a.m. to 4 p.m.

From I-95, take Exit 2 and follow the signs to Route 101 all the way to the ocean. Get on Route 1A, turn left (north), and follow Route 1A for 3.5 miles to Causeway Road in Rye. Go left on Causeway. Go 1 block to the golf course and turn left again. We are the third house on the left, #29. Look for a white house and white fence. *Please park along the road.*

RYE
Jim & Ellen Labrie's Seaside Garden
1451 Ocean Boulevard, Rye

Our garden, overlooking the Atlantic Ocean, features a delightful blend of perennial and annual plantings bordered by a bluestone-capped fieldstone wall. Always a work in progress, for the last two years the garden has shared space with an eight-foot block of Vermont marble being sculpted "in place" into a contemporary spiritual figure. In July, the gaillardia, lilies, and sages will be at their best. A natural stone path leads from the front to the backyard, passing the raised vegetable beds. The rear yard features a stone tower waterfall, weeping cherry, blue hibiscus, and many mature hollies.

Hours: 10 a.m. to 4 p.m.

On Route 1A, just north of Washington Road, 1451 Ocean Boulevard is clearly visible as you round the curve and view the tall stone walls and the "angel." Going south on Route 1A from Portsmouth, the home is .9 mile south of the Pirate Cove restaurant.

Proceeds shared with the Health Support Associates

RYE BEACH
Sal Allocco's Garden
421 South Road, Rye Beach

A seacoast English-style garden awaits you with its fifteen pocket gardens, including a vegetable garden hidden behind a white picket fence. Mainly perennials, special features include a water garden, white garden, and friendship garden. A cluster of large decorative containers overflows with summer annuals. Stone walls, rock formations, and garden art and statuary are featured throughout. Hostas, grasses, and lilies are a few of the hundreds of multicolor combinations that attract many species of birds and butterflies. It is a quiet garden in a natural setting, inviting relaxation and moments of meditation.

Hours: 10 a.m. to 2 p.m.

From *I-95 north (about 60 miles from Boston)*, exit at Seabrook or Hampton and head east on Route 1 (also known as Lafayette Road). Continue north on Route 1 to the Rye/Rye Beach area to North Road (look for a driving range and Rollins Furniture). Turn right onto North Road (about 1.5 miles), which automatically becomes South Road, heading towards the ocean. Look for a Royal Barry Wills Cape on the left side. *Please park on the road.*

Hochschwender Garden
10 Laurence Lane, Rye Beach

Mine is a new garden on half an acre of land, begun when I moved from a much larger property. Different texture and color of foliage give me much pleasure and I am blessed with some beautiful specimens of shrubs and trees, accented with colorful perennials and annuals. A focal point of the backyard is a waterfall and pond, home to goldfish, frogs, and water-loving plants. My goal is to have year-round interest with stone, statuary, curving borders, evergreens, and flowers blooming at different times.

Hours: 10 a.m. to 4 p.m.

From Route 1, turn onto Washington Road (look for Home Center Furniture Store). Turn right at West Road (Christine's Crossing) and turn left at a 4-way stop sign onto South Road. Laurence Lane is on the right after a sharp curve, across from a golf course. My house, #10, is the first house on the left.

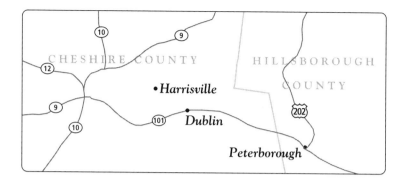

Saturday, July 27

CHESHIRE COUNTY

DUBLIN
Robertson Garden
Gerry Road, Dublin

The inspiration to create this garden came from a trip to England to view several of its creations. The garden is located between a large barn and a pergola. It is surrounded by peach trees, a vegetable garden, and a fairly productive bluebird trail. Peripheral gardens line the juncture of our property with nearby woods and a meadow. It is living proof that a moderately attractive garden can be chiseled from the New Hampshire granite that serves as our "soil."

Hours: 10 a.m. to 2 p.m.

Gerry Road leaves Route 101 about .8 mile west of the junction of Routes 101 and 137. Carr's store and Citgo gas station are located at this junction. Gerry Road, primarily a dirt road through a wooded area, is .7 mile long and dead ends at our property.

Tiadnock
East Lake Road, Dublin

This garden is a slow work in progress. The dramatic views create a sense of remoteness that is hard to find. The gardens are there to complement the site. The main border is yellow, white, and gray with plant material that can flourish in this exposed, windy, dry environment. The front door area is a combination of large-leaved textural plants and a small heath and heather planting with a native shrub border.

Hours: 10 a.m. to 2 p.m.

From Keene, at the intersection of Routes 101 and 10, follow Route 101 east towards Peterborough. Travel 12.5 miles (at which point you have passed Dublin Lake on your right) and turn right onto East Lake Road. Travel .5 mile and look for a large pair of gateposts on the left; the lake will be on your right. Take the dirt driveway immediately past this gate. There is a tree with "Barker," "Townsend," and "Kelly" on it. Travel .4 mile to the top of the hill and turn left. This is our drive and is marked by a signpost that reads "Townsend." Follow this all the way to the end. Our house is brown shingle. Please be careful on the driveway, as it is narrow.

HARRISVILLE
Sky Hill
Mason Road, Harrisville

Located on a high hill facing Mount Monadnock, hardy perennials and roses grow along both sides of a windbreak lattice fence. Another part of the garden features alpines grown in granite and gravel.

Hours: 10 a.m. to 4 p.m.

From Dublin Village, follow Route 101 west for .75 mile (Dublin Lake will be on the left) and turn right onto Old Harrisville Road. Go 2.4 miles to a sign on the right that reads "Single Lane Road." Bear right immediately into Sky Hill driveway. Note: Road name will have changed to Mason Road. *Please park along the driveway.*

HILLSBOROUGH COUNTY

PETERBOROUGH
Gardens of Stan & Cheri Fry
69 Pine Street, Peterborough

The garden consists of forty garden areas spread over a twelve-acre site, some of which is quite steep. The several styles of gardens include a formal one near the wooded areas, a number of water features, and a quite large perennial garden. Some of the gardens have been designed by Gordon Hayward and include such striking features as a 300-foot-long sycamore allée and a series of semicircle terraces bordered by standard Korean lilacs.

Hours: 10 a.m. to 4 p.m.

From Route 101 east in Nashua, proceed to Peterborough, past the intersection of Route 123, and turn right (.5 mile) onto Pine Street. The garden is at the third driveway on the left.

From Route 101 west in Keene, proceed through Peterborough, past the intersection of Route 202. Continue east on Route 101; Pine Street is on the left. The gardens are at the third driveway on the left. *Please park on the street.*

Public Gardens

ROCKINGHAM COUNTY

NORTH HAMPTON

The Fuller Gardens

North Hampton (603) 964-5414 www.fullergardens.org

Fuller Gardens is a formal, turn-of-the-century estate garden that was once an ornament to Alvan T. Fuller's summer home. The area was designed in the Colonial Revival style by noted landscape architect Arthur Shurtleff, with additions in the 1930s by the Olmsted Brothers. More than 2,000 roses of many varieties that bloom all summer, unusual and eye-catching annual and perennial plantings, a hosta display garden, public tropical/desert conservatory, and a Japanese garden are all within the sculpted hedges of this seaside gem.

> *Hours:* Mid-May through mid-October, daily, 10 a.m. to 5:30 p.m.
> *Admission:* $6 adults, $5 seniors, $3 students, $2 children under 12
> *North of the junction of Routes 1A and 111.*

Moffatt-Ladd House & Garden Museum

Market Street, Portsmouth (603) 436-8221

Designed and planted in the late nineteenth century by A. H. Ladd, this garden is one-plus acres of perennials, annuals, bulbs, shrubs, vines, and trees. Two eighteenth-century plantings, the William Whipple chestnut tree and the damask bride's rose, are still alive. A long central path leads from the eighteenth-century mansion through four terraces of formal flower beds, lawns, and pathways. The museum property is owned and maintained by the National Society of the Colonial Dames of America in the State of New Hampshire.

> *Hours:* Mid-June through October, Monday through Saturday, 11 a.m. to 5 p.m., Sunday, 1 p.m. to 5 p.m.
> *Admission:* $5 adults, $2,.50 children
> *In downtown Portsmouth, 2 blocks from Market Square. Take I-95 to the downtown Portsmouth exit. Turn right (left, if traveling from the north) onto Market Street Extension. At the blinking traffic light, the road forks. Keep to the left and follow Market Street. The garden is halfway down the block on the right side of the street.*

PORTSMOUTH

Strawbery Banke Museum

Marcy Street, Portsmouth (603) 433-1100 www.strawberybanke.org

Strawbery Banke, a ten-acre history museum of a seacoast neighborhood, has recreated or restored six period gardens and landscapes. They represent residents' choices in plants, layout, cultural practices, and leisure time, ranging from circa 1720 to 1944. You are invited to stroll the grounds to view them all. Of special merit are the Sarah Parker Rice Goodwin Garden, recreated to its appearance in the 1870s. Based on an 1862 garden plan and the journals and memoirs kept by Sarah Goodwin, the garden contains many unusual heirloom flowers all planted in a high-style bedding design typical of the period. Enter the garden through an eighteen-foot-tall hemlock archway and enjoy the fragrances and richness of color the Goodwin family enjoyed more than 130 years ago. The Thomas Baily Aldrich Memorial Garden appears much as it did in the 1920s, fifteen years after it was laid out as a tribute to Aldrich. True to its roots in the Colonial Revival, the garden contains many classical architectural elements, spaces organized into garden rooms, fragrant perennials, lush roses, and brick pathways. It contains all the plants mentioned in the many poems, novels, and essays Aldrich wrote in the nineteenth century.

Hours: May 1 through October 15, 10 a.m. to 5 p.m.; call for winter hours

Admission: $12 adults, $11 senior citizens, $8 children 7-17, children under 7 free; call for winter hours

From I-95, take Exit 7/Market Street. Follow green signs located throughout downtown Portsmouth. Located on Marcy Street across from Prescott Park and the Piscataqua River.

SULLIVAN COUNTY

NEWBURY
The Fells at the John Hay National Wildlife Refuge
Route 103A, Newbury (603) 763-4789

A PROJECT OF
THE GARDEN
CONSERVANCY

These extensive gardens, developed from 1914 to 1940 as a showplace country estate, had fallen into decline in recent years. Work by the Garden Conservancy staff, current managers, Friends of the John Hay National Wildlife Refuge, and others have revived the historic design of formal naturalized plantings, terraced lawns, and native New Hampshire granite walls. Currently the rock garden, in which Clarence Hay experimented with hundreds of alpine plants for more than forty years, is in its sixth year of rehabilitation.

Hours: Year round, daily, dawn to dusk. House tours available on weekends. Call ahead for special events and educational programs.

Admission: $3 grounds, $4 house and grounds

From the south and east, take I-89 north to Exit 9/Route 103 and go west to Newbury. Take Route 102A north for 2.2 miles. The Fells is on the left.

From the north, take I-89 south to Exit 12/Route 11. Turn right at the end of the exit ramp and make an immediate left onto Route 102A south. Travel 5.6 miles to The Fells on the right. Please park in the parking lot and walk down the driveway to the gardens.

NEW JERSEY

Emer Featherstone's garden, Montclair.

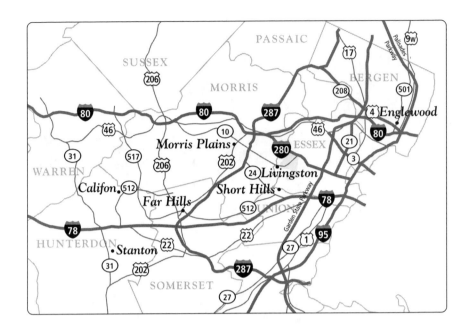

Saturday, May 11

BERGEN COUNTY

ENGLEWOOD

Peggy & Walter Jones

401 Morrow Road, Englewood

This rolling hillside encompasses a variety of gardens, ranging from a formal rose garden to a wild woodland garden where the Japanese primrose and shooting stars dance with the hellebores. Other highlights include a rock garden, a living wall, a small enclosed courtyard with wonderful climbing hydrangeas, and an elliptical herb garden in the center of the back lawn. Come and discover a wealth of unique trees, shrubs, and perennials. Find the split-leaf beech in the expansive front lawn. In the rear of the garden, look for the old moss-covered stone steps, which lead to the outdoor fireplace nestled under a canopy of large oaks. Look to the left and you will see the sorrel tree.

Hours: 10 a.m. to 4 p.m.

From I-95/I-80 east (local lanes), exit at Broad Avenue/Englewood. Follow Broad Avenue north until it ends at a traffic light at Palisades Avenue. Turn left onto Palisades Avenue, then make a quick right at the light onto Lydecker Street. Follow Lydecker to a 4-way stop. Turn right onto Booth Avenue. Head uphill and turn left onto the first road, Morrow Road. Go to the top of the hill. The house, #401, is on the right.

From Palisades Interstate Parkway, take Exit 1/Englewood/Palisades Avenue. Turn right onto Palisades Avenue and go to the light. Turn right onto Lydecker Street and proceed as directed above.

Mercer & Peter O'Hara
251 Glenwood Road, Englewood

Our garden has slowly developed over 25 years. Two years ago, we removed an old arborvitae hedge that divided the property in half. This opened up the garden, revealing a lovely stone wall. The existing perennial garden was retained and backed with a new "hedge" of mixed dwarf conifers that are beautiful in all seasons. The property also includes a woodland garden, butterfly garden, rock garden, and vegetable garden. We practice integrated pest management and use only organic fertilizers.

Hours: 10 a.m. to 4 p.m.

From I-95/I-80 east (local lanes), exit at Broad Avenue/Englewood. Follow Broad Avenue north until it ends at a traffic light at Palisades Avenue. Turn left onto Palisades Avenue, then make a quick right at the light onto Lydecker Street. Follow Lydecker Street to the second stop sign. Turn right onto Glenwood Road. Number 251 is the third house up on the left.

From Palisades Interstate Parkway, take Exit 1/Englewood/Palisades Avenue. Turn right onto Palisades Avenue and go to the fifth light. Turn right onto Lydecker Street and proceed as directed above. This garden is 1 block away from the garden of Peggy and Walter Jones (see preceding entry). *Please park on the street.*

ESSEX COUNTY

LIVINGSTON

Howard P. Fertig
24 Berkeley Place, Livingston

No grass, no front or back lawn, just hundreds of conifers, from *Abies* (firs) to *Tsuga* (hemlocks) and most every variety in between. Many rock garden plants can also be found. There are more than seventy Japanese maples (dwarf to large) in the ground and in pots and more than 100 different hostas. More than fifty azaleas and rhododendrons provide a great amount of beauty and color in this mosaic garden.

Hours: 10 a.m. to 4 p.m.

From I-287, take the I-80 east exit. Take I-80 to I-280 east. Get off at Exit 5A, proceed through 4 traffic lights, and, 1 block after the fourth light, turn right onto Berkeley Place.

From Garden State Parkway, take Exit 145 onto I-280 west. Get off at Exit 5A and proceed as directed above. The house is located on the right in the middle of the block. *Please park in front of the house along the street.*

SHORT HILLS
Winter's Garden
28 Dryden Terrace, Short Hills

This garden is densely packed with conifers ranging from miniature to dwarf, intermediate to full size. Ground covers, perennials, shrubs, and deciduous trees, including dozens of Japanese maples, are incorporated. Weathered limestone is extensively integrated throughout for contrast with the plantings. The arrangements are personal choices for spiritual and aesthetic effect and include many rare and unusual specimens.

Hours: 10 a.m. to 4 p.m.

From Route 24 east, take Exit 8. Go to the second traffic light and turn left. Continue about 6 blocks and turn left onto Dryden Terrace.

From Route 24 west, take Exit 9/Hobart Avenue. Go to the first light and turn right onto Hobart Avenue. Go about 6 blocks to Dryden Terrace. Dryden Terrace is off White Oak Ridge Road between Parsonage Hill Road and Route 24. *Please park on the street.*

HUNTERDON COUNTY

CALIFON
Frog Pond Farm
26 Beavers Road, Califon

In a peaceful countryside hollow, a half-acre spring-fed pond reflects the beauty of the natural scene. The drama is heightened by introduced flowering trees, azaleas, rhododendrons, and uncommon shrubs. There are separate areas for many types of iris, primula, and wildflowers. Crossing a brook on a footbridge, you will see rock gardens and all-season perennial borders, plus a blueberry house. Adding interest to the flag patio during the growing season are many tender container plants started in the small greenhouse.

Hours: 10 a.m. to 4 p.m.

From I-78, take Exit 24. Turn right (if coming from the east) onto Route 523 towards Oldwick. Continue straight ahead as the road becomes Route 517. Continue through the village of Oldwick and on, with no turns (6 miles from the interstate), to the traffic light. This is Fairmont, with Fairmont Church on the right corner. Turn left onto Route 512 and go about 1 mile to Beavers Road (bend in the road with fence). Turn right onto Beavers Road, traveling about 1 mile to #26 at the foot of the hill. The number is on the mailbox and there is a pond in front of the house. *Please park on Beavers Road.*

Stanton
Kallas Garden
91 Dreahook Road, Stanton

Approximately 1.5 acres are under cultivation, with herbaceous borders, annuals, and woody ornamentals in a naturalistic setting with benches for leisurely viewing. The main feature is about 1,000 specimens of 200 different rhododendron and azalea cultivars. The largest number of these is at peak in mid-May.

Hours: 10 a.m. to 4 p.m.

From I-78 west, take the Whitehouse/Oldwick exit and turn left onto Route 523 south. Travel to Route 22 and turn left at the traffic light. Go about 1,000 feet and turn right at the light onto the continuation of Route 523 south. Go about 2 miles to Dreahook Road. Turn right onto Dreahook and travel 2.5 miles to Cushetunk Road. The Kallas driveway is on the right between Cushetunk and Springtown Roads, which are on the left. *Please park on Cushetunk Road (unless handicapped).*

MORRIS COUNTY

Morris Plains
Watnong Gardens
2379 Watnong Terrace, Morris Plains

Watnong Gardens is the former Watnong Nursery made famous by Don and Hazel Smith. The garden now consists of 2.5 acres of collections, including conifers, shrubs, hostas, ferns, perennials, and a water garden. Special plants are added each year. A train, complete with four railroad cars, was made into six-foot and eight-foot-long troughs, all handcrafted by the owner and planted with mini-plants and alpines.

Hours: 10 a.m. to 4 p.m.

From I-80 west, take Exit 43 to I-287 south. Take I-287 south to Exit 39B/Route 10 west. Go about 3 miles west to the third traffic light, Powdermill Road. Take the "jug handle" turn and head east on Route 10. After passing Mountain Club Garden Homes, go slow. Watnong Terrace angles off to the right and parallels Route 10 like a service road. It is .7 mile from the "jug handle" turn. *Please park on the street.*

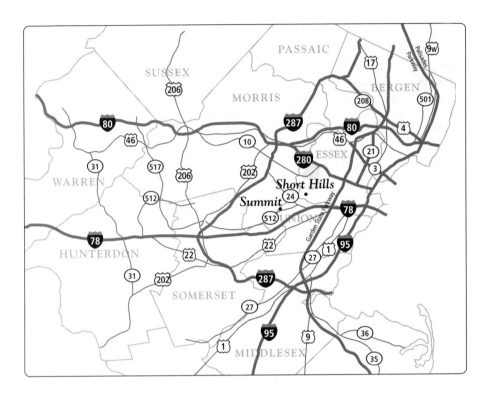

Saturday, June 8

ESSEX COUNTY

SHORT HILLS

Ursula & Andreas Enderlin

8 Taylor Road, Short Hills

I grew up in Switzerland where I was inspired to garden by beautiful flowers and gardens everywhere. My garden here was created over a twenty-year period of failure and success. The seeds fall and grow into an informal, wild colorful display. My garden beds are a continuing show, changing from spring flowers to summer plants into fall color. Two ponds with frogs, lots of birdhouses, and a birdbath add life and happiness to it.

Hours: 10 a.m. to 4 p.m.

From Route 24 west, take the Hobart Avenue exit. Turn right at the traffic light. At the first blinking light, turn right onto Hobart Avenue and drive 1 mile through the next blinking light. As the street curves, Taylor Road is on your left; we are #8, the second house on the right.

From Route 24 east, take the Summit Avenue exit and proceed through 1 light. At the next light, turn left over the overpass and proceed as directed above, from the first blinking light. *Please park on the opposite side of the house only.*

George Sternlieb
66 Old Short Hills Road, Short Hills

A great variety of shade and sun lovers are in troughs, pots, raised beds, and distinct gardens. Roses, clematis, dahlias, and hostas abound, framed by magnolias and Japanese maples. Non-hardy features include orchids, succulents, and a substantial range of vines, as well as begonias and other house/greenhouse plants. Gooseberries and raspberries round out a plantsman's choice.

Hours: 10 a.m. to 2 p.m.

From Garden State Parkway, take Exit 142. Take I-78 west to Millburn and get off at Exit 50B. At the top of the exit ramp, go right on Vauxhall Road and proceed to its end, about .8 mile (Vauxhall twists, so watch out). At the end of Vauxhall, go left on Millburn Avenue. In about .5 mile, the road jogs slightly to the right. Along this road (now called Essex), at the third traffic light you will reach Old Short Hills Road (also called Main Street). Turn right onto Old Short Hills Road and go uphill about .4 mile to #66 on the right.

From New York City, take the Lincoln Tunnel to New Jersey Turnpike/I-95 south. Get off the turnpike at Exit 14/Newark Airport. Stay on the right through the tollbooth, taking I-78 local west to Millburn, and get off at Exit 50B. Proceed as directed above.

Winter's Garden
28 Dryden Terrace, Short Hills

Please see garden description, hours, and directions under May 11

UNION COUNTY

SUMMIT
Abbey's Acre
14 Edgewood Drive, Summit

This garden has grown over the years, creating pleasing views from the house, the patio, and the pool. We needed a welcoming environment for my eclectic worldwide collection of statuary, including a totem pole from Vancouver named Shameesh (in a ceremony held here by the First Nation's artist and his family) and a Ganesh from India. Privacy is created by mature trees and shrubs, with border gardens consisting of many interesting perennials and annuals.

Hours: 10 a.m. to 4 p.m.

From the west, take Route 24 east to the Summit Avenue exit. Follow the access road along Route 24 to the second traffic light. Turn right onto Hobart Avenue. Take the third left onto Springfield Avenue. Take the first right onto Edgewood Road and your first left onto Edgewood Drive. We are the fourth house on the left.

From the east, take Route 24 west (from I-78 west) to the first Summit exit for Millburn/ Springfield/Summit. In the exit curve, follow the sign to Summit. From the sign, go .9 mile to the blinking yellow light. Turn right (not the very sharp right) onto Springfield Avenue. Go under the railroad bridge and to the top of the hill. Turn left onto Edgewood Road. Make the first right onto Edgewood Drive. Our house is the first driveway on the right. *Please park on the street.*

Proceeds shared with the Reeves-Reed Arboretum

Allen Garden

107 Bellevue Avenue, Summit

In 1994, the owners asked Ann Granbery, A.S.L.A., of New Vernon, New Jersey, to design a small garden for three seasons only: fall, winter, and spring. A flat, square suburban backyard featuring a boggy corner, piles of rocks, and some lovely tall, stately trees was transformed. Two small cottage gardens, five apples espaliered against the garage wall, two rockeries, and an evergreen arch leading into the rear garden provide the view from the house required. Much of the design is the addition of many shrubs to provide spring color, an interesting palette of fall foliage color, and architectural style and exfoliating bark for winter. The borrowed landscape provides excellent privacy and a good backdrop for the important view.

Hours: 10 a.m. to 4 p.m.

From Route 24, take the Summit Avenue exit. Go 1 block and turn right onto Bellevue Avenue. Go around the bend to a brick ranch at #107. *Please park on the street.* Walk down the driveway; the garden is through the evergreen arch in the rear.

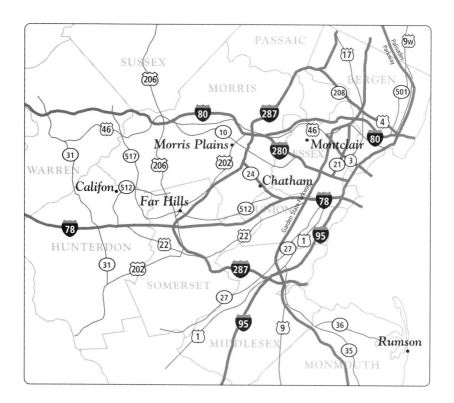

Sunday, June 9

ESSEX COUNTY

MONTCLAIR

Emer Featherstone's Garden

74 Porter Place, Montclair

A hidden garden, very private, 25 years in the making, has been lovingly dug, planted, designed, and weeded by the owner. Flowering shrubs form the backbone of the design (lilacs, crape myrtle, clethra, daphne, and buddleia), complemented by bulbs, hardy perennials, and the occasional annual. Fragrance is a must and the summer lilies are intoxicating. The garden flowers continuously from mid-April to October and species that attract butterflies and birds predominate. Amongst the plantings of old-fashioned moss roses, peonies, astilbes, and forget-me-nots you will find a little pool full of frogs and goldfish, tenanted birdhouses, and a flagstone entryway area festooned with dozens of flower-filled pots.

Hours: 10 a.m. to 4 p.m.

From Garden State Parkway, take Exit 151 to Watchung Avenue west (uphill). Turn left onto Grove Street. Go through 5 traffic lights. The street becomes Elm Street. Make the second right onto Hawthorne. In the fourth block, Hawthorne becomes Porter Place. Number 74 is a red carriage house down a long driveway on the left side of the street.

Proceeds shared with the Van Vleck House & Gardens

HUNTERDON COUNTY

Califon
Frog Pond Farm
26 Beavers Road, Califon

Please see garden description, hours, and directions under May 11

MONMOUTH COUNTY

Rumson
Beliza Ann Furman
8 Woods End Road, Rumson

Over the past nine years, Sam and I have replaced horticultural cliches with our interpretation of a real garden. The focal point is the pond-like swimming pool and waterfall, which are surrounded by several planted areas. In spring, bulbs, azaleas, viburnums, lilacs, astilbes, and rhododendrons stand out. In summer, assorted lilies, spirea, crape myrtle, hydrangea, old roses, and gazillions of perennials fill in the gaps. We are in bloom from February to November. Behind the pool, climbing roses and wisteria standards enhance a columned pergola and seating area. A formal parterre features a stone dining set, standard 'Fairy' roses, and assorted annuals.

Hours: 10 a.m. to 4 p.m.

From Garden State Parkway, take Exit 109. Coming from the north, turn left (east) onto Newman Springs Road, from the south, bear right. Go through 5 traffic lights to the end. Turn right onto Broad Street/Route 35. Go to the next light and turn left onto White Road. Go to the end. Turn left onto Branch Avenue. At the blinking light, turn right onto Rumson Road. Continue straight until you see a sign "Rumson, Settled 1665." The second left is Woods End Road. Our house is the third on the left. *Please park on the street, not in the driveway.*

MORRIS COUNTY

CHATHAM
Jack Lagos
23 Pine Street, Chatham

I have been developing this one-acre property, which backs into a lovely woods, for 25 years. The first garden and island perennial border is now one among many. A 100-year-old barn is backdrop for shade-loving plants and on its sunny sides lies an herb garden and another perennial border. Ten graceful clematis vines climb beautifully designed lattice fencing that defines the dwarf conifer collection. A woodland garden, my latest project, lie beneath a very large white oak and features a natural rock fountain.

Hours: 10 a.m. to 4 p.m.

From Garden State Parkway or New Jersey Turnpike/I-95, take I-78 west to Route 24 west. Take the Chatham exit (immediately after the Short Hills Mall). Follow signs to Route 124 west/Main Street and, at the fifth traffic light, turn left onto Lafayette Avenue. Go all the way to the top of the hill and, when Lafayette Avenue bends to the right, turn right onto Pine Street. Number 23 is the fourth house on the left.

From I-287, exit onto Route 24 east. Continue to The Mall at Short Hills exit. At the bottom of the exit ramp, turn right onto River Road. At the first light, bear right and continue straight (River Road becomes Watching Avenue) to the fifth light. Turn left onto Lafayette Avenue. Proceed as directed above. *Please park on the street.*

MORRIS PLAINS
Watnong Gardens
2379 Watnong Terrace, Morris Plains

Please see May 11 for garden description, hours, and directions.

SOMERSET COUNTY

FAR HILLS
The Hay Honey Farm
130 Stevens Lane, Far Hills

Nestled in a valley with long pasture views, the gardens reflect a diverse range of interests and include an early spring patio garden, a summer-to-fall perennial border, and a wide variety of trees and shrubs. A walk along a stream leads past a wet meadow to a rhododendron glade with year-round interest. There is also a large vegetable and cutting garden.

Hours: 10 a.m. to 4 p.m.

From New Jersey Turnpike/I-95, take I-78 west. Take I-287 north to Exit 22B (or Exit 22 if coming from the north). Stay on Route 206 north. At the fourth traffic light, turn right onto Holland Avenue. At the end, turn left onto Peapack. Turn right onto Willow Avenue. Go 1 mile and turn left onto Branch Road. Follow signs to the garden.

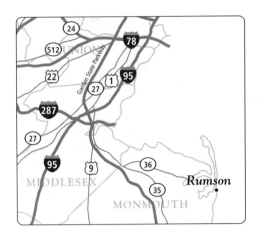

Saturday, June 15
MONMOUTH COUNTY

RUMSON
Linden Hill
138 Bingham Avenue, Rumson

Linden Hill provides a special and unexpected landscape, with numerous garden areas that spread over eight acres. Great specimen trees rise over the level property. No one structure, garden, or style dominates the terrain. The Colonial-style house, built in the early 1890s, is gracefully surrounded by garden beds, impeccably maintained lawns, and arbors of fruit trees. More than 2,500 varieties of flowers, plants, shrubs, and trees infuse this horticulturally rich landscape. Although flowers permeate the entire property, there are ten garden sections that stand out. Reaching beyond traditional forms, Linden Hill provides a horticultural impression that is inventive and pleasurable through an overall effect of cultivated informality.

Hours: 10 a.m. to 4 p.m.

From New Jersey Turnpike/I-95 south, take Exit 11/Garden State Parkway south. At the toll after the Raritan River, stay right on the road marked "Local-All Exits." Take Exit 109/Red Bank, turn left at the traffic light after paying the toll, and follow Newman Springs Road/Route 520 to the end. Turn right onto Broad Street. Turn left at the first light onto White Road. Take White Road to the end. Turn left at the stop sign onto Branch Avenue. Turn right at the blinking light onto Rumson Road. Go about 3.2 miles to the sign for Route 8A. Turn left onto Bingham Avenue. Linden Hill is the third driveway on the left, #138. *Please park in the street, not in the driveway.*

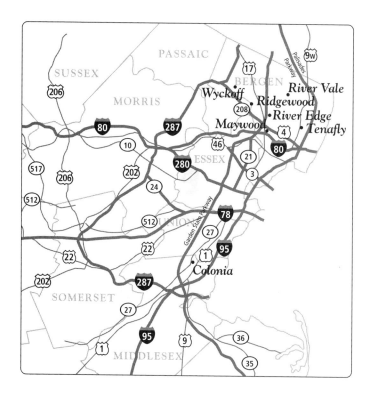

Saturday, June 22

BERGEN COUNTY

Maywood

Dail & Tony's Garden

66 West Magnolia Avenue, Maywood

Ten or so years ago, Tony and I began gardening under the two maple trees that canopy our quite small backyard. Early on, a bluestone path developed, now enticing the visitor beneath a copper arch we created ourselves, alongside another copper piece we built to support tomato plants, beyond to a dwarf weeping crab apple and the rest of the shade beds. The garden has evolved over the years, reflecting our growing fascination with "winter interest," as well as with texture plays both in and out of season. Sedges tuck up to gentians and campanulas, veronica tumbles under a caryopteris. The lavender *Phlox subulata* is later a verdant mat under a lavender callicarpa. Whimsy is all about—an original art piece by Jeanne Wheaton of New Jersey is a focal point in the sun garden, a couple of old candelabrum floor lamps loaded with candles light the way to the wooden rocker hooping a miscanthus. To sit by the three-whiskey barrel water garden, somewhat obscured by mature ficus, schefflera, and draceana houseplants out summering, is to be transported—so small a piece of land, so large the garden.

Hours: 10 a.m. to 4 p.m.

From George Washington Bridge, take Route 4 west to Forest Avenue. Take Forest Avenue north, turn left at the traffic light, and go back over Route 4. The road becomes

Maywood Avenue at Spring Valley Avenue. Continue south for 1 mile and turn right onto West Magnolia Avenue. Ours is the thirteenth house on the left, the second up from the corner of Rampo Avenue.

From Route 208, take Route 4 east to Forest Avenue. Exit to the right and, at the light, turn left. Proceed as directed above. *Please park on the street.*

RIDGEWOOD
The Handley Garden
342 Franklin Turnpike, Ridgewood

John and Sue Handley's garden is set on a one-acre property. The front foundation planting is a mixed border of ornamental trees, shrubs, and flowers and prepares you only somewhat for the beauty of the garden behind the house. A water-and-rock garden is beside the deck. Sunny perennial borders punctuated by garden ornaments extend the length of the path that draws you to the open lawn. Sue Handley has planted a great variety of wonderful plants, some of which may be new to you.

Hours: 10 a.m. to 4 p.m.

From Route 17 south, proceed past Ramsey, Allendale, and Waldwick to the right turn at the Hohokus/Racetrack Road exit. Proceed west for 3 blocks and turn left onto Nagel. Proceed to Franklin Turnpike and turn right. The garden is on the left.

From Route 17 north, go about 4 miles from Route 4 to the Linwood Avenue overpass. Go under the overpass and turn right. Continue to the second traffic light at Pleasant Avenue and turn right. Follow Pleasant Avenue to the end and turn right onto Glen Avenue. Pass the cemetery on the left to a hairpin turn at the beginning of Franklin Turnpike. The Handley Garden is about .75 mile down on Franklin Turnpike, on the left. *Please park on the front lawn.*

Proceeds shared with CAMP-YDP

The Zusy/Ortiz Garden
299 West Ridgewood Avenue, Ridgewood

I have in my garden, a beloved work in progress, plants that lived with me at another Ridgewood home ten years ago. Then we moved to London late one April, and I dug up as many perennials as I could find (having planted many of them and thousands of bulbs the previous fall while nine months pregnant). My mother babysat them at her Kensington, Maryland, home until I moved to Washington, D.C., when we divided the now-bigger plants and I took my share to my new home and then, of course, added more. Three years ago, we moved back to Ridgewood, into an 1870 Italianate Victorian; my perennials came too, the sale contract on our former home stipulating that "the plants do not convey." Many of my flowers are the result of an informal exchange program with gardening friends and I always relish making new ones and adding to my own collection and those of others.

Hours: 10 a.m. to 4 p.m.

From Route 17, take the Ridgewood exit. Follow Ridgewood Avenue directly into the village. Staying on East Ridgewood Avenue, pass the duck pond and go through the commercial area all the way up to the train station. Turn right onto North Broad Street and continue 1 block until you reach Franklin Avenue. Turn left, going under the railroad bridge, and follow the curving road to the traffic light. Turning right, you are now on West Ridgewood Avenue; continue, passing the West Side Presbyterian Church on the left and the Women's Club on the right. Go up the hill to North Murray. Our house, #299, is the only one around that is yellow with white trim and black shutters and stands at the corner of West Ridgewood Avenue and North Murray. (If you go past Ridge School, you've gone too far.)

River Edge
Anthony "Bud" & Virginia Korteweg
800 Summit Avenue, River Edge

Edgecroft is a unique three-acre terraced property laid out in 1910 by Italian artisans, with 100 cararra marble stairs to a swimming pool with a Venetian bridge surrounded by a stone-columned pergola draped in roses, wisteria, and honeysuckle. The property has five garden rooms: a gated brick courtyard entrance with rare *Cryptomeria lubbi*, rhododendrons, azaleas, *Magnolia virginiana*; a centerpiece tiered bronze angel fountain; a Victorian perennial garden with David Austin antique roses and over fifty perennials; a formal garden with crape myrtles, azaleas, a fountain with a copy of Verrochio's fifteenth-century bronze cupid with dolphin; a series of three koi ponds interspersed with nine waterfalls cascading down terraces edged with aged pines, golden larches, flowering cherry trees, dogwoods, *Styrax japonicum*, hydrangeas, wild strawberries, and creeping roses. Look for bronze water statuary, stone benches, and stone statuary throughout the grounds.

Hours: 10 a.m. to 4 p.m.

From George Washington Bridge, take Route 4 west to Route 17 north. Take the Midland Avenue/River Edge exit. Go east about 2 miles to the "T" junction and turn right onto Kinderkamack Road. Travel south to the first traffic light. Turn right onto Lincoln Avenue, up cobblestone hill. The walled property on the right is Edgecroft. Turn right onto Summit Avenue. Edgecroft, #800, is immediately on the right.

From I-80 or Garden State Parkway, get on Route 17 north and proceed as directed above. *Please park along the street and enter through the open gates.*

Proceeds shared with the Beautification of River's Edge

River Vale
Cupid's Garden—Audrey Linstrom Maihack
690 Edward Street, River Vale

With a background of conifers, pines, tall trees, and flowering shrubs, the sun and shade garden at my home is my artistic version of nature's best. It is adorned with rocks, shells, ponds, and driftwood and blended with ground covers, paths, vine-covered trellises, potted tropicals, and bonsai. Spring is color: bulbs, wisteria, azaleas, dogwoods, a weeping cherry, and Scotch broom. Later, iris, peonies, dianthus, roses, and lilacs make way for foxglove and assorted perennials, as well as water plants, daylilies, hostas, ferns, and herbs. Fall color starts the retreat to the potting shed and cedar greenhouse, my winter garden. Outside, under the watchful eye of cupid, hawks and doves, as well as many other birds, frogs, rabbits, chipmunks, "Woody" the chuck, raccoons, and Mr. Skunk all visit the fish in the ponds.

Hours: 10 a.m. to 4 p.m.

From Garden State Parkway north, take Exit 172, the last exit in New Jersey. Turn right onto Grand Avenue eastbound. Pass Kinderkamack Road (railroad tracks) and go over the hill to a "T" (about 3 miles). Turn right onto South Middletown Road, which becomes River Vale Road, for .5 mile to a right on Thurnau Drive (first right after Forcellati Nursery). The first right is Edward Street. Ours is the first house on the right.

From Palisades Interstate Parkway, take Exit 6W. Travel west on Orangeburg Road, to the fourth traffic light and turn left onto Blue Hill Road at the end of the reservoir. Stay on this street 1.4 miles to a stop sign. Turn left onto River Vale Road and go 3 blocks to a right on Thurnau Drive (the first right after Forcellati Nursery) to the first right on Edward Street. Ours is the first house on the right. *Please park on the street.*

TENAFLY
Richard & Ronnie Klein
133 Essex Drive, Tenafly

This is an informal, one-acre plant collector's garden with many rare and unusual flowering shrubs and trees (the garden's primary focus), including collections of magnolias, cercis, styrax, and dogwoods. There are also Japanese maples, fruit trees, and perennial borders in both sun and shade. One third of the garden is a shady woodland and bog area with paths and elevated walks. Garden gates and paths lead the visitor into the next, unseen, part of the garden.

Hours: 10 a.m. to 4 p.m.

From Palisades Interstate Parkway, take Exit 1/Englewood/Palisades Avenue. Circle under the parkway and continue straight to the first traffic light. Turn right onto Route 9W north. Travel north on Route 9W to the fourth light (about 1.6 miles) to East Clinton Avenue. Turn left onto East Clinton, travel 1 short block, and take the next left onto Essex Drive. Go to the second house on the right, #133.

From Tappan Zee Bridge, take the first exit on the right after crossing the bridge, Route 9W south. Follow Route 9W into New Jersey and turn right at East Clinton Avenue. Proceed as directed above.

From I-95/I-80 east (local lanes), exit at Broad Avenue/Englewood. Follow Broad Avenue north until it ends at a light at Palisades Avenue. Turn right onto Palisades Avenue and travel 1 to 2 miles to the second light at Route 9W. Proceed as directed above. *Please park on the street.*

Proceeds shared with Trout Unlimited

Linda Singer
170 Tekening Drive, Tenafly

I designed this romantic garden to include bluestone walks and patios, fieldstone sitting walls, rose-and-vine-covered arbors and trellises, stone ornaments, a swimming pool, and a small vegetable garden enclosed by a white picket fence. There are perennial and mixed borders. A cottage garden is of special interest for a wide variety of flowering shrubs. The greatest challenge is thwarting the legions of moles, voles, field mice, and rabbits that love the garden as much as I do.

Hours: 10 a.m. to 4 p.m.

From Palisades Interstate Parkway, get off at Exit 1/Englewood/Palisades Avenue. Turn right at the first traffic light onto Sylvan Avenue/Route 9W, drive north about 3 miles, and turn left at the light onto East Clinton Avenue. Drive .5 mile and turn right onto Ridge Road. Drive 1 block and turn right onto Berkeley Drive. Drive 1 block and turn left onto Highwood Road. Drive 2 blocks and turn right onto Tekening Drive. The house is the third on the right. A sign with #170 is high on a tree. *Please park on the street.*

Proceeds shared with the Tenafly Nature Center

Tall Trees—Garden of Janet Schulz
16 Colonial Drive, Wyckoff

My creation, Tall Trees, is a wonderful woodland garden featuring shade-loving perennials, bulbs, vines, and shrubs. There is an extensive collection of hostas as well as trough gardens, homemade arbors, and garden statuary. Places to sit have been created so that the garden features can be enjoyed from many areas. Almost all of the plants are labeled. Many of the clematis are growing in other shrubs, which produces an extended season of interest in plants that would have bloomed at another time. An avid plant collector, I am always searching for, and trying to find, plants that may do well in my garden. Plants must be strong to succeed here at Tall Trees, for I do not believe in growing plants that require a lot of spraying or staking.

Hours: 10 a.m. to 4 p.m.

From George Washington Bridge, take Route 4 west to Route 208 north/Oakland, about 7.5 miles to Ewing Avenue. Go down the exit ramp and turn right onto Ewing Avenue. Go to the traffic light and turn right onto Franklin Avenue. Go through 2 lights to the first street on the right, Godwin Drive, and turn right. The first left is Colonial Drive. The garden is at #16 on the right.

From I-287, take Route 208 south. Exit onto Ewing Avenue. Turn left at the stop sign and go to the light. Turn right onto Franklin Avenue. Proceed as directed above.

MIDDLESEX COUNTY
COLONIA
Babbling Brook
335 New Dover Road, Colonia

Babbling Brook is located on 3.5 acres adjacent to the thirteenth hole of the Colonia Country Club. This garden has been in the same family for fifty years. It includes a brook, two ponds, specimen trees, an orchid greenhouse, waterfall with fishpond, perennial borders, wild garden, and indoor and outdoor pools that give this property a uniqueness. All this while sitting majestically on a hill enjoying the expansiveness of the fairways beyond.

Hours: 10 a.m. to 2 p.m.

From Garden State Parkway, take Exit 131. At the end of the exit ramp, make a left onto Route 27 north. Go through the traffic light. Go .25 mile to the overpass. Under the overpass, turn left, go to a stop sign, and turn right onto New Dover Road. Go 1,000 feet. The brick house is on the left, on the golf course. *Please park in the driveway.*

Public Gardens

BERGEN COUNTY

RIDGEWOOD

The James Rose Center

506 East Ridgewood Avenue, Ridgewood (201) 446-6017 www.jamesrosecenter.org

James Rose (1913-1991) was one of the pioneers of applying modern design principles to landscape architecture in the 1930s. Built in 1953, his house and garden were designed to change over time and now reflect more than forty years of evolution at the hands of this creative genius. Stabilization of the house and garden has begun. The property is a unique environment of interwoven garden spaces formed by structure, plants, and water to create a strong fusion between house and garden. In the garden there are scrap metal sculptures and reflecting pools on a floor of fractured bluestone that can only be seen after one has entered the confines of the compound, which seems a world apart from the surrounding suburban landscape.

Hours: April through October, first and third Saturday, 10 a.m. to 4 p.m., by appointment only

From George Washington Bridge, take Route 4 west to Route 17 north. Take Route 17 north to the Ridgewood Avenue/Ridgewood exit. Follow East Ridgewood Avenue towards Ridgewood. The house is on the corner of East Ridgewood Avenue and Southern Parkway.

TENAFLY

Davis Johnson Park & Gardens

137 Engle Street, Tenafly (201) 569-7275

Featuring an award-winning rose garden recognized by the American Rose Society, this 7.5-acre park has many floral beds, paths, and benches. Our gazebo is a favorite place for wedding ceremonies and photos. This former estate has several mature beech trees.

Hours: Year round, daily, dawn to dusk

Admission: free

Take Route 9W to East Clinton Avenue. Go west downhill to the first traffic light (Engle Street). Turn left. The park entrance is on the right, .25 mile from Clinton Avenue.

ESSEX COUNTY

BLOOMFIELD
Oakeside-Bloomfield Cultural Center
240 Belleville Avenue, Bloomfield (973) 429-0960

A three-acre garden near the center of the Township of Bloomfield, Oakeside is on the state and national registers of historic places. The grounds are currently undergoing restoration with assistance from the New Jersey Historic Trust. The Colonial Revival-style mansion was built in 1895. A formal rose garden (1913) and large kitchen garden (1922) were designed by Vitale, Brinckerhoff, and Geiffert. A naturalistic water garden and terrace garden near the solarium date from about 1929.

Hours: Year round, daily, dawn to dusk, except during private events; groups by appointment

Admission: free

From Garden State Parkway south, take Exit 148. Stay straight on J.F.K. Drive to the end, then turn left and make a quick right back onto J.F.K. Drive. At the first traffic light, turn right onto Belleville Avenue. Take the second entrance on the right for parking.

From Garden State Parkway north, take Exit 149. Turn right off the exit ramp onto J.F.K. Drive. Proceed as directed above.

MAPLEWOOD
Durand-Hedden House & Garden
523 Ridgewood Road, Maplewood (973) 763-7712

The house is being restored to reflect the continuum of its life as a farmhouse and residence from the late eighteenth through the mid-twentieth century. The Durand-Hedden House sits on two picturesque acres that include a sloping meadow edged with trees, shrubs, annuals, and perennial beds. The centerpiece is the award-winning educational herb garden maintained by the Maplewood Garden Club. It boasts one of the largest herb collections in the Northeast, with many species and cultivated varieties of thyme, sage, and mint.

Hours: Year round, daily, dawn to dusk

Admission: free

From I-78 west and Route 24 west, take Exit 50B/Millburn/Maplewood. At the top of the exit ramp, turn right onto Vauxhall Road. Continue to the intersection of Millburn Avenue at the third traffic light. Cross Millburn Avenue onto Ridgewood Road. Go 1 mile, past the blinking light. The house is the first on the left after Durand Road and opposite Jefferson School.

MONTCLAIR
Van Vleck House & Gardens
21 Van Vleck Street, Montclair (973) 744-0837 www.vanvleck.org

Begun at the turn of the century, these gardens have been developed by several generations of a family of committed horticulturists. The plan is largely formal, responding to the Mediterranean style of the house. The extensive collection of rhododendrons and azaleas, including several named for family members, is renowned. Also of note are the many mature plant specimens.

Hours: May 1 through October 31, daily, 10 a.m. to 5 p.m., June through October, Thursdays until dusk

Admission: $3 suggested donation

From Garden State Parkway north, take Exit 148/Bloomfield Avenue. Stay in the left lane of the exit ramp through the first traffic light and take the jug-handle under the Garden State Parkway back to Bloomfield Avenue; turn right (west) at the light. Proceed on Bloomfield Avenue for 2.5 miles through Bloomfield, Glen Ridge, and Montclair town centers. Turn right onto North Mountain Avenue (Montclair Art Museum is on the left). Proceed through 1 light (Claremont Avenue) and take the next left onto Van Vleck Street; Van Vleck House & Gardens is on the left.

From Garden State Parkway south, take Exit 148/Bloomfield Avenue. Follow the service road (paralleling the GSP) through 1 stop sign and 2 lights. Turn right (west) at the third light onto Bloomfield Avenue. Proceed as directed above.

From New York City, take the Lincoln Tunnel to Route 3 west. Exit at Grove Street, Montclair. Turn left at the top of the exit ramp onto Grove Street and proceed 3.9 miles to Claremont Avenue. Turn right onto Claremont Avenue and proceed .9 mile to the fifth light.

UPPER MONTCLAIR
The Presby Memorial Iris Garden
474 Upper Mountain Avenue, Upper Montclair (973) 783-5974

The Presby Memorial Iris Gardens is the world's largest display garden of irises, with over 100,000 blooms at peak. The collection of over 2,000 varieties in 29 beds, mostly tall bearded, also contains miniature dwarf bearded, Louisiana, Siberian, Japanese, remontant, and historic irises. A display bed demonstrates the varied landscapes in which irises can grow. Dwarf varieties bloom earlier and some species, such as Japanese and Siberian, bloom through June. Remontants bloom late August through October. The gardens adjoin the Victorian Walther House property, Presby headquarters, and its beautiful surrounding gardens, also open to the public. A small sales area offers iris motif and garden items and rhizomes during the bloom season.

Hours: Tall bearded iris display, May 17 through June 7, dawn to dusk.

Admission: free

Upper Mountain Avenue is bounded by Route 46 on the north, Route 23 to the west, Bloomfield Avenue, Montclair, on the south and is easily reached from Route 3, I-80, I-280, I-287, and the Garden State Parkway. Please call for directions.

MERCER COUNTY

PRINCETON
Historic Morven
55 Stockton Street, Princeton (609) 683-4495 www.historicmorven.org

Home to a signer of the Declaration of Independence and five of New Jersey's governors, the Morven landscape is a composite of 200 years of American history. Once again open to the public, Historic Morven has recently undergone a $2.8 million facelift—the first in a three-phased restoration program. Recent restoration efforts have focused on the gardens, which interpret three distinct periods in Morven's history: a nineteenth-century picturesque entrance lawn, an eighteenth-century horse chestnut walk, and an early twentieth-century Colonial Revival-style garden. These re-created exhibits were designed to depict the changes in horticulture and landscape design in Princeton, New Jersey, and across the nation.

Hours: May through October; call for information about hours and garden tours
Admission: $2 suggested donation
From Somerville Circle, Route 202, and I-287, take Route 206 south for about 17 miles into Princeton. The road (called Bayard Road in Princeton) ends at a traffic light, with Nassau Street (Route 27) to the left and Stockton Street (continuation of Route 206) to the right. Turn right onto Stockton Street. Morven's driveway is the second on the right just past the Princeton Borough Hall and Police Station.

MORRIS COUNTY

BOONTON
The Emilie K. Hammond Wildflower Trail
McCaffrey Lane, Boonton (973) 326-7600

The Dutch word *tourne*, meaning "lookout" or "mountain," aptly describes this 463-acre park of hilly terrain and huge granite boulders. Several mountain trails wind their way through a forest of white oaks, maples, beeches, and hemlocks. A series of niches provides specific microclimates suitable for a wide variety of plant life. There are low, boggy spots and drier upland areas, moist slopes in sun and others in heavy shade, and a fast-flowing brook. Suitable habitats have been found for more than 250 different wildflowers and shrubs native to the eastern United States.

Hours: Year round, daily, 8 a.m. to dusk
Admission: free
From I-80 west, take the Route 46/Denville exit. Take Route 46 east to the Mountain Lakes exit. Turn left onto the Boulevard. Bear left onto Powerville Road. Take the first left onto McCaffrey Lane.

Acorn Hall
68 Morris Avenue, Morristown (973) 267-3465

Acorn Hall, the headquarters of the Morris County Historical Society, is a Victorian Italianate mansion (circa 1853-1860). The gardens have been restored by the Home Garden Club of Morristown to be reflective of the 1853-1888 period. Features include spring-flowering trees, shrubs, and bulbs; more than thirty varieties of authentic Victorian roses; an herb garden and traditional knot garden; and a fern garden.

Hours: Year round, daily, dawn to dusk

Admission: free

From I-287 south, take Exit 37/Route 24 East/Springfield to the first exit (2A) and follow signs to Morristown. Follow Columbia Road to the end traffic light (in front of the Governor Morris Hotel). Turn left at the light into the second driveway on the right.

From I-287 north, take Exit 36A onto Morris Avenue. Take the first right fork onto Columbia Turnpike and make an immediate left at the light. Turn left into the second driveway on the right.

Delbarton
Mendham Road, Morristown (973) 538-3231 www.delbarton.org

Delbarton, the largest estate of Morris County's Gilded Age, was the country home of Luther Kountze, an international banker. Now a private boys' school run by the Benedictine monks of St. Mary's Abbey, the campus occupies more than 380 acres of the original four thousand. A splendid Italian garden with a pergola and statuary flanks the west side of Old Main, the imposing residence built for the Kountze family. Also on the grounds is the striking Abbey Church, designed by Victor Christ-Janer and completed in 1966.

Hours: Year round, weekdays, 9 a.m. to 5 p.m., weekends, 9 a.m. to dusk

Admission: free

From I-287, take Exit 35/Route 124/Madison Avenue. Bear right at the end of the exit ramp onto Route 124 west/South Street. Proceed straight to the Morristown Green. Follow signs for Route 510 west/Washington Street. This becomes Route 24/Mendham Road. Delbarton is on the left, 2.5 miles from the Morristown Green.

MORRIS TOWNSHIP
Frelinghuysen Arboretum
53 East Hanover Avenue, Morris Township (973) 326-7600

The 127-acre Frelinghuysen Arboretum in Morris Township displays a wide range of native and exotic plants in home demonstration gardens of perennials, annuals, plants for shade, ferns, vegetables, and roses. Collections include peonies, dogwoods, crab apples, cherries, and a pinetum. Interpretive materials are available in the Education Center.

Hours: Year round, daily, 8 a.m. to dusk; closed Thanksgiving, Christmas, and New Year's Day

Admission: free

From I-287 north, take Exit 36A. Proceed to Whippany Road. At the second traffic light, turn left onto East Hanover Avenue. The entrance is on the right.

From I-287 south, take Exit 36. Turn right onto Ridgedale Avenue. Turn right at the first light onto East Hanover Avenue. The entrance is on the left.

PASSAIC COUNTY

RINGWOOD
New Jersey State Botanical Garden at Skylands
Morris Road, Ringwood (973) 962-9534 www.njbg.org

This 96-acre Historical Landmark Garden is surrounded by 4,084 acres of woodland with hiking and biking trails. The garden includes a 44-room Tudor-style manor house, generally open on the first Sunday of the month, an arboretum, formal gardens, lilac garden, crab apple allée, water gardens, statuary, wildflower area, rhododendron garden, and heath and heather garden.

Hours: Year round, daily, 8 a.m. to 8 p.m.

Admission: $3

From Route 208 and Skyline Drive, turn right at the end of Skyline Drive onto Route 511. Take the second right onto Sloatsburg Road. Pass the Hewitt School and Carletondale Road. Turn right onto Morris Road; Skylands is 1.5 miles up Morris Road.

From I-287, take Exit 57, then follow the signs to Skyline Drive and proceed as directed above.

From New York State Thruway/I-87 and Route 17, take the thruway to Exit 15A/Route 17, then take Route 17 to Route 72 west, which becomes Sloatsburg Road in New Jersey. Take Sloatsburg Road past Ringwood Manor; Morris Road is on your left and proceed as directed above.

SOMERSET COUNTY

BEDMINSTER
The Upper Raritan Watershed Association
2121 Larger Cross Road, Bedminster (908) 234-1852

The Upper Raritan Watershed Association has established a garden on Fairview Farm Wildlife Preserve to promote the conservation of birds and butterflies, to provide environmental and horticultural education, and to foster an appreciation of nature. The garden offers food, water, protective cover, and a sheltered place for reproduction. A project goal is for visitors and participants to be inspired to add specific plants to their own backyard, creating a habitat for songbirds, hummingbirds, and butterflies.

Hours: Year round, daily, dawn to dusk

Admission: free

From I-287, take the Bedminster exit to Routes 202 and 206 north. Go 5 traffic lights from the exit ramp, bearing left on Route 206 towards Chester. Turn left onto Pottersville Road. Go .8 mile and turn left onto Larger Cross Road. Go .5 mile to URWA's stone pillars on the right.

BERNARDSVILLE
The Cross Estate Garden
Leddell Road, Bernardsville (973) 539-2016 www.nps.gov\morr

Tucked away along the headwaters of the Passaic River, the Cross Estate Gardens go back to the early years of this century when wealthy people built grand country mansions as summer retreats in the "Mountain Colony" located in Bernardsville. Its gardens and buildings provide a glimpse of a lifestyle that is now but a memory.

Hours: Year round, daily, 8 a.m. to 6 p.m.

From I-287 south, take the Harter Road Exit. Turn left at the stop sign onto Harter Road and then left at the stop sign onto Route 202/Mount Kemble Avenue south. Go .9 mile and turn right the traffic light onto Tempe Wick Road and go 2 miles (past the entrance to Jockey Hollow). Turn left onto Leddell Road at the waterfall and go 1.1 miles. Turn left onto the long driveway at the sign "New Jersey Brigade Area—Cross Estate Gardens."

Take I-287 north, to Route 202/North Maple Avenue/Jockey Hollow exit. Turn right at the traffic light onto Route 202 north/Mount Kemble Avenue. Go 1.7 miles and turn left at the traffic light onto Tempe Wick Road. Proceed as directed above.

EAST MILLSTONE
Colonial Park Arboretum, Fragrance & Sensory Garden, Perennial Garden & Rudolf W. van der Goot Rose Garden
156 Mettlers Road, East Millstone (732) 873-2459, TTY (732) 873-0327, or use NJ Relay Service @711

The 144-acre arboretum contains labeled specimens of flowering trees and shrubs, evergreens, and shade trees that grow well in central New Jersey, making this area a valuable resource for homeowners and landscape professionals. The five-acre perennial garden, located next to parking lot F, has as its focal point a gazebo that is surrounded by beds of flowering bulbs, perennials, annuals, trees, and shrubs that provide year-round interest. The Rudolf W. van der

Goot Rose Garden, an accredited All-American Rose Selections display garden, offers a formal display of more than 3,000 roses of 285 varieties from late spring to autumn. Located behind the Rose Garden is the Fragrance & Sensory Garden, designed especially for those with visual impairment or physical handicaps, but available for all to touch, smell, and enjoy. Tours, events, wedding pictures, and ceremonies are by permit only.

Hours: Year round, daily, 8 a.m. to dusk; guided tours can be arranged for groups on weekdays for a small fee

Admission: free, but donations are appreciated

From I-287, take Exit 12. At the end of the exit ramp, turn left onto Weston Canal Road. After 2 miles, turn left before the bridge (do not cross the canal). Continue along Weston Canal Road, which becomes Weston Road. Make the first right onto Mettlers Road. Continue ahead to Colonial Park. The arboretum is the first right (lot F) and second right (lot A). The Perennial Garden is the first right (lot F) and the Rose Garden and Fragrance & Sensory Garden are the second right (lot A).

From Route 206 south, proceed to the Dukes Parkway jug handle (sign says "Manville/Somerville"). Follow Dukes Parkway to the end and turn right onto Main Street. Go through the center of Manville (Route 533) towards Millstone. Turn left onto Route 623/Wilhousky Street. Go over a small bridge and turn right onto Weston Canal Road. Proceed as directed above.

Far Hills
Leonard J. Buck Garden
11 Layton Road, Far Hills (908) 234-2677

The Leonard J. Buck Garden is a nationally known rock garden, developed by its namesake in the 1930s. Designed to be ecologically correct and visually appealing, the garden is as pleasant to walk through as it is to sit in. Buck Garden lies in a woodland stream valley where natural rock outcroppings have been uncovered, providing visual interest as well as planting niches. There are extensive collections of pink and white dogwoods, azaleas, rhododendrons, wildflowers, ferns, alpines, and rock-loving plants. The many outcroppings provide different microclimates and exposures, making his a year-round garden. The garden was presented to the Somerset County Park Commission in 1976.

Hours: March through November, weekdays, 10 a.m. to 4 p.m., Saturday, 10 a.m. to 5 p.m., Sunday, noon to 5 p.m.; December through February, weekdays, 10 a.m. to 4 p.m. Closed on major holidays.

Admission: $1 suggested donation

From I-287 north, take Exit 22B; from I-287 south, take Exit 22. At the end of the exit ramp, take Route 202/206 north, staying right to continue north on 202. Follow the signs to Far Hills and Morristown. At the Far Hills train station, turn right before the tracks onto Liberty Corner/Far Hills Road. Travel .9 mile to Layton Road and turn right. The garden is on the left side.

SUMMIT

Reeves-Reed Arboretum

165 Hobart Avenue, Summit (908) 273-8787 www.reeves-reedarboretum.org

A 12.5-acre former country estate, the Reeves-Reed Arboretum is a national and state historic site and nature conservancy with a focus on horticultural and environmental education for children and adults. It features the newly restored historic 1889 Wisner House. There are azalea, rose, rock, and herb gardens. Thousands of April daffodils are widely naturalized. A double perennial border flowers April through October. Naturalistic areas, a pond, and a glacial kettle provide wildlife habitat.

Hours: Year round, daily, dawn to dusk

Admission: free

From New Jersey Turnpike/I-95, take Exit 14/Newark Airport onto I-78 west. After several miles on I-78 west, take Exit 48/Springfield/Millburn onto Route 24 west. Take the Hobart Avenue exit off Route 24 (Route 124 runs parallel). Go left over the highway and continue straight past the traffic light. Up the hill on the left will be a sign for the arboretum.

WESTFIELD

Mindowaskin Park

11 Kimball Circle, Westfield (908) 233-8110

Mindowaskin Park, in the heart of Westfield, was named for a Lenni-Lenape Indian chief and was established in 1918. In 1994, concerned citizens, The Friends of Mindowaskin Park, raised money to improve the facilities and continue its care. Individuals, corporations, and foundations contributed toward the new Victorian iron lamps, iron and mahogany benches, signage, and various gardens planted with shrubbery, trees, perennials, and annuals. A large lake, fountains, waterways, winding paths, hardwood trees, a bird sanctuary, new playground equipment, flowering gardens, and a large gazebo offer opportunities for walking and watching, ice skating, model boat sailing, performances, art shows, picnics, and relaxation.

Hours: Year round, daily, 7 a.m. to 10 p.m.

Admission: free

From Garden State Parkway, take Exit 137 and head towards Westfield on North Avenue. After 3.1 miles, turn right onto Elmer Street and right again onto East Broad Street. Mindowaskin Park is within 1 block on the left.

NEW YORK

Freckelton Beal gardens, Oneonta.

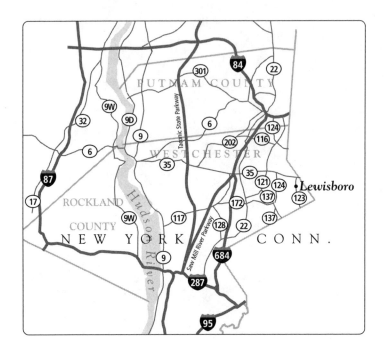

Saturday, April 20

WESTCHESTER COUNTY

LEWISBORO
The White Garden
199 Elmwood Road, Lewisboro

The hardwood forest and native plants provide a "Sacred Grove" setting for the Greek Revival-style house. The gardens, designed by Patrick Chassé, are classically inspired near the house, including a nymphaeum, pergola garden, labyrinth, and theater court. Last year an Oriental garden reached by a bridge was added. More exotic surprises are hidden in separate garden rooms. Sculptures and water features enrich the gardens. In spring, 100,000 daffodils bloom.

Hours: 10 a.m. to 4 p.m.

From Merritt Parkway/Route 15, take Exit 38 and follow Route 123 north through New Canaan to the New York State line. The town of Lewisboro and the village of Vista are the first signs encountered. Go past the Vista Fire Department about .25 mile. Just after the shingled Episcopal church on the right, Route 123 will bear left and Elmwood Road will bear right. Go about another .25 mile just over a hill. At the beginning of a gray stockade fence on the right is the driveway at #199.

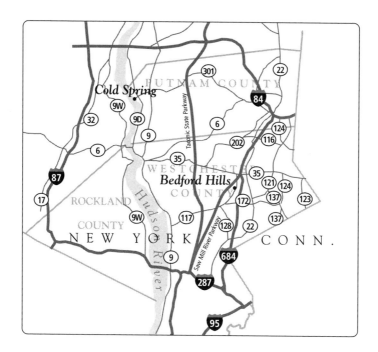

Sunday, April 28

PUTNAM COUNTY

COLD SPRING

Stonecrop Gardens

81 Stone Crop Lane, Cold Spring

Please see the Public Gardens section for garden description, hours, and directions.

WESTCHESTER COUNTY

BEDFORD HILLS

Phillis Warden

531 Bedford Center Road, Bedford Hills

This garden of many facets includes perennial borders, two water gardens, a formal vegetable garden, a wildflower garden, a moss and fern garden, a marsh garden, a tree platform overlooking the marshlands, a woodland walk, and a formal croquet court. The garden extends over seven acres.

Hours: 10 a.m. to 4 p.m.

From Bedford Village, take Route 22 towards Katonah to the intersection at Bedford Cross. The garden is on the left. *Please park at Rippowam School and walk to 531 Bedford Center Road.*

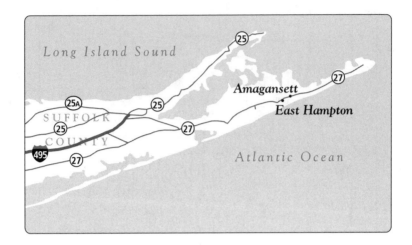

Saturday, May 4

SUFFOLK COUNTY

EAST HAMPTON

Irving & Dianne Benson's Garden

6 Baiting Hollow Road, East Hampton

There are no annuals, no vegetables, and no bedding plants here. This very personal garden is a melange of color coordination, texture variation, and unique plants situated in a chamber-like setting. This environment is host to an assemblage of statuary and other treasures that have been culled from around the world. This continually evolving acre totally engages its gardener twelve months a year. Not only is there the endless search for distinguished and exotic plants, but the rigors of caring for a high-summer tropical garden in Zone 6 are non-stop. There are many gorgeous specimen trees, too.

Hours: 10 a.m. to 2 p.m.

From Montauk Highway/Route 27, pass signs for the Town of East Hampton, then the Village of East Hampton. At the blinking traffic light (Georgica Getty gas station on the left), turn right onto Baiting Hollow Road. The garden is on the second corner on the right. *Please park on adjacent roads and NOT against the direction of traffic (East Hampton police adore giving tickets for that).*

Proceeds shared with the LongHouse Reserve

Mrs. Donald Bruckmann
105 Lily Pond Lane, East Hampton

This seaside location emphasizes traditional and informal plantings of herbaceous borders, woodland, meadow, and rose gardens. Two ponds are surrounded by iris, asters, and other sun-loving plants. An ocean terrace and adjacent dune combine beach vegetation with bright annuals for an interesting contrast of the cultivated and naturalistic.

Hours: 10 a.m. to 2 p.m.

From Montauk Highway/Route 27, proceed to East Hampton. At the traffic light at the head of the pond, turn right onto Ocean Avenue. Take the third right onto Lily Pond Lane. Go .5 mile to the driveway (#105) on the left (oceanside) marked with brick posts and a white gate. *Please park along Lily Pond Lane.*

Margaret Kerr & Robert Richenburg
1006 Springs Fireplace Road, East Hampton

The garden, designed by Kerr, surrounds their house and studios on two acres that extend down to the wetlands of Accabonac Harbor. Kerr's brick rug sculptures, inspired by tribal Middle Eastern carpets, are placed throughout the garden. One, a brick prayer rug, lies in a contemplative glade below the studios. Kerr collects plants grown in the Middle Ages in a courtyard around a fountain and lily pool highlighted with espaliered pear trees. In the spring, drifts of thousands of daffodils bloom in the fields around the house and are left unmowed until late fall. Native grasses and wildflowers make islands of meadow during the summer.

Hours: 10 a.m. to 2 p.m.

From Montauk Highway/Route 27, turn left at the traffic light in East Hampton. Pass the town pond. Continue .9 mile past the next light, taking the immediate left onto North Main Street. Pass the windmill on the right. Go .3 mile, bearing right at the fork onto Springs Fireplace Road. Go 5 miles. The driveway is marked by mailbox #1006. *Please park along Springs Fireplace Road and walk down the dirt road to the second house on the left.*

Proceeds shared with the Horticultural Alliance of the Hamptons

Sunday, May 5

WESTCHESTER COUNTY

MOUNT KISCO

Judy & Michael Steinhardt

433 Croton Lake Road, Mount Kisco

The Steinhardts' love of plants is evident throughout this 55-acre estate. More than 2,000 species of trees, shrubs, and perennials have been incorporated into the gardens. Landscape designer Jerome Rocherolle has created a naturalistic setting with walkways, stream beds, bridges, and ponds where plants can be appreciated and nurtured. There are diverse orchards, a mature perennial bed, and a newly developed alpine and wall garden. Much of the plant material is labeled for the viewer's benefit. Look for extensive use of ferns, moss (a moss bridge), more than 200 cultivars of Japanese maples, and hundreds of varieties of *Hemerocallis*. Wildlife and not-so-wildlife include exotic waterfowl, miniature horses, and more.

Hours: 10 a.m. to 4 p.m.

From Saw Mill River Parkway, take the Kisco Avenue exit (1 exit beyond Mount Kisco). Turn right at the end of the exit ramp and, after a few hundred feet, turn right onto Croton Lake Road. Number 433 is 1.8 miles to the mailbox on the left. *Please park where directed.*

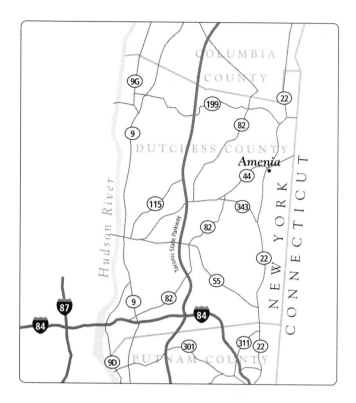

Saturday, May 11

DUTCHESS COUNTY

AMENIA

Broccoli Hall—Maxine Paetro

464 Flint Hill Road, Amenia

Visitors to Broccoli Hall describe this English-style cottage garden as "incredible," "inspirational," "magical"—and they come back again and again. Starting in 1986 with an acre and a half of bare earth, Maxine Paetro collaborated with horticulturist Tim Steinhoff to create a series of enchanting garden rooms. Broccoli Hall offers an apple tunnel, a brick courtyard, a lavish display of spring bulbs blooming with crab apples in May, an extensive border of iris, peonies, and old shrub roses flowering in June, a tree house with long views, and a secret woodland garden. Photos of Broccoli Hall can be seen at www.broccolihall.com.

Hours: 10 a.m. to 4 p.m.

From Route 22 north, go towards Amenia. Go west on Route 44 to Route 83 north/ Smithfield Road. Go 2.5 miles to the dirt road on the right, Flint Hill Road. Turn right. The house (#464) is the first on the left. *Please park on Flint Hill Road. Be careful of ditches.*

Proceeds shared with the Amenia Free Library

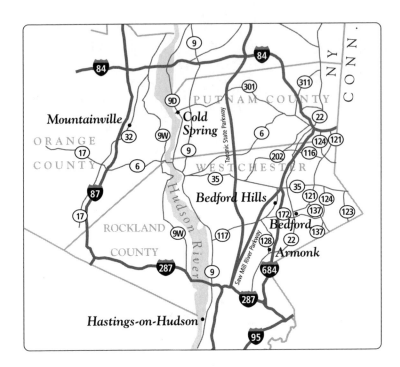

Sunday, May 19

Please also see listings for this date in Connecticut

ORANGE COUNTY

MOUNTAINVILLE
Cedar House—Garden of Margaret Johns & Peter Stern
Otterkill Road at Anders Lane, Mountainville

Mixed perennial borders, "enhanced" meadows, informal flower beds, specimen trees, berries, lilacs, tree peonies, old clipped boxwood, espaliered fruit trees, and a white wisteria-draped pergola are connected by stone walls, trellises, and grass paths. The garden overlooks 200 acres of orchard, farmland, and dogwood-rich forest, as well as the Hudson Highlands to the east and the Moodna Valley to the west.

Hours: 10 a.m. to 6 p.m.

From New York State Thruway/I-87 north, take Exit 16/Harriman/Monroe. Turn right onto Route 32. Travel north for 10 miles to the green metal bridge. Cross the bridge and immediately turn left onto Orrs Mill Road. Take the third left onto Otterkill Road. Follow Otterkill Road .6 mile to Anders Lane (the driveway is on the right). Go up the driveway to the house.

From the Hudson River Valley and Connecticut, travel west on I-84 across the Newburgh-Beacon Bridge. Take Exit 10 south. Travel south on Route 32 for 7 miles. Before you cross the green metal bridge, turn right onto Orrs Mills Road. Proceed as directed above.

Proceeds shared with the Cornwall Garden Club

COLD SPRING

Stonecrop Gardens

81 Stone Crop Lane, Cold Spring

Please see the Public Gardens section for garden description, hours, and directions.

ARMONK

Cobamong Pond

15 Middle Patent Road, Armonk

This is one of the great woodland gardens of the world—a twelve-acre pond is surrounded by twelve acres of naturalistic woodlands with an abundance of flowering shrubs that have been enhanced for almost forty years. It is featured in the book *The Beckoning Path*, with eighty color photographs. The garden has an abundance of rhododendrons, flowering trees, shrubs, and Japanese maples. The garden was also developed to emphasize New England fall color, which is at its most dramatic in October. Cobamong Pond will also be open on October 13th especially for Open Days visitors.

Hours: 10 a.m. to 4 p.m.

From I-684 south, take Exit 4/Route 172. Turn left (east) and continue to the end. Turn right (south) at the Shell gas station onto Route 22. Go 2.2 miles, then turn left onto Middle Patent Road. Take the second driveway on the right, marked by 4 mailboxes. The house, #15, is at the end of a long driveway.

From I-684 north, take Exit 3N and go north on Route 22 for 4 miles, then turn right onto Middle Patent Road and proceed as directed above. *Please park along the driveway near the house.*

Proceeds shared with the Mount Kisco Day Care Center

BEDFORD

Penelope & John Maynard

210 Hook Road, Bedford

We created a garden among rock ledges and oak woods on the steep shoulder of Mount Aspetong. The site is fragmented; thus, the garden areas are designed to flow from one to another, linked together by a ribbon of stone walls. The greatest challenge has been to create some flat, restful spaces. The wide variety of plants must meet one criterion—to prove themselves in dry woodland conditions.

Hours: 10 a.m. to 6 p.m.

From I-684, take Exit 4/Route 172. Turn east onto Route 172. Go 1.5 miles to Route 22. Turn left and drive through Bedford. Just beyond the Bedford Oak Tree, 2.1 miles from Route 172 and Route 22, turn right onto Hook Road. The garden (#210) is almost at the top of the hill. *Please park along the road.*

BEDFORD HILLS
Phillis Warden
531 Bedford Center Road, Bedford Hills

Please see April 28 for garden description, hours, and directions.

HASTINGS-ON-HUDSON
Midge & Dave Riggs
112 Lefurgy Avenue, Hastings-on-Hudson

The house is nestled into a rock ledge with natural outcroppings and niches all planted with choice alpines and rock plants covering one-third acre. A recirculating waterfall built into the ledge is edged with ferns, primroses, creeping phlox, and campanulas planted in the chinks nearby. Alpine plants are nestled in holes drilled into the rocks in the tufa bed. Our great interest in western American plants prompted construction of sand beds to ensure perfect drainage; penstemons, townsendias, acantolimons, oxytropias, and erigoniums grow in them.

Hours: 10 a.m. to 4 p.m.

From Saw Mill River Parkway, turn west onto Farragut Parkway. Go .9 mile to Mount Hope Boulevard. Go up the hill .5 mile to Lefurgy Avenue; turn left. Go to Edgewood and turn right, then turn right onto Sunset Road. *Please park on Sunset Road and walk to the right down the private road.*

Proceeds shared with the North American Rock Garden Society

OSSINING
The Wildflower Island at Teatown Lake Reservation
1600 Spring Valley Road, Ossining

Please see the Public Gardens section for garden description, hours, and directions.

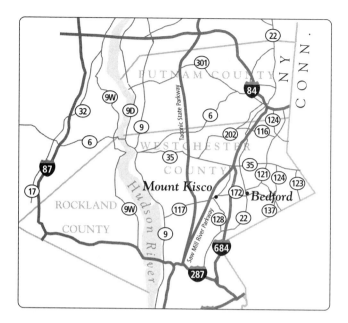

Saturday, May 25
WESTCHESTER COUNTY

BEDFORD
Lulu Farm
614 Croton Lake Road, Bedford

Lulu Farm is a hilltop garden in a park-like setting. This 100-acre property contains ten acres of garden and ninety acres of field and woodland intersected by old stone walls. The gardens are: a dwarf conifer garden, terraces of mixed herbaceous and woody plants, a formal herb garden, a woodland garden walk, a large vegetable garden, and orchards. A pergola, arbors, and antique garden pieces are incorporated throughout the design. The landscape is characterized by diverse plantings of mature trees, some planted when the house was built at the turn of the century. There are many varieties of European beech and a number of unusual Japanese maples. Farm animals, barns, and sheds complete the picture.

Hours: 10 a.m. to 4 p.m.

From Saw Mill River Parkway, take the Kisco Avenue exit (1 exit beyond Mount Kisco). Turn right off the exit ramp, travel a few hundred yards, and turn right onto Croton Lake Road. Lulu Farm is about 1 mile ahead on the right, #614 (mailbox with number is on the left). *Please park on the property as directed.*

Mount Kisco
Rocky Hills—The Gardens of Henriette Suhr

95 *Old Roaring Brook Road, Mount Kisco*

A Project of
The Garden
Conservancy

Rocky Hills is an appropriate name for this property with hills, rocks of all sizes, and a lovely brook. The garden was started by the owner and her late husband over forty years ago. The azalea and rhododendron plantings number in the thousands. There is an extensive tree peony collection, woodland garden, fern garden, wildflower garden, lots of bulbs, and irises of all descriptions. An interesting group of evergreens is planted among rocks. This is a most varied garden in all seasons.

Hours: 2 p.m. to 6 p.m.

From Saw Mill River Parkway, travel north to Exit 33/Reader's Digest Road. At the traffic light, turn left, then make a sharp right onto Old Roaring Brook Road. Rocky Hills, #95, is 1 mile on the right.

From Merritt Parkway/Route 15, travel to I-287 west. Exit I-287 at Saw Mill River Parkway north. Proceed as directed above. *Please park along Old Roaring Brook Road or Lawrence Farms Crossways as directed.*

Proceeds shared with the Friends of Lasdon

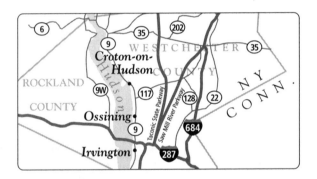

Saturday, June 1
WESTCHESTER COUNTY

Croton-on-Hudson
The Gardens of Dianna & Howard Smith

30 *Fox Run Road, Croton-on-Hudson*

Enter this park-like two-acre property overlooking the Croton Reservoir and follow the paths through undulating woodland gardens to sunny cultivated islands of perennial beds, a hillside grass garden, terraced rock gardens, and a koi pond. Emphasis has been placed on discovering (through trial and error, mostly) and utilizing a huge variety of deer-resistant plants, while creating a haven for birds, frogs, beneficial insects, and other native wild creatures. (Dianna Smith produces a series on gardens and the environment for cable television called SCAPES).

Hours: 10 a.m. to 4 p.m.

From Taconic State Parkway, take the Underhill Road exit towards Croton-on-Hudson. Turn right onto Route 129. Drive 1.9 miles to Fox Run Road, which is the first left after crossing over the reservoir's Hunterbrook Bridge.

From Route 9/9A, take Route 129 3.5 miles through Croton-on-Hudson, past the sign for the town of Cortlandt and Croton Gorge Park towards Yorktown. Fox Run Road is the last street on the right side after passing the "Camp Discovery" mailbox (also on right). *Please park along Fox Run Road or in the cul-de-sac. Enter the path to the gardens from the driveway.*

IRVINGTON

Mary Morrisett

12 Castle Road, Irvington

The garden is set on the grounds of the now-demolished Halsey Castle and has distant views of the Hudson River. Within the remnants of the old estate landscaping, additional paths, steps, walls, and terraces shape the small hilltop property into a series of gardens. The gardens include a lily pond, perennials, roses, vegetables, azaleas and rhododendrons, and various specimen shrubs and trees.

Hours: 10 a.m. to 2 p.m.

From I-287 west, take the right fork leading to New York State Thruway/I-87 north. After joining the thruway, take the first exit (#9). At the end of the exit ramp, turn left onto White Plains Road. At the next intersection (traffic light), turn left onto Broadway/Route 9. Proceed about 2 miles and turn left onto Harriman Road (first light past Main Street). Go up the hill on Harriman and turn right onto Park Road. At the end of Park, turn left onto Palliser Road. Take the first right onto Castle Road. Number 12 is at the end of Castle Road, straight across the circle.

OSSINING

Paul & Sarah Matlock

26 Piping Rock Drive, Ossining

The garden is done in a cottage style on a suburban plot. It is planted for progression of bloom. There are brimming perennial borders, walls, terraces, and walks with numerous thymes and alpines, little secret places, vegetable gardens, and a new trough/gravel garden. We have a collection of old-fashioned daylilies and many old roses, especially climbers. Many unusual plants are started from seed. The garden was built by the owners over twenty years ago and is maintained by them.

Hours: 10 a.m. to 4 p.m.

From I-684 east, take either Route 134 or 133 into the heart of Ossining (134 merges with 133). Turn right onto Route 9. At the far end of town (about 2 miles), turn right onto Piping Rock Drive, which is opposite the green sign for the Cambridge House. The garden is about 5 houses up on the right.

From Route 9 in Tarrytown, proceed north, passing through Ossining. Proceed as directed above.

From Route 9 in Peekskill, proceed on Route 9 south. After passing through Croton, keep right when Route 9A leaves to the left. Go through 1 traffic light and turn left onto Piping Rock Drive, which is opposite the green sign for the Cambridge House. The garden is about 5 houses up on the right.

Proceeds shared with the Taconic Gardeners Club

Friday, June 7

SARATOGA COUNTY

SARATOGA SPRINGS

Brackett House Gardens

605 North Broadway, Saratoga Springs

This is a large city garden designed with the owner and guests in mind. Many details and surprises await all who visit. Blue gates leading to gardens and service areas enhance this visual experience. Visitors who first glimpse the Brackett House Gardens will remember the lush hanging baskets, colorful porch boxes, and formal planting of low hedges, which complement the nineteenth-century house. Formal front gardens lead to a woodland garden, which includes ferns, hostas, and various evergreens and deciduous trees. The path leads to a terraced area in front of the renovated carriage house. Continuing on into the garden south of the carriage house, antique statuary, classic fountains, vine-covered walls, espaliered fruit trees, Alberta spruce, annuals, and perennials all work in harmony to create a distinct English garden. The gardens were designed by Frank Oatman and John Wood of Stones Throw Gardens, Craftsbury, Vermont.

Hours: 11 a.m. to 4 p.m.

Brackett House is located on the corner of Greenfield Avenue and North Broadway. We are 1 block north of the Sheraton Hotel and 4.5 blocks south of Skidmore College.

From the Northway/I-87, take Exit 15 and follow signs towards Saratoga Springs. Once on Route 50, look for a small sign for East Avenue/Skidmore College. Turn right onto East Avenue to the first stop sign. Turn left onto Broadway and go 3 blocks to the corner of Greenfield Avenue and North Broadway. Brackett House is on the corner.

Georgiana Ducas Garden

150 Meadowbrook Road, Saratoga Springs

This garden, at its very best in late spring, is a plant collector's and garden designer's passion. Here you will find pergolas festooned with wisteria and clematis and naturalistic bronze wildlife sculptures. There is a woodland garden with many native treasures, as well as unusual trees and shrubs. Tiered bluestone walls define the sunny, robust perennial beds, which are enhanced by the reflecting lap pool. The garden was designed by the owner and Robin Wolfe, of Wolfe Enterprises, Scotia, New York.

Hours: 11 a.m. to 4 p.m.

From the Northway/I-87, take Exit 14/Union Avenue. Turn left onto Route 9P south/ Union Avenue. The second road on the left is Meadowbrook Road. Turn left and go about 2 miles. Watch for a gray mailbox on the right with "#150." *Please park in the driveway, not on the grass, or on Meadowbrook Road.*

Bruce Solenski

182 Caroline Street, Saratoga Springs

The row of hemlocks serve to create privacy for the Greek Revival-style house (circa 1840). The hedge creates protection for the semi-circle of Madison Snows (earliest blooming rhododendrons). The dogwood, goutweed, pachysandra, and sweet woodruff provide wonderful ground cover under the majestic Norway spruce. Impatiens and browallia are satisfying in this east garden. A short stone path leads to my quiet sitting and reading area. The Concord grapes grow high into the spruce, making a beautiful canopy. My south garden is a sun garden, containing annuals and perennials. The stone wall was added in 1992.

Hours: 11 a.m. to 4 p.m.

From the Northway/I-87, take Exit 14/Union Avenue into Saratoga Springs. Turn right at the third traffic light onto Nelson Avenue. The garden is at the next stop sign. *Please park on the street.*

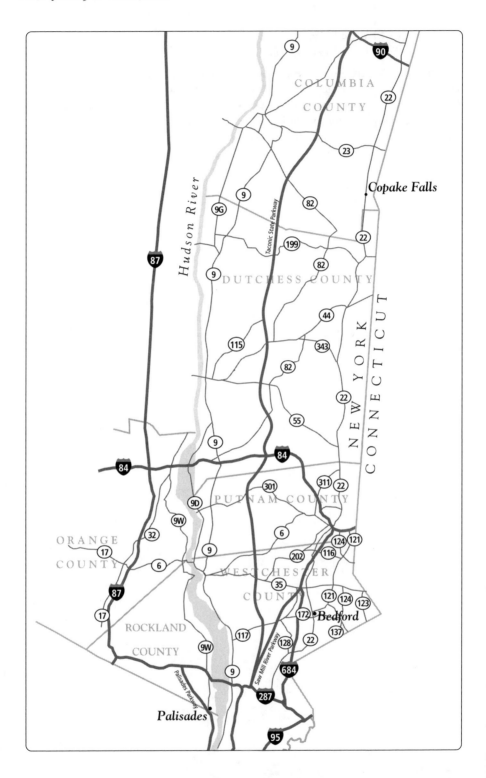

Sunday, June 9

Please also see listings for this date in Connecticut

COLUMBIA COUNTY

Copake Falls
Margaret Roach
Route 344, Copake Falls

This twelve-year-old homemade garden reflects my obsession with plants, particularly those with good foliage or of interest to wildlife (no, not deer!). Sixty species of birds visit. Informal mixed borders, water gardens, paved gardens, and meadow cover this 2.5-acre hillside—a former orchard and pastureland dotted with a simple Victorian farmhouse, barn, and outbuildings, surrounded by the Taconic State Park. Recent collaborations with Glenn Withey and Charles Price of Seattle have smoothed rough edges and helped me begin to realize my hopes for the garden. Expansion continues, with several new areas created in 1999, and more dreams in mind.

Hours: 10 a.m. to 4 p.m.

Off Route 22 (5 miles south of Hillsdale, 13 miles north of Millerton), take Route 343 towards Taconic State Park signs. Bear right after the park and blue deli, over the metal bridge, past the camp. After the High Valley Road intersections on the left, continue right 100 feet more to the barn and house on the left *(park on that side only).*

ROCKLAND COUNTY

Palisades
The Captain John House Garden
20 Washington Spring Road, Snedens Landing, Palisades

A small cottage-style garden with a (too) large diversity of plant material, including petasites, hakonechloa, many yellow-foliaged plants, a rose pergola, and a young triple hedge of peegee hydrangeas, yews, and azaleas. It features interestingly steep topography with a stream that empties into the Hudson River. The garden was featured in the July 1999 issue of *House & Garden* magazine.

Hours: 10 a.m. to 4 p.m.

From Palisades Interstate Parkway, take Exit 4. From the traffic light at the end of the exit ramp, proceed north on Route 9W for about 1 mile. At the first light, where Oak Tree Road and Washington Spring Road cross, turn right onto Washington Spring Road. Follow it down to 2 dead end signs. Bear left. The 3-story white house is at the bottom of the hill on the left. *Please park on the street and enter the garden through the driveway.*

Judy Tomkins Gardens
75 Washington Spring Road, Snedens Landing, Palisades

As a designer, I have become aware of the striking difference in the topography of the land and how important it is for me to learn and observe, depending on where I am, just how the site emerges in its natural perfection—in other words, "the genius of the place"—I feel strongly that gardens should be walked through each day as each day changes and brings delight or sorrow with each of these changes. With this in mind, I am opening three properties that I designed, each different due to the change of land and views. My house is near eighteenth century, looking over the Hudson River. It is nestled by gardens with a garden path approaching the house. The second house is French style, originally the Ferry House, on the Hudson River, with a hidden pool, arbors, and gardens surrounding the house and pool. There is a hillside (old Palisades) with various trees and shade plants. The third house is Victorian, with an apple orchard, wildflower garden, courtyard garden, and cliff side with a small waterfall and a maze of paths leading to different plateaus, all overlooking the Hudson.

Hours: 10 a.m. to 4 p.m.

From Palisades Interstate Parkway, take Exit 4. From the traffic light at the end of the exit ramp, proceed north on Route 9W for about 1 mile. At the first light, where Oak Tree Road and Washington Spring Road cross, turn right onto Washington Spring Road. *Please park at the church on your right and walk down to the house, #75.*

WESTCHESTER COUNTY

Bedford

Ann Catchpole-Howell
448 Long Ridge Road, Bedford

This garden features large perennial borders. It is designed on a central axis with terraces, stone walls, and hidden steps leading to an unusual shrub garden. It was featured in Melanie Fleischmann's *American Border Gardens.* Please come and enjoy a workshop on "Planting a Summer Pot" on June 9 at 11 a.m.

Hours: 10 a.m. to 4 p.m.

From I-684, take Exit 4/Route 172. Take Route 172 east to Route 22. Turn left onto Route 22. In Bedford Village, go right, staying on Route 172 east. Go about .5 mile and turn right at the Mobil gas station onto Route 104/Long Ridge Road (the road to Stamford). Follow 2 miles to the house, #448, on the right. *Please park in the meadow as directed.*

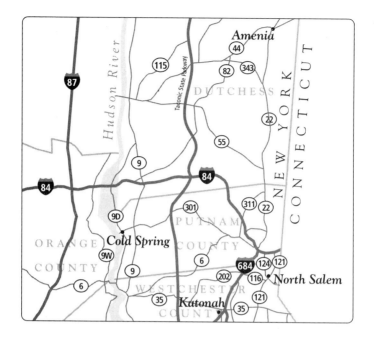

Saturday, June 15

Please also see listings for this date in Connecticut

DUTCHESS COUNTY

AMENIA

Broccoli Hall—Maxine Paetro

464 Flint Hill Road, Amenia

Please see May 11 for garden description, hours, and directions.

PUTNAM COUNTY

Stonecrop Gardens

81 Stone Crop Lane, Cold Spring

Please see the Public Gardens section for description, hours, and directions.

WESTCHESTER COUNTY

KATONAH

Cross River House

129 Maple Avenue, Katonah

Cross River House's gardens are situated on seventeen acres overlooking the Cross River Reservoir in northern Westchester County. The gardens unfold through woodland paths filled with ferns, wildflowers, and large rhododendrons. From the paths, you enter the first of the garden rooms. The hosta or shade garden is surrounded by trellises covered in clematis and wisteria. From the hosta garden, you enter the perennial garden. Low fencing and stonework separate the border from a white azalea allée and a small crescent shade area under the magnolias.

Hours: 10 a.m. to 2 p.m.

From Bedford Village, take Route 22 north out of Bedford approximately 3.3. miles. Maple Avenue is a right turn onto a dirt road at a curved intersection. There are signs for Caramoor at this point, although you don't go towards Caramoor. Once on Maple Avenue, we are .5 mile on the right, #129.

From I-684 north, take Exit 6/Route 35/Cross River/Katonah. Turn right at the end of ramp onto Route 35 east. Take the next right onto Route 22 south. Go 1.8 miles. Turn left at the intersection in the curve onto Maple Avenue (a dirt road), go .5 mile, and the garden is on the right, #129. *Please park along Maple Avenue on either side of the white gates.*

Roxana Robinson—Willow Green Farm
159 North Salem Road, Katonah

A writer's garden, Willow Green Farm has old-fashioned perennial borders, a white garden, an herb/kitchen border, a summer border, a woodland border, meadows, and stone walls on the grounds of a nineteenth-century farmhouse. All organic.

Hours: 10 a.m. to 4 p.m.

From I-684, take Exit 6/Route 35/Cross River/Katonah and go east on Route 35 towards Cross River about 2 miles. Turn left onto North Salem Road (a dirt road). Willow Green Farm, #159, is 1 mile on the right, past Mount Holly Road. *Park along the road.*

Proceeds shared with the Natural Resources Defense Council

NORTH SALEM
Artemis Farm—Carol & Jesse Goldberg
22 Wallace Road, North Salem

Three years ago, I dismantled a barn on our farm and spent this past winter designing a new garden for the site. I created a furnished Victorian garden room featuring many unusual garden antiques that complement our mid-nineteenth-century farmhouse. The property includes a gravel courtyard trough garden, two other large border gardens with a sweeping view of the back pasture, and a kitchen garden. The front of the house, surrounded by maple trees, has primarily shade-loving plants.

Hours: 10 a.m. to 4 p.m.

From I-684, take Exit 7/Purdys. Follow Route 116 east, bearing left where it joins Route 121 north. Travel about 2 miles and turn right onto Route 116 east. Auberge Maxime Restaurant is on this corner. Go .1 mile to Wallace Road and turn left. It is the first house on the left. Note the Artemis Farm sign on the tree. *Please park as directed.*

Proceeds shared with Adopt a Dog

Jane & Bill Bird
6 Spring Hill Road, North Salem

This owner-maintained garden contains one of the nation's largest collections of clematis, including many scarce cultivars not available anywhere in the United States. In addition, the owners have developed new clematis cultivars, which have been planted among the more than 370 clematis featured in the garden. The owner-designed property is sprinkled with multiple garden areas, including a pool garden. It is a plant collector's paradise, featuring about 100 large-flowered dahlias, roughly 100 roses, and hundreds of trumpet, Asiatic, Oriental, and species *Lilium*. Hard-to-find annuals and perennials have been started from seed by the owners, many collected during garden tours in Europe, England, and the United States.

Hours: 10 a.m. to 4 p.m.

From I-684 north, take Exit 8; from I-684 south, take Exit 7. Proceed to the intersection of Routes 22 and 116. From there, proceed east 2.8 miles on Route 116/Titicus Road to Delancy Road on the left. Proceed on Delancy to the first left turn, Spring Hill Road. We are the third house on the left, #6.

From the east, take Route 116 to Delancy on the right. Proceed as directed above.

Lucy Hart Close
June Road, North Salem

Battery Farm has a patterned garden of perennials for shade and sun in a charming early farmhouse setting.

Hours: 10 a.m. to 4 p.m.

From I-684, take Exit 7/Purdys. Take Route 116 east to North Salem. Turn left onto June Road/Old Route 124. Battery Farm is the first driveway on the left.

Page Dickey & Francis Schell
23 Baxter Road, North Salem

At Duck Hill, a series of hedged-in gardens are related to the nineteenth-century farmhouse they surround. They include an herb garden, white garden, and nasturtium garden, described in *Duck Hill Journal, Breaking Ground,* and *Inside Out* by Page Dickey.

Hours: 10 a.m. to 4 p.m.

From I-684, take Exit 7/Purdys. Follow Route 116 east to North Salem. After Route 121 joins Route 116, go .4 mile. At the flagpole, turn left onto Baxter Road. Go to the top of the hill and turn right onto a private road. Duck Hill, #23, is the second house on the left. *Please park along the road.*

Keeler Hill Farm

Keeler Lane, North Salem

Although the land has been farmed since 1731, it is just in the last ten years that gardens have been developed, including the perennial garden, green garden, and white garden. A friendship garden, which provides swimming pool privacy, was planted with friends' castoffs. The vegetable and fruit gardens were placed among the farm buildings. Cutting borders and a lilac walk were added in 1999.

Hours: 10 a.m. to 4 p.m.

From I-684 north, take Exit 7/Purdys. Turn right off the exit ramp onto Route 116 east. Stay on Route 116 east for about 5 miles. Cross over Old Route 124/June Road. Route 116 will join up with Route 121 about 1 mile after the June Road intersection. Bear left at that intersection. About 1 mile up the road, turn right onto Keeler Lane. Continue up Keeler Lane for .5 mile. On the left, you will see 7 yellow barns. Turn in the gate with the sign on the left pillar that reads "Keeler Hill Farm" and "Keeler Homestead" on the right pillar. *Proceed up the driveway to parking.*

Proceeds shared with the North Salem Open Land Foundation

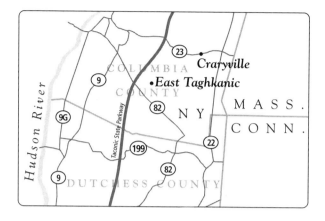

Saturday, June 22

COLUMBIA COUNTY

CRARYVILLE

Susan Anthony & Richard Galef
158 Maiers Road, Craryville

With a view of the Berkshires to the east, the garden has large, exuberant perennial borders, a bog bed with unusual plants and grasses, a flowering shrub border, and pondside beds planted with perennials, evergreens, and specimen trees. A long rock ledge has been exposed and is a backdrop to the lawn and to a large woodland grove that is planted with shade-loving plants and shrubs, a wide variety of small flowering trees, and a number of maple varieties. The grove is terraced with stone walls and crisscrossed with stone paths. Stone walls and terraces also surround the house and a gravel courtyard. And, where there once was a swamp filled with dead trees, a beautiful five-acre naturally landscaped lake has been created.

Hours: 10 a.m. to 4 p.m.

From Taconic State Parkway, exit east at Manor Rock Road. Go 1 mile to the fork and make a right onto Maiers Road. Twenty feet on the left are 5 mailboxes and our driveway with a sign, "158 Maiers Road."

From the junction of Routes 22 and 23 in Hillsdale, proceed west on Route 23 exactly 4 miles to County Route 11/Beauty Award Highway. Go south 2.2 miles to Craryville Road. Make a right and go .8 mile to the fork. Bear right onto Manor Rock Road and proceed 1.5 miles to the Maiers Road fork. Keep left for about 20 feet. Our driveway is just past 5 mailboxes. *Please park on Maiers Road and walk in.*

Proceeds shared with Mothers Voices

Marion & Irwin Kaplan—White Birch Farm
Maiers Road, Craryville

Our twenty-year-old garden contains expansive beds and borders filled with an extensive collection of perennials, American native plants, grasses, and shrubs in a variety of settings, including the banks of a stream, a bog garden bordering a small pond, and several shade gardens. Self-seeding plants, fragrant annuals, herbs, and roses surround the 1840s' farmhouse.

An organic vegetable garden and small orchard sustain us in the summer and the wildflower meadows attract abundant wildlife.

Hours: 10 a.m. to 4 p.m.

From Taconic State Parkway, exit east at Manor Rock Road. Go 1 mile to the fork (intersection with Maiers Road) and bear left. Continue on Manor Rock Road for about 2 miles to a mailbox with a green street sign reading "Manor Rock Road."

From the junction of Routes 22 and 23 in Hillsdale, proceed west on Route 23 exactly 4 miles to County Route 11/Beauty Award Highway. Go south 2.2 miles to Craryville Road. Turn right and go .8 mile to a mailbox at the intersection of Maiers Rock Road. *Please park along the road near the mailbox. Our driveway cannot accommodate cars, but passengers can be dropped off at the entry gates for an easy walk to the garden.*

Proceeds shared with the Columbia Land Conservancy

East Taghkanic
Grant & Alice Platt
41 Tibbet Lane, East Taghkanic

Nestled in the woods at the end of a country lane, this garden takes advantage of a widely varied landscape to create a series of informal gardens that attempt to exploit the beauty of the natural setting. The site contains a series of woodland paths that wander over bridges across a creek and past the remains of old stone walls and natural rock formations. Included in the gardens are sunny herbaceous borders, a rock garden with varied alpine plants, a shade garden, and a park-like hillside garden including a pergola. Out of site but just over a rise is a path that leads to a swimming pond.

Hours: 10 a.m. to 4 p.m.

From Taconic State Parkway north, pass the Route 82 Ancram/Hudson exit and go 1.6 miles. Turn right (east) onto Post Hill Road (coming from the north, turn left). Go .8 mile to a silo at Nostrand Road. Turn left and go .3 mile to Route 27 (no sign). Turn left onto Route 27 and go 1 mile to the Taconic Parkway underpass. Continue for .5 mile to Tibbet Lane. Turn left and *proceed to indicated parking area.*

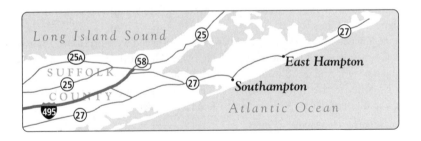

SUFFOLK COUNTY

East Hampton
Irving & Dianne Benson's Garden
6 Baiting Hollow Road, East Hampton

Please see May 4 for garden description, hours, and directions.

Margaret Kerr & Robert Richenburg
1006 Springs Fireplace Road, East Hampton

Please see May 4 for garden description, hours, and directions.

SOUTHAMPTON
Brodsky Garden
251 Murray Place, Southampton

We built our home and garden sixteen years ago on a flat piece of farmland. We carved the land and created a series of rooms punctuated with sculpture. We have several arches with climbers. There is a new (three-year-old) rose garden in a stone-walled area opposite a small reflecting pond and tennis gazebo. Surrounding the swimming pool are borders of mixed perennials with roses and a border of David Austin roses. A striking feature is the newest rose garden with shrub roses climbing up pillars. In recent years, roses have come to rule the garden.

Hours: 10 a.m. to 2 p.m.

Take Route 27 east to Exit 66. Turn left off the exit ramp to the stop sign. Turn left onto Old Montauk Highway. Continue straight and the road becomes Hill Street, Jobs Lane, and Meeting House Lane passing the hospital. At the end, turn right onto Old Town Road. Go to the first left, Wickapogue. Go the third 30 MPH sign to Pheasant Lane (.5 mile). Turn right and go to the end at the fork. Take the left fork to the second house on the right, #251. From Exit 66, it is 8.5 miles to the house.

Kim White & Kurt Wolfgruber—Secret Garden
699 Hill Street, Southampton

Secret Garden is designed and maintained by the owners on weekends. At the middle of the drive, the garden opens to a series of rooms surrounded by evergreens and hedges. An 1866 carriage house sits in the center of the property and is surrounded by perennial island borders filled with flowers. A water garden is at the rear of the house and an herb garden with low boxwood edging lies in front of the living room window. A white garden and perennial beds enclose the pool area. A clipped boxwood path leads to the front door. This is a most varied garden in all seasons.

Hours: 10 a.m. to 4 p.m.

From Route 27, take the Southampton College exit. Turn right 1 block to a stop sign. Turn left onto Montauk Highway, which becomes Hill Street. Look for the blinking traffic light. Go to Lee Avenue on the right side only. The garden is directly across from Lee Avenue. *Please park on Lee Avenue.*

Proceeds shared with the Southampton Fresh Air Home

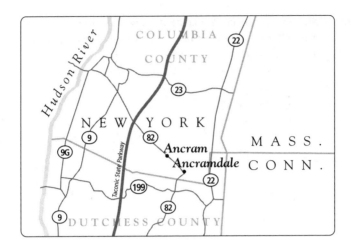

Sunday, June 23

Please also see listings for this date in Connecticut

COLUMBIA COUNTY

ANCRAM
Adams-Westlake
681 Route 7, Ancram

Two writers, garden writer Abby Adams and crime novelist Donald Westlake, authored the various plantings on this former farm in a pastoral Columbia County valley. Perennial borders, a walled swimming pool garden, a cutting/vegetable garden, and an herbary surround the 1835 farmhouse. Paths and strategically placed sitting areas guide a visitor through the landscape to a deep natural ravine, where a spring-fed pond faces a wildflower meadow.

Hours: 10 a.m. to 4 p.m.

From Taconic State Parkway, exit at Jackson Corners; go east on Route 2. At the first "Y," turn left onto Route 7, following the signs for Ancram. At the second "Y," turn left, staying on Route 7. About 7 minutes from the Taconic, the Gallatin Town Hall will be on the left. The garden is next, on the left; look for #681 on a red mailbox. *Please park across the road.*

ANCRAMDALE
Cricket Hill Farm
107 Snyder Road, Ancramdale

An 1844 house and horse farm sit amidst rolling fields with distant views. From the house, with a native fieldstone terrace, an informal kitchen garden of herbs and vegetables flows naturally with the land to the barns and roadside. Lawn, grass paths, and stone walls provide access to fifteen individual beds on five acres. Interesting plant collections include bulbs, perennials, shrubs, evergreens, grasses, herbs, fruits, and vegetables. The gardens, incorporating moss- and lichen-covered rocks, are planned for ease of maintenance, four-season interest, and food and cover for birds. The equestrian center will be open to visitors.

Hours: 10 a.m. to 4 p.m.

From Taconic State Parkway, take the Jackson Corners exit. Turn right at the stop sign. Follow signs to Ancram and Gallatin, going on Route 2 and then Route 7. In Ancram, go straight through the blinking traffic light onto Route 82. Go over a small bridge about 100 yards from the center of town. Go .8 mile to the first left onto Wiltsie Bridge Road; there is a brown house on the corner. Go 1.3 miles to the first right; there is a yellow house on the corner. Go .5 mile to Cricket Hill.

From Route 22, turn onto Route 3 by the Mobil gas station towards Ancramdale. After about 3 miles, passing the Pond restaurant, turn right onto Roche Drive. Go .5 mile to the right fork, then .7 mile to Cricket Farm. *Please park across the road from the house.*

Proceeds shared with the Cricket Hill Academy for Horsemanship, Inc.

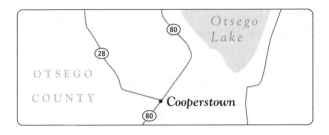

Saturday, June 29

OTSEGO COUNTY

Cooperstown

Fynmere

County Route 33, Cooperstown

This is the ghost of a garden only of interest to garden archaeologists or those interested in Ellen Shipman, who designed it for Mr. & Mrs. James Fenimore Cooper (grandson of the author) in 1912. It was Mrs. Shipman's first commissioned garden and resulted in a long friendship with the Coopers and more garden work in Cooperstown. The property has been long neglected. It was given to the Presbyterian church in 1948, which returned it to the family in 1972, at which time the house was demolished. There will be no charge for visiting this garden, since it is not of horticultural interest, only architectural.

Hours: 2 p.m. to 6 p.m.

The garden is about a .25 mile walk from Heathcote, on Estli Avenue. Please park on Estli Avenue, enter at Heathcote, and follow directions from there.

Heathcote

67 Estli Avenue, Cooperstown

The home of Dr. & Mrs. Henry S. F. Cooper from the 1920s to the late 1980s, this garden was the life's work of Katherine Guy Cooper. Ellen Shipman may have designed the garden house and the layout of the three terraced garden rooms, but the wonderful, highly personal plant selection was all Mrs. Cooper's. It contains magnificent specimen oak trees, large shrubbery, formal borders, waterlily pools, and woodland plantings. Empty for several years after Mrs. Cooper's death, the garden is entering a new life at the hands of garden writer Patricia Thorpe and family.

Hours: 2 p.m. to 6 p.m.

Turn right at Chestnut Street and Main Street and go east on Main Street through town. Cross the Susquehanna River go uphill to the first right turn, marked Estli Avenue. It is the fourth house on the left, a large white house set back behind shrubs and trees. Number 63 appears on the mailbox across from the driveway. *Please park along Estli Avenue and walk up the drive. Elderly or handicapped visitors may drive up.* Admission to this garden includes admission to Fynmere.

Proceeds shared with the Cook Foundation

Frank Kubis

573 Ricetown Road, Cooperstown

A true American cottage garden. Frank has lived on this farm since 1931. His mother originally had a vegetable garden on the present site of the garden and the old fruit trees date from those early days. Hardy roses and old-fashioned perennials gradually won over the vegetables so that today the property is home to more than 250 rose species and varieties, casually mingling with lilies, foxgloves, phlox, and hollyhocks. The garden is a rich and unself-conscious testament to a lifetime of gardening, and a great education on growing roses in an unforgiving climate.

Hours: 10 a.m. to 2 p.m.

Follow directions to Orthwein Garden. Continue up Fish Road for .6 mile to its intersection with Ricetown Road. Turn left onto Ricetown and go .6 mile to the intersection of Ricetown and Ottaway Roads. *Park along the road.* Continue down Ottaway Road to the intersection with Route 33. Turn left onto Route 33 and return to Cooperstown. Turn right onto Route 33 to Cherry Valley and points north.

Proceeds shared with the Cook Foundation

Garden of Loris & Jim Orthwein

230 Fish Road, Cooperstown

The farmhouse porch overlooks a perennial border that meanders 400 feet along the edge of our lake, echoing the natural form of the landscape. Across the water, horticulturist John Gifford has transformed a blackberry and honeysuckle-covered island, once a beaver house, into a perennial and wildflower garden. Accessed by a path around the lake and secret bridge, the woodland side of the island is planted in asters, sedum, iris, hyssop, and *Pontederia cordata*. From the porch, a wild birch, boneset, joe-pye weed, milkweed, woodland ferns, and mallow reflect in the lake. Around the house, hummingbirds, butterflies, and bees enjoy 'Iceberg', 'Saint Cecelia,' and 'Heritage' roses.

Hours: 10 a.m. to 4 p.m.

Drive east on Main Street through Cooperstown, over the river to the first right turn, Estli Avenue. Go up Estli, which ends in a triangle, and bear left onto Route 33 north. Go 3.6 miles to Fish Road on the right. Go .3 mile up Fish Road and look for white fences on the left and #230 on the mailbox. *Please park along the road.*

Proceeds shared with the Cook Foundation

Garden of J. Mason & Rhea Reynolds

50 Lake Street, Cooperstown

The 1804 house had remnants of nineteenth-century planting in meandering island beds, now widened to include a variety of perennials. A muted color plan of rose, pinks, and lavenders is offset by dominant whites, artemisias, and 'Johnson's Blue' geraniums. A comprehensive landscape plan developed by designer Gary Barnum called for a maple grove on the east side of the house, leading to the island beds. On the west side, a curving cobbled path threads through an allée of amelanchier underplanted with hostas and ferns. Fieldstone walls and Federal-style fencing with a rich growth of *Hydrangea petiolaris* surrounds the modern swimming pool.

Hours: 2 p.m. to 6 p.m.

Located at 50 Lake Street, at the intersection of Chestnut and Lake Streets. *Parking may be difficult on the street. Consider parking at the Otesaga Hotel and walking 1 block back.*

Proceeds shared with the Cook Foundation

Riverbrink—Garden of Gail Reid Freehafer & Dr. John Freehafer

7 Main Street, Cooperstown

Riverbrink is a grand Italianate-style house built of pale pink brick in 1853. From the second-story porch one can view its romantic gardens snuggled beside the headwaters of the Susquehanna River. The perennial garden was designed to commemorate the victory of World War I. Recently, the garden has been enclosed to form a triangular shape with three charming seashell paths and a small pool and fountain. Many of the plants in the garden have been collected from old mansions in the area. In the center of the property is the original carriage drive, flanked by sixty magnificent peony bushes leading to the old carriage house and Chinese teahouse.

Hours: 10 a.m. to 2 p.m.

Located at 7 Main Street in the village of Cooperstown. It is the brick house on the right just after the bridge crossing the Susquehanna River.

Proceeds shared with the Cook Foundation

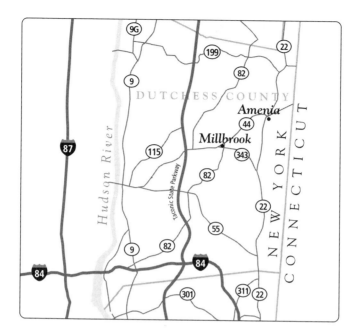

Sunday, June 30
DUTCHESS COUNTY

AMENIA
Jade Hill—Paul Arcario & Don Walker
13 Lake Amenia Road, Amenia

Jade Hill is a hillside stroll garden with a varied collection of exotic plant material. A partial list includes dwarf yellow-stripe bamboo, fountain bamboo, lotus, magnolias, Japanese maples, and conifers. Trees, shrubs, and perennials have been planted to form a tapestry of color and texture. Features include a walk-through bamboo grove and goldfish ponds. An Oriental viewing pavilion cantilevered over a ledge overlooks a gold-themed garden. A new rose garden is in its third year.

Hours: 10 a.m. to 4 p.m.

From the traffic light in Amenia at the intersection of Routes 22, 44, and 343, take Route 44 west. Make the first left after the 55 mph sign onto Lake Amenia Road. A gated driveway is after the fifth house on the right. *Please park on Lake Amenia Road.*

MILLBROOK
Far A-Field
500 Overlook Road, Millbrook

The garden at Far A-Field, most of all, is a collection of ornamental trees planted over the last 25 years in extensive lawns surrounding a small brick Adamesque house built in 1931, which was enlarged in the early 1990s to add a conservatory and library. Protective woods giving the garden privacy and quiet contain another collection of trees, mainly deciduous hardwoods indigenous to Dutchess County. There is a yellow-blossom/silver-foliage garden, a shade garden of large-leaved, mostly white-blossoming plants, a collection of large conifers, a hidden hot colors garden, and the principal border in the garden—a long, curving, richly planted double border in a green/gray/pastel palette accented with wine-colored plants. Up the hill from the front entrance of the house is a small Oriental garden. As you walk back to your car along the drive, there is a small dwarf conifer garden planted in moss beneath native gray birches.

Hours: 10 a.m. to 4 p.m.

From the traffic light at the intersection of Routes 44, 82, and 343 in Millbrook, travel east on Route 343 towards Dover Plains, passing the Millbrook Golf and Tennis Club and a cemetery on the left. Then, almost immediately, turn right onto Altamont Road/Route 96. Follow for just under 2 miles, passing Hoxie Road on the left, then take the next left onto Overlook Road. Proceed up the hill only a short distance to the gravel driveway on the left marked #500. *Please park as posted.*

Proceeds shared with Saint Peter's Episcopal Church

Belinda & Stephen Kaye

658 Deep Hollow Road, Millbrook

This farmhouse garden, designed around a lily pond and Carpenter Gothic-style potting shed, incorporates unusual combinations of annuals, ornamental vegetables, herbs, and perennials. Along the nearby roadside, junipers, native shrubs, grasses, and favorite weeds are naturalized to provide a screen.

Hours: 10 a.m. to 4 p.m.

From Millbrook, take Route 44 east towards Amenia. Continue through Mabbettsville and, about 3 miles beyond, look for Allyn's Restaurant on the right. Take the next right onto Deep Hollow Road. The farm is the first on the left after the church. It is yellow with a yellow barn.

From Amenia, take Route 44 west towards Millbrook, about 5 miles to the hamlet of Lithgow. Turn left onto Deep Hollow Road. *Please park along Deep Hollow Road.*

Proceeds shared with the Wilderstein Preservation

Hamilton & Edith Kean

North Tower Hill Road, Millbrook

Naturalistic landscaping surrounds a wood-and-stone house designed by Edward Knowles in 1982. Shallow-rooted alpine plants on rock ledges are bordered by perennials. A rock path leads through a moist shade garden to two ponds with varied water plants. Distant views are of the Kent Hills.

Hours: noon to 4 p.m

From Millbrook, take Route 44 east towards Amenia. Continue through Mabbettsville and, approximately 3 miles beyond, look for Allyn's Restaurant on the right. Take the next right onto Deep Hollow Road. Take the first right onto North Tower Hill Road. Go 1.7 miles to the top of the hill past the driveway on the left with the mailbox marked "Petersen." The Keans' driveway is the next left. *Please park along North Tower Hill Road.*

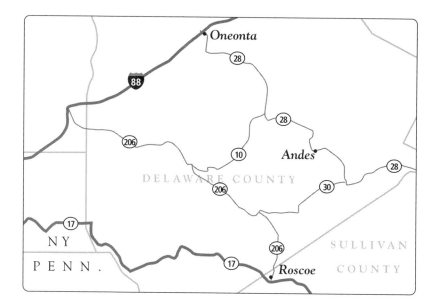

DELAWARE COUNTY

ANDES
Cynthia & Charles Bonnes
265 Bussey Hollow Road, Andes

The garden is centered around a nineteenth-century farmhouse and barn, and consists of a series of spaces defined primarily by native stone walls. The spaces contain formal and informal perennial and shrub borders, a pergola, pool garden, vegetable garden, and an allée of Japanese tree lilacs. The garden is set within a larger, designed landscape of fields, trees, and ponds that open to a view of the Catskill Mountains to the east.

Hours: 10 a.m. to 4 p.m.

From the village of Andes, take Delaware County Route 1/Tremper Kill Road for 5.3 miles to Bussey Hollow Road. Turn right and go for 2.7 miles to the driveway on the right.

From the south, take Route 30 along the Pepacton Reservoir towards Andes. Cross the bridge and turn left. Go 2.7 miles to Bussey Hollow Road. Turn left and go 2.7 miles to the driveway on the right. Cross the cattleguard and *park along the driveway.*

Henry & Judy Jobmann
1811 Bussey Hollow Road, Andes

The garden comprises about five acres of hillside property and has been a work in progress for the past thirty years. One could meander past the vegetable garden to the large perennial garden behind the house with many mature plants and shrubs, or across the lawns sloping down to the stream bordered by bog and water plantings, or stroll along the woodland paths to the gazebo. An abundance of stone has prompted the building of many stone walls.

Hours: 10 a.m. to 4 p.m.

From the village of Andes, take Delaware County Route 1/Tremper Kill Road for 5.3 miles to Bussey Hollow Road. Turn right and go for .9 mile. The house is on the right.

From the south, take Route 30 along the Pepacton Reservoir in the direction of Andes. Cross the bridge and turn left towards Andes. Go 2.7 miles to Bussey Hollow Road. Turn left and continue for .9 mile. The house is on the right. *Please park across the street.*

OTSEGO COUNTY

ONEONTA
Freckelton Beal Gardens
331 Epps Road, Oneonta

Our house, a rebuilt old mill, rises out of the Ouleout Creek and is flanked by a waterfall spilling over a 150-year-old stone dam. The gardens on this many-leveled, rambling property, with terracing and stone walls throughout, include over forty mature varieties of old-fashioned shrub roses, climbers, and ramblers interwoven with clematis, perennials, Japanese peonies, shrubs, and evergreens. As you venture across the stream's footbridge or further away from the main gardens, the grounds give way to native plants with what I call "tuck" planting and selective weeding, to provide a transition to the wild meadow, woods, and pond.

Hours: 10 a.m. to 4 p.m.

From Delhi, take Route 28 west to Meridale. Continue on Route 28 for 4.7 miles; look for a "F&B" sign on the left and turn left onto a dirt road (Epps Road). Go past the first house and drive .25 mile to the end of the road. *Follow the one-way signs to parking.*

From Oneonta, take Route 28 east for approximately 6 miles. Continue on Route 28 past the car lot at North Franklin junction for exactly 3 miles. Look for a "F&B" sign on the right. Turn right onto a dirt road (Epps Road). Go past the first house and drive .25 mile to the end of the road. *Follow one-way signs to the parking area.*

ROSCOE
Berry Brook Farm—Mermer Blakeslee & Eric Hamerstrom
1370 Berry Brook Road, Roscoe

Our garden began twelve years ago on this defunct farm from 1900. It meanders back and forth along a dry stream bed and is headed for the woods, where a large rock has eyed its progress from the start. I love plants both common and rare, so each year a few more paths disappear in the height of summer. The stone work just barely holds together the exuberance, starting from the hand-hewn slates of the terrace interspersed with thyme to the stone walls circling the house. A stone bridge leads to an old milk house where guests stay. Antique trucks have settled in as garden ornaments and our horses grazing in the pastures deliver fertilizer.

Hours: 10 a.m. to 4 p.m.

From Route 17 northwest, take Exit 96. Follow signs to the Beaverkill covered bridge. Go through the bridge and continue (on Berry Brook Road) for 4 miles. Turn right into our driveway, which will be marked.

From Route 17 southeast, take Exit 94. Turn left onto Main Street in Roscoe and left again at the traffic light. Follow Route 206 west out of town for 2.6 miles and turn right onto Beaverkill Road. After 6.6 miles, turn right into our driveway, which will be marked.

From the north, follow Route 30 southwest from Margaretville. Seven miles after crossing the Pepacton Reservoir, turn left onto Holliday Brook Road. In 4 miles, take a sharp left into our driveway, which will be marked. *Please park at the end of the driveway, beyond the horse barn.*

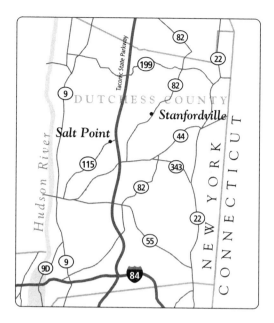

Saturday, July 13

DUTCHESS COUNTY

SALT POINT

Ely Garden

28 Allen Road, Salt Point

Our contemporary gardens have evolved within the original nineteenth-century setting of the house, barn, and woods. These elements are set amid a rolling terrain, which runs down to a five-acre pond surrounded by both native and invasive plants. Between the house and barn we placed large, deep, robust beds, which are bordered by a pergola on one side and an Italianate upper garden on the other. We are now undertaking a new long border leading from the house, parallel to the pond.

Hours: 10 a.m. to 4 p.m.

From the Taconic State Parkway, exit at Salt Point Turnpike. Go west on Salt Point Turnpike/Route 115 for 1.75 miles into the town of Salt Point. Turn right onto County Route 18. Bear right at the fork onto Allen Road. The house is the first on the right. There is a 5-foot-tall white fence along the road in front of the property. *Please enter the south gates and park in the field.*

STANFORDVILLE
Ellen & Eric Petersen
378 Conklin Hill Road, Stanfordville

This is a sunny, sprawling country garden maintained by the owners. We have been adding some structure and shelter over the last few years with rocks, walls, and arbors. I try to blend the garden into its wild surroundings with vigorous native shrubs and perennials, such as bottlebrush buckeye, joe-pye weed, and butterfly weed. I like plants that seed in, such as feverfew, poppies, dill, chamomile, anise hyssop, native bleeding heart, bluebells, columbine, goldenrod, and white wood aster. They provide continuity and act as informal ground covers. I'm planting for winter interest with beautiful bark and conifers; broad-leaved evergreens really struggle on this windy, exposed site. I love yellow, purple, silver, and variegated foliage and any perennial that tops six feet.

Hours: 10 a.m. to 4 p.m.

From Route 82 north, pass the firehouse in Stanfordville. Go 5 miles to Conklin Hill Road and turn right. Continue 2 miles uphill. The house is on the right after a sharp turn. The entrance will be marked. *Please pull into the field on the right.*

Proceeds shared with the American Society of Botanical Artists

Zibby & Jim Tozer
840 Hunns Lake Road, Stanfordville

The gardens at Uplands Farm are surrounded by rolling hills, horse paddocks with grazing miniature horses, Nubian goats, and Belted Galloway cows, grand old trees, and a lush meadow of rye. Among the gardens, the Romantic Garden, with its forget-me-nots, bleeding hearts, blue trapezoidal loveseats by Madison Cox, and blue Moorish gate, is of special interest. The Wedding Folly, built in 1998 for the wedding of Katie Tozer and Jamey Roddy, was inspired by the teahouse at Kykuit and has latticed walls and pagoda lanterns. The images of the fanciful juniper animal topiaries are reflected in the long reflecting pool. Nearby there are large arches, covered with 'William Baffen' roses, which create a path to a meadow. The playhouse has its own charming garden. The main garden is a seventy-foot-long herbaceous border filled with flowering perennials and grasses. Other gardens dot the property.

Hours: 10 a.m. to 2 p.m.

From Taconic State Parkway, take the Millbrook/Poughkeepsie exit. Turn right at the end of the exit ramp onto Route 44. Go about .2 mile. Turn left onto Route 82. Stay on Route 82 for about 8 miles. At the "Y" intersection at Stissing National Bank, bear right onto Route 65. Go 2 miles, passing Hunns Lake on your left. The main house is the third house past the lake on the right. *Please park where indicated.*

Proceeds shared with the Wilderstein Preservation

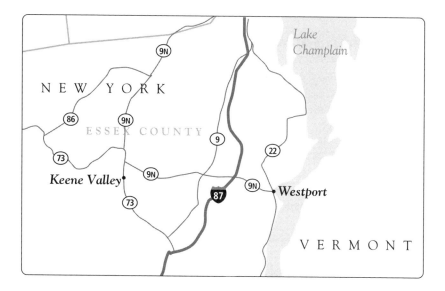

ESSEX COUNTY

KEENE VALLEY

Horse Farm Vegetable Garden
Airport Road, Keene Valley

My gardens, two side-by-side rock-raised vegetable patches, give me such joy and comfort. They are my rich summer painting, one that thrills me because I am partnered with Mother Nature—good earth, the gorgeous backyard, the space in the middle of the mountains. Blessed be the incredible soil (of course, giving credit to the chickens, horses, and sheep). The gardens take on an explosive voluptuousness that is our pleasure to experience and ingest. The sight in the spring of those tiny plants in rows is as thrilling to me as pulling up a baby carrot with its feathery top, bright orange, adorable, covered with root hairs all hanging onto the wonderful soil for dear life.

Hours: 2 p.m. to 6 p.m.

From the Northway/I-87, take Exit 31/Route 9N west through Elizabethtown. From Elizabethtown, turn left onto Route 73 (and from Lake Placid stay on Route 73) and continue over the Ausable River Bridge, passing the Marcy Airfield on the right. Shortly beyond the airfield, there is a long white fence around the horse pasture on the right. Turn right onto a dirt road. Follow the dirt road until it ends at a paved road (Airport Road). Horse Farm Vegetable Garden is directly in front of you.

Woodland Gardens of Mr. & Mrs. Wynant D. Vanderpoel

Interbrook Road, Keene Valley

Overlooking an alpine brook with a scenic mountain view and framed by a stand of towering white pines, the gardens cascade down three levels displaying mixed shrub and perennial beds with annual borders. Flower colors range from blue, purple, white, and deep pink to chartreuse and burgundy shrubs.

Hours: 2 p.m. to 6 p.m.

From the Northway/I-87, take Exit 31/Route 9N west through Elizabethtown to Route 73. Turn left onto Route 73 to Keene Valley, about 3 miles. Turn right onto Adirondack Street (it turns into Interbrook Road) 1 mile. Do not bear off the street. The house is at the third driveway on the left at the "Camp Comfort" sign.

Kenjockety—Phelan-Shapiro

27 Barber Point, Westport

Kenjockety is a complex of Prairie-style stucco-and-banding buildings, built as a summer camp on the shore of Lake Champlain in 1910. The property is approximately nineteen acres of meadows, white cedar forest, and rocky shoreline, as well as a small bay and natural beach. Working with landscape architect Dan Kiley over a number of years to develop a comprehensive plan for the whole property, it is still very much an evolving scheme. There are terraces, pergolas, formal and informal borders, rock gardens, woodland paths, and a large sculpture court.

Hours: 2 p.m. to 6 p.m.

From Northway/I-87, take 9N east to the town of Westport. Travel south on Route 22 towards Port Henry. About 1 mile from downtown Westport, make your first left onto Camp Dudley Road. Take the second left off of Dudley Road. This is Barber Road. Continue on Barber Road to the end. *You may park opposite Barber Point lighthouse* and enter the meadow to start your tour with the formal beds and wisteria pergola *or you may continue through the stone gates and park in the courtyard of the first building you come to* and begin your tour with the sculpture court and woodland gardens and down to the house.

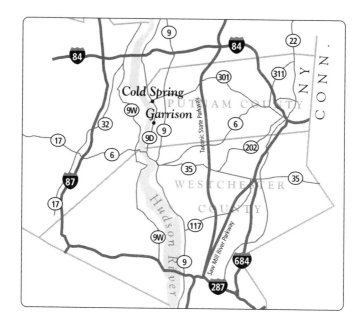

PUTNAM COUNTY

Cold Spring

Stonecrop Gardens
81 Stone Crop Lane, Cold Spring

Please see Public Gardens section for description, hours, and directions.

Garrison

Manitoga/The Russel Wright Design Center
589 Route 9D, Garrison

Please see Public Gardens section for description, hours, and directions.

Ross Gardens
43 Snake Hill Road (Travis Corners), Garrison

This garden is a series of vignettes that flow into each other on five acres overlooking the Hudson River. The gardens are designed and maintained by the owner, Arthur Ross, and include a water garden, a moon (white) garden, a meditation garden, a rock garden, interesting daylilies, a fern garden, a shrub garden, cutting gardens, and garden sculptures, along with a waterfall. Garden paths give easy access to many unusual flowers.

Hours: 10 a.m. to 4 p.m.

Take Route 9 to the Garrison Golf Course. Turn west onto Snake Hill Road. The garden is .25 mile on the left. *Parking is available for 30 cars at any one time.*

Proceeds shared with the Philipstown Garden Club

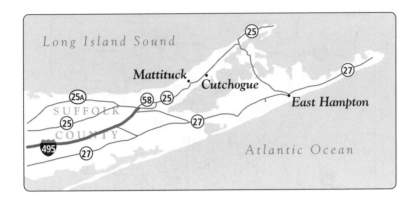

SUFFOLK COUNTY

CUTCHOGUE
Manfred & Roberta Lee
Oregon Road, Cutchogue

Located in the village of Cutchogue, these 2.5 acres of gardens complement the Victorian house and outbuildings. Four large tulip trees punctuate the front lawn. Deep perennial gardens surround the property. Mature azaleas, rhododendrons, roses, hydrangeas, and lilacs are spread throughout the garden. There are unusual conifers and Japanese maples as well as golden chain trees.

Hours: 10 a.m. to 4 p.m.

From Long Island Expressway/I-495, take Exit 73/Route 58. Take Route 58 to Route 25. Go through Mattituck past Love Lane to Wickham Avenue. Turn left onto Wickham Avenue and go past the railroad tracks and traffic light. Stay straight on Wickham Avenue and it will turn into Grand Avenue. Take Grand Avenue about .25 mile to East Mill Road. Turn right onto East Mill Road, keeping to the left, and this will turn into Oregon Road. *Look for signs for parking.*

Alice & Charles Levien's Garden
Antler Lane, Cutchogue

This garden is designed for living—children, grandchildren, guests, frequent outdoor parties. A two-acre mixed border and woodland garden have been planted to provide year-round privacy, continuous blooms in season, many-faceted views, and tranquility during winter. Multi-level decks with a variety of container plantings serve the main house, guest houses, elevated gazebo and pool, and children's playhouse. Occasional saltwater flooding from Peconic Bay Creek made the swimming pool, fishpond, lotus pond, and lawn areas a creative challenge for the designer, Alice Levien.

Hours: 10 a.m. to 2 p.m.

Traveling east on Route 25, turn right at the second traffic light in Cutchogue onto Eugene's Road. Turn right at Beebe Road. Bear right at the fork in the road; Antler Lane is the first street on the right. Look for a hemlock hedge. *Please park along the road.*

Proceeds shared with the Horticultural Alliance of the Hamptons

East Hampton
Ina Garten
23 Buell Lane, East Hampton

This garden, designed by Edwina von Gal, is arranged in squares like a kitchen garden, but is planted with perennials, annuals, roses, vegetables, and herbs. It includes a crab apple orchard and rose and hydrangea gardens and is designed to feel like a traditional East Hampton garden.

Hours: noon to 4 p.m.

From the pond in East Hampton, go north on Route 114 towards Sag Harbor. This is called Buell Lane. The house is the third on the left, #23, past the field. *Please park on the street.*

Bob & Mimi Schwarz
8 Lilla Lane, East Hampton

An explosion of color! The rainbow daylily garden is a sight to see in mid-July. More than 600 named varieties of daylilies are grown in undulating herbaceous borders, backed by cedars, hemlocks, and masses of rhododendrons. More than 5,000 of our own seedlings bloom in the seedling patch. There is also an ornamental grass garden with clumps of miscanthus, panicum, and other grasses. The entire garden has inviting benches and shade.

Hours: noon to 4 p.m.

From Montauk Highway/Route 27, go to East Hampton. Pass the movie theater and continue to the traffic light. Turn left after the light, going under the railroad bridge, leaving the windmill on the right. Continue .5 mile, bearing right at the fork, onto Springs/County Road 41. Go 3 miles and turn right onto Hildreth Place. At the end, turn left onto Accabonac. Go .25 mile and turn right onto Lilla Lane. The house (#8) is 200 yards down on the right. *Please park on the street.*

Mattituck
Maurice Isaac & Ellen Coster Isaac
4835 Oregon Road, Mattituck

This early 1900s' country farmhouse has been designed with two major borders incorporating extensive plantings of unusual combinations of bulbs, perennials, trees, shrubs, and annuals. A pond well-stocked with koi and water plants adds a beautiful and soothing touch. A path leads to a swimming pool and plantings, as well as an old restored barn adjacent to an arbor planted with wisteria, clematis, and several vines offering tranquility, shade, and a view of the extensive nearby farm fields.

Hours: 10 a.m. to 4 p.m.

From Long Island Expressway/I-495, take Exit 73/Route 58. Take Route 58 to Route 25. Go through Mattituck past Love Lane to Wickham Avenue. Turn left onto Wickham Avenue and go past the railroad tracks and traffic light. Stay straight on Wickham Avenue and it will turn into Grand Avenue. Take Grand Avenue about .25 mile to East Mill Road. Turn right onto East Mill, keeping to the left, and this will turn into Oregon Road. *Look for signs for parking.*

Dennis Schrader & Bill Smith
1200 East Mill Road, Mattituck

Set in the heart of the North Fork wineries, the two-plus-acre garden surrounds a restored 1850 farmhouse. The gardens are encircled by fourteen acres of fields. The decks, porches, and terraces are filled with container plantings. There are many perennial and mixed shrub borders, vegetable, herb, and dwarf fruit tree plantings, a formal knot garden, and a woodland shade area. The garden has rustic arbors, trellises, stone walls, a garden pavilion, many sitting areas, and a natural clay pond with a stream and bridge. There are other ponds for waterlilies and papyrus. Many of the plantings contain tropicals, subtropicals, tender perennials, and annuals. Dennis is coauthor of the book *Hot Plants for Cool Climates: Gardening with Tropical Plants in Temperate Zones.*

Hours: 10 a.m. to 4 p.m.

From Long Island Expressway/I-495, take Exit 73/Route 58. Take Route 58 to Route 25. Go through the town of Mattituck past Love Lane to Wickham Avenue. Turn left onto Wickham and go past the railroad tracks and traffic light. Stay straight on Wickham and it will turn into Grand Avenue. Take Grand Avenue about .25 mile to East Mill Road. Turn left onto East Mill and look for #1200. *Please park along the street.*

Proceeds shared with the Horticultural Alliance of the Hamptons

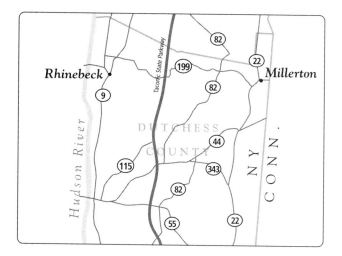

Sunday, July 14

Please also see listings for this date in Connecticut

COLUMBIA COUNTY

MILLERTON
Helen Bodian's Garden
Carson Road, Millerton

In these four gardens, connected by grass paths, we try to use unusual plant varieties. First, along the north side of the house is a large rock garden sheltering small perennials and alpine plants. From there, a path leads to an ornamental vegetable garden also containing cutting flowers and herbs. Across the road are shrub borders and a square garden composed mainly of summer perennials. And next to those is a walled, late summer garden planted with hot-colored annuals and tropicals. Growing in pots set on top of its walls is a comprehensive collection of tender salvias.

Hours: noon to 4 p.m.

From Taconic State Parkway, take the Route 44/Millbrook exit. Turn right towards Millbrook and stay on Route 44 for less than a mile. The first real left turn is Route 82 north. Turn left onto Route 82 and continue north for about half an hour until you reach the traffic light in Pine Plains. Turn right onto Route 199 east. Continue to Route 22. Make a left onto Route 22 north and go straight through the light in Millerton (intersection of Routes 22 and 44). Continue on Route 22 for 4 more miles. On the right, you will see a sign for Columbia County. On the left will be Carson Road. Turn onto Carson Road and go uphill for 1 mile. On the left are a tennis court and metal barn. On the right is a white farmhouse with a modern addition. *Please park along the road or in the field next to the barn.*

DUTCHESS COUNTY

RHINEBECK

Cedar Heights Orchard—William & Arvia Morris

8 Crosby Lane, Rhinebeck

The garden has mixed borders for sun and shade, a pergola with many pots and vines, and a large vegetable garden near the house. Mowed paths through the fields head towards two ponds that are extensively planted. We have made a large wild garden in the woods. There are various structures to provide focus and rest along the way. The orchard hillside faces west to views of the Catskills.

Hours: 10 a.m. to 4 p.m.

From Taconic State Parkway, take the Rhinebeck/Red Hook exit and follow Route 199 west to the traffic light (about 4 miles). Take Route 308 straight for 2 miles to Cedar Heights Road on the right. Turn right and take the second right onto Crosby Lane. Take Crosby Lane all the way to the dead end and into Cedar Heights Orchard. *Please park in the barnyard and in marked areas.*

Amy Goldman

313 Mountain View Road, Rhinebeck

Maps dated 1734 for the partitioning of the Great Nine Partners Patent label this property as "bad" agricultural land. The landscape is wooded overall, with a scattering of open meadows. Situated on a large pond is the Abraham Traver house, a late eighteenth-century farmhouse with an irresistible presence. Improvements to the landscape include a terraced garden and pergola, an Alitex greenhouse, an Adirondack-style lean-to with views of the Catskills, and two large gardens featuring heirloom vegetables.

Hours: 10 a.m. to 2 p.m.

From Taconic State Parkway, take the Bull's Head Road exit heading west towards Rhinebeck. Go 4.2 miles on Bull's Head (also known as Slate Quarry Road or County Route 19) until you see Mountain View Road on your left. Turn left and go 1.5 miles until you see 1,000 feet of split-rail fence on your left and mailbox #313. Turn left into the driveway and go past the red buildings .5 mile to the house.

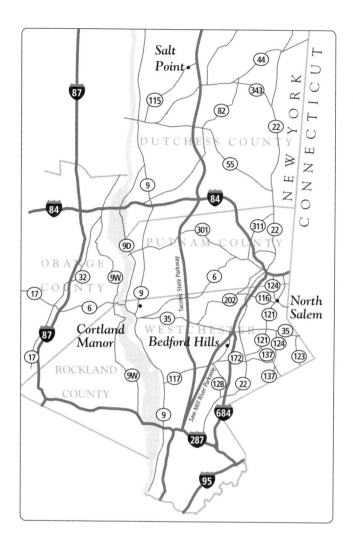

Sunday, July 21

Please also see listings for this date in Connecticut

DUTCHESS COUNTY

SALT POINT
Ely Garden
28 Allen Road, Salt Point

Please see July 13 for garden description, hours, and directions.

WESTCHESTER COUNTY

BEDFORD HILLS
Laura Fisher—Wildflower Farm
44 Broad Brook Road, Bedford Hills

The gardens at Wildflower Farm have recently been laid out to connect the large stone house, built in 1906, with the property's mature trees and open spaces. The new plantings include a Japanese-inspired azalea garden, the intimate studio flower garden, a formal boxwood parterre, and the grand staircase leading to a poolside belvedere and plantings. These are all linked by large open fields, bordered by woodlands and a series of hedges.

Hours: 10 a.m. to 2 p.m.

From I-684, take Exit 4/Route 172. Turn west onto Route 172 (towards Mount Kisco). Go about 1 mile to West Patent Road and turn right (this is the street just after the school crossing sign). Go about 1.5 miles to the second stop sign and turn right onto Broad Brook Road. Wildflower Farm is .2 mile on the left, the second driveway on the left after turning onto Broad Brook Road. *Please park on the road.*

Phillis Warden
531 Bedford Center Road, Bedford Hills

Please see April 28 for garden description, hours, and directions.

CORTLANDT MANOR
Vivian & Ed Merrin
2547 Maple Avenue, Cortlandt Manor

Overlooking a small lake, this garden has unfolded over a rocky wooded site over the last fifteen years, under the guidance of designer Patrick Chassé. New additions include a large variety of azaleas, a tempered glass-enclosed lookout over the lake, and a wooden lotus bridge for perfect lotus viewing on a private pond. Mixed borders line garden rooms that flow among the landforms. Native plants form the framework for a collection that embraces many unusual and rare plants, as well as a large tree peony garden. Several water gardens enhance the site, and greenhouses and a formal kitchen garden provide additional plants, both ornamental and edible. A new parking and entrance garden has been planted. This garden was featured in *House & Garden's* 100th anniversary issue, October 2001.

Hours: 10 a.m. to 2 p.m.

From Taconic State Parkway, exit at Route 202. Turn left (west) towards Peekskill. Go 2.5 miles, then turn left at the traffic light onto Croton Avenue, just past the Cortland Farm Market. Go 1.2 miles to the blinking light/stop sign and turn right onto Furnace Dock Road. Go .8 mile to the blinking light/stop sign, and turn left onto Maple Avenue. Go .9 mile to the private road on the right. Go .2 mile to #2547 on the left. *Please park at house.*

NORTH SALEM
Jane & Bill Bird
6 Spring Hill Road, North Salem

Please see June 15 for garden description, hours, and directions.

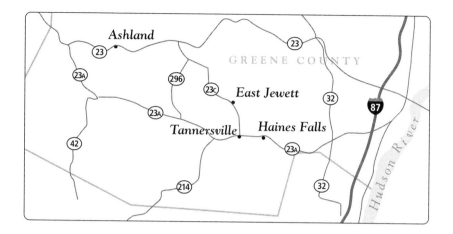

Saturday, July 27
GREENE COUNTY

ASHLAND
Frog Pond Gardens
Pondview Road, Ashland

Our gardens, located in the beautiful northern Catskills, are the results of ten years of taming the one-plus-acre mountainside. Most beds are raised, utilizing tons of local fieldstone and bluestone. Flagstone and gravel paths connect all planting areas. Perennial and annual beds, rock and woodland gardens, as well as many unique flower-filled containers are represented. A large dwarf conifer planting surrounds the "Frog Pond." Come and see the "before" pictures documenting the transition from "lunar landscape" to lush gardens!

Hours: 10:30 a.m. to 4 p.m.

From New York State Thruway/I-87, take Exit 21/Catskill to Route 23 west. Continue on Route 23 for about 22 miles to Windham. Remain on Route 23 to Ashland, continue through the town, and watch for a tractor repair business on the right. About 2 miles past this, you will see a sign for Pondview Road as well as Frog Pond Gardens on the right. Take the dirt road to the top (cul-de-sac). The gardens are located up the only drive off the cul-de-sac. *Please park at the top of the driveway or on the cul-de-sac.*

Proceeds shared with the Mountain Top Arboretum

EAST JEWETT
Daisy & Tom Wenzell's Valley Farm
Alfred O'Bryan Road, East Jewett

Our garden surrounds a farmhouse built in the 1850s and one of the earliest dwellings constructed in what was then the Catskill Wilderness. The views recall the more intimate paintings of the Hudson River School. Most beds host various aconitum, astilbes, campanulas, cimicifugas, delphiniums, thalictrum, phlox, and other perennials that do well at this altitude of over 2,000 feet. Some annuals have been interspersed. There is also a small shade garden and two vegetable gardens, one of which is often ravaged by an indefatigable woodchuck. Two ponds, stretches of ferns, and plantings of indigenous trees and shrubs augment the landscape.

Hours: 10:30 a.m. to 4 p.m.

Take Route 23A west. At Tannersville, turn right at the only traffic light and proceed north on Route 23C. In about 2 miles, you will pass the Mountain Top Arboretum on the right. Continue on Route 23C down a steep hill for another 1.5 miles, passing through the hamlet of East Jewett. Immediately afterwards, turn right onto Alfred O'Bryan Road. In another .3 mile, you reach Valley Farm. *Please park either in front or in back of the house.*

Proceeds shared with the Mountain Top Arboretum

HAINES FALLS
Dunn's Moss Garden
T59 Twilight Park, Haines Falls

Ours is a mountainside moss garden set in a glacial rockfall. A stream bed lined with mountain laurel runs through it. The bordering rock wall is a combination of glacial "pebble rocks" and stones dredged from a local creek. We have accented the rock formation with hostas, astilbes, and daylilies and have used ferns, wildflowers, sedum, a small assortment of other perennials, and a carpet of moss to produce a magically restful space.

Hours: 10:30 a.m. to 4 p.m.

From the east (Palenville), drive west on Route 23A up the mountain to the crest of the hill. Just as the road flattens out, you will see a pair of stone pillars on the left and the "Twilight" sign. (If you pass the Mountain Top Historical Society property on the right, you have gone too far.) Enter Twilight Park and follow the drive to the gatehouse, where you will need to identify yourself. Cross the bridge and bear right up the hill to a dead end. Turn left and follow the road to the next fork in the road. Ours is the brown house on the right at the fork.

From the west (Tannersville), drive east on Route 23A through Haines Falls until you see the Mountain Top Historical Society property on the left. Twilight Park is about 500 feet farther on the right. Turn in at the stone pillars and proceed as directed above. *Please park on the left across from the house or as directed.*

Proceeds shared with the Mountain Top Arboretum

Santa Cruz—Skip & Anne Pratt's Garden
Twilight Park, Haines Falls

This garden overlooks the Kaaterskill Clove, immortalized by the Hudson River artists in the nineteenth century. The house, the former Santa Cruz Inn, was built in 1893 and sits at an elevation of 2,118 feet. The garden has been built, over the past 25 years, in the spaces opened up when the owners dismantled about one half of the former inn. Natural rock formations have lent themselves to using local bluestone to create terraces, steps, and walls for the perennial beds throughout. The lower garden on the south side, although Zone 3 to 4, is protected sufficiently, so that lavender, thymes, sedums, campanula, and scabiosa have reseeded themselves throughout the stone. In the upper garden, tall grasses, rugosa roses, and many other perennials line the pathway leading to a secluded stone bench. This garden is full of monarch butterflies, which arrive at the end of July as bright green caterpillars and spend a week eating parsley before they emerge in all their magnificence. The north side of the garden, with filtered light, has a wide stone path leading from a nineteenth-century gazebo past a wide bed of hosta, rhododendron, epimedium, lily-of-the-valley, goatsbeard, and hemerocallis. There is a covered bridge leading onto a covered porch, where one can not only look down over the gardens, but look out over Kaaterskill Clove to the Hudson Valley and the Berkshires beyond to glimpse the artistic vision that drew the Hudson River School of artists to the area. A full-size copy of an Asher B. Durand painting of the view from this area of the Clove (the original painting hangs in the Century Club in New York City) may be seen in the inn's "social exchange" off the porch.

Hours: 10:30 a.m. to 4 p.m.

From New York State Thruway/I-87, take Exit 20/Saugerties. Follow the signs towards Hunter and Palenville. Take Route 32 north to Route 23A (about 8 miles). Follow Route 23A through Palenville. The road climbs up through the Kaaterskill Clove. As you approach the hamlet of Haines Falls, there are 2 stone pillars on the left with a sign to Twilight Park. There is a gatehouse and there will be instructions to Santa Cruz at that location. If you reach the hamlet of Haines Falls, you have gone too far. At the Twilight Park gatehouse you will be driving over the actual Haines Falls waterfall.

Proceeds shared with the Mountain Top Arboretum

TANNERSVILLE

McCaffrey Garden
40 Parker Road, Onteora Park, Tannersville

The garden was designed in the 1920s by Harold A. Caparn, a well-known landscape architect whose works included the grounds of the House of Representatives Office Building in Washington, D.C., and many features of the Brooklyn Botanic Garden. There is a walled garden with perennial borders, a small pool, and an arbor of arctic kiwi, Himalayan roses, and clematis. Flanking the main house and guest cottage are park-like lawns with stone walks, seats with views of the Catskills, and sculpture bordered by old rhododendrons, mountain laurels, peonies, and hydrangeas. The house was originally constructed by Candace Wheeler in 1893 and was remodeled by Mrs. Ben Ali Haggain in its current shingle style in the 1920s.

Hours: 10:30 a.m. to 4 p.m.

From the traffic light in Tannersville on Route 23C, drive north about 1.5 miles to the entrance of Onteora Club on the left. Proceed on Minwawa Road to the first intersection on the right of Thurber Road. Turn right onto Thurber and proceed to the stop sign. Proceed through the stop sign onto Parker Road (do not go uphill or downhill, only a small jog going straight) and go to house #40 marked on stone pillars flanking the entrance to an oval driveway. The property is called Wildmuir. This garden is next to Bittersweet Cottage.

Proceeds shared with the Mountain Top Arboretum

Minnehaha
Onteora Club, Tannersville

Taking over an existing garden twelve years ago, we first removed all annuals from the flower beds and began cutting back original shrubs, long overgrown, as well as introducing to the vegetable garden triangular beds with roses, herb and cutting garden, and plant storage. Further transformations have been aimed towards bringing the spirit of the property closer to the house, which was designed in the 1890s by Canadian painter George Reid. These have included installing rustic fencing and concentrating on indigenous shrubs and plants as old-fashioned and deer-proof as possible.

Hours: 10:30 a.m. to 4 p.m.

From the traffic light in Tannersville, drive north on Route 23C. Go about 1.5 miles to the entrance of the Onteora Club on the left. Proceed on Minwawa Road to the first intersection on the right at Thurber Road. Turn right there. Minnehaha is the fourth house on the right.

Proceeds shared with the Mountain Top Arboretum

Tony & Rosalyn Smith's Bittersweet Cottage
41 Parker Road, Onteora Club, Tannersville

The garden, beside the original 1890s' farmhouse, is placed against a steep hillside. Multiple terraces take advantage of the hillside's steep descent. The natural rock ledges and boulders are used as boundaries to the planted areas. The palette of colors changes throughout the summer with emphasis on annuals and perennials in the different beds. Trellises of roses and clematis flank the front and sides of the house. The house derives its name from the large bittersweet vine growing along the side of the front porch.

Hours: 10:30 a.m. to 4 p.m.

Take Route 23A west. At Tannersville, turn right at the only traffic light and proceed north on Route 23C. After 1.2 miles on Route 23C, turn left into the Onteora Club. Follow the dirt road (Minwawa Road) for about .25 mile and take the first right onto Thurber Road. Follow Thurber Road for .25 mile. At the first stop sign, keep the same direction by taking a left up the hill, go 10 yards, and turn immediately right. Our home, "Bittersweet," is the fifth house on the left, painted green, up a steep driveway, #41. *Continue up the driveway and park in the large parking area at the top of the hill.* This garden is next to the McCaffrey Garden.

Proceeds shared with the Mountain Top Arboretum

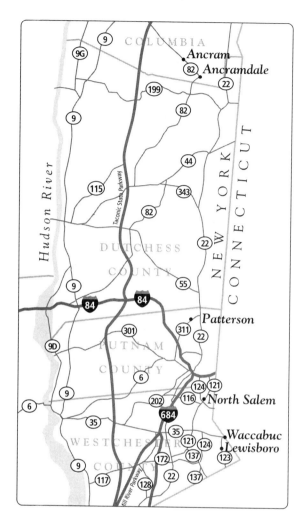

Sunday, September 8

Please also see listings for this date in Connecticut

COLUMBIA COUNTY

Ancram

Adams-Westlake

681 Route 7, Ancram

Please see June 23 for garden description, hours, and directions.

ANCRAMDALE
Cricket Hill Farm
107 Snyder Road, Ancramdale
Please see June 15 for garden description, hours, and directions.

PUTNAM COUNTY

PATTERSON
The Farmstead Garden
590 Birch Hill Road, Patterson
This garden, located on historic Quaker Hill, was planned as a rural landscape in keeping with its 1740 farmstead beginnings. A master plan was commissioned by the owners in 1985 to combine the site's woodlands, wetlands, house gardens, and agricultural fields into a harmonious native plant landscape while preserving the property's horticultural heritage. An heirloom apple orchard greets you as you enter the fieldstone entrance. The driveway is the old stagecoach road, which connected Pawling, New York, with Danbury, Connecticut. Native wildflower meadows now grace the upper and lower fields after decades of haying. A grove of more than eighty mature blueberry bushes tell the story of the acid soil and summers of picking and tasting. The original vegetable garden is anchored by an old majestic quince and the kitchen herb garden is filled with flowering thyme, catnip, and lavender, with a border of germander. A two-acre wetland can be traversed to experience plant and aquatic wildlife. The roadside sloping fields have been mowed to create welcoming paths and sculptural grasslands.

Hours: noon to 4 p.m.

Take I-684 to Pawling. At the intersection of Route 311, turn right onto South Quaker Hill Road. At the first stop sign (2.5 miles), turn right onto Birch Hill Road. Follow the road to #590. The garden is on the left.

From Connecticut, take Route 37 through Sherman and continue to Wakeman Road. The Akin Hall Library is on the right and the Hill Farm on the left. Turn left and continue south. This road becomes Birch Hill Road. *Please park on the road.*

Proceeds shared with the Conservancy for Historic Battery Park

WESTCHESTER COUNTY

Lewisboro
The White Garden
199 Elmwood Road, Lewisboro

Please see April 20 for garden description, hours, and directions.

North Salem
Dick Button—Ice Pond Farm
115 June Road, North Salem

Ice Pond Farm has some interesting topography. It has a valley with an ice pond that some-times gets black ice and a stone wall that pretends it's a rollercoaster. It has an icehouse, smokehouse, springhouse, and an outhouse with a view. It has a pair of perennial borders and a bocce court, a mini-orchard, gazebo, wildflower walk, and stone bridge. If we can get our act together, there will be a better vegetable garden than last year, some interesting plants in the borders, a new orangerie or something that passes for one, and a more developed hillside woodland garden.

Hours: 10 a.m. to 4 p.m.

From I-684 south, take Exit 8/Hardscrabble Road. Turn right onto Hardscrabble Road and go east about 5 miles to June Road/Old Route 124. Turn right onto June Road and go .75 mile to #115.

From I-684 south, take Exit 7/Purdys. Take Route 116 east for about 3 miles to North Salem. Turn left onto June Road/Old Route 124. Go .5 mile to #115. *Please park in the field as directed.*

Waccabuc
James & Susan Henry
36 Mead Street, Waccabuc

A nineteenth-century farm is the setting for perennial gardens, specimen trees, a walled gar-den, cordoned apple trees, a vegetable garden, berries and fruits, a pond in a meadow, and a vineyard producing red and white wines.

Hours: 10 a.m. to 5 p.m.

From I-684, take Exit 6/Route 35/Cross River/Katonah. Follow Route 35 east for 5 miles. After a long hill, look for Mead Street on the left. Take Mead Street .25 mile to #36 on the left. Turn left into the driveway, *then left into the parking area.*

From Connecticut, Mead Street is 4 miles from the traffic light at Routes 35 and 123. *Please park in the field behind the vineyard.*

Proceeds shared with the South Salem Fire Department

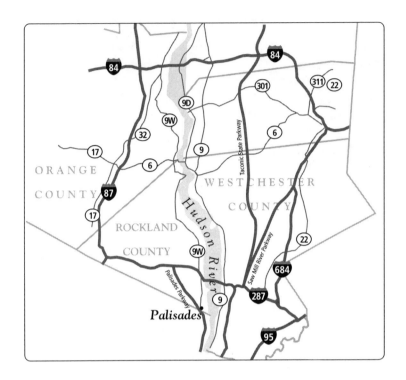

Sunday, September 15

PUTNAM COUNTY

Cold Spring

Stonecrop Gardens

81 Stone Crop Lane, Cold Spring

Please see the Public Gardens section for garden description, hours, and directions.

ROCKLAND COUNTY

Palisades

The Captain John House Garden

20 Washington Spring Road, Snedens Landing, Palisades

Please see June 9 for garden description, hours, and directions.

Judy Tomkins Gardens

75 Washington Spring Road, Snedens Landing, Palisades

Please see June 9 for garden description, hours, and directions.

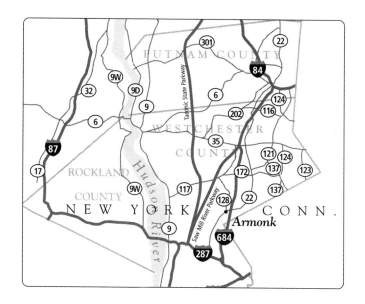

Sunday, October 13

WESTCHESTER COUNTY

ARMONK

Cobamong Pond

15 Middle Patent Road, Armonk

Please see May 19 for garden description, hours, and directions.

Public Gardens
BRONX COUNTY

Bronx
The New York Botanical Garden
200 Street & Kazimiroff Boulevard, Bronx (718) 817-8616 www.nybg.org

The New York Botanical Garden is one of the foremost public gardens in America and a National Historic Landmark. It has some of the most beautiful natural terrain of any botanical garden in the world, with dramatic rock outcroppings, a river and cascading waterfall, undulating hills, wetlands, ponds, and forty acres of historic, uncut forest. Within this grand 250-acre setting in the north Bronx, 48 gardens and special plantings offer stunning seasonal displays, from rainbows of tulips and azaleas in the spring to the rich tapestries of fall foliage. Several noteworthy buildings include America's most beautiful Victorian greenhouse, the Enid A. Haupt Conservancy.

Hours: April through October, Tuesday through Sunday, and Monday holidays, 10 a.m. to 6 p.m.; November through March, 10 a.m. to 4 p.m.; closed Thanksgiving and Christmas Day

Admission: Please call for rates or check the website.

From Westchester County, take Cross County Parkway/I-287 to Bronx River Parkway south. Take Exit 7W/Fordham Road and continue on Kazimiroff Boulevard to Conservatory Gate on the right.

From Connecticut, take I-95 to Pelham Parkway west. Continue for 3 miles. Across from the Bronx Zoo entrance, bear right onto Kazimiroff Boulevard to Conservatory Gate entrance on the right.

From New Jersey, take George Washington Bridge to Henry Hudson Parkway north to the Mosholu Parkway exit. Continue on Mosholu to Kazimiroff Boulevard, turn right, and continue to Conservatory Gate on the right.

Wave Hill

679 West 252nd Street, Bronx (718) 549-3200 www.wavehill.org

Often called "the most beautiful place in New York," Wave Hill is a 28-acre public garden in a spectacular setting overlooking the Hudson River and Palisades. Formerly a private estate, Wave Hill features several gardens, greenhouses, historic buildings, lawns, and woodlands, and also offers programs in horticulture, environmental education, land management, landscaping history, and the visual, performing, and literary arts. All programs focus on fostering relationships between people and nature.

Hours: October 15 through April 14, Tuesday through Sunday, 9 a.m. to 4:30 p.m.; April 15 through October 14, Tuesday through Sunday, 9 a.m. to 5:30 p.m.

Admission: free on Tuesday all day and Saturday until noon, otherwise, $4 adults, $2 senior citizens and students, children under 6 free

From the West Side and New Jersey, take Henry Hudson Parkway to Exit 21/246-250th Street. Continue north to 252nd Street. Turn left at the overpass and left again. Turn right at 249th Street to Wave Hill Gate.

From Westchester, take Henry Hudson Parkway south to Exit 22/254th Street. Turn left at the stop sign and left again at the traffic light. Turn right onto 249th Street to Wave Hill Gate.

BROOKLYN COUNTY

Brooklyn

Brooklyn Botanic Garden

900 Washington Avenue, Brooklyn (718) 623-7200 www.bbg.org

Brooklyn Botanic Garden is a living museum of plants blooming in one of the largest cities in the world. Highlights on our 52 acres include the Japanese Hill-and-Pond Garden, the Fragrance Garden designed for the visually impaired, the children's Discovery Garden, and the Steinhardt Conservatory, displaying tropical, desert, and temperate plants.

Hours: April through September, Tuesday through Friday, 8 a.m. to 6 p.m., weekends 10 a.m. to 6 p.m.; October through March, Tuesday through Friday, 8 a.m. to 4:30 p.m., weekends, 10 a.m. to 4:30 p.m. Closed Thanksgiving, Christmas, and New Year's Day.

Admission: $3 adults 16 and over, $3 children under 16 free, $1.50 seniors and students, seniors free on Friday.

From Brooklyn-Queens Expressway, take the Kent Avenue exit. Follow the service road (Park Avenue) alongside and then under the expressway for 5 blocks. Turn left onto Washington Avenue and continue for 1.75 miles.

By subway, take the Q local or Q express train to the Prospect Park station or the 2 or 3 train to Eastern Parkway.

HUDSON
Olana State Historic Site
Route 9G, Hudson (518) 828-0135 www.olana.org

The flower garden at Olana was added around 1890. Guests would stop to admire the garden on the way up to the house and both family and visitors often walked to it via a footpath from the mansion. The garden was designed in the "mingled garden" style recommended by Andrew Jackson Downing. The garden is 165 feet long and twenty feet wide, with a path up the center and ornamental gates at each end. The flowers are a mix of annuals and perennials, vines and shrubs, laid out in an irregular pattern to create a riot of color.

Hours: Year round, daily, 8:30 a.m. to sunset.

Admission: $3 adults, $2 seniors, $1 children 5-12

From New York State Thruway, take Exit 21/Catskills. Go towards the Rip Van Winkle Bridge. Cross the bridge and go south on Route 9G for approximately 1 mile. The entrance is on the left.

From Taconic Parkway, take the Route 82/Ancram exit. Follow signs for Rip Van Winkle Bridge. At the bridge intersection, go south on Route 9G for approximately 1 mile. The entrance is on the left.

AMENIA
Wethersfield
214 Pugsley Hill Road, Amenia (845) 373-8037

Ten acres of formal classical-style and outer gardens surround Chauncey D. Stillman's Georgian-style brick home. The original garden around the perimeter of the house was created in 1940 by Bryan J. Lynch. Evelyn N. Poehler oversaw the maintenance of the garden from 1952 on and designed the formal gardens over a twenty-year period.

Hours: June through September, Wednesday, Friday, and Saturday, noon to 5 p.m.

Admission: free

From Route 44 east of Millbrook, take Route 86 and turn right onto Pugsley Hill Road. Follow the signs for 1.3 miles to the estate entrance on the left.

ANNANDALE-ON-HUDSON
Montgomery Place
River Road, Annandale-on-Hudson (845) 758-5461 www.hudsonvalley.org

This 200-year-old estate enjoys a picturesque landscape, extolled by Andrew Jackson Downing. Included are ancient trees and vistas of the Hudson River and Catskill Mountains. The early twentieth-century garden includes a wide variety of plants, many unusual. There are also hiking trails, pick-your-own orchards, and waterfalls.

Hours: April 1 through October 31, Wednesday through Sunday; November, weekends only; the first 2 weekends in December, 10 a.m. to 5 p.m.; closed the last 2 weeks of December through March

Admission: $3 grounds only, $6 house and grounds

From New York State Thruway/I-87, take Exit 19/Kingston onto Route 209/199 east across the Kingston-Rhinecliff Bridge. Make a left onto Route 9G and proceed for 3 miles, then turn left onto Annandale Road, bearing left onto River Road to the estate entrance.

HYDE PARK
Vanderbilt National Historic Site: Italian Gardens
511 Albany Post Road, Route 9, Hyde Park (845) 229-6432 www.marist.edu/fwva

This three-level formal garden covers three acres. The rose garden has more than 1,200 plants. The perennial garden, along the cherry walk, includes several hundred perennials, and thousands of annuals are planted each year in the upper beds.

Hours: Year round, daily, dawn to dusk; group tours available by appointment

Admission: free, but donations are appreciated

Located on Route 9, on the left side of the road, just north of the Hyde Park Post Office.

MILLBROOK
Innisfree Garden
Tyrrel Road, Millbrook (845) 677-5286

Innisfree reflects an Eastern design technique called a cup garden, which draws attention to something rare or beautiful by establishing the suggestion of enclosure around it. A cup garden may be an enclosed meadow, a lotus pool, a waterfall, or a single dramatic rock covered with lichens and sedums. Visitors to Innisfree stroll from one 3-dimensional garden picture to another.

Hours: May 1 through October 20, Wednesday through Friday, 10 a.m. to 4 p.m., weekends and holidays, 11 a.m. to 5 p.m. Closed Monday and Tuesday, except holidays.

Admission: $3, Wednesday through Friday; $4, weekends and legal holidays; children under 6 free

Innisfree is on Tyrrel Road, 1 mile from Route 44 and 1.75 miles from the Taconic State Parkway overpass on Route 44.

Mary Flagler Cary Arboretum/Institute of Ecosystem Studies/ New York Botanical Garden

181 Sharon Turnpike/Route 44A, Millbrook (845) 677-5359 www.ecostudies.org

The three-acre perennial garden features ecological demonstration beds. The fern glen is a two-acre display of native plants in natural communities. The greenhouse, open year round, is a tropical plant paradise and includes an "Economic Botany Trail." There are also nature trails, a picnic area, and an Ecology Shop with a plant room.

Hours: Year round, Monday through Saturday, 9 a.m. to 4 p.m., Sunday, 1 p.m. to 4 p.m. Closed major holidays. Grounds open until 6 p.m., May through September. Greenhouse closes at 3:30 p.m.

From Taconic State Parkway, take Route 44 east for 2 miles. Turn onto Route 44A. The Gifford House Visitor and Education Center is 1 mile along Route 44A on the left.

From Massachusetts and Connecticut, take Route 22 to Route 44. Where Route 44 takes a sharp left to the village of Millbrook, continue straight on Sharon Turnpike/ Route 44A. The Gifford House Visitor and Education Center is on the right, just before Route 44A rejoins Route 44.

POUGHKEEPSIE

Springside Landscape Restoration

Academy Street, Poughkeepsie (845) 454-2060

Springside is the only unaltered documented work of Andrew Jackson Downing, one of the most influential landscape architects in American history. Once the summer home of Matthew Vassar (founder of Vassar College), the site was an "ornamental farm." Although unrestored, the landscape bears Downing's undeniable influence, illustrating the principles of the beautiful and the picturesque.

Hours: Year round, daily, dawn to dusk

Admission: free

From Taconic State Parkway, take the Poughkeepsie/Route 44 exit and proceed on Route 44 west through Poughkeepsie until just before the Mid-Hudson Bridge. Stay in the right lane for Route 9 south/Wappingers Falls and proceed on Route 9 for 1 mile to the Academy Street exit. At the bottom of the exit ramp, turn left. Proceed to the first entrance on the right at the bottom of the hill.

Vassar College Arboretum, Native Plant Preserve, & Shakespeare Garden

124 Raymond Avenue, Poughkeepsie (845) 437-5686

The Vassar College campus has a Shakespeare Garden, first planted in 1918, with plants represented in Shakespeare's writings. The garden has brick walks, statuary, knot beds, rose beds, heath and heather beds, and twelve raised-brick beds containing herbs and cottage garden plantings. A hemlock hedge encloses the garden. There is also an arboretum with 220 species of native and non-native trees and shrubs. Arboretum maps are available.

Hours: Year round, daily, dawn to dusk

Admission: free

From Route 44/55 in Poughkeepsie, turn onto Raymond Avenue to the Main Gate, about 3 blocks.

ESSEX COUNTY

ELIZABETHTOWN

Colonial Garden at Adirondack History Center

Adirondack Center Museum, Elizabethtown (518) 873-6466

A formal garden adjacent to the Adirondack Center Museum, the Colonial Garden borrows brick paving and walls, decorative fencing and gates, a summerhouse, fountain, and sundial from Colonial Gardens of Williamsburg. A formal arrangement of hedges, flowering trees, shrubs, and perennials encloses the annual borders, which are planted and maintained by the Essex County Adirondack Garden Club.

Hours: Year round, daily, dawn to dusk.

Admission: free

From the Northway/I-87, take Exit 31/Route 9N. Proceed west on Route 9N about 4 miles to Elizabethtown. Turn left at the blinking traffic light. Take the first left onto Church Street.

From the Essex Ferry via Westport, exit the ferry parking lot. Turn left onto Route 9 and proceed south (the road is also called Lake Shore Drive in Westport). At the stop sign, turn left. Turn right onto Sisco. Follow to the stop sign. Bear right (the fairgrounds are on your right) onto Route 9N and continue past Westport Depot to I-87. Continue as directed above.

WESTPORT

The Depot Theatre Gardens

Route 9N, Westport (518) 962-4449 www.depottheatre.org

Framing the Westport landmark railroad station, which underwent major restoration in 1997-1998, are flower beds with a mixture of annuals, perennials, and shrubs. The station, also known as The Depot Theatre, seats 135 for its summer season equity actors' performances between mid-June and mid-September. Overlooking Lake Champlain, the site is truly unique.

Hours: June through September, daily, dawn to dusk

Admission: free

From the Northway/I-87, take Exit 31/Route 9N. Go east on Route 9N about 3 miles until Route 9N passes under railroad tracks. Westport Railroad Station, aka The Depot Theatre, is on the right on the west side of the tracks.

From the town of Westport, take Route 9N west about 2 miles until 9N passes under the railroad tracks. Westport Railroad Station is on the left on the west side of the tracks.

GREENE COUNTY

TANNERSVILLE
The Mountain Top Arboretum
Maude Adams Road, Tannersville (518) 589-3903 www.mtarbor.org

The Mountain Top Arboretum is a living museum of trees and shrubs created for the education and pleasure of the public. Its founders, the Ahrens family, designed and planted a seven-acre mountain-top area starting in 1977, to display the range of native and exotic trees and shrubs that successfully adapt to the rigorous climate at 2,500 feet above sea level in the northern Catskill Mountains of New York State.

Hours: May through October, daily, dawn to dusk; gate is not locked, so public may visit anytime

Admission: free

From New York City, take New York State Thruway/I-87 to Exit 20/Saugerties. After the tollbooth, turn left at the traffic light and proceed for .1 mile, then turn right onto Route 32. After 6 miles, take a left fork onto Route 32A to Palenville. At the light, turn left onto Route 23A to Haines Falls. Continue west on Route 23A to Tannersville, then turn right at the light onto Route 23C. After 2 miles, turn right onto a dirt road (Maude Adams Road) and proceed 50 yards to the arboretum parking.

From Albany, take New York State Thruway/I-87 south to Exit 21/Catskill. After the tollbooth, turn left and proceed to Route 9W. Turn right onto Route 9W south and take that to Route 23A. Continue west on Route 23A to Palenville and then to Haines Falls. From Haines Falls, proceed as directed above.

NASSAU COUNTY

MILL NECK
The John P. Humes Japanese Stroll Garden
Corner of Oyster Bay Road & Dogwood Lane, Mill Neck (516) 676-4486

A PROJECT OF
THE GARDEN
CONSERVANCY

The Humes Japanese Stroll Garden, a four-acre gem of landscape design, provides a retreat for passive recreation and contemplation. Moving through the garden, where the views, textures, and balance of elements have been planned following Japanese aesthetic principles, visitors experience a walking meditation that can lead to inner peace. The garden symbolizes a mountain beside a sea, where gravel paths represent mountain streams that form pools of cascades, eventually flowing into the ocean, represented by a pond.

Hours: April 29 through October 22, weekdays, 11:30 a.m. to 4:30 p.m.; private tours and tea ceremony can be arranged during the week

Admission: $5 adults, children under 12 free

From Long Island Expressway/I-495 east, get off at Exit 39N. Take Glen Cove Road north to Route 25A/Northern Boulevard, make a right onto Route 25A, pass C.W. Post, pass Route 107, and proceed to the next traffic light—Old Brookville Police Station is on the left—Wolver Hollow Road. Turn left, proceed to the end, make a right onto Chicken Valley Road, pass the Planting Fields Arboretum, and pass a blinking light.

Half mile after the blinking light, you will see a tall pinkish wall on the right. At that corner—Dogwood Lane—turn right and make another right into the parking lot.

From Long Island Expressway/I-495 west, take Exit 41N to Route 106 north to Route 25A. Turn left at the second light onto Wolver Hollow Road. Proceed as directed above.

OLD WESTBURY
Old Westbury Gardens
71 Old Westbury Road, Old Westbury (516) *333-0048 www.oldwestburygardens.org*

North America's most beautiful English-style country estate. Its 160 acres include a walled garden, a sunken parterre rose garden, a boxwood garden, a thatched cottage garden, woodlands, and ponds. A magnificent 1906 mansion contains fine English antiques and decorative arts. Old Westbury Gardens is listed on the National Register of Historic Places.

Hours: Late April through October, Wednesday through Monday, 10 a.m. to 5 p.m.; Sundays in November 10 a.m. to 5 p.m. Holiday Celebration December 6 through 16, 11 a.m. to 4 p.m.

Admission: $8 adults, $6 senior citizens, $3 children 6-12

From Long Island Expressway/I-495, take Exit 39/Glen Cove Road south. Stay on the service road of Long Island Expressway. At the third traffic light, turn right onto Old Westbury Road. The entrance to Old Westbury Gardens is .25 mile on the left.

ORANGE COUNTY
WEST POINT
Anna B. Warner Memorial Garden
Constitution Island at the U.S. Military Academy, West Point (845) *446-8676*
www.constitutionisland.org

Old-fashioned perennial and annual border garden lining a fifty-yard path, planted in nineteenth-century style with flowers described by Anna Warner in her book *Gardening by Myself* written in 1872. Cared for by dedicated volunteers, this garden received the Burlington House Award.

Hours: Mid-June through October. Tours to Constitution Island are available on Wednesday and Thursday, mid-June through September. Reservations required.

Admission: $10 adults, $9 senior citizens and students, children under 4 free; present this book and admission will be reduced to $5

From the south, take Route 9W or Palisades Parkway to Bear Mountain Bridge Circle. Go 2 miles north on Route 9W, then take Route 218 through Highland Falls to West Point. After Hotel Thayer, take the first right (Williams Road) downhill. Cross the railroad tracks. Park north of South Dock.

From the north, take Route 9W south. Take the first sign to West Point. Drive through West Point on Thayer Road. After the road goes under a stone bridge, take the first left (Williams Road) downhill. Proceed as directed above.

COOPERSTOWN
Brookwood
West Lake Road, Cooperstown (607) 547-1402

Brookwood Point had several owners after William Cooper sold this part of his large land patent in 1799. It was not until 1915 that Brookwood's then owners, Frederic dePeyster Townsend (a landscape architect from Buffalo) and his wife, Katharine, designed and built its formal garden and garden house. The original outlines of the formal garden are still visible and the original pools and fountain are in operation. The garden overlooks a spectacular view of Otsego Lake and the village of Cooperstown, and work is underway to restore its plantings. Today, the Cook Foundation owns and operates Brookwood for the enjoyment of local residents and visitors to the area.

Hours: Year round, daily, 10 a.m. to 5 p.m. Due to a wedding on June 29, scheduled visitors will be admitted between 10 a.m. and 2 p.m. only.

Admission: Suggested donation $5

The driveway is located on the right side of West Lake Road (at 6000 S.R. 80), 1.4 miles north of the Cooperstown village limits. Look for #6000 on the mailbox and stone pillars along the drive. Follow the drive straight towards the lake. Please park in the field across from the sailing club.

Fenimore Art Museum Terrace Garden
Route 80, Cooperstown (607) 547-1400 www.fenimoreartmuseum.org

The Fenimore Art Museum Terrace Garden is, in reality, a rooftop garden, although it is not immediately perceived as such. The bluestone terrace, which tops the museum's American Indian Wing, is divided into mirror-image garden rooms by a patterned central walk, which terminates with a spectacular view of Otsego Lake. Each lower terrace room is dominated by a classical white pavilion, which faces, across simple grass parterres, a balustraded garden wall and five elegant, topiary-filled white *caisses de Versailles* on plinths set in a sixty-foot linear bed of *Euonymus fortunei* 'Green Lane'. This gray-green architectural garden is different in every season but always subtle.

Hours: Year round, daily, dawn to dusk

Admission: grounds are free

Proceed west on Cooperstown's Lake Street, passing the Otesaga Hotel. Lake Street becomes Route 80. Continue .5 mile past the hotel, traveling the full length of the golf course to the right. The Farmer's Museum buildings will be seen on the left. The entrance to Fenimore House Museum is on the right, just after the golf course. The garden is to the rear of the museum.

PUTNAM COUNTY

Cold Spring

Stonecrop Gardens

81 Stone Crop Lane, Cold Spring (845) 265-2000 www.stonecropgardens.org

At its windswept elevation of 1,100 feet above sea level in the Hudson Highlands, Stonecrop enjoys a Zone 5 climate. The display gardens cover an area of about twelve acres and include a diverse collection of gardens and plants: woodland and water gardens, a grass garden, raised alpine stone beds, a cliff rock garden, perennial beds, and an enclosed English-style flower garden. Additional features include a conservatory, display alpine house, pit house with an extensive collection of choice dwarf bulbs, and a series of polytunnels for overwintering half-hardy plants.

Hours: Open Days events, April 28, May 19, June 16, July 13, and September 15; otherwise, by appointment only, April through October, Tuesday, Wednesday, Friday, and the first and third Saturday of each month, 10 a.m. to 4 p.m.

Admission: $5

From Taconic State Parkway, take the Route 301/Cold Spring exit. Travel 3.5 miles to Stonecrop's entrance on the right. A street sign reading "Stonecrop Gardens" marks the driveway.

From Route 9, take Route 301 east for 2.4 miles. Our driveway will be on the left marked by a street sign reading "Stonecrop Gardens."

Garrison

Manitoga/The Russel Wright Design Center

589 Route 9D, Garrison (845) 424-3812 www.russelwrightcenter.org

A premier example of naturalistic landscape design, Russel Wright's woodland garden invites active participation in the 2.5 miles of trails open regularly to the public. This is a landscape not just to be seen but to be experienced, with feature highlights that Russel Wright wanted you to notice. The 75-acre site, including Wright's house, is listed on the National Register of Historic Places.

Hours: Open Day event July 13, 10 a.m. to 2 p.m.; otherwise, year round, weekdays, 9 a.m. to 4 p.m.; April through October, also weekends and holidays, 10 a.m. to 6 p.m.

Admission: Suggested donation $4

Located on Route 9D, 2.5 miles north of the Bear Mountain Bridge and 2 miles south of the intersection of Routes 403 and 9D.

SARATOGA SPRINGS

Yaddo

Union Avenue, Saratoga Springs (518) 584-0746

The former estate of Katrina and Spencer Trask is now a world-renowned working artists' community with only the gardens open to the public. Presently being restored by the Yaddo Garden Association, the Rose Garden is based on Italian classical-style gardens, which the Trasks had seen on their tours abroad. The adjoining Rock Garden expresses, in contrast, an Anglo-American tradition of interest in indigenous landscape. The 1899 Garden was meant to be a garden of romance and delight, an expression of Katrina's own life.

Hours: Throughout the growing season, daily, dawn to dusk. Informal tours available mid-June through September, on Saturday and Sunday, and Tuesday during racing season. Meet at 11 a.m. at the large fountain.

Admission: $3

From Exit 14 of the Northway/I-87, take Union Avenue/Route 9P west crossing over the Northway. Yaddo is the first entrance on the left. Union Avenue goes into town and ends at Congress Park.

BAYPORT

Meadow Croft, The John E. Roosevelt Estate

138 Bayport Avenue, Bayport (631) 472-9395

This nature preserve, consisting of 75 acres of woods and tidal wetlands, was the summer home of John E. Roosevelt, a first cousin of President Theodore Roosevelt. The privet and lattice-enclosed kitchen garden adjacent to the Colonial Revival home was planted and is maintained by the Bayport Heritage Association and contains plant material that would have been available in 1910, the year to which the house is restored. Included are 24 varieties of heirloom roses, heirloom vegetables, annuals, and more than sixty varieties of perennials.

Hours: The third Sunday in June through third Sunday in October, Sunday, noon to 5 p.m., with tours at 1 p.m. and 3 p.m.; closed weekends of July 4th, Labor Day, and Columbus Day

Admission: free

From Sunrise Highway/Route 27, take the Lakeland-Ocean Avenue/Route 93 exit southbound for approximately 2 miles to Main Street. Turn left onto Main Street and immediately bear right onto South Main Street/Middle Road. Continue on Middle Road for .5 mile and turn left at the estate entrance.

BRIDGEHAMPTON
Bridge Gardens Trust
36 Mitchell Lane, Bridgehampton (631) 537-7440 www.bridgegardens.org

The gardens on these five acres were designed and installed by Jim Kilpatric and Harry Neyens. They include a formal knot surrounded by herbal beds, perennial mounds, topiaries, specimen trees, expansive lawns, aquatic plantings, woodland walks, a bamboo "room," a lavender parterre, and hundreds of roses. A 750-foot-long double row of privet hedge—with fifteen viewing ports in its fifteen-foot-high walls-encloses a pavilion-like garden house (not open to the public). Bridge Gardens Trust, a charitable foundation, was created in 1997 to preserve the gardens and to encourage the accumulation of gardening knowledge.

Hours: Late May through late Septemeber, Wednesday, and Saturday, 2 p.m. to 5 p.m.

Admission: $10 adults, $9 senior citizens

From Montauk Highway/Route 27, go to Bridgehampton. At the blinking traffic light at the western edge of the village, turn left onto Butter Lane. Go .25 mile and under the railroad bridge; turn left immediately onto Mitchell Lane. Bridge Gardens, #36, is the first driveway on the left. Please park along Mitchell Lane with the flow of traffic.

EAST HAMPTON
LongHouse Reserve
133 Hands Creek Road, East Hampton (631) 329-3568 www.longhouse.org

Sixteen acres of gardens are punctuated with contemporary sculpture. Landscape features include a pond, numerous allées and walks, a dune garden, and 1,000-foot-long hemlock hedge that follows the boundaries of farm fields that occupied the site until it was abandoned for agricultural use in the nineteenth century. There are collections of bamboo and grasses, 200 varieties of daffodils with more than 1 million blooms, and numerous irises, conifers, and broadleaf evergreens. The large new house (not open to the public) was inspired by the seventh-century Shinto shrine at Ise, Japan. LongHouse Reserve was established in 1991 to reflect founder Jack Lenor Larsen's professional interests and his desire to encourage creativity in gardening, collecting, and everyday living with art. The majestic 25-feet-tall, 33-feet-in-diameter *Fly's Eye Dome* by Buckminster Fuller has been added to a selection of almost 50 sculptures throughout the gardens.

Hours: Late-April through mid-September, Wednesday and Saturday of each month, 2 p.m. to 5 p.m.

Admission: $10, free to members

From East Hampton Village, turn onto Newtown Lane from the intersection at Main Street. Go to Cooper Street, turn right, and go to the end. Turn left onto Cedar Street and bear right at the fork in the road onto Hands Creek Road. Go .7 mile to #133

SAGAPONACK
Madoo Conservancy
618 Main Street, Sagaponack (631) 537-8200 www.madoo.org

This two-acre garden is a virtual compendium of major garden styles, including an Oriental bridge, box-edged potager, renaissance-perspective rose walk, knot garden, laburnum arbor, hermit's hut, and grass garden, as well as an Italianate courtyard and a user-friendly maze. It is fountained, rilled, and pooled. It is noted for its innovative pruning techniques and striking colors (a gazebo is in three shades of mauve). Sculptures are by Matisse, Bourdelle, and Soriano. Rare trees and plants abound. A copse of fastigiate ginkgos rises above box balls like the handles of mallets about to strike boules or hedgehogs. A staircase going nowhere is another of its whimsical features, as is a fifth-century B.C. Greek exedra. The garden has been much published.

Hours: May through September, Wednesday and Saturday, 1 p.m. to 5 p.m.; tours of 10 or more may be arranged at other times

Admission: $10

From Long Island Expressway/I-495, take Exit 70 and follow signs to Montauk. Sagaponack is on Route 27, 1 mile east of Bridgehampton. Turn right at the traffic light (the first light east of Bridgehampton on Route 27). Madoo Conservancy is a little over 1 mile from the highway and is 3 driveways after the post office on the right.

WESTCHESTER COUNTY

CROTON-ON-HUDSON
Van Cortlandt Manor
South Riverside Avenue, Croton-on-Hudson (914) 271-8981 www.hudsonvalley.org

This restored Federal period manor complex includes a border of period ornamentals of interest throughout the growing season, a large tulip display, a vegetable garden, an orchard, and narcissi naturalized at the woodland's edge. An extensive culinary and medicinal herb garden is also noteworthy.

Hours: April through October, daily, except Tuesday, 10 a.m. to 5 p.m.; November, weekends only

Admission: $4 for grounds

Take Route 9 to Croton Point Avenue. Go east on Croton Point Avenue to the first traffic light. Turn right at the light onto South Riverside Avenue. Van Cortlandt Manor is at the end of the road, past the Shop Rite shopping center.

KATONAH

Caramoor Gardens

Girdle Ridge Road, Katonah (914) 232-1253 www.caramoor.com

Located throughout the 100 acres are the Sunken Garden, Spanish Courtyard, Butterfly Garden, Sense Circle for the visually impaired, Cutting Garden, Medieval Mount, Woodland Garden, Cedar Walk, and numerous antique containers planted in creative ways.

Hours: May through October, Wednesday through Sunday, 1 p.m. to 4 p.m. Group tours by appointment; call to reserve.

Admission: $7

Girdle Ridge Road is off Route 22. Enter through Main Gate.

Lasdon Park, Arboretum & Veterans Memorials

2610 Amawalk Road/Route 35, Katonah (914) 232-3141 www.westchestergov.com/parks/ locationpage/lasdonsanctuary.htm

Lasdon Park, Arboretum & Veterans Memorials is a magnificent 243-acre property consisting of a 22-acre arboretum and formal azalea garden. The park has woodlands with hiking paths and open grass meadows. There are many picturesque locations from which to view the gardens and various tree, shrub, and flower specimens from all over the world. Special focal points are the Azalea Garden, Historic Tree Trail, Lilac Collection, Magnolia Grove, Dwarf Conifer Collection, a collection of more than sixty varieties of dogwood from around the world, the Chinese Culture Garden, and the Veterans Memorial with the Trail of Honor. Investigative research is done in conjunction with different governmental research institutions on the American chestnut and butternut. The Friends of Lasdon Park & Arboretum is a not-for-profit volunteer organization for the sole support of Lasdon Park & Arboretum. The Friends sponsor horticultural workshops, provide horticultural information, and oversee the horticultural library. The volunteers maintain the greenhouse to raise plants for sale. As their yearly main fundraiser, they sponsor a plant sale and maintain a plant shop.

Hours: Year round, daily, 8 a.m. to 4 p.m.; the plant shop is open April through mid-December, weekends, noon to 4 p.m.

Admission: free

The entrance is on Route 35, 2.5 miles west of the intersection of Routes 100 and 35.

Muscoot Farm

Route 100, Katonah (914) 232-7118

Muscoot is a Westchester country gentleman's farm circa 1880-1950. The herb garden on the property is cared for by the Muscoot Naturalist. The garden displays beds with tea, dye, fragrance, and cooking herbs to be used for programs and workshops.

Hours: Year round, daily, 10 a.m. to 4 p.m.

Admission: free, but donations appreciated

From I-684, take Exit 6/Route 35/Katonah/Cross River and go west on Route 35 for 1.3 miles. Turn left (south) onto Route 100. Muscoot Farm is on the right after 1.5 miles.

NORTH SALEM

Hammond Museum Japanese Stroll Garden

Deveau Road, North Salem (914) 669-5033 www.hammondmuseum.org

A 3.5-acre garden with thirteen different landscapes, the Japanese Garden is a living collection. The stroll garden contains a pond and waterfall, a garden of the Rakan, a red maple terrace, a Zen garden, and many species of trees and flowers, including cherry, katsura, quince, azalea, peony, and iris. The café serves lunch on the terrace.

Hours: May through October, Wednesday through Saturday, noon to 4 p.m.

Admission: $4 adults, $3 seniors citizens and students, children under 12 free

From I-684, take Exit 8/Hardscrabble Road. Turn right off the exit ramp and continue 4 miles to the end. Turn right onto June Road. Take the second left onto Deveau Road. The garden and museum are at the top of Deveau Road.

OSSINING

The Wildflower Island at Teatown Lake Reservation

1600 Spring Valley Road, Ossining (914) 762-2912 www.teatown.org

The island is a woodland garden of more than 200 species of native flowers. Several hundred pink lady's slippers make a spectacular display in May. In late summer, the sunny shores of the island are ablaze with cardinal flowers, lobelia, ironweed, and other bright, moisture-loving flowers. A small interpretive museum is at the entrance to the bridge leading to the island. Visitors are guided along narrow paths by experienced volunteers. Call for tour schedule.

Hours: Open Day event, May 19, 10 a.m. to 2 p.m.; otherwise, May through September, Monday through Saturday, 9 a.m. to 5 p.m., Sunday, 1 p.m. to 5 p.m. Wildflower Island tours: April and June, weekends, 2 p.m.; May, Saturday, 10 a.m. and 2 p.m., Wednesday, 7 p.m.; July through September, Saturday, 10 a.m.

Admission: $3

Take the Major Deegan Expressway to New York State Thruway/I-87 north to Exit 9/ Tarrytown (last exit before the Tappan Zee Bridge). Take Route 9 north to Ossining. Watch for Route 133 on the right. At the third traffic light after Route 133, turn right onto Cedar Lane. Cedar Lane will become Spring Valley Road. Teatown is on the left, 3.8 miles from Route 9.

POCANTICO HILLS

Kykuit, The Rockefeller Estate

Pocantico Hills (914) 631-9491 www.hudsonvalley.org

The extraordinary early twentieth-century gardens at Kykuit, The Rockefeller Estate, were designed by William Welles Bosworth. Included are a formal walled garden, woodland gardens, a rose garden, fountains, and spectacular Hudson River views. Important twentieth-century sculptures were added by Governor Nelson Rockefeller, including works by Alexander Calder, Henry Moore, Pablo Picasso, Louise Nevelson, David Smith, and many others.

Hours: May through October, daily, except Tuesdays, 10 a.m. to 3 p.m., no reservations needed

Admission: $20 adults, $19 senior citizens, $17 children

All tours begin at historic Philipsburg Manor, located on Route 9 in the village of Sleepy Hollow.

PURCHASE

The Donald M. Kendall Sculpture Gardens at PepsiCo

700 Anderson Hill Road, Purchase (914) 253-2000

One hundred and twelve acres of landscape designed by Russell Page surround the world headquarters of PepsiCo, Inc. Spacious lawns and shrubs, plantings of trees, and small gardens provide settings for 45 sculptures by renowned twentieth-century artists.

Hours: Year round, daily, dawn to dusk

Admission: free

From I-84, take I-684 south to the Westchester Airport exit. Take Route 120 south to Anderson Hill Road to PepsiCo on the right.

From Merritt Parkway/Route 15 south (which becomes the Hutchinson River Parkway), take Exit 28/Lincoln Avenue/Port Chester. Turn left onto Lincoln Avenue and proceed 1 mile to PepsiCo on the right.

TARRYTOWN

Lyndhurst

635 South Broadway/Route 9, Tarrytown (914) 631-4481 www.lyndhurst.org

The grounds at Lyndhurst are an outstanding example of nineteenth-century landscape design. Elements include a sweeping lawn accented with shrubs and specimen trees, a curving entrance drive revealing "surprise" views, and the angular repetition of the Gothic roofline in the evergreens. The rose garden and fernery are later Victorian additions.

Hours: Mid-April through October, Tuesday through Sunday, 10 a.m. to 4:15 p.m.; November through mid-April, weekends only, 10 a.m. to 3:30 p.m.

Admission: $4

From New York State Thruway/I-87, take Exit 9/Tarrytown/Route 9. Turn left at the end of the exit ramp onto Route 119 and continue to the traffic light at Route 9/Broadway. Turn left onto Route 9 and proceed .5 mile to the Lyndhurst gates on the right side.

VALHALLA
The Lady Bird Johnson Demonstration Garden— The Native Plant Center
75 Grasslands Road, Valhalla (914) 785-7870

This two-acre garden, installed in 1998 on the campus of Westchester Community College, contains only native American plants indigenous to the northeastern United States. The perennial and shrub beds are designed to show how these beautiful and vigorous American species can be used in the home landscape. There are also two demonstration meadows, planted one year apart using different management techniques. The garden is designed for summer and fall color but is interesting all year. No pesticides or fertilizers are used in this garden. Wheelchair accessible; woodchip paths.

Hours: Year round, daily, dawn to dusk

Admission: free

From I-287, take Exit 4/Route 100A. Turn north onto Route 100A. The college is .5 mile on the right. At the end of the entrance road, turn right.

From northern Westchester, take Taconic State Parkway south to Sprain Brook Parkway. Exit at Eastview. Turn left onto Route 100. Enter at East Grasslands Gate and bear right at the fork.

From southern Westchester, take Sprain Brook Parkway and exit at Eastview. Turn right onto Route 100. Enter at East Grasslands Gate and bear right at the fork. Follow the road to parking lot 1 on the right. The path through the woods on the far right of the lot leads to the garden.

NORTH CAROLINA

OPEN DAYS:

April 13
May 18
July 13
September 14
September 15

Kenilworth Gardens, Asheville.
Photo © John Dickson, 2001.

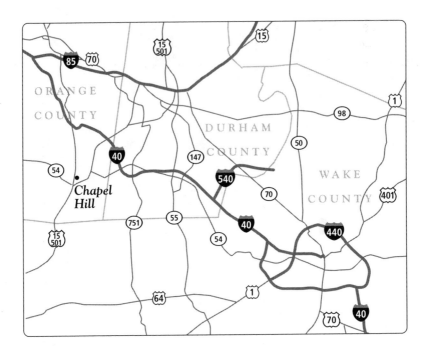

Saturday, April 13

ORANGE COUNTY

CHAPEL HILL

Boyd-Martin Garden

313 Country Club Road, Chapel Hill

Countless azaleas, camellias, ferns, and rhododendrons cascade through trees down a rocky hill, which the original owner, UNC professor Bernard Boyd, tamed in the 1950s with winding paths and an intricate drainage system. We have exhilarated in the maintenance and rejuvenation of this delightful, orderly forest which startles the busy university traffic with its early spring spectacle. Bulbs, hostas, hellebores, foamflower, phlox, and other perennials defy shade and the earth's crust to fill rock gardens and beds in the more mercifully flat areas around the house.

Hours: 10 a.m. to 4 p.m.

From I-40, take Exit 273/Route 54 west to Chapel Hill. This later becomes Raleigh Road. Continue straight for 3.5 miles (passing the Glen Lennox Shopping Center and the junction of Route 15-501) to the traffic light at the intersection of Raleigh and Country Club Roads. Turn left (south) onto Country Club Road. Go straight (past Ridge Road) for .1 mile to a "Private Drive" sign on your left. At the bottom of "Private Drive" is our house/garden (313 Country Club Road, which is behind 307 Country Club Road). *Please park on Country Club Road in the weekend/legal university spaces on the right, slightly beyond the "Private Drive" sign and walk back to "Private Drive," or, as you come in from I-40, at 3.4 miles, there is a pay-UNC visitor parking lot across from the hill entry to the garden.*

The Robertson Garden
520 Hooper Lane, Chapel Hill

In 1995, Wyndham Robertson began the renovation of this house and garden in the heart of Chapel Hill's oldest and most beautiful neighborhood. Created by Chip Calloway of Greensboro and Mary Jane Baker of Spring Branch Landscapes, the new gardens weave comfortably among the wonderful old camellias, boxwoods, magnolias, oaks, and hollies that preceded them. The front entry to the garden is a classic mixed border of roses, hardy geraniums, phlox, herbs, tulips, and annuals. Many varieties of hydrangeas and unusual flowering trees and shrubs fill the garden with bloom and fragrance throughout the four seasons.

Hours: 10 a.m. to 4 p.m.

From East Franklin Street, the main downtown street, turn south at the traffic light onto Boundary Street. The garden is on Hooper Lane, which is the next right, but *parking is ahead on Boundary in the parking lot on the left. It is a short 50-yard walk to the house and garden.*

Tenney Farmhouse Garden—Elizabeth Pringle
381 Tenney Circle, Chapel Hill

In 1993, John and I restored the 1810 Tenney farmhouse and I began a love affair with my "new old garden" containing a few treasures from earlier gardeners. Much of my garden design and many of the plants I selected could have been used in the nineteenth century. The front porch looks over low shrubs to the perennial beds of the parlor garden, which has a deciduous shrub border along the old stone wall near the street. An arch leads to the herb garden and stone terrace, which overlooks the back wildflower garden with a small pond, a semi-bog, a moss garden, and a fern bower amongst woodland paths. The evergreen shrub border on the west side surrounds the rock garden under the large oak tree in the center. Scented plants and attractions for butterflies and birds are numerous and many plants are blooming all year.

Hours: 10 a.m. to 4 p.m.

Follow signs to Chapel Hill. In the center of town, at the intersection of Franklin and Columbia Streets, go east on East Franklin Street. Pass through the traffic light at Hillsborough Street and turn left at the next light, which is Boundary Street. Go 2 blocks and turn right onto North Street for 1 block. Turn left onto Tenney Circle and follow the curve to the right. The second house is #381.

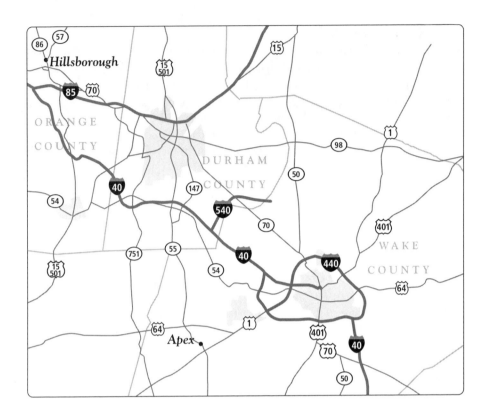

Saturday, May 18

ORANGE COUNTY

HILLSBOROUGH

Chatwood Garden

1900 Faucette Mill Road, Hillsborough

The garden surrounds a nationally listed Federal house, dated 1806, in the North Carolina Piedmont. It is situated on the old Colonial King's Highway and the Eno River. Dr. and Mrs. Charles Blake bought the property, which is currently twenty acres, in the mid-1950s and developed the extensive gardens over a period of forty years. Mrs. Blake was one of the earliest "rose rustlers" and saved many old roses from cemeteries and old homes in Hillsborough. There are over 250 different kinds of roses and English roses are currently being added to extend the bloom season of the gardens. The roses are principally in three Williamsburg-style walled gardens. There is a wonderful Long Border, added in 1998, which is 12 feet x 70 feet and planted in yellow, blue, and white. In addition, there is an heirloom vegetable garden, bulb beds, a sanctuary garden, several specialty beds, and two long meadows leading towards the river. The new owners are renovating much of the garden, in an effort to make it more historically accurate. The Woodland Garden, which was heavily damaged in a storm in 2000, has been extensively reworked to reflect the changed environment.

Hours: 10 a.m. to 4 p.m.

From I-85, take Exit 164 onto old Route 86 north. Follow Route 86/Churton Street through downtown Hillsborough to the intersection with Route 70 (do not turn left onto Corbin/Business 70; continue 200 yards further to the larger intersection). Turn left onto Route 70 west and follow it for about 1 mile to the traffic light. Make a right onto Faucette Mill Road. Follow for 1.6 miles. There is an old barn to the left where Faucette Mill Road turns right into Frank Perry Road. *Parking is immediately to the left after making the right onto Frank Perry. There will be signs.* Chatwood is marked by a sign at the point where Faucette Mill becomes a lane. Walk 100 yards down the lane to the house on the left.

From I-40, take Exit 261 onto old Route 86 north and proceed as directed above.

Fairmount
4600 Old NC 86, Hillsborough

Completed in 1999, the rambling white house was styled after the 1928 Gregory farmhouse by the late West Coast architect William Wilson Wurster. Landscape architect Richard Bell designed the Fairmount site with its meandering, climbing drive and compound-style garden. The pastoral site, with its view towards sunset, is a natural park-like setting with its original, dilapidated tenant house purposely featured in the design for its history of the land. An auto courtyard entrance is planted as a response to Rowand's trips to Provence. A gurgling, 24-foot cement cattle tank gives focus and sound to the "L"-shaped courtyard. There are four trellised arbors to walk through as one circumvents the geometric gravel walkway that surrounds the house. Each arbor is designed for fragrance and seasonal color as well. Along with a rose garden, there are rose arbors, wisteria arbors, and others planted with grapes and trumpet vines. Carolina jasmine intertwines with climbing annuals in the trellis of the owner's private, outdoor, walled shower patio. The Friendship Garden features hundreds of gift plants from a wide circle of friends. Iris and peonies from Rowand's Illinois birthplace, mixed with other perennials, are constantly being heeled in for rooting and groomed for cut flowers for the house. Outdoor sculptures by artists that Rowand represents in his gallery are placed strategically throughout the hilltop grounds.

Hours: 10 a.m. to 4 p.m.

From I-40, take Exit 261 to Old NC 86 and go 1.5 miles south. Fairmount is on the left (you will see a sign at the entrance).

From I-85, take Exit 164 to Old NC 86 and go 2.5 miles south. Fairmount is on the left (you will see a sign at the entrance).

Pleasant Green Farm

4500 Schley Road, Hillsborough

Set on 500 rolling acres in northern Orange County, the house and gardens that make up part of Pleasant Green Farm came into being in 1984. The husband and wife designed the stone walls and all of the gardens without the benefit of a landscape plan—not something they recommend! There is a large vegetable garden, an orchard, an herb garden, and many perennial beds, all of which frame long views across horse and cattle pastures to two lakes.

Hours: 10 a.m. to 4 p.m.

From the main street of Hillsborough (Churton Street/Route 86), go north through town. Cross over Route 70 and make an immediate right onto Route 57. Go 5 miles and turn right onto Schley Road (church on the left). Travel 1 mile and turn left into the driveway. The mailbox reads "Box 4500, Pleasant Green Farm." Stay on the paved driveway all the way to the house at the top of the hill.

Proceeds shared with the Historical Hillsborough Commission

WAKE COUNTY

Aᴘᴇx

The Gardens at Rosecroft

404 Wooded Lake Drive, Apex

Rosecroft is a six-acre property on a small lake, bordered by woods. The garden was designed by Bridget Hutchinson, who has also designed gardens in Switzerland and Canada. The European flavor comes from the shaped hedges and geometric patterns, but is softened by mixed borders and beds of blooms. Some of the features are a parterre garden with rose trees, hedges, and gravel paths, seven rose towers with garlands of roses spanning the five feet between the towers, and a wedding cake staircase to a grass path leading to a gazebo overlooking the lake. The garden has over 200 rosebushes, many of which are David Austin shrub roses. The garden changes from a more formal style near the house to a naturalistic style near the water and woods.

Hours: 10 a.m. to 4 p.m.

Take Route 751 (south from I-40, north from Route 64) to Lewter Shop Road, which is almost directly across from a large nursery and dead ends at Route 751. Take Lewter Shop Road to Barbee Road (about 1.5 miles). Turn left onto Barbee Road to the entrance to the Wendy Hill subdivision (about .75 mile) on the left. Enter and stay on Wooded Lake Drive to #404 on the right. You'll see brick pillars and roses. *Please park on the shoulder across from the house.*

Proceeds shared with the Chapel Hill Garden Club

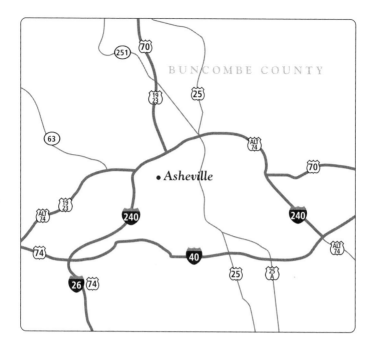

Saturday, July 13

Please start your tour at the Richmond Hill Inn where you may pick up a map and coupons for all of the Asheville garden. See the Public Gardens section for description, hours, and directions.

BUNCOMBE COUNTY

ASHEVILLE

Albemarle Inn

86 Edgemont Road, Asheville

When we purchased the Albemarle Inn, the grounds had not been cared for in many years. Our goal was to create a horticultural frame to set off the 1909 Greek Revival-style mansion. To that end, an elegant front lawn now sweeps down from the massive stone veranda and stops at a stone bench surrounded by an arbor draped with a hyacinth bean vine. Classic mixed English herbaceous borders flank the lawn. Formal English boxwoods and lavender line the driveway to the period *porte-cochère*. An herb garden is used daily for the inn breakfasts.

Hours: 10 a.m. to 4 p.m.

Traveling east on I-40 on I-26, take I-240 east to Exit 5B/Charlotte Street. Turn left to travel .9 mile to Edgemont Road. Turn right to travel .2 mile to the inn.

John & Curry Jamison

100 Windswept Drive, Asheville

Our garden meanders along the shady ridge of 2,800-foot Beaucatcher Mountain, overlooking Asheville and the Great Smoky Mountains beyond. It's a challenging place to make and nurture a garden, but we are here for the views. This garden celebrates the views! The centerpiece is a luxuriant rockery and waterfall formed with great schist boulders—a magnet for visitors who gather on a deck that hangs from the edge of a cliff, affording a memorable view of Mount Mitchell and the Blue Ridge Mountains. This is a visitor-friendly and peace-giving garden with hundreds of collector species, a blend of natives and exotics that keeps us interested from very early spring until the fading of leaf color.

Hours: 10 a.m. to 4 p.m.

From I-240 in Asheville, take Exit 5B/Charlotte Street. Turn south onto Charlotte Street, then left at College Street. After the next traffic light (Martin Luther King Boulevard), get in the right lane, then turn right onto College Street. Follow this up the mountain .4 mile and take the third street to the right, Windswept Drive. Follow this .3 mile and look for the Garden Conservancy sign at #100.

Kenilworth Gardens

175 Lakewood Drive, Asheville

Kenilworth Gardens was created by Doan Ogden, a renowned landscape architect. The nine-acre garden was his home and botanical experimentation site from 1950 through 1989. He planted more than 18,000 plants, many natives and exotics. The twelve or so garden rooms, or areas, are united by a mile of moss-covered trails. The foremost gardens on the property are the moss garden and the colorful annual and perennial garden. The home is wonderfully sighted overlooking Kenilworth Lake. John Cram, an avid gardener and current owner, has worked extensively reinterpreting the gardens over the last twelve years.

Hours: 10 a.m. to 4 p.m.

From I-240, take Exit 6/Chuns Cove Road. Turn left onto Tunnel Road. Go 2 blocks to Kenilworth Road and turn right. Go about 1.5 miles, past Harvest House. Just beyond Harvest House, turn left onto Lakewood Drive. Go .5 mile, to a sharp turn to the left. The first drive on the right is #175, directly next to Lake Garden. *Please park on the street and walk down the driveway.*

The Lake Garden

185 Lakewood Drive, Asheville

This garden has a number of rooms, one overlooking the dam and another, the lake. There is an eclectic mix of plants, many planted with an eye to textures. Some plants are rare, others native wildflowers.

Hours: 10 a.m. to 4 p.m.

From I-240, take Exit 6/Chuns Cove Road. Turn left onto Tunnel Road. Go 2 blocks to Kenilworth Road. Turn right onto Kenilworth and go about 1.5 miles. Pass Harvest House and just beyond turn left onto Lakewood Drive. Go .5 mile, to a sharp left turn. Ahead is #185, a flat-roofed stone house with a bronzed-glass greenhouse.

Proceeds shared with the Friends of the Pack Library

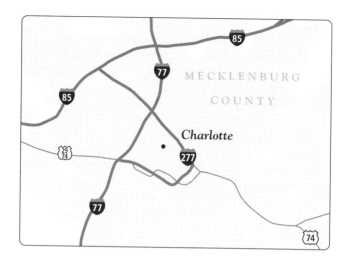

Saturday & Sunday, September 14 & 15

MECKLENBURG COUNTY

BELMONT

Daniel Stowe Botanical Garden

6500 South New Hope Road, Belmont (704) 825-4490

Daniel Stowe Botanical Garden is a private, nonprofit, public garden. The gardens consist of the Four Seasons, Color Walks, Cottage Garden, Canal Garden, four perennial gardens, and numerous fountains.

Hours: Year round, daily, 9 a.m. to 5 p.m.

Admission: Weekdays, $6 adults, $3 children, children under 4 free; weekends, $8 adults, $4 children, children under 4 free.

From I-85 south, take Exit 27/Belmont/Mount Holly/Highway 273. Turn left towards Belmont. Travel 8.3 miles following Highway 273 to Belmont. Turn right onto NC279/ New Hope Road. Go .3 mile. The garden will be on the left.

CHARLOTTE

The Cooper Gardens

637 Hungerford Place, Charlotte

This 6.5-acre garden, located in the Eastover neighborhood of Charlotte, was originally an undeveloped portion of the current owner's parents' grounds. The unique and personal garden has dramatically evolved over the past thirty years and now includes formal gardens extending from the house, woodland gardens (with azaleas, rhododendrons, wildflowers, and spring bulbs), large perennial beds, and two rose gardens. Incorporated throughout both the formal and woodland gardens are fountains, reflecting pools, statuary, and over 1,000 English boxwoods. There is always something special in bloom every month of the year and the passion with which this garden was created is transferred to all its visitors.

Hours: 10 a.m. to 4 p.m.

From the north, take I-85 south to Exit 38/Statesville/Columbia/I-77 south. Bear left on the exit ramp onto I-77 south. Get in the right lane and take Exit 11 to Brookshire Freeway (Routes 16 and 177). Bear left upon exiting and, while on Brookshire Freeway, stay to the right. Go 2 miles and exit onto John Belk Freeway. Take Exit 2A/Fourth and Third Streets. Go down the exit ramp to the first traffic light. (Here you may make a U-turn onto Third Street or turn left onto Fourth Street, take the next left onto McDowell Street, and take another left onto Third Street.) Go to the seventh light and turn left onto Cherokee Road, bearing right to stay on Cherokee Road. Turn left onto Eastover Road. At the end of Eastover Road, you are at the back of the Mint Museum on Hempstead Place. Turn right, then make an immediate left onto Museum Place and a right onto Museum Drive. Take the first left onto Hungerford Place.

Duncan Garden

2408 Westfield Road, Charlotte

Our garden is a study in contrasts; it is a reflection of its urban setting and a secluded sanctuary. It is home for a family with small children and an ambitious plant collector. Exuberant plantings abound within a formal framework. Ours is a small garden to contain such large collections, particularly of Japanese maples and climbing roses. Stone walls define the front and side gardens; roses, clematis, and the children's swings hang from an arbor in the front yard. A screened summerhouse covered with roses provides us with a gathering place regardless of sun, rain, or mosquitoes. Our garden reflects the diverse needs and interests of our family.

Hours: 10 a.m. to 4 p.m.

From I-77, take Exit 6A/Woodlawn Road/Queens College. Stay straight on Woodlawn for 2.8 miles. You will go through several traffic lights. Pass through South Boulevard, Scaleybark Road, and Park Road intersections. Turn left onto Selwyn Avenue after you have passed Park Road Shopping Center. Go 1 mile to Westfield Road. Turn left onto Westfield. The garden is .1 mile down on the right. *Please park on the street with the traffic; avoid blocking the road with cars parked on the other side. The street is narrow.*

Hampton Gardens

3034 Hampton Avenue, Charlotte

This small urban "test" garden was created over twenty years by this garden writer-lecturer and her retired physician husband. There is always something of interest year round, with emphasis on contrast and textures. A collection of Japanese maples adds graceful charm to the series of small gardens. The entire property is under cultivation with a street-side border and a vegetable/cutting garden. A charming pool forms the centerpiece of the often-photographed rear walled garden.

Hours: 10 a.m. to 4 p.m.

From I-85, take Exit 36/Brookshire Freeway east/Route 16 south. Go southeast towards the uptown on Brookshire Boulevard/Route 16 south. Take Exit 2A/Route 16/Fourth Street. Turn left onto East Fourth Street. At the next traffic light, turn left onto South McDowell Street. At the next light, turn left onto Third Street/Route 16. (Third Street changes into Providence Road/Route 16 south after 2.5 miles.) Turn right onto

Beverly Drive (just past Christ Church). Take the first left onto Hampton Avenue. The garden is the last on the right.

From I-77, take Exit 11/Brookshire Freeway east/I-277/Route 16 south. Go southeast towards the uptown on Brookshire Boulevard/Route 16 south. Proceed as directed above. *Please park on Hampton Avenue only.*

Minor Manor
1929 East Eighth Street, Charlotte

When I moved to this small urban bungalow in 1991, the garden was an overgrown mess. (What a difference a little muscle and manure can make!) Mature hardwood trees provide dappled shade and safe haven for birds and other wildlife. Underneath are a series of lush green rooms connected by pea gravel pathways and rustic metal sculptures designed by local artisans. Through the side gate, on the right, sits a wonderfully whimsical water fountain leading to what I call "the dance floor," with plenty of seating to enjoy the show.

Hours: 10 a.m. to 4 p.m.

From I-85, take Exit 36/Brookshire Freeway east/Route 16 south. Go southeast towards the uptown on Brookshire Boulevard/Route 16 south. Take Exit 3B/Davidson Street/College Street/McDowell Street. The exit ramp becomes 11th Street. Go straight to the sixth traffic light (the street curves and changes names to McDowell Street). Turn left onto Seventh Street. Go about 1 mile to Clement Avenue. Turn left onto Clement Avenue. Go to Eighth Street and turn right. Go one half block to #1929.

From I-77, take Exit 11/Brookshire Freeway east/I-277/Route 16 south. Go southeast towards uptown Brookshire Boulevard/Route 16 south. Proceed as directed above. *Please park along the street.*

Gardens on Valleybrook
7432 Valleybrook Road, Charlotte

Cross the bridge over the stream and enter our multi-level gardens, which meander over 2.5 acres with paths designed to lead you to each garden area. Larry designed and implemented each area and constructed the entry, arches, benches, and all embellishments. His extensive collection of conifers and woody plants forms the backbone of each garden area. I designed the placement of plant material and each year add to the perennial collection of both sun and shade plants. My dahlia collection enhances the fall garden. As with gardens everywhere, this is a work in progress. Since we both enjoy the creativity of design and passion for collecting, I doubt we will ever complete this garden. And, as a wildlife habitat, we plant for the birds and butterflies and welcome all creatures that call our garden home. There is much to see. Sit "a spell" and let the birds entertain you. Enjoy the plants as you walk the paths. Walk the bamboo trail. Explore the woods. Linger. Enjoy.

Hours: 10 a.m. to 4 p.m.

From I-85, take Exit 36/Brookshire Freeway east/Route 16 south. Go southeast towards the uptown on Brookshire Boulevard/Route 16 south. Take Exit 2A/Route 16/Fourth Street. Turn left onto East Fourth Street. At the next traffic light, turn left onto South McDowell Street. At the next light, turn left onto Third Street/Route 16. Third Street changes into Providence Road/Route 16 south. After about 7 miles, turn left onto Sardis Lane (Sardis Lane dead ends into Providence). Go about .5 mile to the third stop sign and turn right onto Valleybrook Road.

From I-77, take Exit 11/Brookshire Freeway east/I-277/Route 16 south. Go southeast towards the uptown on Brookshire Boulevard/Route 16 south. Proceed as directed above. (704) 364-5369. *Please park on the street.*

Garden of Genie & Jim White
2924 Saint Andrews Lane, Charlotte

This one-acre city garden is composed of a series of varied garden rooms, including a winter walk with a diverse collection of plants with winter interest, a perennial area, woodland with moss garden, small pools, native ferns and wildflowers, and a terrace garden featuring old roses. The potager contains vegetables in formal raised beds with old roses and flowers enclosing them. An herb garden centered with an old millstone adjoins the kitchen garden.

Hours: 10 a.m. to 4 p.m.

From I-85, take Exit 36/Brookshire Freeway east/Route 16 south. Go southeast towards the uptown on Brookshire Boulevard/Route 16 south. Take Exit 3B/Davidson Street/ College Street/McDowell Street. The exit ramp becomes 11th Street. Go straight to the fifth traffic light. Turn left onto East Tenth Street. Tenth Street becomes Central Avenue. Turn left onto The Plaza. Turn right onto Belvedere and keep on Belvedere (turning left at the stop sign). Turn right onto Saint Andrews Lane.

From I-77, take Exit 11/Brookshire Freeway east/I-277/Route 16 south. Go southeast towards the uptown on Brookshire Boulevard/Route 16 south. Proceed as directed above. *Please park on the street, along one side only.*

The Garden of Lindie Wilson
348 Ridgewood Avenue, Charlotte

Enter this garden, created by the late Elizabeth Lawrence, and you will find a magical sanctuary that has been expanded and restored by its current owner. An arched iron gate opens to a path of rustling bamboos. The garden is screened from the street by a tall *Camellia sasanqua* hedge and features a geometric design, reminiscent of Mediterranean gardens. A pond edged in stone serves as the focal point. The mixed borders of woody and herbaceous plants are informally planted within this formal design. Paths lead to a small, serene woodland garden under pines.

Hours: 10 a.m. to 4 p.m.

From I-77, take Exit 6A/Woodlawn Road/Queens College. Stay straight on Woodlawn for 2.8 miles. You will go through several traffic lights. Pass through South Boulevard, Scaleybark Road, and Park Road intersections. Turn left onto Selwyn Avenue after you have passed Park Road Shopping Center. Go .5 mile to Ridgewood Avenue. Turn left onto Ridgewood. The garden is .3 mile down on right. *Please park on the street.*

Public Gardens

BUNCOMBE COUNTY

ASHEVILLE

The Biltmore Estate

1 North Pack Square, Asheville (800) 543-2961 www.biltmore.com

Frederick Law Olmsted, designer of New York's Central Park, created the stunning backdrop for George W. Vanderbilt's chateau. The 250 acres of landscaped gardens, grounds, and park are as spectacular as the house itself. From manicured grounds to forests and fields, the landscape was shaped by Olmsted's naturalistic vision.

> *Hours:* Year round, daily, 9 a.m. to 5 p.m.; closed Thanksgiving and Christmas Day
> *Admission:* $32 adults, $24 students 10-15, children under 10 free
> *From I-40*, take Exit 50 or 50B, then follow the signs.

The Botanical Gardens at Asheville

151 W. T. Weaver Boulevard, Asheville (828) 252-5190 botgardens@main.nc.us

The Botanical Gardens at Asheville is a ten-acre community of plants, shrubs, and trees native to the southern Appalachian Mountains. Located adjacent to the University of North Carolina at Asheville, the gardens are dedicated to the preservation and display of the plants of the region.

> *Hours:* Year round, daily, dawn to dusk
> *Admission:* free
> *From Route 19/23*, take the UNC-Asheville exit. Turn right onto Broadway and make

a left at the second traffic light onto W.T. Weaver Boulevard. The entrance to the gardens is the first driveway on the left.

The North Carolina Arboretum

100 Frederick Law Olmsted Way, Asheville (828) 665-2492 www.ncarboretum.org

Visiting the North Carolina Arboretum is the perfect way to experience the natural beauty of western North Carolina. Miles of nature trails offer leisurely walking, as well as challenging hiking; cultivated gardens reflect the unique culture and craft of the southern Appalachian Mountains; a state-of-the-art greenhouse complex is fascinating to visitors; and the National Native Azalea Repository is covered with azaleas. A tour may last 45 minutes or half a day.

> *Hours:* Year round, daily, 8 a.m. to 9 p.m.
> *Admission:* free
> *From Blue Ridge Highway*, exit at mile marker 393, where there are signs for the arbo-

retum, Highway 191, and I-26. On the exit ramp, the entrance to the arboretum is on the left, before Highway 191.

> *From I-40*, merge right into I-26 east. Take Exit 2/Blue Ridge Parkway/Brevard Road/

Highway 191 and turn left (south) onto Highway 191. Proceed for about 2.1 miles (you will pass Biltmore Square Mall). Highway 191 will merge from 4 to 2 lanes. Look for the brown signs for Blue Ridge Parkway and NC Arboretum. Turn right at the traffic light and the entrance to the arboretum will be ahead on the right.

> *From Asheville*, take I-240, which merges into I-26 east. Proceed as directed above.

The Richmond Hill Inn

87 Richmond Hill Drive, Asheville (828) 252-7313 www.richmondhillinn.com

Shortly after the historic Richmond Hill Mansion opened in 1989 as an inn, the Michel family began working with landscape designer Chip Callaway from Greensboro, North Carolina, to create a world-class Victorian landscape for the ten-acre estate. What evolved is a spectacular Victorian garden that is reminiscent of the year in which the mansion was built, 1889. Today, our landscape features English cottage-style gardens, spacious lawn areas, a croquet court, monuments, a mountain brook, and a waterfall. The crown jewel of the gardens is the Parterre Garden, a simple, geometrically landscaped garden.

Hours: Open Day event, July 13, 10 a.m. to 4 p.m.; otherwise, year round, daily, dawn to dusk

Admission: $5 on the Open Day; otherwise, free, but docent-led tours only available on the Open Day

Richmond Hill is located 3 miles northwest of downtown Asheville. From Route 19/23, take the Highway 251/UNC-Asheville exit and follow the signs.

DURHAM COUNTY

CHAPEL HILL
Sarah P. Duke Gardens

Anderson Street, Durham

The Sarah P. Duke Gardens are often spoken of as the "crown jewel" in the heart of Duke University's West Campus, immediately adjacent to the Duke University Medical Center. It is recognized as one of the premier public gardens in the United States, renowned both for landscape design and the quality of horticulture, each year attracting more than 300,000 visitors from all over the world. Duke Gardens provides a place where people of all backgrounds and ages come for beauty, education, horticulture, solitude, discovery, study, renewal, and inspiration.

Hours: Year round, daily, 8 a.m. to dusk

Admission: free

From I-85, take the Hillandale Road exit. Turn east at the top of the exit ramp onto Hillandale Road. Continue on Hillandale Road until it merges with Fulton Street (at the Highway 147 overpass). Proceed on Fulton Street to the intersection with Erwin Road. Turn left onto Erwin Road and proceed to the second traffic light; turn right onto Anderson Street. The entrance is about .5 mile on the right (a half-circle drive with stone walls).

From Raleigh, take I-40 west to the Route 147/Durham Freeway split; follow Route 147 into town and take the Swift Avenue exit. Turn left onto Swift Avenue and proceed to Campus Drive (a 4-way stop). Turn right and go to the first light at Anderson Street and turn right.

North Carolina Botanical Garden

CB 3375 Totten Center, Chapel Hill (919) 962-0522 www.unc.edu/depts/ncbg

The North Carolina Botanical Garden includes nearly 600 acres, including our Main Visitor Area and Piedmont Nature Trails, Coker Arboretum, Mason Farm Biological Reserve, and other lands. We specialize in the display, conservation, and interpretation of plants native to the southeastern United States. The Main Visitor Area includes the Coastal Plain Habitat Garden, Piedmont Habitat Garden, Mountain Habitat Garden, Shade Garden, Fern Collection, Carnivorous Plant Collection, Garden of Flowering Plant Families, Herb Garden, Wildflower Border, plant sales, and gift shop. The garden, part of the University of North Carolina at Chapel Hill, is supported by the State of North Carolina and the Botanical Garden Foundation, Inc.

Hours: Year round, weekdays, 8 a.m. to 5 p.m.; daylight savings time, Saturday, 9 a.m. to 6 p.m., Sunday, 1 p.m. to 6 p.m.; standard time, Saturday, 10 a.m. to 5 p.m., Sunday, 1 p.m. to 5 p.m.

Admission: free

From I-40, take Exit 273 from the west, Exit 273B from the east. Turn right onto Highway 54W and proceed 2.4 miles; turn left at the traffic light onto Finley Golf Course Road. Go .6 mile and curve right onto Old Mason Farm Road. Go .7 mile and look for the North Carolina Botanical Garden sign on the left; turn left into the parking lot.

From the 15-501 Bypass/Fordham Boulevard, look for the brown landscaped highway wall on the south side of Fordham Boulevard, .6 mile west of the Highway 54 overpass. Turn onto Old Mason Farm Road at the east end of the wall. Look for the garden sign immediately on your right and turn right into the parking lot.

MECKLENBURG COUNTY

CHARLOTTE

UNC-Charlotte Botanical Gardens

9201 University City Boulevard, Charlotte (704) 687-4055 www.bioweb.uncc.edu/gardens

We have 5,000 square feet of greenhouse displaying tropical plants from around the world in habitats such as tropical rainforest, desert, orchid jungle, seven acres of hybrid rhododendrons and native azaleas, plus 1,000 species of native plants including wildflowers and ferns of the Carolinas, and three acres of exotic hardy plants suitable for landscape used in the Southeast, including a winter garden, the Butterfly and Hummingbird Pavilion, and Rock Garden.

Hours: Open Days events, Saturday and Sunday, September 14 and 15, 10 a.m. to 3 p.m.

Admission: free

From I-85, take Exit 46. Turn right onto Mallard Creek Church Road and go 1.5 miles to the second traffic light. Turn right onto Mary Alexander Road. Go .5 mile and turn right onto Craver Road. Turn right into the visitor parking opposite McMillon Greenhouse.

Wing Haven Gardens and Bird Sanctuary

248 Ridgewood Avenue, Charlotte (704) 331-0664 www.winghavengardens.com

Wing Haven has been a unique part of Charlotte since its creation in 1927 by Elizabeth and Edwin Clarkson. The gardens, enclosed on all sides by brick walls, encompass approximately three acres in the heart of Charlotte and include both formal and woodland areas. Throughout the emphasis is on plantings for birds and other wildlife, providing cover, nesting sites, and food. Plaques and statuary, integrated into the garden walls and paths, reflect the spirit and beauty of Wing Haven and its creators.

Hours: Open for Open Days Program on September 14 & 15, 10 a.m. to 4 p.m.; otherwise, year round, Sunday 2 p.m. to 5 p.m., Tuesday, 3 p.m. to 5 p.m., and Wednesday, 10 a.m. to 2 p.m.

Admission: free

From I-77, take Exit 6A/Woodlawn. Follow Woodlawn for about 3 miles and turn left onto Selwyn Avenue. Follow Selwyn for .5 mile and turn left onto Ridgewood Avenue. Wing Haven is at #248.

WAKE COUNTY

RALEIGH

J. C. Raulston Arboretum at North Carolina State University

Beryl Road, Raleigh (919) 515-3132 http://arb.ncsu.edu/arboretum

Be sure to visit the JC Raulston Arboretum the next time you are in Raleigh. The arboretum features over 5,500 different types of trees, shrubs, vines, ground covers, herbaceous perennials, and annual bedding plants displayed in a beautiful garden setting. Stroll through our new cutting-edge plants that are released to the nursery industry.

Hours: Year round, daily, 8 a.m. to 8 p.m.

Admission: free

From I-440, take Exit 3/Hillsborough Street. Turn left onto Hillsborough Street and proceed to Beryl Road. Turn right onto Beryl Road (you will see a restaurant called Waffle House). Go over the railroad tracks and straight ahead. We are located on the left side of Beryl Road across from Capital City Lumber.

OHIO

OPEN DAYS:

April 21
June 15
July 7

Beechwood Gardens, Cincinnati

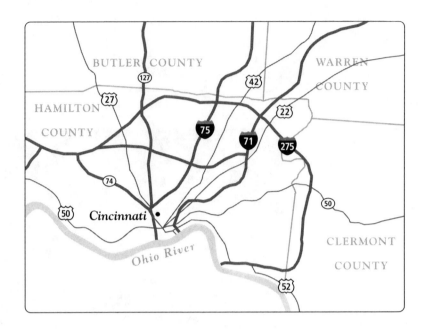

Sunday, April 21

HAMILTON COUNTY

ANDERSON TOWNSHIP

Judy Brandenburg's Garden

1260 Apple Hill Road, Anderson Township

I garden on a hillside with giant oaks, tall pines, and spruces. There is an understory of redbuds and dogwoods. I have added lots of crab apples, magnolias, rhododendrons, and azaleas, as well as a variety of flowering trees and shrubs. There are paths that wander throughout the gardens. In the spring, there are thousands of bulbs, wildflowers, primroses, iris, and tree peonies. A wide variety of early perennials makes a real splash. At this time of year, the rock garden is lovely. The sunny summer garden becomes a tapestry of color and texture with daylilies, phlox, and all the wonderful perennials of the season. The woods offer a cooler contrast, with ferns, astilbes, pulmonaria, and hosta. The small pond is always delightful. This garden never ceases to thrill my soul! It is my passion and my love!

Hours: 10 a.m. to 4 p.m.

From I-275, take Exit 73/Kellogg Avenue west. (This is the last exit before you go over the bridge to Kentucky; if you are coming from Kentucky, it is the first exit after you go over the bridge.) Go west on Kellogg for about 1 mile. You will see the Cincinnati Water Works on the left; at the bend, Apple Hill Road goes to the right. At the fork, bear left. Go about .8 mile. I'm the first driveway on the right after the River Hills subdivision. There is a sign by the road for #1260; you will see flowers but won't be able to see the house.

HYDE PARK
The Robertson-Conway Garden
1322 Delta Avenue, Hyde Park

This is a lovely collection of shade-loving plants set off by an abundance of azaleas and rhododendrons. The garden is a great blend of plantscapes and hardscapes with intimate gathering places and unique statuary. Brick pathways lead you through multi-level planting areas that create a sense of peace and tranquility. In the summer months, colorful annuals provide a vibrant splash of color against the dense green background of the spring-blooming azaleas.

Hours: 10 a.m. to 4 p.m.

From I-71, take Exit 5/Dana Avenue. Turn left at the end of the exit ramp onto Duck Creek Road. Go about .7 mile and turn right onto Dana Avenue. At the traffic light at Madison Road, Dana becomes Observatory Avenue. Travel 2 miles on Observatory to Delta Avenue. Turn right onto Delta and go to the sixth house on the left. There is a large hedge along the front property line. *Please park on the street.*

Proceeds shared with the Cincinnati Horticultural Society

WYOMING
Nancy & Ed Rosenthal's Garden
223 Hilltop Lane, Wyoming

This is a large garden with a wide variety of plants and trees, both native and species not indigenous to this area. Much survives of the original plantings, which were done by noted Cincinnati landscape architect Richard Grant in 1937. In late April, you will see spring in all her glory with many flowering trees, shrubs, and bulbs. There is a lilac garden and a hillside of Exbury azaleas. You may meander the woodlands and find most species of wildflowers native to the area. By July, the perennials are in full stride in the many gardens of roses, daisies, monarda, lilies, and hostas. There are gardens from full sun to full shade, rolling lawns, deep woods with stone-lined paths and a covered bridge, butterfly gardens, numerous annuals, and even sculpture.

Hours: 10 a.m. to 4 p.m.

From I-75 north, take Exit 10/Galbraith Road on the right (going west). Continue several miles to Congress Run Road on the right. Congress Run will make a bend and turn onto Hilltop Lane shortly after the stop sign. Go .5 block (note the street sign that reads "Slow-25 miles"). Turn left down the unmarked private lane. Go to #223, the last house on the private lane.

Proceeds shared with the Cincinnati Horticultural Society

Saturday, June 15

MONTGOMERY COUNTY

Dayton

The Larkins Garden

41 Stonemill Road, Dayton

This classic, urban Dayton property has been divided into three garden areas, all designed around the use of roses. Each garden uses a different variety of fence design for definition and backdrop for pockets of color and privacy. The first garden is of borders layered with shrubs and trees, leading to the patio garden. This small garden, entered and exited though arches, features a boxed herb garden and uses roses as accents in a border reflecting an English influence. The lower garden is separated from the main yard by a low brick wall and is defined at the rear by a tall arbor and latticed fence, which forms the frame for a variety of climbing roses.

Hours: 10 a.m. to 4 p.m.

From I-75, take the Main Street exit. Go south on Route 48 to Stonemill Road (3 streets past the traffic light at Stewart Street) and turn east for 1 block. Our house, #41, is on the northwest corner of Stonemill and Rubicon Roads.

Proceeds shared with the Garden Club of Dayton, Marie Aull Tribute Garden

The Patterson Homestead

1110 Rubicon Road, Dayton

The Patterson Homestead offers a variety of gardens to explore and enjoy. A rose bed displays hybrid, moss, Bourbon, and several grandiflora roses all vying for the visitor's attention. The west side of the home is a backdrop for a profusion of colorful spring bulbs and the striking red foliage of oak-leaf hydrangeas in autumn. Around the corner are a flourishing shade garden and a kitchen garden, which provides an abundant harvest of tomatoes, peppers, Swiss chard, and rhubarb. An overflowing perennial garden cascades down the southern slope. The spectacular plant materials represent a lifetime of effort and love of flowers by Edna Ostendorf. Ms. Ostendorf, upon selling her home, donated her entire garden to the Homestead, including dozens of fifty-year-old peonies.

Hours: 10 a.m. to 4 p.m.

From I-75, take the Main Street exit and go south on Route 48 to Springhouse Road (.25 mile past Stewart Street). Turn left and go 1 block to Rubicon Road. Turn left onto Rubicon to the entrance to the garden.

Proceeds shared with the Patterson Homestead and Aullwood Gardens.

Gloria B. Richardson Garden

30 Stonemill Road, Dayton

This is a patio garden where every bulb, herb, and flowering perennial becomes as important as the one older tree, the boxwood, and the ornamental firs. I first wanted scent, then color and texture. From early spring through the fall, a leisurely rest as well as afternoon tea or a cocktail party in the garden affords sensual pleasure.

Hours: 10 a.m. to 4 p.m.

From I-75, take the Main Street exit and go south on Route 48 to Stonemill Road (3 streets past the traffic light at Stewart Street). Turn east; #30 is in the middle of the first block on the south side.

Proceeds shared with the Garden Club of Dayton, Marie Aull Tribute Garden

Ellie Shulman's Rose Terrace

253 Schenck Avenue, Dayton

My garden style has been influenced by extensive English, French, and American garden touring and by collaboration with garden designer Ziggy Petersons. In front is a shaded "garden within a garden," all green plant material but no lawn. Challenges of difficult terrain and mostly full sun to the south and west have resulted in a terraced rose garden and several "garden rooms" with perennials, topiary, espalier, and a start at pleaching. There is an unusually large amount of plant material on less than an acre of property and I am always working toward that elusive goal of continuous color, bloom, and fragrance.

Hours: 10 a.m. to 4 p.m.

From I-75, take the Edwin Moses Boulevard/University of Dayton exit and go east on Edwin Moses .8 mile to Stewart Street (the first traffic light). Turn right onto Stewart and proceed .6 mile (the third light). Turn right onto Brown Street and proceed .7 mile (4 lights plus 2 more streets). Turn left onto Schenck Avenue and proceed to #253.

Proceeds shared with the Garden Club of Dayton, Marie Aull Tribute Garden

Wessex

758 Plantation Lane, Dayton

As its name suggests, this garden mirrors an English cottage garden, for it is dense with greenery. Its beds contain herbs alongside swaths of flowers chosen for their subtle coloration, gray tones, or leaf formation. Old roses and flowering vines grow into trees and up walls. This one acre also includes a rock garden, hydrangea collection, and redbud grove with wildflowers underfoot. As the land falls away at the back of the yard, a wisteria pergola overlooks a swimming pool with Italian overtones. A bust of David is flanked on one side by a curved brick wall and a crescent of pleached lindens on the other.

Hours: 10 a.m. to 4 p.m.

From I-75 north, take Exit 47/Dixie Drive/Mordine/Kettering. Follow this road north to the second traffic light and make a right onto West Stroop Road. Turn left at the third light onto Southern Boulevard. Turn right onto Blossom Heath Road and drive up the hill. Turn left onto Plantation Lane. *Please park on Plantation Lane or Blossom Heath Road.*

Proceeds shared with the Garden Club of Dayton, Marie Aull Tribute Garden

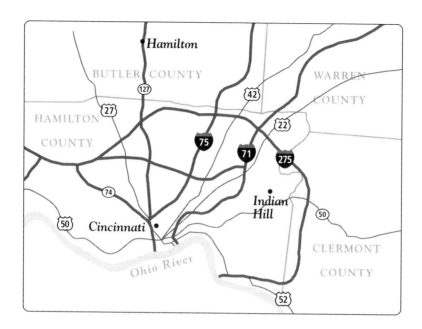

Sunday, July 7

BUTLER COUNTY

HAMILTON

Joan Day's Garden

6215 Cavalcade Drive, Hamilton

This well-established and lovingly tended garden is situated on a little more than three quarters of an acre. Inviting paths (including one composed entirely of crushed terra-cotta pots) draw the visitor into a serene woodland setting. There are also high color sun beds, as well as a dainty fairy garden tucked into the top of a living stone wall. An eclectic collection of over fifty hypertufa trough gardens and numerous birdhouses are encountered at every turn. Many genera of plants are featured (over 600 hosta cultivars), in addition to rare alpines, conifers, ornamental shrubs, and Japanese maples.

Hours: 10 a.m. to 4 p.m.

From I-75, take the "new" exit Route 129 west to Hamilton. Go about 3 miles to Exit 747. Turn right (north) for about .25 mile to the first traffic light. Turn left onto Princeton Road. Go 1 mile to the blinking light to Liberty-Fairfield Road, turning right. Continue for .5 mile and turn left onto Stoneybrook Drive, then turn right onto Calvacade Drive. Go to the fifth house on the left, #6215. *Please park on the street.*

Proceeds shared with the Hamilton Garden Club

HAMILTON COUNTY

AMELIA

The Gardens of Brenda & John Demetriou

1065 Gaskins Road, Amelia

The front gardens include an English herb garden, along with a formal miniature rose garden. The two-story brick house is covered with English ivy and the planting around the house has a cottage garden look, with a wide variety of perennials mixed with annuals. The back gardens are shade gardens and feature over 400 varieties of hostas with companion plants—ferns, hydrangea, pulmonaria, Solomon's seal, and more. Brenda's original birdhouses are featured throughout the gardens, as are several butterfly gardens and theme gardens.

Hours: 10 a.m. to 4 p.m.

From I-275, take the Beechmont/Amelia exit. Go towards Amelia. You will be on State Route 125. Go about 3 miles to Merwin-Ten Mile Road. Skyline Chili is on the corner. Turn right onto Merwin-Ten Mile Road. Go about .25 mile to the first road on the right. Turn right onto Gaskins Road. Go to the third house on the left, #1065.

Proceeds shared with the Greater Cincinnati Daylily & Hosta Society

ANDERSON TOWNSHIP

Judy Brandenburg's Garden

1260 Apple Hill Road, Anderson Township

Please see listing under April 21 for garden description, hours, and directions.

INDIAN HILL

Kurtz's Garden

4770 Burley Hills Drive, Indian Hill

This garden is a succession of garden rooms, including a shrub and small tree border, the Celtic garden (a quadrant of perennials each in a different color scheme with steps leading to an herbaceous border), a garden filled with tropical and subtropical woodland plants, a woodland garden walk and resting area, a water garden, and an herb and vegetable garden beside a patio garden. The site is a rather steep hillside, which has posed many challenges yet has given definition to each room. I have also never met a plant I could do without and am always experimenting with new varieties.

Hours: 10 a.m. to 4 p.m.

From I-71 north, take Exit 11/Kenwood/Madeira to Kenwood Road. Turn right off the exit ramp to the first traffic light, Euclid Road. Turn left onto Euclid, go to the second light at Miami Road, and turn right. Madeira Fire Department in on the left and City Hall on the right. Pass through 3 lights and enter Indian Hill (St. Gertrude's Church is on the right and a BP gas station is on the left). Stay on Miami to the first red blinking light, Indian Hill Road, and turn right. Burley Hills Drive is the first street on the left. Total miles from I-71, 4 miles.

From I-71 south, take Exit 12/Montgomery Road/Kenwood Mall. Turn left off the exit onto Montgomery Road to the second set of lights. Turn right onto Hosbrook Road and go to the end. Turn left onto Euclid Road and, at the next light, turn right onto Miami

Road. Stay on Miami Road through 3 lights until you reach a red blinking light at Indian Hill Road. Turn right. Burley Hills Road is the first street on the left. *Please park on the street or in the driveway.*

HARTWELL
Amy & John Duke's Daylily Gardens
223 Kearney Street, Hartwell

Our American Hemerocallis Society Display Garden features 500 different daylily cultivars, including a complete Stout Medal collection. Pathways will lead you through rooms that feature over 100 hosta varieties, many woody shrubs, and perennials. Plantings are arranged around statuary, pathways, stone walls, and elements of whimsy. You will see our Child's Garden, Fairie Gardens, and miniatures. Many plants are labeled. We plant over 1,000 annuals and many containers to carry color through fall. We welcome visitors (and cameras) and provide a tour guide write-up intended to be both informative and entertaining.

Hours: 10 a.m. to 4 p.m.

From I-75, take Exit 10/Galbraith Road. Turn west. The first street is Woodbine Avenue at the traffic light. Turn left (south). Kearney Street is the next hard left turn. We are at #223, about the third house on the right, the white Victorian with two tall Norway spruces in front. *Please park on the street.*

Proceeds shared with the Greater Cincinnati Master Gardener Association

HYDE PARK
Julie Mahlin's Garden
2500 Observatory Avenue, Hyde Park

This is a sixteen-year-old English cottage garden enhanced by a wrought iron fence. It sits on a corner lot in a turn-of-the-century neighborhood. The garden flows in large, graceful curves and is edged with silver lamb's ear. There are more than 165 different perennials, including achillea, astilbe, thalictrum, helianthus, aster, boltonia, buddleia, clematis, and brunnera. Each year I add about 2,000 annuals to ensure constant color in a scheme of pink, purple, white, and lemon yellow. Within the beds are small trees and shrubs including Carolina silverbell, Tanyosho pine, Korean fir, vitex, *Chamaecyparis* 'Boulevard' and 'Fernspray Gold', viburnums, and *Cornus mas*. A rear brick patio backs up to a brick garage wall that has a fountain on it. Thirty containers give color to this secret garden. This garden will be featured in *Better Homes & Gardens* magazine in the summer of 2002.

Hours: 10 a.m. to 4 p.m.

From I-71 north, take Exit 5/Dana Avenue. At the end of the exit ramp, turn left onto Duck Creek Road. Go .7 mile and turn right onto Dana Avenue. At the traffic light at Madison Road, Dana changes to Observatory Avenue. Go past the light to the corner of Berry Avenue on the left. Look for the house with a wrought-iron fence and lots of flowers.

From I-71 south, take Exit 5/Dana Avenue. At the end of the exit ramp, turn left onto Dana, then proceed as directed above. *Please park either on Observatory Avenue or Berry Avenue.*

Proceeds shared with the Cincinnati Horticultural Society

INDIAN HILL
Beechwood Gardens
6900 Given Road, Indian Hill

This is an informal cottage garden of wildflowers, bulbs, and perennials amid annuals on five acres of beech forest. Garden accents include an antique iron fence, a pond with a Robinson iron fountain, stone benches and urns, bridges and creeks, and meandering paths through the woods and gardens. This garden was visited by *Rebecca's Garden* in May 2000 and was filmed for her TV series. It was also featured in *Ohio Magazine* in May 2000.

Hours: 10 a.m. to 4 p.m.

From I-75 or I-71, take I-275 east to the Loveland/Indian Hill exit. Turn right onto Loveland Madiera Road (pass a major intersection at Remington Road). Proceed .25 mile past Remington and turn left onto Spooky Hollow Road. Turn right (at a stop sign) and continue on Spooky Hollow. Turn right (at a stop sign) onto Given Road. Go 2.4 miles to #6900. *Please park in the driveway.*

Proceeds shared with the Cincinnati Horticultural Society

J. Louis & Beth Karp's Garden
5875 Mohican Lane, Indian Hill

This amazing three-acre garden is maintained by Beth and Jay alone and has been created over the last five years. This garden has many separate garden rooms. A formal blue-and-white garden is enclosed by boxwood and brick. Raised beds with stone walls contain vegetables, herbs, and flowers. Between the raised beds is an area with a bench, roses, and sundial. Gardens by the pond are colorful and feature plants that can survive "wet feet" during the winter. Several shade gardens feature hostas, ferns, and flowering trees and shrubs. Trees, which include stewartia, black gum, Japanese maple, bald cypress, and weeping dogwood, are featured throughout the garden. There is a new conifer garden, as well as a new raised bed next to the brick terrace, which is enlivened by gorgeous containers. Foliage color and texture are an important part of this garden's appeal.

Hours: 10 a.m. to 2 p.m.

From I-71 south, take Exit 12/Montgomery Road/Kenwood Hall and turn left; if coming from the north, turn right. Go about .5 mile and turn right onto Galbraith Road. Continue to the second traffic light, Miami Road, and turn right. Go about 1 mile to Euclid and Miami. Stay in the right lane and continue on Miami Road. Drive about 1.4 miles (past Camargo and Shawnee Run Road) and turn left onto Graves. Drive .6 mile and turn left onto Mohican Lane. The garden is at #5875, the third house on the left. *Please park on the street.*

WYOMING
Nancy & Ed Rosenthal's Garden
223 Hilltop Lane, Wyoming

Please see April 21 for garden description, hours, and directions.

Public Gardens

FRANKLIN COUNTY

NEWARK

Dawes Arboretum

7770 Jacksontown Road S.E., Newark (800) 443-2331 www.dawesarb.org

Established in 1929, the Dawes Arboretum is dedicated to education in horticulture, natural history, and arboretum history. It includes 1,149 acres of horticultural collections, gardens, natural acres, a Japanese garden, the Daweswood House, and collections of hollies, crab apples, rare trees, and rhododendrons. A 4.5-mile auto tour and eleven miles of trails provide easy access.

Hours: Year round, grounds, daily, dawn to dusk; visitor center open Monday through Saturday, 8 a.m. to 5 p.m., Sundays and holidays, 1 p.m. to 5 p.m.; closed Thanksgiving, Christmas, and New Year's Day.

Admission: free

Located 30 miles east of Columbus and 5 miles south of Newark on Route 13, north of I-70, off Exit 132.

WESTERVILLE

Inniswood Metro Gardens

940 Hempstead Road, Westerville (614) 895-6216

Originally the home of Grace and Mary Innis, Inniswood is a balance of colorful, landscaped garden and natural areas, yet it captures the warmth and serenity of a long-established estate garden. The herb, rock, and rose gardens fit the contours of the land and are in harmony with the meadow and woodlands. Cultural and educational programs and tours are offered for all ages. Fall is celebrated with "An Affair of the Hort," held the last full week of September.

Hours: Year round, daily, 7 a.m. to dusk

Admission: free

From I-270, take the Westerville exit. Turn left onto Westerville Road. Turn left at the first traffic light onto Dempsey. Turn left at the second light onto Hempstead Road. The road will veer to the right after the fire station and the entrance to the garden is on the right.

CINCINNATI
Cincinnati Zoo & Botanical Garden
3400 Vine Street, Cincinnati (800) 944-4116

Among the finest horticultural display gardens in the country, the Cincinnati Zoo & Botanical Garden features over 3,000 varieties of trees, shrubs, tropical plants, bulbs, perennials, and annuals. Arranged in gardens and in naturalistic settings simulating animal habitats, many of the plants are labeled, providing identification and interesting information for the garden enthusiast. The zoo boasts one of the largest and finest spring gardens in the country, with over a million spring bulbs and thousands of colorful, early-blooming shrubs and trees. The zoo's outstanding butterfly and pollinator gardens include interpretive signs providing information about butterflies, flowers, and gardening, as well as the importance of the symbiotic relationships of plants and pollinators. The zoo is home to the largest collection of hardy bamboo species in any Midwest botanical garden. Also see the endangered species garden and display at the zoo's Center for Conservation and Research of Endangered Species (CREW).

Hours: Memorial Day through Labor Day, daily, 9 a.m. to 6 p.m.

Admission: $11.50 adults, $9 senior citizens, $6 children 2 p.m. to noon

From I-74, go east to I-75 north. Take I-75 north to Mitchell Avenue. Turn right onto Mitchell Avenue. Turn right onto Vine Street. Turn left onto Forest Avenue. Turn right onto Dury Avenue. The auto entrance is on the right.

From I-75 north, take Mitchell Avenue. Proceed as directed above.

Civic Garden Center of Greater Cincinnati
2715 Reading Road, Cincinnati (513) 221-0981

The Civic Garden Center of Greater Cincinnati is located in the Hauck Botanic Gardens, also known as "Sooty Acres." The property was donated to the center by Cornelius Hauck, who developed the property into an urban oasis. The garden includes rare and historic trees, an herb garden, a hosta garden, a dwarf conifer collection, and a butterfly garden.

Hours: Year round, daily, dawn to dusk

Admission: free

From I-71 south, take the William Howard Taft exit to Reading Road. Turn right and go 1 block to Oak Street. Turn left onto Oak Street and take an immediate left into the Civic Garden Center parking lot.

From I-71 north, take the Reading Road exit and proceed north on Reading Road to Oak Street. Turn left onto Oak Street and take an immediate left into the Civic Garden Center parking lot.

Spring Grove Cemetery & Arboretum

4521 Spring Grove Avenue, Cincinnati (513) 681-1526 www.681-PLAN.org

Since its founding over 150 years ago, Spring Grove has remained a leader in cemetery design and management. The landscape "lawn plan" concept was created here and, although it was considered a radical concept of cemetery design at that time, it later became accepted almost universally as the model plan. Spring Grove remains a masterwork of the landscaping art, studied by horticulturists and admired by thousands of visitors. The Cincinnati Chamber of Commerce lists it among the city's outstanding attractions, proudly quoting the praise of an artist who once said, "Only a place with a heart and soul could make for its dead a more magnificent park than any which exists for the living." With over 733 acres, fifteen lakes and one waterfall, three expansive floral borders, 21 champion trees and more than 1,000 labeled woody plant specimens within the arboretum, Spring Grove truly is one of Cincinnati's best-kept secrets.

Hours: Year round, daily; front gate, 8 a.m. to 6 p.m.; north gate, 8 a.m. to 5 p.m.

Admission: free

From downtown, take I-75 north. Proceed to Exit 6/Mitchell Avenue. Turn left (west) onto Mitchell Avenue. Travel Mitchell Avenue to Spring Grove Avenue, turn left onto Spring Grove (in center lane), and go past 3 traffic lights (including the light at Mitchell). Pass under the third light (Winton Road) and get into the curb lane as you pass under light. The entrance to cemetery is approximately 500 feet ahead on the right.

From Dayton, I-75 south to Exit 6/Mitchell Avenue. Bear right (west) on Mitchell Avenue. Follow as directed above.

From Indiana, I-74 east to I-75 to Exit 6/Mitchell Avenue. Follow as directed above. From Columbus, I-71 North to Exit E562/Norway Lateral. Follow the lateral to I-75 south to Exit 6/Mitchell Avenue. Turn right onto Mitchell Avenue and follow as directed above.

MONTGOMERY COUNTY

DAYTON

Aullwood Garden

930 Aullwood Road, Dayton

Aullwood Garden Metro Park is a 1920s' country estate garden. The shady woodland combines native wildflowers, bulbs, and exotic plants. A meadow has some native prairie species. Peak bloom is in spring, especially April and May. There is something in bloom most of the year from *Helleborus, Narcissus, Mertensia,* and *Syringa* to *Echinacea, Lycoris,* and *Colchicum.*

Hours: March 1 through December 16, Tuesday through Sunday, 8 a.m. to 7 p.m.

Admission: free

From I-75, take Route 40 west, then take Aullwood Road south at Englewood Dam. Pass the Aullwood Audubon Center and turn right into the garden parking via the sign.

Cox Arboretum & Gardens

6733 Springboro Pike, Dayton (937) 434-9005

The Cox Arboretum exhibits landscaped and natural areas on 175 rolling acres. Garden features include the Edible Landscape Garden, Herb Garden, Founders Water Garden, and the Shrub Garden. Woody plant collections include crab apples, magnolias, lilacs, maples, oaks, and conifers. Hiking trails traverse about seventy acres of woodlands and ten acres of prairie and wetland. Tulips and daffodils afford a major spring display.

Hours: Year round, daily, 8 a.m. to dusk; closed Christmas and New Year's Day
Admission: free

From I-75, get off at Exit 44. Go east on Route 725 for 1 mile to Route 741/Springboro Pike, then go south for 2 miles to the entrance.

Wegerzyn Gardens MetroPark

1301 East Siebenthaler Avenue, Dayton (937) 277-9028

These formal gardens feature Federal, English, and Victorian theme gardens, as well as rose, shade, and children's gardens, all flanking the Garden Green with an ash allée. This MetroPark also features the scenic Stillwater River, the Marie Aull Nature Trail, and a mature lowland forest, or wetland wood, through which meanders a 350-foot-long boardwalk. The center presents programs on horticulture.

Hours: Year round, daily, 8 a.m. to dusk; closed Christmas and New Year's Day
Admission: free

Located 1.5 miles west of I-75 and 4 miles south of I-70. Take I-75 to Exit 57B/Wagoner Ford Road. Turn west onto Siebenthaler Avenue, continue west on Siebenthaler Avenue, and turn right into the Cultural Arts Complex, before the Siebenthaler Bridge. Follow the drive .5 mile to the horticultural center.

OKLAHOMA

The Gardens of Bonnie & Joe Klein, Tulsa

Saturday, May 18

TULSA COUNTY

Tulsa
The Gardens of Bonnie & Joe Klein
2508 East 30th Street, Tulsa

Peacefulness defines this lovely historic section of Tulsa and the Klein residence is no exception to the rule. Prevailing upon the landscape is a magnificent river birch, which overarches this stately English Tudor manor house. A curved limestone walk leads to the front of the house and flanking it to one side are three mature 'Yaupon' hollies and a dogwood tree that has graced the lawn for many a season. Interspersed amongst the azaleas that help to define the entrance are 'Densaformis' yews and a weeping juniper. Two magnificent 'Foster' hollies stand as sentries on each end of the front of the home. The long driveway leads to a beautiful back lawn and gardens. In serpentine fashion, 'Helleri' holly with 'Capitata' yews serving as punctuation points wind their way against the pierced red brick formal wall. Seasonal pots of ferns and annuals lend interest to the flagstone terrace complete with a stone barbecue and seating for many a hungry guest. Here, once again, are yews and dogwoods in graceful contrast to beds of lush ferns and perennials. Lovely oak-leaf hydrangeas thrive in this setting and native trees can be viewed for as far as the eye can see. An architectural cabana with a timbered roof overlooks the lagoon pool. A peaceful border-encased pool flows through a stone bridge enabling the water to spill over larger native stones into the pool below. A *dissectum* 'Crimson Queen' Japanese maple provides a softening touch among the rust-hued stones, which serve as a beautiful complement to the dappled turquoise water. Magnificent pots hold huge balls of colorful burgundy and yellow mums. Perimeter Asiatic lily gardens appear before one proceeds further into extensive areas of hostas, astilbes, iris, spirea, dicentras, and roses. An intimate enclosed side patio to the east of the house is completely done in antique wicker and a small circular pool is the focal point of interest to those who are seated in this cozy shaded area. Tucked into various corners are antique iron planters, which hold one-of-a-kind urns spilling over with ivy and flowers. Grandchildren find the secret gardens to be enticing and many a fanciful dream has been born in this place so finely and intricately wrought.

Hours: 10 a.m. to 4 p.m.

From I-44, exit onto Lewis Avenue. Go north on Lewis Avenue to the 31st Street intersection. Go straight on Lewis for 1 block and turn right (east) onto 30th Street. Go 1 long block to the residence. *Please park along the street.*

The Gardens of Breniss & Daniel O'Neal

2451 East 40th Street, Tulsa

Forest Hollow Estate is the vision which has become reality for Breniss and Daniel O'Neal. Owning a landscape design business has enabled them to bring fantasy to life in their home and gardens, which are located on a one-acre plot in the heart of one of Tulsa's most beautiful areas. This estate has been certified by the State of Oklahoma as a wildlife habitat and upon entering there is an immediate sense that this is far more than home and garden, it is an artful preservation of nature in its most complete and natural form. Upon entering, the sloping fescue lawn leads the eye to the rose garden. Canopied beneath the evergreen trees are stone stairways leading into Chapel Hill, that area where songbirds provide pause for a meditative moment. On almost any given day, the gentle sound of leafy branches blowing carries one away while experiencing each distinct sensation of sight, smell, and sound. Interlaced throughout the garden are 387 cultivars of evergreen trees and shrubs, each one lending its special architectural and textured grace to the total scheme. It is this sense of formality which enhances the veritable arboretum in the midst of other fluid forms of nature. Nestled amongst a backdrop of cherry laurels, tsuga hemlocks, and viburnums is an extensive area of *macrophylla* hydrangeas mingled into the rock-delineated beds. Defining the upper lawn and gardens from the more colorful azalea-filled back gardens is an antique iron gate, which opens onto a curving flagstone pathway between walls that may serve as seating. While seated on the flagstone terrace, which provides a link to various backyard areas of interest, one may look up to the dry stream bed filled with many forms of perennials spilling their purple and yellow petals upon the stream-worn stones beneath. Looking to the lower area, an azure pool provides that soothing water element so necessary to any total landscape. Monarch butterflies dart amongst the perennials and no season is without its special tranquil moments. 'Zéphirine Drouhin' roses cascade over an arbor and provide an entrance into the Moonlight Garden. Many special plants and shrubs are grown as specimens in various urns and time-worn pots, yet there is a touch of whimsy provided by a multitude of birdhouses. Forest Hollow provides a peaceful setting in which all forms of life may harmoniously co-exist.

Hours: 10 a.m. to 4 p.m.

From I-44, exit onto Lewis Avenue. Go north on Lewis Avenue to 40th Street (the number streets run consecutively). Turn right (east) and go 1 long block. Fortieth Street will dead end into Forest Hollow's circular driveway. *Please park in the driveway and along the street.*

The Burke Reynolds Garden
1824 East 31st Place, Tulsa

One waxes poetic upon first glimpse of the Reynolds home, nestled amidst a towering native canopy of green, which is echoed in the expanse of bright green Bermuda lawn beneath. There is an immediate approach of lush banks of azaleas massed beneath one of several specimen dogwoods. A large moss-laden boulder is naturalized into the bed with perennial and annual color. Dwarf nandinas provide a curving border of contrast in front of 'Joseph Coat' roses, punctuated by more azaleas. Providing a crisp, straight line of relief in front of the porch are precisely clipped boxwoods, while 'Capitata' yews in antique urns stand at either side of the impressive front entrance. Burke is especially proud of the antique coach lights, which echo the appeal of the symmetry on either side of the entrance as well. Oak-leaf hydrangeas provide lush blooms in this landscape so beautifully defined in green and white, which complements the dusty red brick of this English cottage-style residence. The flowing, park-like setting is enhanced by a shaded border plot to the east, comprised of yews, azaleas, 'Cayuga' viburnums, and Japanese maples beneath the graceful branches of yet another dogwood. On either side of the charming chimney window are 'Welchi' junipers and more oak-leaf hydrangeas. A large gas lantern stands as gatekeeper to the more intimate backyard, encircled with Carolina jessamine. Echoing the azure tones of the rectangular pool are stands of slash pines, which line both the east and west sides of this area. A cedar deck overlooks the pool where an urn spilling water into a small pond causes one to take note of the border of azaleas and perfectly formed clusters of bird's-nest spruce. Shiny leaved Russian laurels add an architectural element to the winding paths of this garden, providing a harmonius blend of earth, tree, and sky.

Hours: 10 a.m. to 4 p.m.

From I-44, exit onto Lewis Avenue. Go north on Lewis Avenue to 31st Street. Turn left (west) onto 31st Street. Go 2 short blocks to Zunis Avenue and turn left. Turn right onto 31st Place to #1824. *Please park along the street.*

Public Gardens
TULSA COUNTY

Tᴜʟsᴀ
Gilcrease Museum

1400 Gilcrease Museum Road, Tulsa (888) 655-2278 www.gilcrease.org

Gilcrease Museum houses the world's largest, most comprehensive collection of art of the American West. In addition, Gilcrease offers an unparalleled collection of Native American art and artifacts; a hands-on, interactive exhibition highlighting the art, culture, and history of Mexico; and a distinguished collection of historical manuscripts, documents, and maps. Using the Gilcrease collections as a guide, historical theme gardens have been developed on 23 of the museum's 460 acres. These gardens enhance the museum's collections by reflecting gardening styles and techniques from five time periods in the American West: Pre-Columbian, Pioneer, Colonial, Victorian, and Rock. Gilcrease is the only known art museum to have these educational and inspirational gardens on one site. Special care of the grounds began with the museum's founder, Thomas Gilcrease, who encouraged the growth of native plants and introduced numerous exotic specimens, including the southern magnolia.

Hours: Tuesday through Saturday, 9 a.m. to 5 p.m., Sunday and holidays 11 a.m. to 5 p.m. Also open Monday, Memorial Day through Labor Day, 9 a.m. to 5 p.m., closed Christmas Day.

Admission: Suggested admission donation $3 adults, $5 for a family

From downtown Tulsa, take Highway 51 west. Exit onto Gilcrease Museum Road. Follow signs to the museum, about 1.5 miles.

Philbrook Museum of Art and Gardens

2727 South Rockford Road, Tulsa (918) 749-7941 www.philbrook.org

The Philbrook gardens offer the most breathtaking views in Tulsa! Twenty-three acres of formal gardens, sweeping lawns, and sloping woodlands in the center of town are an unexpected oasis on the prairie. Highlights include a reflecting pool and classic Tempietto.

Hours: Year round, Tuesday through Sunday, 10 a.m. to 5 p.m., Thursday until 8 p.m.

Admission: free

From I-44, take the Peoria exit. Go north on Peoria for 2.5 miles. Turn right onto 27th Place. There are signs at 27th Place and Peoria. Go 1 block and Philbrook will be at the end of 27th Place.

Tulsa Garden Center

2435 South Peoria, Tulsa (918) 746-5125

Built in 1919 as a 21-room private residence, this splendid Italian renaissance villa was home to three different prominent Tulsa families. The Tulsa Garden Center was originally one of the most elegant homes in Tulsa, sitting on thirteen country acres within the city. The estate was comprised of the main house, two greenhouses and a solarium, a swimming pool, two five-room cottages, and two barns. Renovated in the early thirties by George and Geraldine Snedden and interior decorator Louis Perry, today the Tulsa Garden Center stands as a beautiful and grand reminder of their endeavor. In 1954, the city of Tulsa purchased the home and ten acres of adjoining property. Today, the nonprofit organization Tulsa Garden Center, Inc. strives to support, preserve, and enhance the historic building in which it is housed.

Hours: Year round, daily, 9 a.m. to 4 p.m.

Admission: free

From I-44, take the Peoria exit. Go 2.75 miles north on Peoria. Turn right into the villa's driveway. There is a sign on Peoria.

Woodward Park

Peoria Avenue, Tulsa (918) 746-5125

The Woodward Park Complex encompasses areas including Woodward Park, the Municipal Rose Garden, and the Tulsa Garden Center. The arboretum is a collection of trees and shrubs that do well in the Tulsa area. The conservatory is a Victorian-style Lord and Burnham structure featuring rotating displays and permanent collections of cacti, succulents, and tropical plants found in major rainforest regions of the world. The rock garden contains streams, pools, and statuary among thousands of blooming spring bulbs, spring annuals, and summer floral plantings blooming from mid-March until frost. The azalea garden features 17,000 plants in a wooded setting enjoyed from meandering paths. The iris display bed includes over 200 plants with a peak bloom in early May. The Municipal Rose Garden contains over 9,000 rose plants and more than 250 varieties over a 4.5-acre terraced slope. Peak blooming periods are mid-May and again in mid-October.

Hours: Year round, daily, 6 a.m. to 11 p.m.

Admission: free

From I-44, take the Peoria Avenue exit. Go north on Peoria 2.75 miles. Pass the Garden Center Villa's driveway entrance and take the first right into Woodward Park.

OREGON

OPEN DAYS:

April 27
June 15
June 16
July 21
August 4

Russell Archer garden, Portland.

Saturday, April 27

Please visit the Cecil & Molly Smith Garden and Kaiser Permanente's Tualatin Poison Prevention Garden both open today especially for the Open Days Program. You will find descriptions, hours, and directions for these gardens in the Public Garden section.

WASHINGTON COUNTY

AURORA

Huntington Garden at the Case House

20755 Case Road, Aurora

The Case House is a Greek Revival-style farmhouse dating from the 1850s and influenced by Louisiana prototypes. The restoration of the house and beginnings of the garden date from 1977. The garden, in keeping with the house, is formal, with spaces defined by boxwood but with a relaxed formality more akin to English country houses than to Williamsburg. Historic accuracy has prompted me to plant "old-fashioned" plants appropriate to the period of the house (lilacs, hydrangeas, spireas, and shrub roses), but being a plant collector, I've added magnolias, stewartias, eucryphias, azaras, etc. The site, in French Prairie, is attractive, having old growth Douglas firs, rich soil, and views of hop fields, filbert orchards, and Mount Hood.

Hours: 2 p.m. to 6 p.m.

From I-5, take Exit 278/Aurora Donald. Proceed west, bypassing Donald, and, at 3.5 miles, turn left onto Case Road. Go about .65 mile to #20755 and turn right into a gravel driveway, keeping straight at the fork.

SHERWOOD
Bella Madrona
24050 S.W. Baker Road, Sherwood

Set amidst towering firs and beautiful madrones, this six-acre garden features several rooms divided by clipped hedges, each with its own character. Many unusual shrubs and trees have matured over the twenty years' creation of the garden. Included are mixed borders, a conifer garden, a Mediterranean slope, color themes, allées, and tapestry hedges. A three-acre enhanced swamp and scrubland has become a magnet and refuge for diverse wildlife during our dry summers.

Hours: 2 p.m. to 6 p.m.

From I-5 south, take Exit 28/Tualatin/Sherwood. Go right (west) off the exit ramp and follow signs to Sherwood for 3.4 miles. Turn left onto Oregon Street, go .7 mile, turn left onto Murdock Rock, and go .8 mile. Go through the 4-way stop and in .3 mile turn left into a pasture.

Proceeds shared with the Berry Botanic Garden

Cavender Garden
15920 S.W. Oberst Lane, Sherwood

This is a well-established collector's garden of about an acre. It features more than 400 species and hybrid rhododendrons and azaleas, many magnolias, Japanese maples, and other unusual flowering trees. A large collection of herbaceous material including several species of hardy orchids, *Arisaema*, cyclamen, lilies, and other treasures complements the trees and shrubs. A rock garden and pond round out the garden set on a sloping site with a panoramic view of four snowcapped mountains. A warm greenhouse contains a large collection of tropical rhododendrons and other tender plants. A cool greenhouse contains the largest collection of pleione orchids in North America. An additional two acres is planted with new hybrid rhododendrons.

Hours: 10 a.m. to 4 p.m.

From I-5, take Exit 289/Tualatin/Sherwood. Go west towards Sherwood about 5 miles. Turn left onto Oregon Street. There is a traffic light and signs read "Old Town Sherwood." Half a mile on Oregon, turn left onto Murdock Road (the second left). Go .5 mile to a stop sign. Turn right onto Sunset and go .5 mile to the second stop sign at the bottom of the hill. Turn left onto Ladd Hill Road. Go up Ladd Hill Road .75 mile to Oberst Lane, the second left off Ladd Hill Road. Oberst Lane is a one-lane paved road with a street sign on the power pole. Go down Oberst Lane 1 block to the big driveway on the right. There is a "Red's Rhodies" sign on the corner. Go up the driveway to the end.

From Route 99W, eastbound from Newberg, go about 7 miles east towards Tigard. Turn right onto Sunset, which is just beyond a sweeping right curve. There is a light at Sunset and it is the first light since leaving Newberg. A YMCA is on the corner. Go 1.5 miles on Sunset to the first stop sign. Turn right onto Ladd Hill Road. Proceed as directed above.

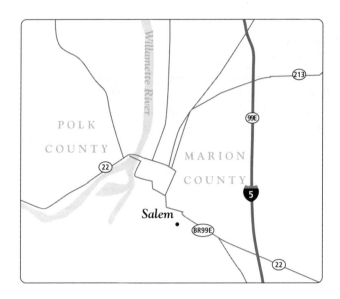

Saturday, June 15

MARION COUNTY

SALEM

Garry Oaks

8038 Mosier Street S.E., Salem

A five-acre mix of shade and sunshine, here are woodland gardens among oaks and cedars. Spruce and sequoia—and a sunny potager combining herbs, flowers, fruits, and vegetables— pools, arbors, a rockery, and a lot of birdlife are in this peaceful retreat.

Hours: 10 a.m. to 4 p.m.

From I-5, take Route 22 east towards Stayton for about 5 miles to Exit 7/Silver Falls State Park. Take a right at the bottom of the exit ramp and make the next left onto Aumsville Highway. Turn right onto 81st Street, which becomes Mosier Street. The garden is located at #8038.

Lord and Schryver

545 Mission Street, Salem

This garden was the home of landscape architects Lord and Schryver and was built in 1932. The original garden design, with brick paths, ornamental boxwood, intricate lattice fencing, and grape arbor, has been maintained, as has the shrubbery. There are mature rhododendrons, azaleas, and many varieties of camellias. We have a good variety of perennials blooming in June and, although the spring-flowering shrubs are over by then, the garden is still special. This secret garden on a half-acre lot in the heart of Salem shows how a small garden can be designed to look spacious. A Salem Heritage Tree, a 300-year-old Oregon white oak, is on the lot and Deepwood Gardens, also designed by Lord and Schryver, is close by. Deepwood Gardens and Bush Park Rose Garden, just across the street, are both public gardens. Our garden was featured in *Pacific Horticulture* magazine, Winter 1990.

Hours: 10 a.m. to 4 p.m.

From I-5, take Exit 253. Turn west onto Highway 22/Mission Street and go 2.5 miles. The house is on the right side of the street, 545 Mission. *Parking is available 1 block before the house at Bush's Pasture Park.*

Proceeds shared with the United Animal Nations

Villa Bacca Collina Estate Garden
4095 Illahe Road South, Salem

Beyond the graceful Italianate entrance, the hand-stamped design on the ebony drive leads you through a garden collage of ever-changing colors. As the driveway sweeps on towards the villa, you pass a grand wisteria-covered arbor opening onto a sunken professional croquet court. Beyond this is a view of the oak-covered hillsides and mountain vistas. The many features of this fabulous estate garden, designed by Ron Thompson, include a magnificent stone temple overlooking the Willamette River, a large azure lake, and a woodland shade garden. The extensive use of French limestone terraces envelopes the home, highlighting the cabana and sunken grotto pool.

Hours: 10 a.m. to 4 p.m.

From I-5, take the Salem exit and travel west about 3 miles to Mission Street to Commercial Street. Turn left onto Commercial Street and continue south 3 blocks, turning right onto Owens Street. Follow Owens, which becomes River Road, about 3.5 miles past the Wild Pear Restaurant (blinking traffic light), staying right at the fork. Continue over the railroad tracks and continue straight onto Illahe Road South. Take the second right (not the first to the Clubhouse) and follow to #4095 (the second gate on the right after the road curves left).

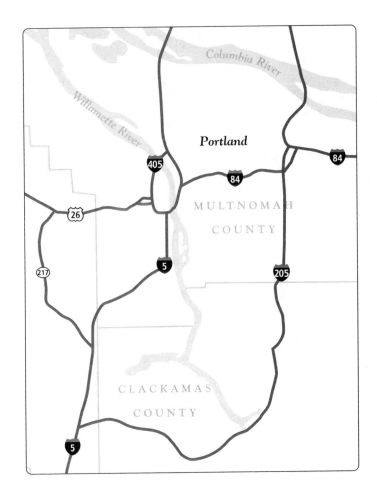

Sunday, June 16
MULTNOMAH COUNTY

PORTLAND
Russell Archer Garden
10745 S.W. 71st Avenue, Portland

Sitting on a half acre, a homey 1940s' bungalow is surrounded by my fifteen-year-old garden. Half of the garden is open and bright with ornamental grasses, a pumpkin patch, and a vegetable plot, while the other half presents a series of outdoor spaces creating intimacy and enclosure. Many of the plants and trees were collected over fifteen years ago with plantsman James Walker. Some of the earlier plantings include a thirty-foot *Eucalyptus pauciflora niphophila* started from seed, an *Acca sellowiana* (*Feijoa sellowiana*), a *Grevillea victoriae*, and a *Trachelospermum jasminoides* 'Madison' growing happily to the top of a 25-foot chimney. A collection of lagerstroemias have aged enough to show the beauty of their multicolored bark. Gravel and grass paths meander throughout and every corner opens to a new view.

Hours: 10 a.m. to 2 p.m.

From I-5, proceed 6 miles south of Portland to Exit 294/Route 99W. Turn right onto 71st Avenue at the Burger King sign and make another left onto Spruce Street. The house and garden are the first driveway on the right, located on the corner of Spruce and 71st. *Please park along Spruce Street.*

Proceeds shared with Our House of Portland

June Collins' Garden
7320 S.W. Newton Place, Portland

My one-acre garden has evolved over thirty years, from firs, lawn, rhodies, and pieris, to accommodate the needs of this intensely passionate propagator. Extra plants are sold during my annual garden party to benefit Hoyt Arboretum Friends Foundation. Approximately ninety percent of the trees, shrubs, climbers, and perennials are propagated by me. Features include a redwood greenhouse, a rock garden, many mixed borders and beds, and a sixty-foot arbor planted with clematis and roses. The many copper structures located throughout the garden were designed and created by me. A new front woodland garden with paths is currently in progress. Attracting birds and butterflies is a very important part of my garden, as is sharing seeds, plants, knowledge, etc. with other gardeners. Annually my granddaughter plants one sunflower for each of her years in my vegetable garden.

Hours: 2 p.m. to 6 p.m.

From downtown Portland, follow Highway 26 west, through the tunnel and past the zoo. Take the next exit (Sylvan), turning left over the freeway, and follow the signs toward Raleigh Hills, where my home and garden are located. At the bottom of the hill, just a few feet before the huge intersection, turn right (north) onto S.W. Fogwood Lane, located at the west end of Parr Lumber Yard. The first left is onto Newton Place; continue until the street ends. My house is a gray two-story Colonial on the left. *Please park on Newton Place or Charming Way.*

Proceeds shared with the Hoyt Arboretum Friends Foundation

Sara Mauritz Garden
7405 S.W. Newton Place, Portland

My garden is a very personal one, which has been developed over the past thirty years. Throughout the years, it has grown and changed with my interests from a "yard" with a perennial border to a "garden" full of unusual trees, shrubs, and perennials. A plantlover's garden, it reflects my natural tendency to collect and features large collections of iris, many of which should be in bloom in June, and ornamental grasses. It is an eclectic, half-acre garden with over 800 species tucked into mixed and shrub borders, as well as a small rock garden.

Hours: 2 p.m. to 6 p.m.

From Highway 26/Canyon Road west, take the Sylvan exit and go left down Scholls Ferry Road about 3 miles to the bottom of the hill. At the traffic light, turn right up Dogwood Lane (behind Parr Lumber Yard) and go 1 block. Turn left onto Newton Place. The house is the next to the last house on the right at the dead end.

The Jane Platt Garden
4550 S.W. Humphrey Boulevard, Portland

Many specimens in this sixty-year-old garden are among the oldest and largest to be seen outside their native ranges. Designed with a painter's eye, the plantings feature trees and shrubs whose bark and foliage provide interest in all seasons. The 2.5-acre garden surrounds a house designed in 1940 by Pietro Belluschi and a large rock garden filled with treasures from around the world. In 1984, the Garden Club of America awarded Jane Platt the Mrs. Oakleigh Thorne Medal "for the establishment of an exquisite garden incorporating rare and difficult botanic material into a design of incredible harmony, beauty, and distinction."

Hours: 10 a.m. to 4 p.m.

Heading west out of Portland on Highway 26, take the Sylvan exit and turn left over the highway. Go through the traffic light and onto Scholls Ferry Road, then take an immediate left onto S.W. Humphrey Boulevard. Continue on Humphrey Boulevard for .8 mile, then turn right into the drive across from 4 black mailboxes. *Follow signs to parking in the field or right below the hedge.*

The Schatz/Spendelow Garden
533 N.W. Miller Road, Portland

Our home, which once was the Miller horse barn, is on an idyllic four acres, ten minutes from downtown Portland. Native woodland screens us from the road, opening onto a large garden anchored and terraced by expansive stone walls and a massive arbor. Habitats range from full shade to Mediterranean, and the extensive plant collection reflects a balance between foliage, fragrance, and flower. Beyond the main garden and a native hedgerow is the old orchard garden, where every tree provides a mount for climbing and rambling roses.

Hours: 10 a.m. to 4 p.m.

From Highway 26 west, take Exit 69B/Barnes Road, or follow Highway 217 north to the very end. From Highways 26 or 217, turn right onto Barnes and head east about 1.3 miles to Miller Road (a major intersection). Turn left and go .9 mile. Our driveway is on the left, just past Ash Street/Taylor Crest. *Please park on the shoulder beyond the driveway unless you have limited mobility.*

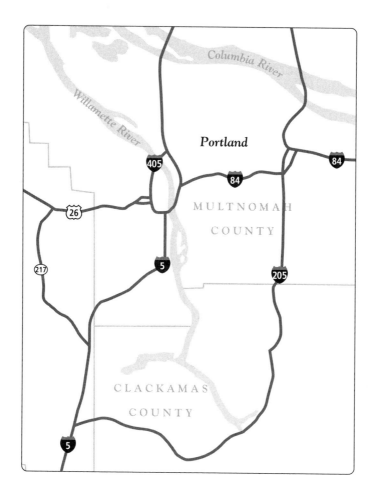

Sunday, July 21
MULTNOMAH COUNTY

PORTLAND
Jeffrey Bale
1222 N.E. Fremont Street, Portland

My ghetto oasis surrounds two small houses built in 1917. I have been gardening around one for seventeen years. The other was a crack house until I purchased it condemned three years ago. The gardens are small, so I am encrusting them like jewelry, with intricate pebble mosaics, carved stone, and bronzes. The layout is cosmic in its meaning and intended to be a manifestation of paradise. The plants are a blend of natives and collected specimens, leaning towards a lush, tropical look. Pools, fountains, a clawfoot tub for bathing, and a bed make being in this garden a taste of heaven in the city.

Hours: 10 a.m. to 4 p.m.

Located north of N.E. Fremont Street between 12th and 13th Avenues, about 1 mile north of Lloyd Center. From I-5 south, take the Rose Quarter exit. Make the first right, then go left onto Seventh to Fremont.

From I-405, take the Kerby Street exit off Fremont Bridge. Turn left for 2 blocks, then go left on Williams and right on Fremont.

Proceeds shared with the Filmarts Foundation

Catswalk Cottage—JoAnn & Roger Thomas
2804 N.E. 46th Avenue, Portland

A passion for purple describes our garden starting with the periwinkle fence and arbors that greet you and continuing to the back cottage garden. Our garden is on a standard 50 x 100-foot city lot and invites you in with roses, clematis (purple, of course), dahlias, sunflowers, salvias, and more. Look for hidden doors and windows, garden art, and painted signs to destinations around the world. Color abounds in all seasons! Enjoy sitting in the secluded woodland garden or on the front terrace, where the fragrance of thymes and lavender surrounds you.

Hours: 2 p.m. to 6 p.m.

From downtown Portland, take I-84 east to the 39th Avenue exit. Turn left onto 39th Avenue. Turn right onto Sandy, then go to 47th Avenue and turn left. Go to the stop sign and head uphill on Wyberg. At the top, turn right onto Alameda and then immediately left onto 46th Avenue. We are the second house on the right with the purple fence. *Please park along the street.*

Proceeds shared with the Hardy Plant Society of Oregon

Nancy Goldman Garden
4527 N.E. Skidmore Street, Portland

This whimsical urban garden with a strong background of perennials is accented with showy annuals and unique elements: trellises, arbors, chairs, doors, old lawnmowers, and even bicycles. The back garden, edged with fifty-year-old *deodora* cedars, features espalier, hidden rooms, a fence made of old pickets and garden tools, and a jewel-tone lower garden contained by an "L"-shaped fence full of objects of "art" and an unusual tea kettle fountain. The front garden features gravel beds resplendent with broken pots and other interesting garden accents (that most people would have thrown out!). The garden was featured in the August 2000 issue of *Country Living Gardener* magazine, the January 2001 issue of the Royal Horticultural Society's *The Garden*, and the Canadian television series *Weird Homes*.

Hours: 10 a.m. to 4 p.m.

Take I-84 east to the 33rd Avenue exit. Turn left (north) at the top of the exit ramp. Proceed north on 33rd Avenue for 1 mile to Fremont Street. Turn right onto Fremont to 42nd Avenue. Turn left onto 42nd Avenue (north) for .5 mile and turn right onto Skidmore Street. The home has a red brick front and red-and-white-striped awnings.

Proceeds shared with the Portland State University Library

Goodman-Schultz Garden
7228 North Hurst Avenue, Portland

It was an exciting challenge to co-design and construct this walled courtyard garden. Our goal was to entirely reform the traditional "grassy" backyard of this 1944 bungalow. We wanted to create a mixed-use outdoor living space as a backdrop for our subtropical garden. We've incorporated pavers, cobbles, stones, and acid-washed concrete into the overall structural design. A tiered twelve-foot-tall Dutch cast-iron fountain in the courtyard center serves as the primary focal point. A nine-foot-high arbor supported by ten cast concrete columns frames the garden.

Hours: 10 a.m. to 2 p.m.

From I-5, take the Portland Boulevard exit. Head west to Willamette Boulevard. Turn right onto Willamette. Continue to Hurst Avenue and turn right. The garden is the second house on the right, #7228. *Parking is best along Willamette Boulevard.*

Hogan/Sanderson
2822 N.E. 11th Avenue, Portland

Small, urban, having spread to most of the block, the garden is designed to create many spaces, each with a different feeling—the Moon Garden (silver, variegated, and blues, fragrance in the evening), Blood 'n' Guts Border, Smoke Screen, and two courtyards of tropicals with an enclosed feeling. Mostly the garden serves as trial grounds for new plants to horticulture, or just to Portland—many hundreds a year. The plants range from trees—especially broad-leaf evergreens—to shrubs and perennials. Mediterranean, southern hemisphere, native, and subtropicals make up the majority of the palette.

Hours: 10 a.m. to 4 p.m.

From I-5, take the Weidler Avenue exit (Rose Quarter). Go east to Martin Luther King Boulevard. Turn right onto N.E. Knott and left onto N.E. 11th Avenue. Continue to #2822. *Please park on the street.*

Sunday, August 4
WASHINGTON COUNTY

SHERWOOD

Bella Madrona
24050 S.W. Baker Road, Sherwood

Please see April 27 for garden description, hours, and directions.

Cavender Garden
15920 S.W. Oberst Lane, Sherwood

Please see April 27 for garden description, hours, and directions.

Public Gardens
MARION COUNTY

SALEM
Bush's Pasture Park
600 Mission Street S.E., Salem (503) 838-0527

Originally the home of Asakel Bush, pioneer banker and newspaperman, the park now boasts a delicious mix of open spaces, walking paths, perennial and annual gardens, and a Victorian greenhouse. Native garry oaks tower over the main axis of the park, while a spectacular well-labeled collection of unusual flowering shrubs and trees surrounds the house and rose gardens. The latter date from the 1950s and include extensive older hybrid tea plantings as well as the Fartar Old Rose Collection, the finest collection of old roses on public property in the Northwest.

Hours: Year round, daily, dawn to dusk. Greenhouse open 9 a.m. to 4 p.m. weekdays, afternoons on weekends.

Admission: free

From I-5, take Exit 253/Mission Street and head west on Mission over the overpass to High Street. Turn left onto High Street and take the first left (opposite Bush Street) to the parking lot. This park in a neighbor of Historic Deepwood Gardens.

Historic Deepwood Gardens
1116 Mission Street S.E., Salem (503) 363-1825 www.oregonlink.com\deepwood

The English-style gardens of Historic Deepwood Estate were created by Lord and Schryver in 1929. The estate consists of a series of beautifully designed garden rooms (Hollow Tree, Great Room, Spring Garden, Tea House Garden, 1905 Gazebo, Scroll Garden, Shade Garden, Secret & Border Gardens). Extensive use of evergreen plant material and the excellence of design make it a place of interest all year round. Near the 1894 Queen Anne house and greenhouse is a 3.5-acre Nature Area with numerous gravel paths winding through a stand of tall trees along Pringle Creek.

Hours: Year round, daily, dawn to dusk

Admission: free

From I-5, take Exit 253/Mission Street and continue west over the overpass. Turn left onto 12th Street and then take the next right onto Lee Street. The parking lot is at that corner and well marked. This park is adjacent to Bush's Pasture Park.

Willamette University—Martha Springer Botanical Garden

900 State Street, Salem (503) 838-0527 www.willamette.edu/dept/plant/grounds/botanical

Three special gardens have been created amidst the beautifully landscaped 61-acre campus which spans the Mill Race along with more than 1,000 trees and several sculptures. The Springer Botanical Garden has twelve acres, including a butterfly garden, herb garden, alpine rock garden, theme borders, and an Oregon native area. There are other smaller gardens within the campus.

Hours: Year round, daily, dawn to dusk

Admission: free

From I-5, take Exit 253/Mission Street and go west on Mission. As you approach the overpass, bear right, then left following the signs to Willamette University. After crossing 12th Street, take the first right opening into a parking lot. The garden is north of Sparks Gym.

SILVERTON

The Oregon Garden

879 West Main Street, Silverton (503) 874-8264 www.oregongarden.org

The Oregon Garden is a world-class botanical display garden in the making with 65 acres of an ultimate 240 acres well designed and landscaped. Special gardens include the Conifer Garden, the Northwest Garden, the Oak Grove which features a collection of 150-year-old Oregon White Oaks, a Children's Garden, the Oregon Way, the Rediscovery Forest, the Amazing Water Garden, the Jackson and Perkins Rose Garden, and the wetlands. The garden is a public/private partnership with the City of Silverton and the Oregon Garden Foundation.

Hours: March through October, daily, 9 a.m. to 6 p.m. November through February, 9 a.m. to 3 p.m.; closed Thanksgiving, Christmas, and New Year's Day

Admission: $6 adults, $5 senior citizens and students, $3 children 8 -13, children 7 and under free

From I-5, follow signage to Silverton and the Oregon Garden. Oregon 213 from I-205 in the Portland area to the garden.

From Stayton, take the Cascade Highway from Stayton northward.

From Bend, follow Oregon 20 and 22 to Stayton and turn north towards Silverton.

From Woodburn, take Oregon 214 to Mount Angel and then to Silverton.

MULTNOMAH COUNTY

PORTLAND

The Berry Botanic Garden

11505 S.W. Summerville Avenue, Portland (503) 636-4112 www.berrybot.org

Nestled in the hills of southwest Portland, the Berry Botanic Garden is a wonderfully natural place to visit. Guide yourself through this six-acre historic garden, created by renowned plantswoman Rae Selling Berry. The gentle style of specialty gardens from the 1940s features choice plants, many taking their forms from those found in nature. The curving herb lawn features a border of mature specimens of some of the best shrubs and trees grown in gardens today. Explore the 150-tree rhododendron forest, a secluded and shady fern garden, our water garden with native water-loving plants, a native plant trail, the sunny quarter-acre rock garden, and moist border areas featuring species primroses. Most of all, savor the garden flavor of an earlier time, when gardeners like Rae Berry pursued their gardening dreams of excellence.

Hours: Open Days on July 21 and August 4, dawn to dusk; otherwise, year round, daily, dawn to dusk, by appointment only

Admission: free

From I-5, take Exit 297/Terwilliger Boulevard/Lewis & Clark College and follow the signs for Lewis & Clark. Turn right onto Terwilliger Boulevard and cross the freeway. Drive through a small business district. Keep left at the forks at Boones Ferry and at Terwilliger Boulevard/Lake Oswego. This puts you on Palatine Hill Road. Go past the college on Palatine Hill Road. Turn right onto Military Road. Summerville Avenue is about .5 mile on the left. Follow Summerville to the end and go down the left driveway with the arrow that reads "Botanic Garden."

From downtown, take Front Avenue or First Avenue south and follow the signs for Highway 43/Lake Oswego. It is in the same vicinity as the on-ramp to the Ross Island Bridge so you can follow those signs too. Take Highway 43 south through Johns Landing. At the Sellwood Bridge, keep right and follow the sign for Lake Oswego. If you count the light at the bridge as the first turn right at the third light. The sign there reads "Breyman Avenue/Palatine Hill Road/Lewis & Clark College." Go uphill and keep left until you reach Riverdale School. Turn right onto Military Road and proceed as directed above.

Crystal Springs Rhododendron Garden

S.E. 28th Avenue, Portland (503) 771-8386

This is a unique seven-acre garden with 2,000 rhododendrons and azaleas, 145 different tree species, and numerous companion plants. The rhododendrons bloom February through June. Winter trees add color and structural interest. A lake surrounds the garden, attracting waterfowl to nest in this natural habitat. Ninety-four different bird species have been observed. Three waterfalls and a tall fountain add pleasure. A photographer's dream.

Hours: Year round, daily, dawn to dusk

Admission: free to all from Labor Day through February. March through Labor Day, Thursday through Monday, there is a $3 fee between 10 a.m. and 6 p.m.

We are a 10-minute drive from the city center, nearly surrounded by Eastmoreland Golf Course and across the street from Reed College.

Elk Rock, The Garden at the Bishop's Close

7405 S.W. Newton Place, Portland (503) 297-2857

Secluded at the end of a small lane and nestled on a cliff overlooking the Willamette River, Elk Rock is a jewel of a garden. Begun in 1912 by an avid plantsman, the 6.5-acre English-style garden is a treasure trove of rare and unusual plants. Broad sweeps of lawn, a delightful rock garden, a woodland garden and fishpond, and a cascade garden are all features of this garden, which was innovative in its blending of new plant introductions from around the world with Northwest natives. A renowned collection of *Magnolia* species provides spectacular interest from March through June. A garden for all seasons, Elk Rock is beloved for its quiet, contemplative nature as well as its rare plant collection.

Hours: Year round, daily, 8 a.m. to 5 p.m.; closed some holidays. No buses.

Admission: free

From downtown Portland, take Route 43 south to S.W. Military Road (traffic light) about 1.5 miles south of the Sellwood Bridge. Turn left and then immediately right onto S.W. Military Lane. The garden is at the end of the lane. Parking is limited and guests are asked to park in the upper lot only on weekdays. There are no restroom facilities and no food or drink is permitted. Children must be accompanied by parents and should be reminded that this is not a playground or a park. The garden is not wheelchair accessible. No buses!

Hoyt Arboretum

4000 S.W. Fairview Boulevard, Portland (503) 228-8733 www.hoytarboretum.org

Hoyt Arboretum is a treasured living museum close to the city center, with trails, majestic groves, and sunny clearings. The arboretum is home to 900 species of trees and woody shrubs, providing a living classroom for students from pre-school through college. Twelve miles of trails are a favorite place for walkers, joggers, and people who enjoy and appreciate the world of plants.

Hours: Year round, daily, 6 a.m. to 10 p.m.; visitor center daily, 9 a.m. to 4 p.m., except Thanksgiving, Christmas, and New Year's Day.

Admission: free

From downtown Portland, take Route 26 to the Washington Park/Oregon Zoo exit and follow signs to Hoyt Arboretum. TriMet bus #63 stops directly in front of the visitor center and the Max Light Rail station is nearby at the zoo. During the summer, a shuttle bus runs regularly among the many attractions in Washington Park.

International Rose Test Gardens

400 S.W. Kingston Street, Portland (503) 823-3636

Portland is home to one of the world's most famous rose gardens, the International Rose Test Gardens in Washington Park. Each year hundreds of thousands of visitors from around the world visit this garden. This popular tourist site, with spectacular views and more than 8,000 roses, is one of Portland's most notable signature landmarks.

Hours: Year round, daily, 6 a.m. to 9 p.m.

Admission: free

From West Burnside, turn left onto Tichner Avenue. At the stop sign, turn right. The Japanese Garden parking lot is on the right, tennis courts on the left. You can park there or go to the next stop sign, turn left, and go into garden parking lot.

Japanese Garden Society of Oregon

611 S.W. Kingston, Portland (503) 223-1321 www.japanesegarden.com

The Japanese Garden is nestled in the scenic west hills of Portland. It encompasses 5.5 acres and is composed of five garden styles: Tea Garden, Strolling Pond Garden, Natural Garden, Karesansui Dry Meditation Garden, and Flat Garden. It is the most authentic Japanese garden outside of Japan.

Hours: April 1 through Sept 30, daily, 10 a.m. to 7 p.m.; October 1 through March 31, 10 a.m. to 4 p.m., Mondays, noon to 7 p.m.

Admission: $6 adults, $4 seniors, $3.50 college students, children under 5 free

From Route 26 westbound, take the 200 exit and follow the road past the 200, Forestry Center, and Vietnam Memorial. Turn right onto Kingston, follow 1.6 miles and continue left on Kingston to the garden's parking lot on the left across from the Rose Garden Tennis Courts. A shuttle bus takes visitors to the main entrance or there is a walking path.

Ladd's Addition Rose Gardens

400 S.W. Kingston Street, Portland (503) 823-3636

Ladd's Addition Rose Garden, the smallest and most intimate garden, is located in an historic southeast residential area just across the river from downtown. Displaying many varieties popular earlier in this century, this garden contains about 3,200 roses.

Hours: Year round, daily, 6 a.m. to 9 p.m.

Admission: free

Located between S.E. Hawthorn and S.E. Division, S.E. 12th Avenue and S.E. 20th Avenue. Like a spoke on a wheel are the four separate gardens around a large center circle.

Leach Botanical Garden

6704 S.E. 122nd Avenue, Portland (503) 823-9503

The fifteen-acre garden with a half acre in cultivation is located in a riparian drainage with a dense overhead canopy of evergreen and deciduous specimens, therefore, the major plant collections are adapted to shade. The garden's focus is on Pacific Northwest native species and historic collections displayed with like genera. There is a nursery on the premises with display beds of unusual plants.

Hours: Year round, Tuesday through Saturday, 9 a.m. to 4 p.m., Sunday, 1 p.m. to 4 p.m.; extended summer hours, Wednesday, 9 a.m. to 8 p.m.

Admission: free

Located 4 blocks south of 122nd Avenue and Foster Road S.E. The closest interstate is I-205. We are 3 miles east of the Foster Road exit.

Peninsula Rose Garden

400 S.W. Kingston Street, Portland (503) 823-3636

Peninsula Park Rose Garden, with more roses than the International Rose Test Gardens, is a treasure located just a few minutes from the city center. More than 8,800 fragrant roses engulf the visitors of this sunken garden of distinct early twentieth-century design.

Hours: Year round, daily, 6 a.m. to 9 p.m.

Admission: free

From I-5, take the Portland Boulevard exit. Go east to Albina and turn right. The garden is at the south end of Peninsula Park.

Portland Classical Chinese Garden

239 N.W. Everett, Portland (503) 228-8131 www.portlandchinesegarden.org

Discover Portland's newest garden, the Garden of Awakening Orchids. The largest Suzhon-style urban garden outside of China is waiting for you to explore. An infinite number of views unfold from each vantage point. Pavilions, a teahouse, rugged rocks, and serpentine walkways reflect in the lake. This is an ever-changing poetic landscape to revive your spirit and touch your soul. Calm yourself.

Hours: November 1 through March 31, daily, 10 a.m. to 5 p.m.; April 1 through October 31, daily, 9 a.m. to 6 p.m.

Admission: $6 adults, $5 students and senior citizens, children under 5 free

From I-405, take the Everett Street exit east. Travel down Everett until you reach Third and Everett. We are located on the corner of N.W. Third and Everett.

Saint Paul

Cecil & Molly Smith Garden

14635 S.W. Bull Mountain Road, Saint Paul (503) 590-2505

The Cecil & Molly Smith garden has charmed and delighted visitors from around the world. The wooded setting of native firs creates an ideal environment for a natural garden of rare beauty, featuring superior forms of species and hybrid rhododendrons. Complementing the rhododendron collection are choice trees, shrubs, wildflowers, and bulbs. Each pathway reveals its own visual treat—a moss-covered log with plants tucked into bark crevices, plants thriving in tree stumps, drifts of wildflowers. Plants flourish here!

Hours: March, April, and May, Saturdays (except last Saturday in May), 10 a.m. to 3:30 p.m., or by appointment. Special guided available on April 27.

Admission: $3 for non-ARS members

Located 3.5 miles south of Newberg. Take Route 219 to Champoeg Road. Turn right onto Ray Bell Road.

TUALATIN

Kaiser Permanente's Tualatin Poison Prevention Garden

19185 S.W. 90th, Tualatin (503) 813-4820

Opened in 2001, the garden was designed by Kaiser Permanente to educate the public about common poisonous plants and how plant poisoning can be prevented. Plants are labeled with both their botanical Latin and English names. Native and introduced ornamentals are featured, including three dozen different kinds of trees, shrubs, and perennials. The garden is adjacent to Kaiser Permanente's Tualatin Medical Office, which also features native plant gardens and a neighboring wetland.

Hours: Open Days event, April 27, 10 a.m. to 2 p.m.; otherwise, year round, weekdays, 8 a.m. to 5 p.m.; tours led by master gardeners on fourth Saturday of the month, April through October, 11 a.m. Otherwise, please call the office to arrange guided tours for 4 people or more.

Admission: free

From I-5, take the Tualatin/Sherwood exit westbound onto S.W. Nyberg Street. Proceed west across the railroad tracks and past S.W. Boones Ferry Road. About 1 mile from the freeway, turn right at the intersection onto S.W. 90th. The first driveway on the left leads into the Kaiser Permanente Tualatin Medical Office. The poison prevention garden is to the left of the building's main entrance.

Pennsylvania

OPEN DAYS:

May 5
June 2
June 9
June 29
July 6
July 28

Gulph Mills, Gulph Mills. Photo by Ralph Schumacher.

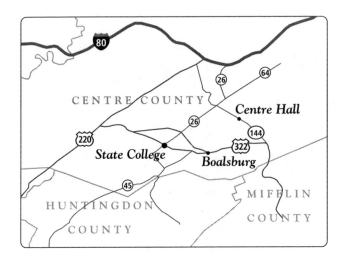

Sunday, May 5
CENTRE COUNTY

BOALSBURG

Darlene & Paul's Gardens

1023 Torrey Lane, Boalsburg

Our mountainside flower and vegetable gardens are a blend of the whimsical and the practical, the unusual and the commonplace. We believe there is beauty everywhere, if only we know where to look and how to appreciate it. And surprises, too. So our many, mostly small, gardens are filled with beauty and surprises, including lots of spring bulbs, native plants, wildflowers, grasses, magnificent vegetables, and herbs. We added a spring-fed pond last year; in the summer it is surrounded by blue vervain, cardinal flowers, and great lobelia.

Hours: noon to 4 p.m.

At the corner with the Exxon gas station and Omega Bank on Business 322/South Atherton Street on the east outskirts of Boalsburg, turn onto Main Street. Go 1 block, turn left onto Loop Road, go approximately .25 mile, and turn right onto Torrey Lane. Go to the top of the hill; we're the last house on the right, a big blue house with a barn with a bright blue door. Pull in the drive and go as far up the lane as possible (there will be signs).

Proceeds shared with the Clearwater Conservancy

State College
Deno's Garden
139 Lenor Drive, State College

There will be 100 to 150 different botanical species in flower on the visitation dates. There are large colonies of many eastern U.S. species and colonies of three endangered species. The garden has small cliffs, many rock outcroppings, steep hillsides, woods, a marsh, a spring, and more than 200 yards of trout stream.

Hours: 10 a.m. to 4 p.m.

Located only 2 blocks from the intersection of Routes 322 and 26. From this intersection, proceed 1 long block southwest on Route 26 (towards State College) to Puddintown Road. Turn right onto Puddintown Road. Turn onto the first road on the left (Lenor Drive). This is a dangerous turn, as cars come up a hill. We are the second house on the right, #139. *Please park along the road in front of the house.*

Gabriel & Jill Welsch Garden
533 Glenn Road, State College

A lattice panel fence encloses a plot of perennials, herbs, vegetables, fruit, and grasses—all of which comprises the view from a relaxing bench surrounded by plants chosen for their scents. A path winds to a patio garden below, a strip of sun garden inspired by Shakespeare, and other beds in progress. I am a published poet and writer, and ours is a garden I turn to again and again in my work.

Hours: 10 a.m. to 4 p.m.

From the north and west, take Business Route 322/Atherton Street south towards State College and Penn State University. At the traffic light at Hillcrest Avenue, turn right. The road will fork in front of a church. Bear right to a stop sign. Drive straight through the stop sign and onto Martin Terrace. Martin Terrace curves left and becomes Glenn Road. Number 533 is at the crest of a slight incline on the right. The garden is fenced and the house is a white contemporary.

From the south and east, take Business Route 322/Atherton Street north past the Penn State campus. Turn left at the Hillcrest Avenue light. Continue as directed above.

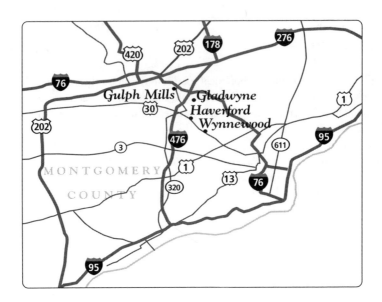

Sunday, June 2

MONTGOMERY COUNTY

GLADWYNE

Fernside Cottage

1485 Mill Creek Road, Gladwyne

Primarily a shade-woodside garden, this property consists of seven acres, two of which are developed every month and present new and different flowering plants and foliage. The entire garden is practically self-maintaining, other than irrigation and an annual weeding. Purposely, no lawn exists, nor dedicated flower garden. The landscape is planted so as to appear to blend naturally from one plant type to another.

Hours: 11 a.m. to 4 p.m.

From the center of the town of Gladwyne, going west on Route 23, turn right onto Youngsford Road and make another right onto Rose Glen Road. At the stop sign, turn onto Mill Creek Road and go about 500 feet to #1485. Look for a cobblestone driveway on the left.

Mr. & Mrs. John W. Powell II

412 Youngsford Lane, Gladwyne

The sign reads "Caution Pig Zone" but "Deer Zone" may be more apt. Those of you who are so afflicted must not miss the non-intrusive barrier the Powells have erected, without which there would be no garden. As you enter the property beneath a canopy of oak and white pine, glance downward to find an exquisite combination of ground covers, textures, and colors provided by hostas, ferns, ajuga, and sweet woodruff. Pause at the garden gate to take in the expansive sloping lawn with its collections of beds and borders and varieties of woodies and trees. Make sure to capture the front beds around the front door with shade lovers and companion plants.

Hours: 11 a.m. to 4 p.m.

Go to the main intersection of Youngsford Road and Route 23/Conshocken State Road in the center of Gladwyne. Continue south on Youngsford Road and look for Youngsford Lane on the right (a small cul-de-sac). Proceed to #412 at the end of the cul-de-sac on the left side. Look for a pig on the mailbox.

Gulph Mills
Gulph Mills
947 Longview Road, Gulph Mills

Rising behind the house over the past 33 years we have gradually developed a terraced hillside garden with seven separate levels. Directly behind the house is a shaded patio and small fountain surrounded by beds of shade-tolerant plants. Along the paths, we have areas with many varieties of rhododendrons and azaleas, viburnums, dwarf evergreens, a variety of ground covers, annual beds, and, at the very top, a shrub and perennial border. There is a small waterfall leading into a fish pool, a Japanese-style house, distinctive ornaments, often from our travels, and secluded areas with spots to sit and contemplate. We are especially interested in trees with great bark and winter interest and have collected many beautiful specimens.

Hours: 11 a.m. to 4 p.m.

From I-476 north, take Exit 16B/I-76 west towards Valley Forge. Take Exit 330 towards Route 320/Gulph Mills. Keep left at the fork in the exit ramp. Merge onto Balligomingo Road. Turn right onto Trinity Lane/Route 320. Bear left onto Trinity Lane. Turn right onto South Gulph Road. Turn left onto Gypsy Lane. Turn left onto Longview Road and look for #947.

Haverford
Baruch Garden
230 Laurel Lane, Haverford

Traditional landscaping in the front of my house hints at the bountiful gardens that await the visitor who passes through the gate to the back yard. The design has evolved during the past fifteen years as a result of many trials and quite a few errors. Planting situations range from moist and shady to dry and sunny, providing me with the opportunity to experiment with a wide selection of perennials and shrubs. My favorite species include hostas, hellebores, heucheras, and sedums. Birdhouses and iron sculptures provide interesting accents. I enjoy my garden from every window of my home.

Hours: 11 a.m. to 4 p.m.

From the intersection of Montgomery and Morris Avenues in Bryn Mawr, head east on Montgomery Avenue. At the second traffic light, turn left onto Grays Lane (Merion Cricket Club is on the far left corner). At the top of the hill, turn left onto Laurel Lane. The Baruch home is #230, the fifth house on the left.

WAYNE
Frogsleap—Mr. & Mrs. John D. Borne
113 Banbury Way, Wayne

From many acres to one-half acre—that was the challenge which faced this couple twelve years ago. This "convenient to everything" walled property is only about 100 x 200 feet but has been carefully planned to contain several varied exterior living spaces, including a place to sun and swim. To replicate the spirit of their larger place, the gardens have been developed along strong architectural lines and have been enhanced with the addition of several outbuildings that stylistically complement the whole composition. A change in levels underscores the division of the garden into separate rooms and enhances the illusion of more space. Both walls and a layering of planting assure privacy from three streets and hide the reality of being in the center of town. In this case, less really is more.

Hours: 11 a.m. to 4 p.m.

Take I-476/Blue Route to Exit 13/Saint David's/Villanova. Take Route 30/Lancaster Avenue west for 2 miles to the center of Wayne (you will see Wayne Avenue, a movie theater, and a bank). Continue west on Lancaster Avenue to the next traffic light and turn right at the Wawa onto Banbury Way. Number 113 is at the end of the street (1 block) on the right. *Please park on the street.*

WYNNEWOOD
Gillean's Wood
139 Cherry Lane, Wynnewood

The garden of Bill and Elizabeth McLean was created on the bones of a garden landscape designed in the late 1920s by Thomas Sears. When the McLeans built their house (on the site of the original tennis court) 33 years ago, Fred Peck designed a "low-maintenance" landscape for the then non-gardening family, busy raising five children. When the gardening interest hit, the garden gradually expanded to almost five acres, including an herbaceous border, woodland gardens, meadows, a gazebo and pond, and small collections of magnolias, azaleas, witch hazels, and viburnum.

Hours: 11 a.m. to 4 p.m.

From Montgomery Avenue east, pass Lower Merion High School on the left and then Wister Road. Cherry Lane is the next left at the traffic light. Coming down Cherry Lane from Montgomery Avenue, you pass 4 small streets on the left; we are the next house on the right, #139. There are two wooden gateposts with black lanterns, rather like a Japanese priest's hat. The sign reads "Gillean's Wood."

From West Chester via Lawrence Road (off Route 320), cross the West Chester Pike, following the bend to Eagle Road, which becomes West Wynnewood Road. Follow Wynnewood Road across Lancaster Avenue and take the first left under Wynnewood Station/Penn Road. Penn Road becomes Cherry Lane when it crosses Montgomery Avenue. Proceed as directed above.

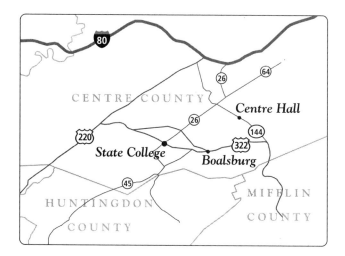

Sunday, June 9

CENTRE COUNTY

STATE COLLEGE

Deno's Garden

139 Lenor Drive, State College

Please see May 5 for garden description, hours, and directions.

Olgi Draper's Garden

450 East Irvin Avenue, State College

I started working with soil after my husband passed away of cancer in 1987. Gardening—I found—is very therapeutic. My idea was to create an English garden—namely, informal, a bit wild, and colorful. Every year I added something new, a path, a small rose garden, a few butterfly bushes for colorful visitors, a sitting area. Perhaps my favorite flowers are the deep blue delphiniums, red bee balm, and Oriental lilies. But many other flowers contribute to a colorful, happy garden.

Hours: 10 a.m. to 4 p.m.

In State College, take University Drive to East Irvin Avenue. Number 450 is a 2-story white house with a red roof and a 5-foot-tall white fence out front. *Please park on the street.*

Rae's Garden

705 Holmes Street, State College

My ten-year-old garden contains 400 rose varieties, most of which are old and species roses in a community of perennials, shrubs, small trees, grasses, and animals. I rely on heterogeneity, compost, and manure and do not use pesticides or commercial fertilizers. The roses are large shrubs, hardy, disease resistant, and entangled with companion plants. Variety helps prevent disease and insect concentrations and encourages pest-prey interactions. Close planting inhibits weeds, conserves moisture, and moderates soil temperatures. Birds provide spirit and song, help to keep insects in check, and are as important to the garden as plants. Complexity, chaos, and twisting paths allow for wonderful surprises.

Hours: 10 a.m. to 4 p.m.

In State College, enter East Park Avenue from North Atherton Street/Route 322 or from University Drive. Turn north off East Park Avenue onto Holmes Street and go 2 blocks. Number 705 is on the right. *Please park on the front street.*

Proceeds shared with Clearwater Conservancy.

Gabriel & Jill Welsch Garden

533 Glenn Road, State College

Please see May 5 for garden description, hours, and directions.

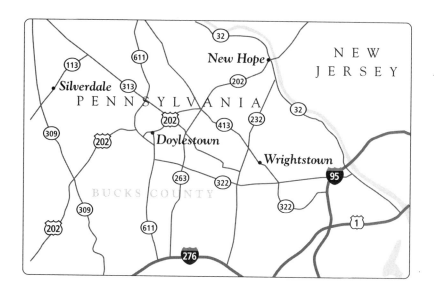

Saturday, June 29

BUCKS COUNTY

DOYLESTOWN

Fordhook Farm of the W. Atlee Burpee Company

105 New Britain Road, Doylestown

Here at Fordhook Farm, you will have the opportunity to take a "behind the scenes" tour of the company's famed trials and testing operations. In 1888, W. Atlee Burpee acquired several hundred acres of farmland in bucolic Bucks County. Today at Fordhook Farm, as before, thousands of new vegetables, annuals, and perennials are grown, tested, and evaluated to see if they meet Burpee's high standards for quality. Once home to the Burpee family, the eighteenth-century manor house now operates as the Inn at Fordhook Farm. Designated a National Historic Site, the inn features the richly paneled study where W. Atlee Burpee compiled and edited the first Burpee catalogs. Burpee Hall, located in a stone bank barn adjoining the inn, has been fully renovated as a conference center. The main conference room features a hand-painted mural of Fordhook Farm during the late nineteenth century. Once the hub for seed processing at Fordhook Farm, the Seed House is located across the drive from the manor. Be sure to visit the restored heirloom greenhouses, kitchen garden, and perennial demonstration garden, as well as the trial gardens—birthplace of culinary favorites such as the Big Boy tomato, Iceberg lettuce, and Fordhook lima bean.

Hours: 10 a.m. to 4 p.m.

From Philadelphia, take I-95 north to Route 332 west towards Newtown. Take Route 332 3.7 miles to Route 413 north. Take Route 413 10.4 miles to Route 202 south. Take Route 202 3.5 miles to State Street. Follow State Street south past the hospital and over Route 611, then go .25 mile and turn left onto New Britain Road (the first road on the left next to Delaware Valley College). The entrance to Fordhook Farm is .25 mile on the left through 2 stone pillars. Follow the drive over the little bridge to the large stone house on the right.

From New York and points north, take I-287 south to Route 202 across the Delaware River to Doylestown (about 45 miles from Somerville). Proceed as directed above.

From Baltimore/Washington, D.C., take I-95 north. At Chester, Pennsylvania, exit onto I-476, towards Plymouth Meeting. Stay on I-476, then exit onto I-276 east. Take I-276 to Exit 27/Doylestown. Follow Route 611 north 11 miles to Route 202 south. Proceed as directed above.

New Hope
Jericho Mountain Orchards
Buckmanville Road, New Hope

This is a delightful, terraced country garden surrounding a seventeenth-century stone-and-timber farmhouse on extensive acreage. Many varieties of old garden roses and climbers ramble over eighteenth-century walls, barns, trellises, and tuteurs, leading to lovely perennial borders and formally parterred beds. There are also charming shade pond and stream gardens, as well as a sizeable nineteenth-century apple orchard.

Hours: 10 a.m. to 4 p.m.

From New Hope, take Route 232 south about 4 miles to Street Road. Turn left onto Street Road, then take your first right onto Buckmanville Road. Jericho Mountain Orchards will be about .5 mile down on the right.

From Hortulus Farm (see next page), turn right out of the drive onto Thompson Mill Road. Continue to the stop sign, then turn left onto Pineville Road. Buckmanville Road will be about .5 mile down on the right. Turn right and continue .5 mile to Jericho Mountain Orchards on the right.

Proceeds shared with the Riverside Symphonia

Silverdale
Carol A. Pierce
839 Callowhill Road, Silverdale

This is a series of vignette gardens set on 1.3 acres designed to flow from one to another. Perennials and flowering shrubs combine to attract birds and butterflies. Featured is a beach theme garden packed with ornamental grasses, boulders, and perennials for a burst of color. There are two water gardens, one of traditional design to be viewed from the home's breakfast area and a second of contemporary design built into the entranceway deck accenting the home's summer living space.

Hours: 2 p.m. to 6 p.m.

From I-276, take the Fort Washington exit. Take Route 309 north to the Route 113 exit. Turn right onto Route 113. At the fifth traffic light, turn right onto Callowhill Road. Number 839 is 1 mile on the left.

From Doylestown, go north on Route 313 through Dublin. Turn left onto Route 113. Travel to the first light and turn left onto Callowhill Road. Number 839 is 1 mile on the left. *Please park on the right, next to the detached garage.*

WRIGHTSTOWN
Hortulus Farm
62 Thompson Mill Road, Wrightstown

Our garden appears as an integral part of the Pennsylvania landscape as befits an eighteenth-century farmstead with barns and a healthy population of animals. We are lucky enough to be nestled in our own little valley, quite far off the road and unusual for a house of this age. Our 72 acres try to respect the integrity of the farm's historical significance and the natural landscape, with the occasional whimsical or formal statement thrown in. There are lots of woods and pasture, lots of shrubs and naturalized perennial plantings in the stream and woodland gardens, yet also formal borders, follies, and gazebos, and sizeable herb and vegetable gardens. All is anchored by the formal simplicity of classic Bucks County architecture.

Hours: 10 a.m. to 4 p.m.

From New Hope, take Windy Bush Road/Route 232 south out of New Hope for approximately 5 miles. At the "Wrightstown Township" sign on the right, turn immediately left onto Pineville Road. Go on Pineville Road for about 1 mile to a right onto Thompson Mill Road. Continue over the bridge through a series of steep, winding, uphill turns and up into a clearing and straightaway.

From Philadelphia, take I-95 north towards Trenton for about 40 miles to Exit 31/New Hope. Turn left at the end of the exit ramp onto Taylorsville Road. Go north for 3 miles to Wood Hill Road on the left. Stay on Wood Hill Road for about 2.7 miles to the first stop sign. Turn right onto Eagle Road and go .3 mile to the first left onto Pineville Road. Proceed as directed above.

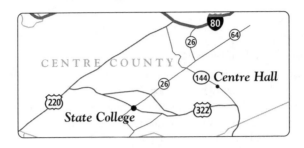

Saturday, July 6

CENTRE COUNTY

STATE COLLEGE
Olgi Draper's Garden
450 East Irvin Avenue, State College

Please see June 9 for garden description, hours, and directions.

Rae's Garden
705 Holmes Street, State College

Please see June 9 for garden description, hours, and directions.

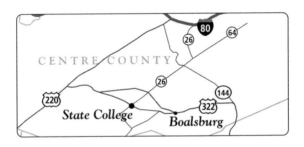

Sunday, July 28

CENTRE COUNTY

BOALSBURG
Darlene & Paul's Gardens
1023 Torrey Lane, Boalsburg

Please see May 5 for garden description, hours, and directions.

STATE COLLEGE
Gabriel & Jill Welsch Garden
533 Glenn Road, State College

Please see May 5 for garden description, hours, and directions.

Public Gardens

CENTRE COUNTY

CENTRE HALL

Rhoneymeade Arboretum, Sculpture Garden & Labyrinth

Rimmey Road, Centre Hall (814) 364-1527 www.rhoneymeade.org

Rhoneymeade is an intimate public garden that provides sites for a variety of sculpture. Century-old hemlocks, spruces, arborvitaes, and maples tower around massings and specimens of deciduous and evergreen trees planted since 1984. Paths reveal an old orchard, gazebos, ponds, limestone walls, a brick garden, and an 1853 brick farmhouse. These create spaces for abstract and figurative sculpture in wood, stone, and metal. Because the garden straddles a high north-south ridge, it offers outstanding views to surrounding farm fields, forests, and sky. The new studio is a treat and don't miss the labyrinth down in the woods.

Hours: Open Days events May 5, June 9, and July 6 with house tour 12:30 p.m. to 4:30 p.m.; otherwise, garden only open the first weekend of each month, April through October, 12:30 p.m. to 4:30 p.m.

Admission: free

From State College, take Route 322 south/east. At the Exxon gas station in Boalsburg, go east on Route 45 for 4.4 miles. Make a sharp left turn onto Rimmey Road and, after .6 mile, turn in at the "Rhoneymeade Arboretum & Sculpture Garden" sign.

UNIVERSITY PARK

Penn State Horticulture Trial Garden

Bigler Road & Park Avenue, University Park (814) 863-2190

The Penn State Horticulture Trial Garden is one of the premier cultivar evaluation sites in the Northeast. This seven-acre garden is planted with over 1,500 types of annual and perennial flowers, vegetables, and woody plants. New plants from all over the world are planted side by side with some of the best available cultivars. A walk through the garden is like a stroll through a seed catalog. The garden also features a replica medieval garden, including medicinal, culinary, and ornamental plants used in medieval Europe.

Hours: Throughout the growing season, daily, dawn to dusk

Admission: free

Located on the Penn State Campus on the corner of Bigler Road and Park Avenue in the shadow of the football stadium.

CHESTER COUNTY

CHADDS FORD

Brandywine Conservancy

Route 1, Chadds Ford (610) 388-2700

Begun in 1974, the gardens feature indigenous and some naturalized plants of the greater Brandywine region displayed in natural settings. The gardens use wildflowers, trees, and shrubs in landscaped areas. Plants are selected to provide a succession of bloom from early spring through the first killing frost. Each is located in a setting akin to its natural habitat: woodland, wetland, flood plain, or meadow.

Hours: Year round, daily, dawn to dusk

Admission: free

From I-95, take the Route 141 exit north to Route 52 north. Follow Route 52 until it intersects with Route 1. Turn right onto Route 1 north. Travel 2 miles to the conservancy.

Kennett Square
Longwood Gardens

Route 1, Kennett Square (610) 388-1000 www.longwoodgardens.org

One of the world's premier horticultural displays, Longwood offers 1,050 acres of gardens, woodlands, and meadows; twenty outdoor gardens; twenty indoor gardens within four acres of greenhouses; 11,000 types of plants; spectacular fountains; extensive educational programs, including career training and internships; and 800 events each year, including flower shows, gardening demonstrations, courses, children's programs, concerts, musical theater, and fireworks displays.

Hours: Year round, daily, 9 a.m. to 5 p.m.; frequently open later for seasonal displays

Admission: $12 adults ($8 on Tuesdays), $6 students 16-20, $2 children 6-15, children under 6 free

Located on Route 1, 3 miles northeast of Kennett Square and 12 miles north of Wilmington, Delaware.

DELAWARE COUNTY

Swarthmore
Scott Arboretum of Swarthmore College

500 College Avenue, Swarthmore (610) 328-8025 www.scottarboretum.org

The Scott Arboretum is a green oasis uniquely situated on the Swarthmore College Campus. More than 300 acres create the college landscape and provide a display of the best ornamental plants recommended for Delaware Valley gardens. There are more than 3,000 different kinds of plants grown on the campus. Major plant collections include flowering cherries, crab apples, hydrangeas, lilacs, magnolias, rhododendrons, tree peonies, viburnums, wisteria, and witch hazels. Special gardens include the Rose Garden, Fragrance Garden, Teaching Garden, Entrance Garden, Winter Garden, Nason Garden, Harry Wood Courtyard Garden, and Cosby Courtyard.

Hours: Year round, daily, dawn to dusk

Admission: free

From I-95, take Exit 7/I-476 north/Plymouth Meeting. Take I-476 to Exit 2/Media/Swarthmore. Turn right onto Baltimore Pike and follow the signs for Swarthmore. Stay in the right lane for .25 mile and turn right onto Route 320 south. Proceed through the second traffic light at College Avenue to the first driveway on the right.

WAYNE
Chanticleer
786 Church Road, Wayne (610) 687-4163 www.chanticleergarden.org

This 32-acre pleasure garden was formerly the home of the Rosengarten family. Emphasis is on ornamental plants, particularly herbaceous perennials. The garden is a dynamic mix of formal and naturalistic areas, collections of flowering trees and shrubs, a pond, a meadow, wildflower gardens, and a garden of shade-loving Asian herbaceous plants.

Hours: April 1 through October 31, Wednesday through Saturday, 10 a.m. to 5 p.m.

Admission: $5

Take I-76 to I-476. Turn south onto I-476 going towards Chester. Take Exit 5 towards Villanova. Turn right at the intersection of Routes 30 and 320 south. Turn right at the next traffic light onto Conestoga Road. Turn left at the second light onto Church Road. Go .5 mile to Chanticleer.

MONTGOMERY COUNTY

MEADOWBROOK
Meadowbrook Farm & Greenhouse
1633 Washington Lane, Meadowbrook (215) 887-5900

This beautiful garden is the life work of J. Liddon Pennock. Designed as a series of outdoor rooms, each garden is unique and very comfortable, with the emphasis on design. The public display garden leads to the greenhouse, where plants and garden gifts of all types are available. Meadowbrook Farm has long been known for special horticulture activities, including lectures and workshops to visiting groups.

Hours: Year round, Monday through Saturday, 10 a.m. to 5 p.m. Tours for groups of 15 to 40 people of the house and private gardens by appointment only; call for details and reservations.

Admission: $10 for tour

From I-76, take Exit 27. Take Route 611 south and turn left onto Route 63. After about 1.5 miles, turn right onto Washington Lane. The Meadowbrook Farm sign is located about .75 mile on the left.

PHILADELPHIA

Fairmount Park Horticulture Center & Arboretum

Belmont Avenue and North Horticultural Drive, Philadelphia (215) 685-0096

The arboretum covers 22 acres and boasts an assortment of trees, many of which have been labeled with both common and botanical names. The display house is the first greenhouse you enter from the lobby. Its permanent display includes olive and fig trees, oleander, and bougainvillea. The next greenhouse contains a magnificent collection of cacti and succulents. There are also many statues and perennial gardens on these grounds. Come and visit!

Hours: Year round, daily, 9 a.m. to 3 p.m.

Admission: free

From I-76/I-276, take Exit 35/Montgomery Drive. Turn left at the traffic light onto Montgomery Drive and travel 1 block, turning left onto Horticultural Drive. Drive through the front gates on the left; the building is on the right.

Historic Bartram's Garden

54th Street andLindbergh Boulevard, Philadelphia (215) 729-5281 www.libertynet.org/ bartram

Historic Bartram's Garden is America's oldest living botanical garden, founded in 1728 by John Bartram, America's first great botanist, naturalist, and plant explorer. The 45-acre site on the banks of the Schuylkill River includes the furnished Bartram house and other unique eighteenth-century farm buildings, a botanical garden, historic trees, a fifteen-acre wildflower meadow, a water garden, a wetland, a parkland, and a museum shop.

Hours: March through December, Tuesday through Sunday, 10 a.m. to 4 p.m.; January and February, group tours by reservation

Admission: grounds are free

Located less than 15 minutes from Center City Philadelphia and convenient to I-76 and I-95. Please call for detailed directions.

Morris Arboretum of the University of Pennsylvania

100 Northwestern Avenue, Philadelphia (215) 247-5777

The Morris Arboretum of the University of Pennsylvania is an historic Victorian garden and educational institution dedicated to understanding the important relationships between people and plants. Its living collection contains about 2,532 taxa and more than 14,000 accessioned and labeled plants from the temperate northern hemisphere, parts of Asia, Europe, and North America. The arboretum collection consists of 92 acres that include gardens in the Victorian eclectic style. Handicapped accessible.

Hours: Year roundweekdays, 10 a.m. to 4 p.m.; April through November, also open weekends, 10 a.m. to 5 p.m.

Admission: $6 adults, $5 senior citizens, $4 children 6-12, children under 6 free

From I-76/Schuylkill Expressway, exit at the Blue Route/I-476 north. Take Exit 8/Plymouth Meeting and follow the signs for Germantown Pike east. Proceed on Germantown Pike for 4 miles and turn left onto Northwestern Avenue. The arboretum entrance is .25 mile on the right.

Tennessee

OPEN DAYS:

May 18
May 19

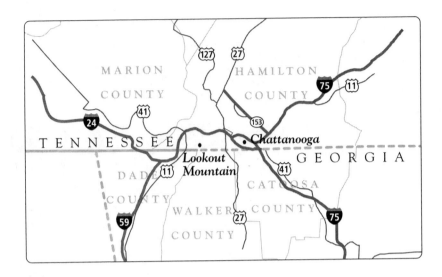

Saturday, May 18

HAMILTON COUNTY

CHATTANOOGA

The Garden at Skillet Gap

1000 Skillet Gap, Chattanooga

This meandering garden sprawls from the shady front pond to a rock garden full of blue and purple flowers at the side of a woodsy, contemporary home. There are three outdoor garden "rooms" as well. On the south side, in back of the home, are three paths at varying levels above the Tennessee River. Each one offers a different perspective, from natural woodland to cultivated lilies, hydrangeas, and azaleas. The garden offers a peaceful feast every season.

Hours: 10 a.m. to 2 p.m.

From downtown Chattanooga, go west on I-24 to Exit 175/Brown's Ferry Road about 4 miles from downtown. Turn right at the exit and go to Elder Mountain Road on Brown's Ferry Road, about 1 mile. Turn left onto Elder Mountain Road and travel 2 miles. At the top of the mountain, you will come to a guardhouse and a stop sign. Turn right onto Cumberland Road. Stay on Cumberland for 2 miles. Just past a cellular tower but just short of the very end, turn left onto Skillet Gap, a half-gravel, half-paved road. Two thirds of a mile later, after you pass a white gate on the left, you will come to 1000 Skillet Gap. The driveway is through the stone columns.

LOOKOUT MOUNTAIN

The Garden of Connie & John Higgason

415 Park Road, Lookout Mountain

Our old English garden was inherited from the previous succession of owners beginning in the 1930s. The graceful curvature of the beds highlights and enhances the natural beauty of this primarily free-form garden. The garden is abundant with wildflowers and perennials. Resplendent with native mountain laurel and rhododendron, this mature and unstructured garden also boasts of mayapple and Solomon's seal.

Hours: 10 a.m. to 4 p.m.

From I-24 into Chattanooga, take the Lookout Mountain exit. Follow Rock City/Ruby Falls signs down South Broad Street. At the last traffic light, follow signs up Lookout Mountain to Ruby Falls. Pass Ruby Falls and cross over the bridge over the incline tracks. At the top of the mountain, proceed through the flashing caution light to the intersection in front of the large stone water fountain. Turn right onto West Brow Road and proceed around West Brow Road past signs for "Sunset Rock" on the left. Turn right onto Maple Avenue and take a quick left back onto Maple Avenue. At the intersection of Park Road, Maple Avenue, and Laurel Lane, look for a white stucco English Tudor house with gray trim. *Please park along the street.*

Reilly Garden

407 Park Road, Lookout Mountain

Our front garden is a balance of evergreens and perennials. The boxwood along the north fence outlines the drive to the carport. Fronting the house are again boxwood, juniper, laurel, and azaleas surrounding a fringe tree. A little path of marble leads you to the backyard. A weeping cherry and dogwood are surrounded by pieris, 'Princess' spirea, rhododendrons, and hemlocks. Hollies and oak-leaf hydrangeas with laurel give balance to the south fence. The 'Foster' hollies follow the path to the back garden. The south fence is fronted by a 'Shasta' viburnum and hollies. In the corner section are blue lace-cap hydrangea, oak-leaf hydrangea, and 'Conroy' viburnum. Below the bedroom balcony are hosta and boxwood. Just off the deck stairs are boxwood azalea and a mix of camellias. A little herb garden is nestled near to be easy access from the kitchen and sunroom door. These gardens have been "remodeled" for easy maintenance and simplicity for the owner, who likes to be in constant motion.

Hours: 10 a.m. to 2 p.m.

From Scenic Highway, go up Lookout Mountain, passing Ruby Falls. At the stop sign, stay on Scenic Highway, past Stonedge on the left. Follow the road to the fountains and turn right. Pass city hall on your left; this is West Brow Road. You will pass Wataugu Road on the right and the next road on the right is Laurel Lane. Take this road to the stop sign. Turn right and follow north to the fork. Turn right onto Park Road and go north. Number 407 is the third house on the right with a white picket fence. *Please park on Park Road.*

Yates Garden

119 Dogwood Lane, Lookout Mountain

Our garden is small, with raised beds and attractive stone walls and parts being natural woods. The area in the center of the driveway is somewhat naturalized with azaleas, hellebores, ferns, and spring bulbs. In back, separating the woods from the lawn, are shrubs for use in flower arrangements, along with several for attracting butterflies and hummingbirds. On the lowest level there is a small perennial bed, along with well-established peonies.

Hours: 10 a.m. to 4 p.m.

Take Highway 58 north up Ochs Highway to Lookout Mountain, which deadends (into Lula Lake Road). Turn right and go to the 4-way stop with the blinking traffic light. Continue straight (road name changes to Scenic Highway). Dogwood Lane is the first street on the left. Come uphill, bearing to the right, to the third house on the right, #119. *Please park on the street.*

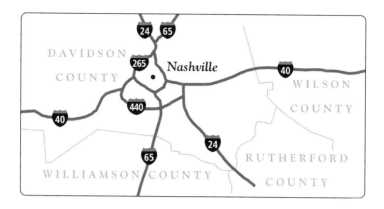

Sunday, May 19

DAVIDSON COUNTY

NASHVILLE

Fletcher-Chapman Garden

3717 Princeton Avenue, Nashville

A beautiful 1918 Craftsman-style bungalow provides the setting for an intimate casual garden composed of a broad spectrum of shade-tolerant native Tennessee wildflowers and indigenous shrubs. The expansive screened porch in the rear of the house provides an almost year-round outdoor entertaining space and a wonderful vantage point to watch the passing of the seasons in the gardens.

Hours: 1 p.m. to 4 p.m.

From I-65, take I-440 west to Exit 1/West End Avenue. Travel west .4 mile to Craighead and turn right. Go .2 mile to Princeton and turn left. Go .3 mile on Princeton. The garden is on the left

Proceeds shared with Cheekwood

Follin Garden

4416 Gerald Place, Nashville

A charming white frame cottage reveals its secrets to the first-time visitor with a pair of garden gates opening into a series of interwoven specialty gardens. Having been greeted by a choice collection of roses, the visitor is then led by a walkway to the pool. This entire space is totally engulfed in a magnificent perennial border with a low retaining wall that showcases an extensive succulent collection and moves the visitor through an array of rare Tennessean wildflowers. Finally, a secret walk meanders through a collection of shrubs and ornamental trees and returns the visitor to the garden gates.

Hours: 1 p.m. to 4 p.m.

From I-65, take I-440 west to Exit 1/West End Avenue. Travel west 2.1 miles to Belle Meade Boulevard and turn left. Go 1.2 miles on Belle Meade Boulevard and turn left onto Gerald Place. *Please park in the empty field on the corner and walk to the second house on the left.*

Proceeds shared with Cheekwood

Martin Garden
610 Belle Meade Boulevard, Nashville

A stroll across gracious lawns dotted with specimen trees leads to a stately southern mansion, with classic columns and a cobblestone-lined drive. The home and grounds have been the residence of several generations of prominent Nashvillians. In contrast to the sweeping, park-like expanse at the front of the property are the secluded formal spaces found tucked around the western side of the house. Carefully maintained hedges of boxwood and yew create elegant garden rooms centered on the delicate tracery of a wrought-iron gazebo and an armillary sphere encircled by beds of roses, hostas, and other subtle plantings.

Hours: 1 p.m. to 4 p.m.

From I-65, take I-440 west to Exit 1/West End Avenue. Travel west 2.1 miles to Belle Meade Boulevard and turn left. Go 1.2 miles on Belle Meade Boulevard and turn left onto Gerald Place. *Please park in the empty field on the corner.* The garden is across the street at 610 Belle Meade Boulevard. Access the garden through the drive off Gerald Place.

Proceeds shared with Cheekwood

Simons Garden
502 Park Hill, Nashville

After gardening for more than 25 years, the owner knew exactly what she wanted when she moved into her present home. An old family tradition of croquet on Sunday afternoons gave shape to the central lawn with a sixty-foot border focusing on summer color and winter structure. A sunken white garden, a kitchen garden, and colorful poolside plantings complete the picture.

Hours: 1 p.m. to 4 p.m.

From I-65, take I-440 west to Exit 1/West End Avenue. Travel west 2.1 miles to Belle Meade Boulevard and turn left. Go .8 mile on Belle Meade Boulevard to Deer Park Drive and turn right. Travel .1 mile and turn left onto Park Hill. Proceed .1 mile to #502 on the left.

Proceeds shared with Cheekwood

Public Gardens
DAVIDSON COUNTY

NASHVILLE
Cheekwood
1200 Forrest Park Drive, Nashville (615) 356-8000 www.cheekwood.org

At Cheekwood, you'll find collections of dogwoods, wildflowers, herbs, iris, roses, peonies, magnolias, daylilies, ferns, hydrangeas, and much more. Specialty gardens include the Color Garden, showcasing gardening as a year-round activity, water gardens, the Japanese Garden, and the Trial Garden, where annuals are tested for performance in the mid-South. The perennial gardens are at their peak in June and July. The original Bryant Fleming-designed gardens around the Cheek mansion, which now houses the Museum of Art, are fully restored to their former elegance, with lovely vistas, boxwood gardens, Italianate water features, and spectacular stonework.

Hours: Year round, Monday through Saturday, 9:30 a.m. to 4:30 p.m., Sunday, 11 a.m. to 4:30 p.m.

Admission: $10 adults, $7 senior citizens, $5 children 6-17, children under 6 free

From I-65, take I-440 west to Exit 1/West End Avenue. Travel west 5.1 miles to Belle Meade Boulevard and turn left. Go 2.8 miles to Page Road. Turn right onto Page Road, go .2 mile, and turn left onto Forrest Park Drive. Follow Forrest Park Drive .2 mile to the Cheekwood entrance.

HAMILTON COUNTY
CHATTANOOGA
Reflection Riding Arboretum & Botanical Gardens
400 Garden Road, Chattanooga (423) 821-9582

Reflection Riding is a 300-acre landscape park, nature preserve, and historic site nestled between the western slope of Lookout Mountain and Lookout Creek. Sixteen miles of roads and trails offer visitors an opportunity to enjoy dramatic vistas, thousands of wildflowers, and flowering trees and shrubs along the way in woodland gardens, meadows, mountain ravines, and slopes. More than 500 species and a rich selection of southern Appalachian plant life grow here, and more than 200 are propagated on site. The Philp Garden features all the evergreen rhododendrons and all but two azaleas native to the eastern United States.

Hours: May 18, 10 a.m. to 5 p.m.; otherwise, year round, weekdays, 9 a.m. to 5 p.m., Sunday, 1 p.m. to 5 p.m.

Admission: $6 per car

From downtown Chattanooga, take I-24 west to Exit 175/Brown's Ferry Road and turn left at the traffic light. At the next light, turn left onto Cummings Highway. Travel about 1 mile and turn right at the signs for Reflection Riding and the Tennessee Wildlife Center. Follow Garden Road to the end and turn left at the sign to the Humphreys House.

LOOKOUT MOUNTAIN
Tennessee River Gardens & Wildlife Preserve
1002 Scenic Highway, Lookout Mountain (423) 821-1538

Tennessee River Gardens is a wildflower and native plant garden on a spectacular site along the Tennessee River. More than 500 species are individually identified with colored pictures along a trail that winds through a meadow and forest and by streams, fifteen-foot waterfalls, and trout ponds. River Gardens overlooks a private fifty-acre lake with a dramatic view down the Tennessee River Gorge with 1,200-foot mountains rising on each side. Here you may also see great blue herons working out of their rookery, Canada geese, kingfishers, ospreys, and sometimes wild turkeys and bald eagles. The wildflowers in the meadows in May are spectacular.

Hours: May 18, 10 a.m. to 5 p.m.

Admission: free

Go west on I-24 6 miles from downtown Chattanooga. Take the Lookout Valley exit and go right onto Cummings Highway/Route 41. Go 2.7 miles and turn right through the stone gates to River Gardens (250 yards past TVA Racoon Mountain Facility Road).

Texas

OPEN DAYS:

April 13
April 14
May 18
September 28

Tony Cerbone's Exotic Dallas garden, Dallas.

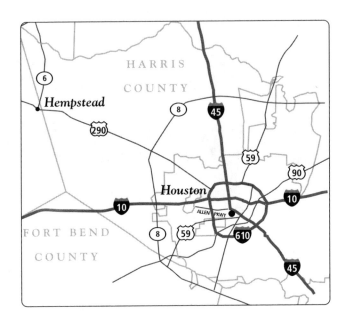

Saturday, April 13

HARRIS COUNTY

HOUSTON
1411 North Boulevard
1411 North Boulevard, Houston

The garden has evolved since 1927 under three owners and three landscape architects. It is an arrangement of garden rooms relating to the house and formed by various garden features— motor court and drive, south terrace and pergola, pool terrace and screened porch, east live oak/camellia garden and fountain, west lawn and herb border, secret or shade garden, and walk. The Birdsall Brisco Residence was placed on the site to allow for maximum exposure for the South Garden.

Hours: 10 a.m. to 2 p.m.

We are located near Rice University and the Museum District. The closest freeway is I-59. Exit at Greenbriar and head south to the second street, which is North Boulevard. Turn left and travel through 5 stop signs. Number 1411 is on the corner of West Boulevard and North Boulevard on the south side of the street.

Benton Residence

3395 Del Monte, Houston

This newly established garden was designed by the homeowner as part of a major remodeling and renovation (1999-2000) of the house, built in 1936. Planting in the front and side yards is intentionally austere, with 'Mrs. G.G. Gerbing' azaleas and Japanese boxwood setting a formal tone under a canopy of oak, pine, and magnolia trees. The back garden is divided into four "garden rooms" and is entered through a gate on the east side. The first room is a shady fern garden with a small fountain. Beyond an arch planted with white-flowered vines, the second is a narrow garden planted to attract birds and butterflies. It is bordered by a hedge of Japanese yew, which separates the butterfly garden from the main part of the back garden. The greatly enlarged terrace and formal parterre anchoring this area replaced a large swimming pool and pool house. This room is the result of a desire for more space to plant in the English manner—exuberant planting of formal beds with an axial arrangement. The "L"-shaped beds around a "dipping pool," with its ornamental water jets, contain several species of native Texas plants, as well as other Houston-reliable perennials. Each of these beds is a mirror image of those on either side. A simple border of perennials and elaeagnus frames a small folly built into the handsome brick wall at the back of the garden. The fourth room, the area closest to the new garage, is dominated by narrow beds of shrubs, old garden roses, and shallow-rooted plants (dictated by a large existing water oak) surrounding a gravel terrace with a distinctly Mediterranean feel. Outside the walls of the garden proper, on Mockingbird Lane, is a cottage-style garden of native Texas flowering plants and a stylized brick terrace outside the west-side door.

Hours: 2 p.m. to 6 p.m.

From Southwest Freeway/I-59, take the Buffalo Speedway exit and go north. Cross Richmond, Alabama, Westheimer (after which the street name changes to Claremont Lane), and San Felipe (all intersections with traffic lights). Claremont dead-ends into Chevy Chase Drive. Turn left onto Chevy Chase, then make the next right onto Mockingbird Lane. The next intersection is Del Monte. We are located on the near right corner. *Turn right and park on Del Monte.*

Brennan Residence

2337 Tangley, Houston

This young garden was given compelling tenor by responding to the cosmopolitan interiors. The home and garden became integrated once appropriate garden planning was employed two years ago. An acutely Provençal-inspired style ensued. Gravel use addresses the utilitarian requirements of the home while giving a seamless continuity to the garden aesthetic. Delicate grays and blues, subtle reds, lavender, and pink correspond to the sublime colors and textures inside the home. Deliberate selection and strategic placement of trees, shrubs, and perennials summon the Provençal experience. At the same time, the garden appears to belong to the home and site due to the willful cultivation of natives alongside ornamentals.

Hours: 10 a.m. to 2 p.m.

From Southwest Freeway/I-59, take the Shepherd/Greenbriar exit. Go south on Greenbriar to Tangley. Turn right. Tangley is 6 blocks south of Bissonnet; it runs east to west and is between Bissonnet Street and Rice Boulevard.

Casey Residence
2818 Ferndale, Houston

Sculpture from the studio of local artist Tim Glover sets the tone of this home and garden. Since the owners were moving from a more traditional and spacious garden, they decided to embark on a new garden style for their new home. The entrance garden was composed to gently differentiate between public and private space. One normally does not experience the west garden until observing it from inside on the second floor, the public area of the home. The garden had to read boldly from this perspective. Hence the obtuse scale of the various elements. Illusion of depth and scale is achieved by pulling the composition away from the perimeter fence. A steel screen conceals awkward fencing at an important tree. An out-sized stone mesa supports potted flowers, a cushion for lounging, and a four-foot-wide bowl fountain.

Hours: 10 a.m. to 2 p.m.

From Southwest Freeway/I-59, take the Kirby exit. Go left on Kirby to Kipling. Turn left and turn right onto Ferndale.

From downtown, take Allen Parkway, which turns into Kirby, and pass through the traffic lights at Inwood, San Felipe, and Westheimer. Turn right onto West Alabama, go 3 blocks, and turn right onto Ferndale.

Corn-Parker Garden
616 Harvard Street, Houston

The charming front garden beckons neighbors and strangers as well as nature's delightful creatures. The fragrance of antique roses draws the visitor along the pathway to a delightful cottage garden and a lush bed of ferns, gingers, and Louisiana iris. Recycled materials lend a touch of whimsy to the garden. Seating areas have been designed to invite the visitor to stop and savor the wonders of the garden. A small pond leads the visitor through a garden gate to the tropical courtyard garden. The play of dappled shade from the nearly 100-year-old pecan tree enhances the various textures and colors of ginger, fern, and bromeliad. Again, the use of recycled materials and personal touches brings a smile to the visitor's face. The sound of several water features and the fragrance of honeysuckle, plumeria, and jasmine make this a delightful surprise.

Hours: 2 p.m. to 6 p.m.

Located in the historic Houston Heights, take I-10 downtown and exit at Studemont/Yale/Heights. Reverse circle under the freeway. Travel north on Frontage Road and turn right onto Heights Boulevard. Turn right onto White Oak and turn left onto Harvard Street. A white cottage sits back from the street on the right, #616. *Please park along the road.*

Proceeds shared with the Houston Heights Association

The DeGeurin Garden
2106 Persa, Houston

This is a garden that provides a refuge for both wildlife and people. The city is screened from the house by intensely planted gardens of underutilized native and rare plants. The house and hardscapes are meant to be a part of the planting rather than standing apart from it. The border between the interior space of the garden is softened. The pool garden is planted with the plants of South Texas and the high chaparral of Mexico. Another garden has plants of the eastern timber belt of Texas and the mountains of Mexico. It is a landscape that hopes to awaken a feeling of being in the forest away from the city.

Hours: 2 p.m. to 6 p.m.

From Allen Parkway, turn left onto Shepherd Drive about .6 mile, after San Felipe turn right onto Avalon Place. The second block is Persa. Turn left onto Persa. The garden is the second house on the right, #2106. *Please park along the street.*

Kainer Residence
2029 Albans Road, Houston

Hidden completely from public view, this unassuming yet seductive garden is an experience likened to a symphony, sequentially soft, low, loud, fast, stimulating, and finally soothing. Off the tree-lined sidewalk, one steps up to the hidden gate, deeply shaded by a rose bower. Once through the gate, the garden blazes in colorful, sunlit splendor. East or west the mature garden path narrows and becomes a moist fern glade or a shaded grove of guavas. The effusive personality of the inhabitants is evident in this perpetually evolving garden best illustrated in the water garden. The architectural components, accessories, and the complex horticultural tapestry create a depth and warmth unique to this intimate garden. Our favorite detail is how this garden is afforded privacy by way of the lushly planted metal fencing. The limits of the gardens seem boundless.

Hours: 10 a.m. to 2 p.m.

From Southwest Freeway/I-59, take the Greenbriar exit. Go south on Greenbriar to Albans Road. Turn left onto Albans Road and go 3 blocks. Albans is 7 blocks south of the freeway; it runs east to west and is between Bissonnet Street and Sunset Boulevard.

Garden of Karen & John Kelsey
2112 Westgate, Houston

Our garden is an Italian design, with formal beds trimmed with boxwood and filled with old roses. Native Texas plants are used for ease of care and maintenance.

Hours: 2 p.m. to 6 p.m.

Westgate runs north and south and crosses Westheimer between Kirby and Greenbriar (where the French Gourmet Bakery is). Turn north off Westheimer onto Westgate. Stay on Westgate almost until the intersection with Avalon. Number 2112 is on the west side of the street, three lots from the corner. It is a three-story stucco house with palm trees on the third-floor terrace. *Please park on the street.*

Pinson Residence

3311 Del Monte Drive, Houston

Subtle gradations of cool colors and manipulation of natural light, distinct formal garden rooms where large and small groups of guests can be at ease, and design motifs which are compatible with the owners' lifelong interest in theater, opera, and the visual arts provide the first impressions of this garden. The blue and lavendar flowering plants infilling chipped boxwood beds flanking the entrance walk reflect the Baroque French idiom suggested by the house. On the west side of the front garden is an allée of Mexican plums with their lovely pale pink spring flowers and later, delicately colored fruit. The beds surrounding the lawn in this area are informally planted within a fairly formal design to provide a habitat for birds, among them Indigo buntings, a fmaily favorite. This relaxed and slightly disheveled planting scheme surrounding the allée and west of the fragrant crape myrtle garden lends a romantic Southern air, reinforced by deciduous and Robin Hill azaleas in deliberate stylistic contrast to the formality of the front garden. This garden in progress is well underway to fulfilling the Pinsons' vision of a setting that expresses their aesthetic interests, respects gardening traditions of River Oaks, and invites guests to share their love for being together outdoors.

Hours: 2 p.m. to 6 p.m.

Follow directions to the Benton Garden. The Pinson garden is located on the same block as the Benton garden, on the same side of the street, but at the opposite end of the block, on the corner of Del Monte and River Oaks Boulevard. *Please park along the street.*

Simon Residence

2003 Dunstan, Houston

A mature live oak canopy characterizes this splendid urban garden. The site was redeveloped five years ago and preservation of these trees was the driving force behind the layout of the home and garden. Refinement is initially evident in the entrance garden along Dunstan. A contemporary interpretation of a French parterre is revealed as one approaches the garden door. Through this door the deftly composed walled garden rests in association with the breezeway, terraces, and galleries of the home. The pool was set where once the previous structures stood. A delicately cultivated shade garden was placed along the pool. At the opposite end of the walled garden is a gravel terrace, which affords the garden strong composition yet minimizes maintenance and impact on the trees. A utilitarian herb garden has good exposure in the alley. Through the westernmost pedestrian alley garden vignettes opposite windows are employed alongside the necessary household mechanical equipment.

Hours: 10 a.m. to 2 p.m.

From Southwest Freeway/I-59, take the Greenbriar exit. Go south on Greenbriar to Dunstan. Turn left onto Dunstan and go 3 blocks. Dunstan is 7 blocks south of Bissonnet Street; it runs east-west and is between Bissonnet Street and Rice Boulevard.

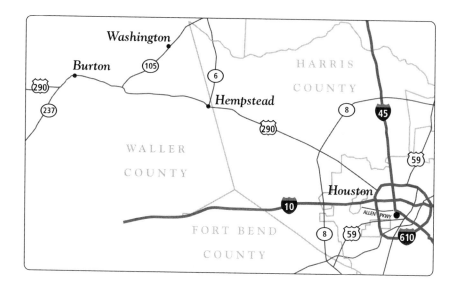

Sunday, April 14

WASHINGTON COUNTY

BURTON

Jacomini 5J Farm

10205 Mayer Cemetery Road, Burton

Ninety miles outside of Houston, in the gentle rolling hills between Brenham and Round Top, is the 100-acre farm of the Jacomini family. The farmhouse, dating from 1857, faces a three-acre pond and restored log cabin. The pond is fed by a well and stocked with catfish and bass. The property abounds in many species of oaks (burr, chinkapin, Durand, Mexican blue, overcup, Shumard, and water). The garden is a traditional cottage garden with flowers and herbs planted along with vegetables. The landscape is sympathetic with the home and surrounding countryside and rich in native wildflowers.

Hours: 2 p.m. to 6 p.m.

Take Highway 290 west towards Austin approximately 70 miles. Take the Blinn College exit or FM 389. Go left over the highway (at Diamond Shamrock Station). Proceed approximately 8.7 miles. Turn right onto Greenvine Road or FM 2502. Proceed approximately 1.5 miles. Turn left onto Wickel Road. Proceed approximately 2.4 miles. Turn left onto Mayer Cemetery Road. Proceed approximately 2.9 miles. The 5J Farm will be on your left.

From Rocking "S" Ranch & Garden, take FM 1948 to Route 290. Exit onto FM 2502. Turn right onto Wickel Road and proceed as directed above.

Rocking "S" Ranch & Garden

2866 FM 1948N, Burton

My garden is a secondary effort around the old (begun in 1835) house on my ranch. I have planted Texas perennials, bulbs, and roses, hoping to foil the armadillos, rabbits, dogs, and summertime invasions of grasshoppers. My family, consisting of four children and three of their spouses, enjoy their own Houston gardens. While at the Rocking "S," they ranch! All of us enjoy sitting on a big old porch and admiring what the critters have left, as well as the huge live oak trees all around the property.

Hours: noon to 4 p.m.

Take Highway 290 west from Houston and go around Brenham towards Austin. Twelve miles beyond Brenham, turn right off Highway 290 onto FM 1948. Rocking "S" Ranch is 3 miles from Highway 290 down FM 1948. There is a sign over the gate. The house is about .4 mile on the right. *There is plenty of parking outside the fence.*

From Independence, take Route 390 west, crossing Route 36 to FM 1948. Turn right into Rocking "S" Ranch & Garden.

Proceeds shared with the Burton Cotton Gin & Museum

WASHINGTON

Peaceable Kingdom Farm

11111 Mount Falls School Road, Washington

The gardens of Elizabeth Winston Mize and Jerald Mize, set on 152 acres of rolling, partially wooded land, are on the grounds of a former organic gardening school. The main garden comprises a mix of perennials, annuals, roses, herbs, and, especially in spring, bulbs. Nearby is the greenhouse berm, having dryland plants and native species. Water gardens are in progress. Across from the persimmon, jujube, peach, pomegranate, and fig orchard is the kitchen garden, featured in *Southern Living* magazine in 2000. The ornamental cedar fences and trellises were featured in a separate article. Around the main house is a cottage garden which includes plants dating from before 1862. There are woodland nature trails and a growing native plant herbarium with more than 450 pressed species.

Hours: 10 a.m. to 2 p.m.

From Houston, take Highway 290 to Hempstead. Take Exit 6 towards Navasota and Bryan/College Station. Go 19.1 miles to the Brenham/Washington-on-the-Brazos exit and take Route 105 west. Go under Highway 6 to the left for 7.3 miles to Pickens Road. Turn right and go .5 mile to Mount Falls School Road. Turn right and go 1 mile to the cattleguard. Turn left into Peaceable Kingdom Farm.

From Austin/Roundtop, take Highway 290 east to the Brenham city limits (just past the Route 190/36 overpass). Continue on Highway 290 Business east to Route 105 east (just past the square). Follow signs to the corner of Chappel Hill and Academy. This will be 2.1 miles. Continue right on Route 105 east from this corner and go 17.2 miles to Pickens Road. Turn left and go .5 mile to Mount Falls School Road. Proceed as directed above.

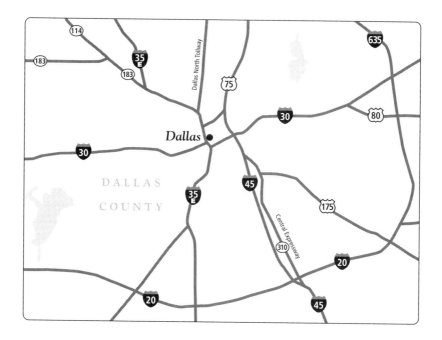

Saturday, May 18

DALLAS COUNTY

DALLAS
Tony Cerbone's Exotic Dallas Garden
6641 Highgate Lane, Dallas

This Dallas garden specializes in cold hardy plants that evoke a tropical atmosphere. Everything is hardy to a Zone 8A climate. It contains the largest collection of cold hardy palm trees in north Texas. In addition, there are many flowering plants from the tropics that do well in Dallas's summer heat, die down to the ground during winter, and return from their roots the next spring like perennials. Several vignettes have been created throughout the garden and include a tropical rainforest area, southwestern desert, annual and perennial color section, and bamboo collection. The garden was established fourteen years ago and includes several large oleanders that have been trained to tree form shapes and are spectacular during peak bloom in mid-May. Dallas's transitional climate has been highlighted and the garden showcases the unique types of plants that are possible in this area. Winters are mild enough to grow several species of cold hardy palms, dry enough to allow for cacti and agaves, and cool enough to provide chilling for warm temperate plants. The climate is wet enough to allow for luxuriant bamboo and trees such as live oak and crape myrtle.

Hours: 10 a.m. to 4 p.m.

Take Central Expressway/Route 75 to Lovers Lane and go east on Lovers Lane past Greenville, Skillman, and Abrams. Continue to a stop sign, which is Fisher Road, and turn right onto Fisher. Proceed for 2 blocks and turn left onto Highgate Lane. Number 6641 is less than 1 block after the turn onto Highgate.

Michael Cheever's Garden

618 Valencia Street, Dallas

A charming garden of perennials, flowering shrubs, and small trees, this garden reflects the owner's sixteen years of work as a botanical garden professional. Surrounding a Tudor cottage in an historic Old East Dallas neighborhood, the plant collection includes many Texas native plants, unusual perennials, and unique species from botanical gardens and collecting trips. A shady back garden with large pecan trees, lovely decomposed granite paths, and a patio provides a cool refuge in summer for the owner and his guests.

Hours: 10 a.m. to 4 p.m.

This garden is located about 3 miles east of downtown Dallas in the Hollywood Heights neighborhood (south of White Rock Lake and adjacent to Samuell-Grand Park). From I-30, take the Winslow exit and turn north. Turn right onto East Grand at the stop sign, then proceed north to Clermont Street. Turn left onto Clermont to go through Samuell-Grand Park. Turn left onto southbound East Grand, go 2 blocks to Valencia Street, and turn right. The garden is on the north side of Valencia 3 blocks up from East Grand.

Proceeds shared with the Texas Discovery Gardens

Einspruch Garden

3505 Lindenwood Avenue, Dallas

The garden was designed by David Rolston, landscape architect, as a series of outdoor rooms/ spaces, each with a different sense of enclosure and intimacy. The borders of perennials, both native and adapted, create a contrast to the structure provided by the decomposed granite walks, wall, gate, hedges, and parterres. Plants were chosen for texture and form, to attract butterflies, and to provide fall and winter interest.

Hours: 10 a.m. to 4 p.m.

From Central Expressway/Highway 75, take the Mockingbird Lane exit west; from the Dallas Tollroad, exit onto Mockingbird Lane east. Follow Mockingbird to Hillcrest. Turn south onto Hillcrest. Go to Beverly Drive. Turn west onto Beverly to Auburndale. Turn south onto Auburndale to Lindenwood Avenue and turn right. Number 3505 is on the south side 3 houses from the Auburndale/Linwood corner.

Judy Fender's Garden
9019 Fringewood Drive, Dallas

Visitors delight in my hidden backyard gardens, which I built entirely myself. Creating a "Garden of Eden" as a place of relaxation and beauty for my enjoyment, there are three water gardens, waterfalls, and a 46-foot-long stream. To entice birds and other suburban wildlife, there are over 100 roses scattered among native plants, perennials, and herbs. A certified Wildlife Habitat and Butterfly Habitat, take time to meander along the paths. Delight in the vast variety of plants, whimsical garden statuary, and artistic touches. Sit a while at various locations in the gardens and watch the koi and goldfish.

Hours: 10 a.m. to 4 p.m.

From I-30, take the Buckner Boulevard exit. Take Buckner north (past 3 traffic lights) to Ferguson Road West. Turn west onto Ferguson Road. Drive about .5 mile (past churches) to Lanecrest (at the bottom of a slight hill) and turn left. Take the first left onto Ripplewood. Make the first right onto Glenmont. Make the first left onto Fringewood. The house is the fourth on the left side. Walk down the driveway to the gardens.

From North Central Expressway/Highway 75, travel south to I-30 (downtown Dallas) or exit at either Northwest Highway or Mockingbird Lane and drive east (past White Rock Lake) to Buckner Boulevard. Take Buckner south. You will pass Garland Road (at a light) and continue to Ferguson Road West. Turn right onto Ferguson Road West. Proceed as directed above. *Please park on the street.*

Proceeds shared with the Dallas County Master Gardeners

Rolston/Cohn Garden
7206 Tokalon Drive, Dallas

The garden is a composition of formal garden design and informal plantings. The plantings consist of easily obtainable material, combined in mass quantities. This approach allows the garden to be low maintenance with maximum visual impact. I maintain the garden myself on weekends. If plant material is not adaptable or suited to this schedule, I re-evaluate the selection. There are fountains, a stream, and two small formal garden pools throughout this two thirds of an acre.

Hours: 10 a.m. to 4 p.m.

From Central Expressway/Highway 75, take Mockingbird Lane east to Abrams. Turn right onto Abrams. Go through 2 traffic lights; at the third light, turn left onto Lakewood Boulevard. Go .7 mile until Lakewood veers to the left. At that point, veer to the right onto Tokalon Drive. We are the second house from the lake on the right side at #7206. *Please park on the street.*

Peter & Julie Schaar

3515 Haynie Avenue, Dallas

The garden of Peter and Julie Schaar is an inner city garden on a small lot. It is a mixed planting of roses, trees, shrubs, palms, perennials, bulbs, and containers, and includes a wide variety of native and adapted plants. The Schaars maintain their garden organically, using no sprays, fungicides, or insecticides, and fertilize only with manure, compost, and other organic products. The garden is watered only occasionally, usually five to eight times per year. The front yard is an informal design inspired by cottage gardens in order to conform to the cottage house. The backyard has many touches of formality and structure while still presenting exuberantly planted beds. Recent plantings have spilled out into both sides of the alley. Roses, gardenias, and camellias in containers line the driveway in the back near the garage. Fragrance is an important part of this garden's appeal, there being a large number of fragrant trees, shrubs, vines, roses, herbs, and bulbs that perfume the garden at almost every time of the year. The Schaars welcome you to their garden and hope you have an enjoyable visit. They ask only that you refrain from smoking and that you ask for starts of any plants you are interested in.

Hours: 10 a.m. to 4 p.m.

From the intersection of Hillcrest and Lovers Lane, drive south on Hillcrest to the SMU Campus (4 to 5 blocks). Turn right onto Haynie Avenue, which is the street just before University Boulevard. The Schaar garden is in the second block, between Dickens and Thackery, at #3515. *Please park on the street or in the driveway.*

Southbrook Gardens

5120 Southbrook Drive, Dallas

Southbrook Gardens is a study in contrasts: sun and deep shade, geometrically arranged raised beds and winding mulched pathways, formal and naturalistic styles. The garden was designed as a teaching tool for visitors of all ages and interests, from preschoolers learning to scratch and sniff fragrant herbs to amateur artists studying the basics of botanical illustration. Herbs dominate the plant palette and range from familiar parsley to patchouli and papaloquelite. At the center of the enclosed formal area is a large limestone sculpture by a local artist, Eliseo. The garden is a certified Texas Wildscape and Butterfly Habitat.

Hours: 10 a.m. to 4 p.m.

Southbrook Drive is located 1 block south of the intersection of Inwood Road and Northwest Highway. From Inwood, turn west onto Southbrook. Southbrook Gardens are behind the second house on the left. *Parking behind the house is reserved for visitors with disabilities. Others may park on the street or in the small off-street area in front of the house.*

Proceeds shared with the Dallas County Master Gardeners Association

Terry Garden
6001 Revere Place, Dallas

As a result of our love for the Texas Hill Country and Santa Fe, we were inspired to create a homestead ambiance in our surroundings with native plants in an older urban setting here in Dallas. The sway of the upright verbena and Mexican feather grass dance with birds and butterflies in total harmony with nature. Grasses, perennials, and succulents were carefully chosen to accentuate a native and drought-tolerant environment. The large stones and rocks lend an aura of permanence and coherence to the garden, as does the long stone wall across the front. The rustic backdrop of antiques and vintage vessels harmonizes with the natural beauty of the garden to create a calm and soothing effect. The garden invites you to come in and wander along the granite-and-flagstone path to a small pond with the serenity of water cascading over the natural stone. The majestic pecan tree casts sun and shade throughout the day; many niches draw you in to sit and take in your lush surroundings. A myriad of native plants forms a rich tapestry as you leisurely stroll around the garden. Come and have a unique opportunity to visit a magnificent garden habitat.

Hours: 10 a.m. to 4 p.m.

From North Central Expressway/Highway 75, take the Mockingbird Lane exit. Go east on Mockingbird Lane to Skillman Avenue (about 5 traffic lights). Turn right (south) onto Skillman; go 7 blocks to Revere Place. Turn right (west) onto Revere and go 1 block to the corner of Revere and Concho. The house is on the northeast corner. *Please park along the street.*

Saturday, September 28

TRAVIS/WILLIAMSON COUNTY

AUSTIN

James deGrey David & Gary Peese

8 Sugar Creek Drive, Austin

This is a collector's garden with Mediterranean elements. It includes a series of terraces and courtyards. Water features include a native limestone water staircase extending to a creek bed. A special feature is a vegetable garden with a collection of exotic, hard-to-find edibles. The garden integrates and flows with this architecturally acclaimed home.

Hours: 10 a.m. to 6 p.m.

Travel south on Mo-Pac Expressway/Route 1. Go west on Route 2244, commonly known as Beecave Road. Turn right onto Edgegrove at the Texaco gas station. Turn right onto Rollingwood Drive and then make a quick left onto Gentry. Turn right onto Sugar Creek Drive. *Please park along the road.*

Deborah Hornickel

3206 Oakmont Boulevard, Austin

A long gravel drive lined with roses (*Rosa chinensis mutablis*) leads you to the entry of the garden, which originates in back of the house. The cool greenery and unexpected size and formality of this garden greet you as your eyes behold the ultimate surprise, a *Pyrus calleryana* allée. This is a garden with many elegant touches and made with economy in mind.

Hours: 10 a.m. to 6 p.m.

Travel north on Mo-Pac Expressway/Route 1 to the 35th Street exit. Go east on 35th Street and turn right onto Oakmont Boulevard.

Old Ziller House Garden

Our garden surrounds a charming early Texas cottage (circa 1877). When we acquired the property in 1993, the house was in severe disrepair and the garden had been untended for several years. Surprisingly, many plants survived this neglect. Rather than starting from scratch, we incorporated these survivors into our new garden plan. We also employed many old favorites, including camellias, azaleas, boxwood, iris, spider lilies, daylilies, asters, altheas, spireas, and nandina. We're especially pleased with our towering Sabal palm and our ancient wisteria, which engulfs a full-grown oak. Our old-fashioned garden is lush and abundant, the plants spill into one another, giving it a very familiar, comfortable feeling.

Hours: 10 a.m. to 6 p.m.

Take I-35 to Austin. Take the Sixth Street exit (Third to Eighth Streets) going west. Go through downtown Austin, past Congress Avenue, past Lamar Boulevard, to Blanco Street (about 2 miles). Turn right at the traffic light onto Blanco Street. Go 4 to 5 blocks to 12th Street. Our garden is on the left side of the near corner. *Please park along 12th Street or Blanco, but watch for No Parking signs.*

Possumhaw Hollow—The Spencer-Martinez Garden

4913 Finley Drive, Austin

Surprisingly large for a central Austin garden, Possumhaw Hollow is a series of interconnected garden rooms organized around long view corridors. The dominant feature of the garden is an allée of bald cypress trees inspired by the stream courses of the Texas Hill Country. The other features of this new garden (started in late 2000) include a stone-lined pond, a circle of possumhaw hollies, and Mexican folk art. Tom Spencer, host of KLRU-TV's *Central Texas Gardener* and creator of www.soulofthegarden.com, is the co-owner and designer.

Hours: 10 a.m. to 6 p.m.

From Mo-Pac Expressway/Route 1, take the 45th Street exit and go east towards Lamar Boulevard. Go 2 blocks to the traffic light at Bull Creek Road. Turn left onto Bull Creek and go 2 long blocks on your right to 49 1/2 Street. Turn right onto 49 1/2 and go 1 block to Finley Drive (the first street that you will encounter). Turn left onto Finley Drive and the house will be on your right, #4913. Look for the grove of elm trees. *Please park along the street, being careful not to block the driveways.*

Proceeds shared with the Seton Cove

Bill & Anna Prothro

2204 Hopi Trail, Austin

This garden is a Texas version of the traditional English cottage garden. The front yard is informally planted, while the backyard is more formal. The design is based on the circle, which appears in the planting and also in the many circular topiaries throughout the garden. Special features include two ponds, a grotto on the side of the house, and hand-crafted ornaments, including a majestic bottle tree.

Hours: 10 a.m. to 6 p.m.

From Mo-Pac Expressway/Route 1, take the Windsor exit. Go west on Windsor past Exposition to Hopi Trail. Turn left onto Hopi Trail to #2204, the second house on the right. *Please park along the street.*

Webber Garden
806 West 31st Street, Austin

An intense interest in trying to grow every kind of plant I've come across has resulted in some surprising successes and unusual plant choices and combinations, particularly in regard to dryland tropicals. Native limestone boulders with sculptural agaves and succulents in full sun transition to single roses, grasses, and perennials to shaded beds, stone patios, and walks ringing the 1933 frame house. The preservation and integration of 1930s' rock work—tiled columns, dry stack walls, and seating—were important to the ordering of the garden design. In the back is a brilliantly sunlit gravel terrace, backed by a stucco wall with built-in stone shelves and a waterfall.

Hours: 10 a.m. to 6 p.m.

Located in central Austin, 2 blocks east of Lamar Boulevard, at 806 West 31st Street. Please park along the street.

Proceeds shared with Doctors without Borders

Public Gardens

COLLIN COUNTY

McKINNEY
The Heard Museum Texas Native Plant Display Garden
One Nature Plaza, McKinney (972) 562-5566 www.heardmuseum.org

The Heard Natural Science Museum and Wildlife Sanctuary has a two-acre Texas Native Plant Display Garden. It is home to over 200 native species, including 26 trees, 29 shrubs, 15 vines, 20 grasses, and over 100 varieties of perennial and annual wildflowers. The purpose of the gardens is to educate the public about the beauty and diversity of our native plants and how they may be used in urban landscapes.

Hours: Year round, Monday through Saturday, 9 a.m. to 5 p.m., Sunday, 1 p.m. to 5 p.m.; closed major holidays.

Admission: $4 adults, $2 children

From Route 75, take Exit 38A and follow the brown-and-white highway signs. The Heard Museum is located 1 mile east of Highway 5 on FM 1378, southeast of McKinney.

DALLAS COUNTY

DALLAS
Dallas Nature Center
Mountain Creek Parkway, Dallas (972) 296-1955 www.dallasnaturecenter.org

The Dallas Nature Center is a 630-acre wilderness sanctuary that provides vital habitat for several endangered plants and animals, including the black-capped vireo. In addition to prairie wildflower areas, the Dallas Nature Center also features a butterfly garden landscaped with native plants.

Hours: Year round, Tuesday through Sunday, dawn to dusk

Admission: $1 suggested donation

From I-20, take the Mountain Creek Parkway exit. Travel south on Mountain Creek Parkway for 2.5 miles. The Nature Center entrance is just south of the intersection with Wheatland

Texas Discovery Gardens, Fair Park
3601 Martin Luther King Jr. Boulevard, Dallas (214) 428-7476

The Texas Discovery Gardens is the second oldest botanical institution in Texas and has 7.5 acres of gardens. Plant collections and specialized gardens include a Butterfly Garden, the Benny J. Simpson Texas Native Plant Collection, antique fragrant roses, perennials, and an African plant collection in the tropical conservatory.

Hours: Year round, daily, dawn to dusk; visitors center and conservatory open Tuesday through Saturday, 10 a.m. to 5 p.m., Sunday, 1 p.m. to 5 p.m.

Admission: free

From I-30 east, take the Second Avenue exit, curve to the right, and turn left at the second traffic light, which is Martin Luther King Jr. Boulevard.

From I-30 west, take the First Avenue exit, turn under the freeway to Exposition Avenue, and turn right onto Parry Avenue. Turn left at the fourth light which is Martin Luther King Jr. Boulevard.

From I-45 south, take the Martin Luther King Jr. Boulevard exit, curve to the right, and turn left at the light.

HARRIS COUNTY
HOUSTON
Bayou Bend Collection & Gardens
Westcott Street, Houston (713) 639-7750 www.bayoubend.uh.edu

Bayou Bend, now the American Decorative Arts wing of the Museum of Fine Arts, Houston, is located within the fourteen-acre estate of Miss Ima Hogg. The regional bayou woodland has been interplanted with a diverse collection of native Gulf Coast and ornamental plants. The horticultural collection is framed in a series of formal garden rooms, woodland gardens, ravines, and paths. The integrated house/garden composition is a significant example of a regional historic landscape of the American Country House movement. The gardens feature one of the most extensive collections of azaleas and camellias in Texas.

Hours: Year round, Tuesday through Saturday, 10 a.m. to 5 p.m., Sunday, 1 p.m. to 5 p.m. Guided tours available at 10 a.m. and 11 a.m. on Tuesday and Friday; reservations required.

Admission: $3 adults, children under 11 free

Approach Bayou Bend via Memorial Drive in Houston, turning south at Westcott Street. Please park in the free lot and cross the footbridge to enter the gardens.

Rienzi

1406 Kirby Drive, Houston (713) 639-7800 www.mfah.org

Rienzi, the European Decorative Arts wing of the Museum of Fine Arts, Houston, is the former home of Carroll Sterling and Harris Masterton III. The residence and its gardens opened to the public in March 1999. Set in 4.4 acres of wooded ravines on Buffalo Bayou, Rienzi's gardens are an artful combination of formal spaces compatible with its Palladian contemporary exterior and its wilder native ravines. Azaleas, camellias, gingers, and roses flourish in settings surrounded by native magnolias, conifers, and oaks.

Hours: Year round, except August, docent-led tours Monday, Thursday, Friday, and Saturday, 10 a.m. to 4 p.m.; Sunday, open-house format, 1 p.m. to 5 p.m.

Admission: $6 adults, $5 senior citizens and students over 12; Sundays, $5 general admission, $10 for group of up to 4, $15 for group of up to 6

Rienzi is located in River Oaks, west of downtown Houston and north of Highway 59. From downtown, take Allen Parkway west. As it crosses Shepherd, Allen Parkway becomes Kirby Drive. Rienzi is on the right.

From Highway 59, take the Kirby Drive exit and drive north. Rienzi will be on the left. Bayou Bend is nearby.

TARRANT COUNTY

FORT WORTH

Fort Worth Botanic Garden

3220 Botanic Garden Boulevard, Fort Worth (817) 871-7686 www.fwgarden.com

The Fort Worth Botanic Garden is the oldest botanic garden in Texas. Covering an area of 109 acres, the botanic garden features a world-renowned Japanese Garden, an historic Rose Garden, one of the few floral clocks in the nation, a tropical conservatory, a restaurant, and meeting facilities.

Hours: Year round, weekdays, 8 a.m. to 9 p.m., Saturday, 8 a.m. to 7 p.m., Sunday, 1 p.m. to 7 p.m. (summer); weekdays, 8 a.m. to 9 p.m., Saturday, 8 a.m. to 5 p.m., Sunday, 1 p.m. to 5 p.m. (winter); conservatory closes at 6 p.m. in summer, 4 p.m. in winter, opens at 10 a.m. Closed Christmas Day.

Admission: $1 conservatory, $1.50 to $3 Japanese garden.

Located 1.5 miles west of downtown Fort Worth at the intersection of I-30 and University Drive. Turn north onto University and the garden may be reached by turning left on the first 2 streets north of I-30.

AUSTIN

Lady Bird Johnson Wildflower Center

4801 La Crosse Avenue, Austin (512) 292-4100 www.wildflower.org

The Lady Bird Johnson Wildflower Center maintains a native plant botanical garden with acres of designed gardens, courtyards, and natural areas, showcasing the magnificent native plants of the Texas Hill Country in a variety of styles from naturalistic to formal. Highlights of the grounds include a Visitors Gallery with exhibits and a video presentation, Wild Ideas: The Store, a terraced café, a 45-foot observation tower, a children's discovery room, home comparison gardens, and nature trails. The center also has one of North America's largest rooftop rainwater collection systems, with a series of aqueducts, beautiful stone cisterns, and waterways.

Hours: Year round, Tuesday through Sunday, 9 a.m. to 5:30 p.m.

Admission: varies depending on season

From I-35, take Exit 227/Slaughter Lane. Bear west off the exit ramp and travel 6 miles west to the intersection of Slaughter Lane and Mo-Pac Expressway/Route 1. Turn left onto the expressway and left again onto La Crosse

ROUND MOUNTAIN

Westcave Preserve

24814 Hamilton Pool Road, Round Mountain (830) 825-3442 www.westcave.org

Westcave preserve is a thirty-acre natural sanctuary protected for future generations. It is a delight for wildflower enthusiasts, hikers, birders, or anyone who loves the natural beauty of the Texas Hill Country.

Hours: Year round, weekends, 10 a.m. to noon, 2 p.m., and 4 p.m. Weekday programs scheduled in advance.

Admission: donations welcomed

Take Highway 71 west from Austin to the village of Bee Cave. Turn left onto Ranch Road 3238 (Hamilton Pool Road) and travel 14 miles, crossing the Pedernales River. Look for the first gate on the right.

WALLER COUNTY

HEMPSTEAD

Peckerwood Garden

20571 FM 359, Hempstead (979) 826-3232 www.peckerwood.org

A PROJECT OF
THE GARDEN
CONSERVANCY

Peckerwood Garden is an artist's garden set in a natural landscape. It holds an unduplicated collection of native rarities from Texas and Mexico interspersed in the garden with their Asian counterparts. This garden also serves as a horticultural laboratory where unusual plants and innovative techniques are tested. At present, the cultivated garden occupies about seven acres of the twenty-acre site and includes a woodland garden along the banks of a creek, a higher dry garden on the north slope of the creek, and a recently established meadow garden and arboretum on acreage to the south. More than 3,000 species and cultivars can be found here, including significant collections of *Quercus*, agaves, yuccas, and related plants, *Acer*, *Magnolia*, *Ilex*, *Styrax*, *Bauhinia*, rare bulbs, and conifers.

Hours: March 16 & 17; April 6 & 7, April 20 & 21, May 4 & 5, May 11 & 12, May 18 & 19, 1 p.m. to 5 p.m.; June 15 & 16, July 20 & 21, from 9 a.m. to 1 p.m.; October 5 & 6, October 19 & 20, from 1 p.m. to 5 p.m. November 2 & 3, 9 a.m. to 1 p.m.

Admission: $6 adults, $5 senior citizens and students over 12; Sundays, $5 general admission, $10 for groups of up to 4, $15 for groups of up to 6

From Houston, take Highway 290 west past Prairie View. Before reaching Hempstead, take Exit FM359 toward Brookshire. Proceed through the traffic light at the intersection with Business 290. The garden is located 1.7 mile past this intersection, on the right. Look for a small sign. Please park at Yucca Do Nursery, which is located just south of the garden.

WASHINGTON COUNTY

INDEPENDENCE

The Antique Rose Emporium Display Gardens

10,000 Highway 50, Independence (979) 836-5548

The site of an early settler's homestead in Independence is the location of our Texas display gardens. A variety of restored buildings, some dating back to the 1850s, have given us the opportunity to incorporate roses, perennials, herbs, and native flora into many varied garden settings. The gently rolling hills of Washington County covered with the spring display of bluebonnets surround the nursery. Each fall, these gardens are the focus for our Festival of Roses.

Hours: Year round, Monday through Saturday, 9 a.m. to 5:30 p.m., Sunday 11:30 a.m. to 5:30 p.m.

Admission: free

Located 10 miles northeast of Brenham at 10,000 Highway 50 which is .25 mile south of FM 390 and Highway 50.

From Washington, take Highway 105 to Highway 50. Turn right onto Highway 50 and proceed as directed above.

VERMONT

OPEN DAYS:

June 8
July 13

Joan & Lee Fegelman's garden, Manchester Center.

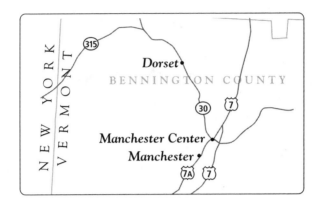

Saturday, June 8

BENNINGTON COUNTY

DORSET

Westerly

159 Danby Mountain Road, Dorset

Everything you see, except the large native trees, has been added by us since 1993. The garden is composed of several "rooms," which deliberately shift in mood as you progress around the house. At the entryway is a green garden, with a small pool and rare and native plants. Next is a working area with fruit and nut trees, rhubarb, asparagus, grapes, elderberry and blueberry plantings, and raised beds for annuals. Then comes a circular contemplative garden planted with *Physocarpus opulifolius*, because the deer loved the *Taxus* with which we started. Finally, through a giant gateway on which are espaliered two *Larix* x *pendula*, comes the largest room, the south lawn. There is a view of mountains to the south, while the house is framed by raised beds. A pentagonal folly, with its own different view of mountains, is tucked into the southwest corner. One surprise (herein revealed) follows another. Note the use of bluestone and natural stone to create gardens where the soil is practically "undiggable."

Hours: 10 a.m. to 4 p.m.

Take Route 30 north from Manchester to Dorset, about 6 miles. At the Dorset Inn, continue north 1.1 miles to Danby Mountain Road and turn right. Go up the first pitch, about 200 yards. On the left is a sign for #159. Enter and turn left before the first house you see, which will take you to our house.

MANCHESTER
Glebelands
4263 Main Street/Route 7A, Manchester

Our garden was started in the 1930s with perennials and a long allée of peonies. We later added marble defining walls, two gazebos (a Temple of Love and a Moorish-style with tassels), statues, and a tiled pool. I've incorporated a large reflecting pool with fountains at each end, antique iron (New Orleans) gates and grills, urns, and statuary from my former house. The grounds, totaling thirty acres, encompass an orchard underplanted with narcissus (a fairyland in springtime), a folly pavilion, two large ponds created by a 100-yard-long nineteenth-century marble dam (the area was a marble mill), two miles of woodland trails, brooks, and fine trees, including a *Chamaecyparis* collection I've raised from cuttings that I propagated.

Hours: 10 a.m. to 4 p.m.

Take Route 7A from the Equinox Hotel in Manchester Village. Travel north for .7 mile. Orvis Company will be on the right. Look for a dirt driveway within a spruce and pine grove on the left. A Glebelands sign with "4263 Main Street" on it will be in the middle of the drive. The house cannot be seen from the road.

From the north, take Route 7A south past the junction of Routes 11 and 30 in Manchester Center. Travel .6 mile south. Glebelands will be on the right. *Please follow signs for parking.*

Proceeds shared with the Bennington Garden Club

White Tree Farm
1166 West Road, Manchester

Our garden is a quadrangle surrounded by stone walls that sits behind an early farmhouse. Three quarters of the beds are herbaceous perennial borders supplemented by annual cutting areas and a small herb patch. The house and garden are Vermont vernacular in character and could easily have been here 100 or 200 years earlier. Within the garden walls is a unique birch tree of great age and beauty that adds much charm to the garden. Beyond the garden walls are areas of interest, including an old corncrib and barn, a vegetable garden, and small pond. The grounds are particularly attractive because of the venerable native trees on the property.

Hours: 10 a.m. to 4 p.m.

Take Routes 11 and 30 into Manchester. At the blinking traffic light turn south (left) onto Route 7A. Proceed through the roundabout and take the first right onto Way Lane. Follow to the stop sign and turn north (right) onto West Road. Pass Brightwood Road on the right. Next, pass Village Glen Road and the very next driveway on the right will be White Tree Farm, with white wooden gates. Number 1166 will be on the gate. *Please park in the driveway or on the lawn.*

MANCHESTER CENTER
Edwards' Garden
67 Coventry Lane, Manchester Center

The siting of my informal garden to run the length of the back of the house, surrounding the low deck, means that, when outside, one lives in the garden, rather than looks at it. Likewise, from inside the house, the garden is constantly in view from most windows. Such scrutiny requires attentive maintenance. The garden was designed to disappear in winter, with one's attention directed past it to the woods beyond. It is a work in progress and will be extended with the remodeling of the east end of the house.

Hours: 10 a.m. to 4 p.m.

Located in the northeast section of Manchester. Take Route 7A/Main Street north to Barnumville Road. Proceed .5 mile to Canterbury Road on the left. Climb Canterbury until the pavement ends. One hundred feet beyond the end of the pavement is Coventry Lane on the right. My house is the first house on the left. The garden is reached around the back side of the garage.

Joan & Lee Fegelman's Garden
42 Coventry Lane, Manchester Center

In the spring of 1991, our gardens began as three large perennial beds on a former horse pasture. Today our gardens encompass over an acre. As you meander through the perennial garden room on wide grass pathways, you will witness a riot of color that is in various stages of bloom from spring until frost. Leaving the perennial garden through an arbor, you wander along a peony/daylily walkway, the vista opens, and, to the right, you see a pergola garden room featuring rocks, a sundial, and interesting shrubs. From there, meander on a thyme-scented stone path through the herb garden, which then flows into the grass and annual garden. The rose garden features roses that are at home in Vermont. Unusual hostas enhance the beauty of the pool area.

Hours: 10 a.m. to 4 p.m.

From Manchester Center, take Route 7A north to Barnumville Road. Go .7 mile to Canterbury Road, which will be your second left. Go .6 mile to Coventry Lane, which will be your second right. Our home is the first driveway on the right.

MANCHESTER VILLAGE
The Sunken Garden
2234 River Road, Manchester Village

Remains of old foundations delineate some of my garden. My garden design has been guided by the walkways and stone walls that were once part of the model working farm on the Wilbur estate. My house (circa 1790) was the gardener's cottage. The old potting shed and greenhouse (near the study) had large glass structures coming out from them. The outlines of these glass structures are still visible on the buildings and the old foundations are still evident on the lawn. The remains of a pool and foundation have become a daylily bed and the old stone wall foundation has become my main garden. Because of the age and size of my property, I wanted the feeling to remain small and informal—old-fashioned and casual, like an English cottage garden.

Hours: 10 a.m. to 2 p.m.

From Route 7A south in Manchester, go 1 mile down River Road. The driveway is the second on the left past the entrance to the Wilburton Inn. Look for "J.B. Wilbur" on the stone pillars. Please park along the driveway.

Proceeds shared with the Federated Garden Club of Vermont, Inc.

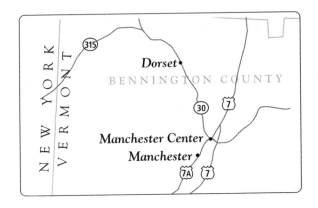

Saturday, July 13
BENNINGTON COUNTY

DORSET
Westerly
159 Danby Mountain Road, Dorset

Please see June 8 for garden description, hours, and directions.

MANCHESTER
Glebelands
4263 Main Street/Route 7A, Manchester

Please see June 8 for garden description, hours, and directions.

White Tree Farm
1166 West Road, Manchester

Please see June 8 for garden description, hours, and directions.

MANCHESTER CENTER
Edwards' Garden
67 Coventry Lane, Manchester Center

Please see June 8 for garden description, hours, and directions.

Joan & Lee Fegelman's Garden
42 Coventry Lane, Manchester Center

Please see June 8 for garden description, hours, and directions.

MANCHESTER VILLAGE
The Sunken Garden
2234 River Road, Manchester Village

Please see June 8 for garden description, hours, and directions.

Public Gardens

BENNINGTON COUNTY

Manchester
Hildene

Manchester (802) 362-1788 www.hildene.org

Robert Todd Lincoln's Hildene was the home of Abraham Lincoln's descendants until 1975. This Georgian Revival mansion is situated among formal gardens that have been restored to their original beauty. Many of the original plantings remain and the location on a promontory in the valley provides a splendid view of the mountains on either side of Hildene's meadowlands below. A peony festival is held in June.

Hours: Mid-May through October, daily, 9:30 a.m. to 4 p.m.; tours available by appointment

Admission: $8 full tour, $4 grounds only

Located just 2 miles south of the junctions of Routes 7A and 11/30.

Shelburne
The Inn at Shelburne Farms

1611 Harbor Road, Shelburne (802) 985-8442 www.shelburnefarms.org

The gardens at the Inn at Shelburne Farms, originally designed by Lila Vanderbilt Webb, feature lush perennial borders inspired by the English cottage style of Gertrude Jekyll. The peak of the gardens' bloom is early June, when the 'Queen Victoria' peonies are in their glory, through July, when delphiniums bloom in front of a backdrop of tall plume poppies. Low brick walls provide the formal architectural structure to define the "rooms" within the garden and create multiple levels for the rose garden, the lily pond surrounded by Dutch and Japanese iris, and an herb garden. Continuing Lila's tradition to welcome the community into her gardens, we invite you to visit. Shelburne Farms is a 1,400-acre working farm, a national historic site, and a nonprofit environmental education center whose mission is to cultivate a conservation ethic by teaching and demonstrating the stewardship of natural and agricultural resources.

Hours: Year round, daily, 10 a.m. to 2 p.m.; garden tours available

Admission: $5

From I-89, take Exit 13 to Route 7 west at the traffic light in the center of Shelburne. Drive 1.6 miles to the entrance of Shelburne Farms. Turn right into the Welcome Center parking area before entering the gates. Tickets may be purchased there.

CHITTENDEN COUNTY

Essex Junction
The Inn at Essex

70 Essex Way, Essex Junction (802) 878-1100 www.innatessex.com

The Inn at Essex, Vermont's only AAA four-diamond hotel, built in 1989, is also home to the Essex campus of the acclaimed New England Culinary Institute. The gardens are designed to complement the large Colonial Revival-style Federal and Georgian buildings and reflect the unique partnership of the culinary school and the inn. Over 35 flower boxes grace the windows of the Governor's Mansion, the inn, and the Manor on the Green. Two generous beds filled the annuals flank the top of the green in front of the inn and many large pots filled with flowers decorate the walkways. Behind the inn is a large tented atrium/patio with stone steps leading down to the East Lawn, a welcoming expanse bordered by eighty-foot-long hedge-lined perennial beds with a wedding gazebo at the far end. Between the patio and Butler's Restaurant is a formal herb garden for use by the chefs and their students. The herb garden has a stone wall at one end with steps leading down to an allée of green ash trees. On the other side of the patio is a partially shaded bed with a mix of woody flowering shrubs, roses, and perennial phlox complemented by flowering shrubs and other perennials and annuals. At one end of the pool is a fountain sculpted by the late Paul Aschenbach, his last work, accentuated by a semi-circle of flowering annuals.

Hours: Year round, daily, 10 a.m. to 4 p.m., except during private parties

Admission: free

From I-89 south, take Exit 17/Colchester, Vermont. Turn left, then right onto Routes 2 and 7 at the traffic light. Go 3 miles, then bear left onto Route 2A south, go 5 miles to Exit 10/Route 289 east/Essex Way, and turn right. The inn is .25 mile on the left.

From I-89 north, take Exit 11/Richmond, Vermont. Turn right and then make an immediate right again onto Route 117 west. Go 6 miles to Exit 10/Route 289 west/Essex Way and turn left. The inn is .25 mile on the left.

FERRISBURGH

The Gardens of Basin Harbor

Basin Harbor Road, Ferrisburgh (802) 475-2311

Gardens at the Basin Harbor Club are a central part of the property's history. Established in 1886, the landscape vision of Basin Harbor came from our grandfather, Allen Penfield Beach. Through his vision we have made the preservation of the landscape an integral part of our philosophy. Much of what you see today is from the bones laid out by our grandfather. Over-looking Lake Champlain, Basin Harbor's gardens comprise 20,000 square feet of annuals, the largest display of unusual annuals in Vermont. Spread throughout our property you will dis-cover gardens varying in size, color, and design. Our head gardener, Joanne Cummings, is always looking for new and innovative ways to improve and show our gardens while keeping Basin Harbor's tradition and history alive.

Hours: Year round, daily, 9 a.m. to dusk

Admission: free

From the Essex, New York-Charlotte, Vermont, ferry, follow Route F5 east to Route 7. Turn right (south) onto Route 7. Turn right onto Route 22A into Vergennes. Go through town, down the hill, over the bridge, and take the second right at the blinking traffic light onto Panton Road. Follow the signs to Basin Harbor Club and Lake Champlain Maritime Museum. Go west about 1 mile and turn right onto Basin Harbor Road. Pro-ceed 6 miles to the Basin Harbor Club entry sign. Follow the signs to the lodge.

From the Lake Champlain Bridge on Route 17, continue northeast on Route 17 for about 2 miles. Take the left fork at Addison Gas Station and Store onto Lake Street. Follow the signs to Lake Champlain Maritime Museum. Stay on the paved road about 5 miles and fork left at Panton Store and gas pump. Stay left, go about 1 mile past Button Bay State Park, turn left onto Basin Harbor Road, and follow to the Basin Harbor entry sign. Follow the signs to the lodge.

Virginia

Garden of Linda Scott & Mary Dufour, Arlington.

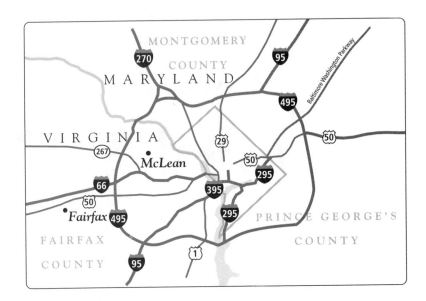

Saturday, June 15

Please also see listings for this date in Maryland

ARLINGTON COUNTY

ARLINGTON
Burnet-Deutsch Garden
716 North Edgewood Street, Arlington

This intimately structured outdoor living space appears deceptively larger than its modest 7,800 square feet. Extensive renovations to the 1920s' bungalow and garden occurred simultaneously as one design effort. The result of this multi-disciplined effort is a seamless flow of hardscapes and landscape beds strategically integrated with the main house structure. Three separate and distinct "garden rooms" extend indoor entertaining to the outdoors. The sunken garden, the oval garden, and the family garden and patio all offer individualized environments in which diverse rich plantings are artfully displayed. Throughout the garden are elements of surprise, delights, vistas, and focal points. The major component of the sunken garden is a round water feature offering a neutralizing effect on the surrounding quasi-urban setting. Surely, this creation is proof that grand solutions can be achieved in restricted spaces.

Hours: 10 a.m. to 4 p.m.

From the Beltway/I-495 in Virginia, go east on Route 267 to Route 66 east to Exit 71/ Glebe Road/Fairfax Drive. Stay straight on Fairfax Drive, crossing Wilson Boulevard (a Merit gas station is on the right corner); the street name changes to North 10th Street.

Go to the second traffic light and turn right onto Northern Washington Boulevard. Go to the next light (about .25 mile) and turn right onto North Pershing Drive to the first right, North Edgewood Street. Go to #716 (sixth house on the left).

From Washington, D.C., cross into Virginia from Georgetown via the Key Bridge. Proceed and, at the slight fork, veer right under overpass and, at the top of the hill, merge to the right lane to access Route 50 west. At the first light (about 1 mile), turn right onto North Pershing Drive. Go through the first intersection and turn right at the first street, North Edgewood. Go to #716 (sixth house on the left). *Please park on the street.*

Proceeds shared with the Lyon Park Citizens Association

Cozy Shack
3219 North Fourth Street, Arlington

Cozy Shack is a small natural garden featuring a large fishpond, Tennessee crab paving, sweeps of perennials, grasses, and sedges, and lots of informal plantings. The garden won a 1999 Grand Award in The Landscape Contractors Awards competition (MD, DC, VA). Garden owners are Doug Mearns and Tom Mannion of Tom Mannion Landscape Design, Inc.

Hours: 10 a.m. to 4 p.m.

Ashton Heights, Arlington, is a northern Virginia suburb of Washington, D.C. The garden is near the intersection of North Jackson Street and Pershing Drive. *Please park on the street.*

Proceeds shared with the Ashton Heights Civic Association

Garden of William A. Grillo
606 North Edgewood Street, Arlington

Approach this Arlington shade garden over a cobblestone drive court, past the front porch covered in cypress louvered shutters. The handcrafted gates welcome visitors to walk down the stone path along a dry creek to the recesses of this shade garden. This open-air room is framed by two outbuildings and two ponds. One pond is a simple square located close to the dining pavilion. The other is centered in the flagstone patio and is populated with koi swimming through the gentle current of a waterfall. The studio offers respite with different views of this space. Ferns, astilbe, hostas, liriope, crape myrtle, oak-leaf hydrangeas, and Japanese maples fill the garden and are accentuated by a backdrop of 35-foot-high bamboo and Leyland cypress. Several seating areas near low stone walls allow visitors to reflect and enjoy the essence of this intimate retreat.

Hours: 10 a.m. to 4 p.m.

From Washington, D.C., take Route 50 west to Pershing Drive; turn right. At the intersection of Pershing Drive and Washington Boulevard, continue on Pershing. Make the first right onto North Edgewood Street to the second house on the left.

From I-395, take the Washington Boulevard/Columbia Pike/Route 27 exit about 1.8 miles to Washington Boulevard. Turn left onto Pershing Drive, then make the first right onto North Edgewood Street to the second house on the left.

Garden of Linda Scott & Mary Dufour

3216 North Fourth Street, Arlington

Our garden has been evolving. First we said goodbye to our lawn efforts and dug a large bed. Then came hardscapes to ease a difficult transition to street level and create paths. Our back patio was enlarged, including a much larger water garden. Our new beds are filled with perennials that change with the seasons. Plantings were selected to help achieve our overall goals, beautiful space that is also attractive to wildlife and relatively easy care or, as Mary and I crafted our mission statement, "animal friendly, year-round color, and low maintenance." Blueberries, a crab apple, and buddleia in the front, and a mulberry in the back ensure a constant visitation of birds and butterflies. We have lovely large trees and the new garden blends beautifully with our small, semi-urban lot. Cedar fencing and a small iron gate to finish the pen for the summer run of our African spotted leopard tortoise, Monroe, complete the boundaries. There is even a little space for cutting flowers and herbs. This garden, designed and assisted in evolution by our friend and neighbor, landscape designer Tom Mannion, is truly a work of natural art and pleasure.

Hours: 10 a.m. to 4 p.m.

Ashton Heights, Arlington, is a northern Virginia suburb of Washington, D.C. The garden is near the intersection of North Jackson Street and Pershing Drive. *Please park on the street.*

Proceeds shared with the Ashton Heights Civic Association

FAIRFAX COUNTY

FAIRFAX
Dorothy & Art Phinney

3212 Chichester Lane, Fairfax

We've gardened here for three decades. We focused primarily on having color and interest in every season, in both sun and shade, in curving beds and borders, preferably including something unusual. Recently European Garden Design helped us to add more order and formality and to emphasize structure, height, and vistas. With their guidance, we've added pergolas, stone walls, pools, and some secluded, hidden retreats, which we hope will tempt you to dally awhile.

Hours: 10 a.m. to 4 p.m.

From the Beltway/I-495, take Exit 8/Arlington Boulevard/Route 50. Proceed west, towards Fairfax. Go through 5 traffic lights. The fifth light is Cedar Lane. Go less than 100 yards beyond the light to the first left turn, Chichester Lane. Number 3212 is on the right near the end of the second block. *Please park on the street.*

MCLEAN
Hilltop Cottage

2046 Rockingham Street, McLean

We bought an old house with an even older, very neglected, once-great garden. Its strength was classic Virginia: one dramatic spring display of hundreds of azaleas, rhododendrons, and mountain laurel. To enjoy the garden throughout the year, we have redesigned it, adding two water gardens (one for koi, one for goldfish), two perennial gardens, shade gardens, and an evergreen hillside—all connected by paths, focal points, and rest spots. The garden today is a complex series of rooms on different levels that have to be sought out to be enjoyed. Intentionally, one cannot read the garden with a single glance or from a single perspective. In 1999, the garden was described as a standout by the *Washington Post*. The garden was published in *Big Ideas for Small Spaces: Pocket Gardens*, edited by James Trulove. Last year the ponds were profiled in *Water Gardening* magazine's September/October 2001 issue. The garden is owned by Philip Metcalf and his wife, Patricia Galagan.

Hours: 10 a.m. to 4 p.m.

From Washington, D.C., take Route 66 west. Exit at Sycamore Street and turn right onto Sycamore. Go 1 mile to the traffic light at Williamsburg and the Williamsburg Shopping Center. Go straight on Williamsburg for 5 blocks. Turn left onto Kensington. Go 5 blocks and turn left onto Rockingham. Hilltop Cottage is the second house on the right after Rhode Island.

From the Beltway/I-495, take Route 66 east and exit at Westmorland Street. Turn left onto Westmorland. At the first light, turn right onto Williamsburg. Go .75 mile. At the light at the Williamsburg Shopping Center, turn left to continue on Williamsburg for 5 blocks. Proceed as directed above.

Ridder Garden

1219 Crest Lane, McLean

The garden slopes down to the bluffs of the Potomac River just below Little Falls. Much of the beauty of the garden derives from its views of the falls, the rapids, and an unspoiled island that is part of George Washington Park. The garden was probably started in the twenties, after farming on the rocky river bank was abandoned, so there are many mature trees, tulip poplars, oaks, and beeches, also old rhododendrons and azaleas. My effort has been to grow regionally appropriate flowers and vegetables and have a garden that flowers from March to November. The garden is divided between a woodland walk with wild and shade flowers and a series of parterres with perennials.

Hours: 10 a.m. to 4 p.m.

From Washington, D.C., take Canal Road to Chain Bridge. Turn left across the bridge. Take the first right at the traffic light onto Chain Bridge Road/Route 123. At the top of the hill, after passing Merrywood, turn right onto Crest Lane (just before George Washington Memorial Parkway). Take the third right off Crest Lane onto a small roadway. Number 1219 is a yellow house, the third on the right between #1260 and #1211.

From Maryland, take the Beltway/I-495 south to Virginia. Take the first Virginia exit onto George Washington Memorial Parkway. Exit the parkway at Chain Bridge Road/Route 123. Follow the exit ramp to Route 123. Take the first left onto Crest Lane. Proceed as directed above.

Proceeds shared with the Potomac Conservancy

Public Gardens

ARLINGTON COUNTY

ALEXANDRIA

American Horticultural Society at George Washington's River Farm

7931 East Boulevard Drive, Alexandria (703) 768-5700 www.ahs.org

Once part of George Washington's property, this 27-acre garden overlooking the Potomac River now serves as headquarters for the American Horticultural Society. The gardens include the Interactive Children's Gardens; the George Harding Memorial Azalea Garden; the Wildlife Garden; herb, perennial, and annual display beds; a picnic area; art exhibits; a visitor's center; and a gift shop.

Hours: Year round, weekdays, 8:30 a.m. to 5 p.m.; April 1 through October 31, Saturday, 9 a.m. to 1 p.m. ; closed on holidays

Admission: free, but donations are appreciated

River Farm is located about 4 miles south of Old Town Alexandria, just off George Washington Memorial Parkway. Exactly .5 mile after going under Stone Bridge, make a left off the parkway at the Arcturus/East Boulevard/Herbert Springs exit. Turn left at the stop sign. The entrance is on the right.

WASHINGTON

Geller-Irvine garden, Seattle. Photo by Keith Geller.

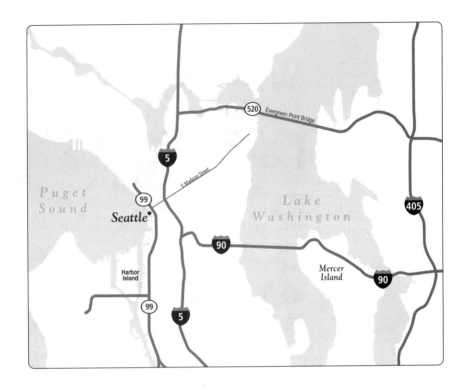

Saturday, June 1

KING COUNTY

SEATTLE
Noel Angell & Emory Bundy
270 Dorffel Drive East, Seattle

The residence is a 1905 Craftsman-period home on the National Historic Register. From the street, the home is approached by a river rock pathway through a light woodland garden. Granite steps lead down along a granite boulder waterfall, reflecting the region's hilly topography. An upper patio in the front of the house is nestled into a dense planting of sun-loving plants. After walking through a river rock archway to the back, the gardens have a more rustic appeal, with edible berries and fruit trees.

Hours: 10 a.m. to 3 p.m.

From I-5 south, take Highway 520 to the Montake exit. Travel south and east on Lake Washington Boulevard, through the arboretum. Cross Madison Street and continue on Lake Washington Boulevard. After about 4 blocks, pass Bush School and turn right onto 37th East. After about 50 feet, 37th East curves and becomes Dorffel Drive East. Number 270 Dorffel Drive East is the first house on the left, brown with white trim.

From I-5 north, take the first Madison Street exit and travel east on Madison Street. At Lake Washington Boulevard, turn right and proceed as directed above. *Please park along the street.*

Geller-Irvine Garden

1725 26th Avenue, Seattle

I started the garden in 1981, when there were only two trees on the property. Today, the woodland cottage garden reminds me of my native New England. The placement of the main structure of trees and shrubs naturally defines the interconnected outdoor rooms. A walk through the property brings you up a steep hillside entry garden, through the woodland canopy, and onto two brick terrace gardens surrounded by perennials. The 60 x by 120-foot garden feels larger than it is due to the changing feeling and flow of the spaces.

Hours: 10 a.m. to 3 p.m.

From I-5, take the Madison Street exit. Turn east onto Madison towards Lake Washington. Turn right onto 25th Avenue east (heading south). Turn left onto East John Street and proceed down the hill. Take the first right onto 26th Avenue and continue a couple of blocks past East Denny and East Howell. Number 1725 is on the right side just past East Howell. Look for a wooden staircase.

Carol Henderson

530 McGilvra Boulevard, Seattle

A long brick wall separates the sidewalk from the house, creating a private brick courtyard. Several large shore pines (*Pinus contorta*) were brought in to create the bones of the front garden and to add depth to the open space. A walk under large rhododendrons and down stone steps to the back garden reveals the magnificent setting overlooking Lake Washington and Mount Rainier. Stone paving, ornamental grasses, and ground cover take the place of formal lawn areas.

Hours: 10 a.m. to 3 p.m.

Take I-5 to Madison Street. Head east towards Lake Washington on Madison to McGilvra Boulevard. Turn right onto McGilvra to #530.

Carol Isaacson-Rawn

453 McGilvra Boulevard, Seattle

The house and garden have a sunny Mediterranean feeling through the use of terra-cotta stone paving and the abundance of white flowers and variegated foliage. While walking up the front stairway, several terraces allow for a pause and changing views of the surrounding garden. The back terrace is an extension of the home, where the garden acts mostly as a backdrop for the terrace. Large terra-cotta containers placed within the garden and a small sitting alcove add to the depth of the narrow space.

Hours: 10 a.m. to 3 p.m.

Take I-5 to Madison Street. Head east towards Lake Washington on Madison to McGilvra Boulevard. Turn right onto McGilvra to #453.

Carlo & Lalie Scandiuzzi

1215 41st Avenue East, Seattle

We have tried to create a landscape that reminds us of an Italian country home within an urban setting. Through the garden's different rooms, the details of plants and architecture reveal cross-cultural lifestyles that blend with the Pacific Northwest. For example, a walled morning garden off the kitchen creates a sense of privacy and reflection. The front hillside garden of upright blue junipers is reminiscent of the Italian countryside, with its vertical Italian cypresses. And the back garden features a terraced deck transitioning onto a stone-and-gravel patio surrounded by several smaller intimate spaces.

Hours: 10 a.m. to 3 p.m.

From I-5, take the to Madison Street exit. Head towards Lake Washington. Turn right onto 41st Avenue. *Please park along the street.*

Public Gardens

CLARK COUNTY

VANCOUVER

1845 Period Garden at Fort Vancouver

1100 East 5th Street, Vancouver (360) 696-7659

Fort Vancouver's 1845 Period Garden recreates the flower and vegetable gardens planted by the British Hudson's Bay Company. The original garden was the first formal garden in the Northwest. The National Park Service manages the five-acre site organically and plants only heirloom or historic varieties.

Hours: March 1 through October 31, daily, 9 a.m. to 5 p.m.; November 1 through February 28, daily, 9 a.m. to 4 p.m.; closed Thanksgiving Day, Christmas Eve, and Christmas Day.

Admission: free

From I-5, take Exit 1-C and follow signs to Fort Vancouver.

From I-205, follow SR14 West to I-5 north, take Exit 1-C, and follow signs.

Kaiser Permanente's Salmon Creek Poison Prevention Garden

14406 N.E. 20th, Vancouver (503) 813-4820

Opened in 1997, the garden features common garden trees, shrubs, and perennials harmful to humans. More than three dozen species are represented, from horse chestnuts to daphne and autumn crocus. All plants are labeled in botanical Latin and English. A plant list is available inside the adjacent Salmon Creek Medical Office.

Hours: Special Open Days event, May 11, 10 a.m. to 2 p.m.; otherwise, year round, weekdays, 8 a.m. to 5 p.m. (except holidays). Tours led by master gardeners on the second Saturday of each month, April through October; otherwise, call office for guided tours for 4 people or more.

Admission: free

From Portland, take I-5 north. Take the N.E. 134th Street exit and go 2 blocks east on N.E. 20th. Turn left (north) on N.E. 20th. The poison prevention garden is located on the campus of Kaiser Permanente's Salmon Creek Medical Office. The garden is to the left of the building (see Community Garden sign).

COWLITZ COUNTY

WOODLAND

Hulda Klager Lilac Gardens

115 South Pekin Road, Woodland (360) 225-8996

The gardens are really an arboretum with many flowers, shrubs, and exotic trees, besides the lilacs. The house has been restored and made into a museum honoring the "Lilac Lady." Also, the woodshed, water tower, and carriage house have all been restored. The Lilac Garden is a nonprofit organization with an approximately 90% volunteer work force, which puts in many hours keeping the gardens as Hulda Klager kept them.

Hours: Year round, daily, dawn to dusk

Admission: $3 per person

From I-5, take Exit 21. Coming south, go about .5 mile to a stop sign. There will be a sign on the street leading to the garden. Coming north, turn left at the bottom of the exit at the traffic light. At the next light, there will be a sign pointing to the Lilac Garden. Follow signs to the garden.

KING COUNTY

ORTING

The Chase Garden

A PROJECT OF
THE GARDEN
CONSERVANCY

17904 Brittany Drive S.W., Orting (206) 242-4040 www.chasegarden.org

Recently featured in *Earth on Her Hands: The American Woman in Her Garden* by Starr Ockenga, this naturalistic style garden on 4.5 acres has been created and tended by Emmott and Ione Chase since 1960. The area surrounding the house was designed by Rex Zumwalt, evoking the simplicity of a Japanese garden by use of raked pea gravel, moss-covered boulders, and a reflecting pool. A forest of native trees is carpeted with wildflowers. There are perennial shade borders, a rock garden, and a ground cover meadow inspired by the alpine meadows of Mount Rainer. Visitors may enjoy the mountain as part of the panoramic view of the Puyallup River Valley.

Hours: By appointment only from mid-April to mid-May.

Admission: $5

From Highway 161 (Meridian), turn east onto 264th Street east, which is about 1 mile south of the town of Graham. Continue for 3.5 miles. Watch for the driveway directly across from a road sign indicating 10 mph (with a crooked arrow).

From Seattle, go south on Highway 167. Take the Puyallup/Olympia exit onto Highway 512 south. Remain on Highway 512, bypassing Puyallup, and take the South Hill/ Eatonville exit. Turn left at the traffic light to access Highway 161 (Meridian). Proceed as directed above.

From Tacoma at I-5, take Highway 512 east to the Eatonville exit. Turn right at the light to access Highway 161 (Meridian). Proceed as directed above.

From Olympia, follow signs to Eatonville. Go north from Eatonville via Highway 161 (Meridian). Proceed as directed above.

Seattle
The Dunn Gardens
Seattle (206) 362-0933 www.dunngardens.org

In 1915, the Olmsted Brothers designed a summer country place for the Arthur Dunn family on a bluff overlooking Puget Sound. The estate has remained in the private ownership of the family and, with the passage of time, has come to reflect the mature grace which the designers and owners desired for a rural retreat. The Olmsted ideals of naturalistic groupings of trees amid broad lawns and flowering borders of shrubs and ground covers continue to be as vibrant and compelling today as they were at the turn of the century.

Hours: April through September, guided tours only, Thursday, 2 p.m., Friday, 10 a.m. and 2 p.m.

Admission: $7 adults, $5 students and senior citizens

Please call for directions.

Washington Park Arboretum
2300 Arboretum Drive East, Seattle (206) 543-8800 http//depts.washington.edu/wpa

Washington Park Arboretum is a living plant museum emphasizing trees and shrubs hardy in the maritime Pacific Northwest. Plant collections are selected and arranged to display their beauty and function in urban landscapes, to demonstrate their natural ecology and diversity, and to conserve important species and cultivated varieties for the future. The arboretum serves the public, students at all levels, naturalists, gardeners, and nursery and landscape professionals with its collections, education programs, and interpretation and recreational opportunities.

Hours: Year round, daily, dawn to dusk

Admission: free

From I-5, take Exit 168-B/Bellevue/Kirkland east. Take the very first exit, Montlake Boulevard/UW. At the traffic light, go straight. You are now on Lake Washington Boulevard East. Follow for 1 mile until you come to the stop sign with the left-turn lane. Turn left onto Foster Island Road and follow the signs to the visitor's center.

West Seattle
Village Green Perennials
10223 26th Avenue S.W., West Seattle (206) 767-7735

An English country garden and cottage nursery owned and operated by Teresa Romedo. A rich tapestry of color and texture, the garden hosts High Tea for the Daughters of the British Empire twice a year. Flowers, foliage, artworks, and a soothing pond, Village Green Perennials is on oasis in a suburban neighborhood. Explore the intoxicating garden, then visit the nursery to add your favorites to your own garden.

Hours: Year round, Saturday, 10 a.m. to 4 p.m., and Sunday, 11 a.m. to 4:30 p.m.

Admission: free

From I-5, exit at the West Seattle Freeway heading west. Once in West Seattle, turn left at 35th Avenue S.W. Continue south to the intersection with S.W. Roxbury. Turn left onto Roxbury and travel west to 26th Avenue S.W. Turn right onto 26th Avenue S.W. and travel south 3 blocks to the Village Green Perennials sign at the curb. *Please park along 26th Avenue S.W.*

KITSAP COUNTY

BAINBRIDGE ISLAND

Bloedel Reserve

7571 N.E. Dolphin Drive, Bainbridge Island (206) 842-7631 www.bloedelreserve.com

The Bloedel Reserve is a 150-acre former residence, now a public access garden and nature preserve. The primary purpose of the reserve is to provide people with an opportunity to enjoy nature through quiet walks in the gardens and woodlands.

Hours: Year round, Wednesday through Sunday (except federal holidays)

Admission: $6 adults, $4 senior citizens and children 5-12

The reserve is located about 8 miles north of Winslow (Bainbridge Island Ferry Terminal) off Highway 305. Phone for reservations and directions.

BELLEVUE

The Bellevue Botanical Garden

12001 Main Street, Bellevue (425) 452-2750 www.bellevuebotanical.org

The Bellevue Botanical Garden comprises 36 acres of display gardens, rolling hills, woodlands, meadows, and wetlands offering an ever-changing panorama of greenery and color. A unique combination of horticulture education, scenic beauty, special events, and volunteer opportunities creates a focus of community pride. Since opening in 1992, the Bellevue Botanical Garden has become a major center community activity.

Hours: Year round, daily, dawn to dusk

Admission: free

From I-405, exit onto N.E. Eighth east. Follow N.E. Eighth to 120th and turn right onto 120th. Turn left onto Main Street. The garden is located on the right at #12001.

FEDERAL WAY

Rhododendron Species Botanical Garden

Federal Way (253) 661-9377 www.rhodygarden.org

The Rhododendron Species Botanical Garden features one of the finest collections of rhododendrons in the world. Enjoy more than 10,000 rhododendrons growing in a beautiful 22-acre woodland setting with exotic and unusual companion plants. Year-round features include scenic beauty, alpine, pond, and woodland gardens, a hardy fern collection, and a gazebo.

Hours: March through May, daily, except Thursday, 10 a.m. to 4 p.m.; June through Febuary, Saturday through Wednesday, 11 a.m. to 4 p.m.

Admission: $3.50

From I-5, take Exit 143/Federal Way/South 320th Street. Turn west onto 320th Street. At Weyerhaeuser Way South, turn right. Bear left at the fork and turn left at the stop sign. Take the first right and follow signs for parking.

SHOHOMISH COUNTY

LAKEWOOD

Lakewold Gardens

12317 Gravelly Drive S.W., Lakewood (253) 584-4106 www.lakewold.org

A beautiful ten-acre estate garden showcasing stunning formal gardens as well as naturalistic displays. This includes woodland areas, aquatic displays, waterfalls, rock and alpine gardens, a knot garden, kitchen garden, shade garden, rose garden, and fern garden. Lakewold also is a splendid example of noted landscape architect Thomas Church's residential designs.

Hours: April through September, Thursday, Saturday, Sunday, Monday, 10 a.m. to 4 p.m., Friday, noon to 8 p.m. October through March, Friday through Sunday, 10 a.m. to 3 p.m.

Admission: $5 adults, $3 senior citizens, students, and military; children under 12 free

From I-5, take Exit 124/Gravelly Lake Drive. Follow signs for 1 mile. Lakewold is only 10 miles south of the Tacoma Dome.

WEST VIRGINIA

Photo by Clara Thomas

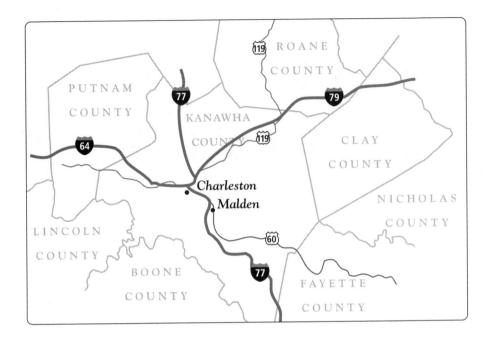

Saturday, June 29

KANAWHA COUNTY

CHARLESTON

Laughinghouse—the Giltinans' Garden

800 Louden Heights Road, Charleston

Our gardens at Laughinghouse reflect old and new approaches. We have sited a new house in an old 1.5-acre woodland, attempting a new naturalistic habitat on areas disturbed by construction. Lawns are of mixed clovers and lespedeza. Roof drains are piped to an underground cistern and rain water is pumped to garden hydrants. Surface water from the sloping site seeps to a bog garden beside the creek that borders the property. Native trees and shrubs, wildflowers, seed-propagated deciduous rhododendrons, and mixed perennial borders attract pollinators, songbirds, and indigenous wildlife, providing safe haven for their cycles and great pleasure for the gardeners! A small pond, fed by a watershed stream, overflows to a rocky watercourse spanned by a footbridge leading to the woodland paths.

Hours: 10 a.m. to 4 p.m.

From downtown Charleston, cross Southside Bridge (Dickinson Street) toward Louden Heights. At the end of the bridge, turn left at the traffic light and go up Louden Heights Road. Continue .7 mile to #800 on the left. Just past Bougemont Road (a private drive where you may not park) are the stone gate posts marking the driveway at Laughinghouse. *Please park in the driveway.*

Proceeds shared with the Kanawha Garden Club

The Garden of Bill Mills & Thomas Gillooly
729 Gordon Drive, Charleston

As a garden designer, I (Bill) greatly enjoy having my own laboratory to work in. The garden never remains static and I like being able to constantly expand and recreate the space. Covering close to an acre of property with varying terrain, from the sunny beds to the shaded woodland hillside, the space offers many horticultural experiences. As one strolls up the gravel drive, several different borders come into view. Through the gate, one enters into a circular white garden with a small circular pool. This leads to a serpentine perennial border and then on to another shaded, circular space. Access to the extensive woodland garden is through a breezeway laden with assorted pots, haymows, and a water feature. Continue up the steps lined with potted and planted topiary. The woodland garden is home to many herbaceous perennials, shrubs, and conifers. Throughout the property you will find many unusual trees and conifers, as well as sculptures, urns, and specimen tropicals.

> *Hours:* 10 a.m. to 4 p.m.

> *From I-64*, take the Oakwood exit to Route 119. Turn right onto Cantley Drive. From Cantley, turn right onto Wilkie Drive. Make the second left turn onto South Fort Drive. South Fort turns into Gordon Drive. Our residence, 1 mile further at 729 Gordon Drive, is on the left, a small cottage up a gravel drive. *Additional parking may be found just past the residence at Weberwood Elementary School.*

> *Proceeds shared with the Kanawha Garden Club*

Governor's Mansion—State of West Virginia
1716 Kanawha Boulevard East, Charleston (344) 558-3588

This red-brick walled garden combines woody plants, perennials, and annuals around an open courtyard. An informal dining area overlooks a small herb and garden garden in the summer, and chrysanthemums and Japanese anemones in the autumn. The focal point is a wall fountain with a faux marble finish and surrounded by blue atlas cedars. The west wall contains climbing hydrangea and is underplanted with hellebores, narcissus, and native creeping phlox.

> *Hours:* 10 a.m. to 4 p.m.

> *Exit I-64* at the airport and State Capital Building. Turn right, and at the first traffic light, turn left into the parking area for the cultural center. Continue on foot for one half block toward the Kanawha River. The mansion faces the river and Kanawha Boulevard.

Dr. & Mrs. George E. Toma
12 Quail Cove Road, Charleston

A dramatic natural setting from which to overlook two converging streams, especially as seen from a high lookout called "The Point." One of Charleston's longest herbaceous borders, a wooded moss garden, carefully planned flowering shade gardens, and specimen-size ornamental shrubs and trees are handicapped accessible. The canyon on the rear of the property, housing a wildflower garden aproned in front of a long cave and colonies of native cucumber magnolias, can be observed from a spacious deck at tree-top level. Outstanding plant species include hardy orchids, large golden false cypresses, massed azaleas, hypericum, and a bank of

Stephanandra incisa 'Crispa'. The gardens are good examples of properly siting ornamental plants and ground covers on steep and heavily shaded hills to maximize serenity and privacy.

Hours: 10 a.m. to 4 p.m.

From downtown Charleston, cross Southside Bridge and immediately bear left onto Louden Heights Road. At about 2 miles, turn right onto Hampton Road at Holz Elementary School. Continue on Hampton Road for about .75 mile and turn right onto Stonehenge Road. At the stone pillars, bear left into Fairfax Estates. Turn right onto Quail Cove Road to #12.

Proceeds shared with the Kanawha Garden Club

Zeb & Sara Sue Wright's Garden

1525 Clark Road, Charleston

The home of a garden designer, retired garden writer, and avid collector, displaying over 1,500 species and cultivars of shrubs, orchids, dwarf conifers, perennials, wildflowers, and water/bog plants sited in a figure-eight pattern that meanders among rock, mixed border, carnivorous, and water gardens. Especially recommended are large colonies of hardy orchids and 240 species and cultivars of conifers landscaped among companion astilbes, hostas, dwarf shrubs, heathers, and ground covers. Well-established gardens include a large perennial and alpine garden, as well as areas of native plants and wildflowers. Some areas of the garden go back as far as thirty years; the bog and water gardens are new additions. Most plants are labeled and a computer printout will be available upon request.

Hours: 10 a.m. to 4 p.m.

From downtown Charleston, take I-64 towards Huntington. Take the Oakwood exit and turn right onto Route 119. Continue to the top of the hill and the second traffic light (about 1 mile). Turn left onto Oakwood Road to the George Washington High School intersection. Turn right onto Clark Road to the fourth house on the right, #1525.

Proceeds shared with the Kanawha Garden Club

MALDEN

Kanawha Salines—Garden of Mrs. Turner Ratrie

Kanawha Salines, Malden

Kanawha Salines, one of the most historic properties in the Kanawha Valley, was built by a pioneer in the exploitation of the abundant resources of salt brine beneath the earth. The original house was built in 1815 and remodeled in 1923. The owner, Mrs. Ratrie, is a direct descendent of the first salt producers and has been the garden designer since 1958. An allée of cherry trees on either side of an old brick walk leads to an enchanting white garden surrounding a rectangular pool filled with white waterlilies. There is a formal rose garden surrounded by an English boxwood hedge, an extensive vegetable garden, and a beautiful herbaceous border. The property encompasses 1.5 acres.

Hours: 10 a.m. to 4 p.m.

From I-64 /I-77, take Route 60 east to the Malden exit. Turn left after the underpass and proceed through the town of Malden. Turn right onto a gravel road east of town. Look for a sign at the gravel driveway. *Please park as directed.*

Proceeds shared with the Kanawha Garden Club

Wisconsin

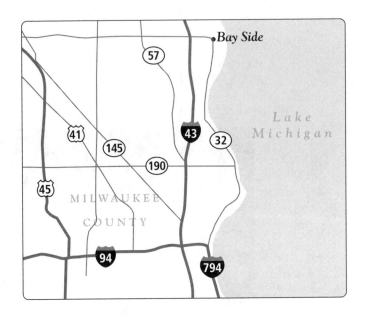

Sunday, July 21

MILWAUKEE COUNTY

BAYSIDE
Coffman-Morrison Gardens
301 West Fairy Chasm Road, Bayside

We approached the yard as a blank canvas. Only two old crab trees and a garden house remain. The front garden invites you to rest on the bench while watching the fish cavort in a small pond. A vine-covered cedar fence encloses the backyard. Upon entering, a path must be chosen. Will it be the shade bed graced by an old willow tree? Or the patio, filled with unique container plantings? Choosing the patio leads one's eyes to a cedar arch covered in honeysuckle. Below is a copper cattail fountain that fills the air with the sounds of dancing water. The arch is surrounded by four perennial beds, an invitation to butterflies, humming-birds, and gardeners. The next path may lead you past the herb bed, under an archway, and into the garden house. But before you leave, one last path, a quaint goodbye past the grasses and apple espalier, leaving you with a sweet scent by which to remember your visit.

Hours: 10 a.m. to 4 p.m.

From Highway 43 north, take Exit 82A/Brown Deer Road. Travel east on Brown Deer Road for .25 mile. At the first 4-way stop sign, turn left onto Port Washington Road. Travel for .5 mile and turn right onto Fairy Chasm Road. Travel .5 mile to 301 West Fairy Chasm Road. Look for a lannon stone Cape Cod on the right. _Please park on the side streets and at Community Center just off Fairy Chasm Road._

RIVER HILLS
David Knox's Garden
1000 West Bradley Road, River Hills

My gardens are set on ten acres of lawn, woods, and ponds with unobstructed natural vistas. The gardens surround a Colonial Revival house designed by Andrew Hepburn of Perry, Shaw, and Hepburn, the Boston architects responsible for the restoration of Colonial Williamsburg. Included are a formal rose garden, perennial gardens, vegetable and herb gardens, pond gardens, and an orchard. The property remains a garden in progress and includes a small arboretum.

Hours: 10 a.m. to 4 p.m.

Take Highway 43 north from downtown Milwaukee to the Good Hope Road exit, about 10 miles. Turn left onto Good Hope Road and take the first right onto Pheasant Lane. Travel north about 1 mile to West Bradley Road. *Turn right onto West Bradley and park. Walk down the long entrance road at #1000.*

Proceeds shared with the Friends of Boerner Botanical Gardens

The LaBahn Garden
1400 West Calumet Court, River Hills

Formal gardens complement this red brick Georgian-style home. The scale is large, the design calmly understated, and the planting restrained. Brick walks and patios are laid out along formal axes. The result is elegant simplicity. A custom-built screened gazebo echoes the stately lines of the house, featuring a cupola, cedar shakes, and Neoclassical pillars and posts. The meadow beyond is bordered by an allée of trees, providing a formal invitation to wander into the woods beyond.

Hours: 2 p.m. to 6 p.m.

From downtown Milwaukee, go north on I-43 to the Good Hope Road exit, about 10 miles. Turn left (west) onto Good Hope Road and travel about .25 mile to River Road. Turn right (north) for .5 mile to Calumet Court. Turn left onto Calumet Court.

Russell Garden
3000 West Brown Deer Road, River Hills

Twenty years ago, the owner set out to transform a large, white frame house on seven acres. It continues to be a work in progress! A perennial garden surrounded by a picket fence to contain the rampant black-eyed Susans, phlox, and bee balm, a small "pinch and sniff" garden, a small pond, a formal garden with a fountain, arbor, lattice fence, and pots around the pool are the main attractions. As the homeowner does all the work, it has a casual feel. One can always find a weed to pull!

Hours: 10 a.m. to 4 p.m.

Take I-43 north to the West Brown Deer Road exit. Proceed west to #3000. The house is uphill and on the north side. *Please park on the property unless it is full. If the barricade is up, there are directions to a nearby parking lot and a shuttle will be provided.*

Public Gardens

MILWAUKEE

HALES CORNERS
Boerner Botanical Garden
5879 South 92nd Street, Hales Corners (414) 425-1130

Internationally recognized, fifty-acre formal gardens set within a 1,000-acre arboretum park. Collections are displayed in beautifully landscaped settings including a Perennial Mall, Herb Garden, Rose Garden, Annual Garden, Rock Garden, and Shrub Mall. Seasonal displays of wildflowers, tulips, crab apples, peonies, iris, roses, and daylilies are among the popular attractions. Boerner Botanical Garden is an All-American Selections Flower Trial Judging Ground and an All-America Rose Selections Test Site, and displays All-American Flower Trial and Vegetable Trial Winners.

Hours: Mid-April through November, daily, 8 a.m. to dusk

Located southwest of Milwaukee. Take I-894 to Exit 5A/Forest Home. Take Forest Home southwest to 92nd Street and go south about 1 mile to the College Avenue entrance.

MILWAUKEE
Mitchell Park Horticultural Conservatory
524 South Layton Boulevard, Milwaukee (414) 649-9830

Three large domes seven stories tall house a rainforest, a desert, and a themed floral show. There are orchids, a 35-foot waterfall, more than 6,000 plants, and cacti from around the world. Five themed floral shows feature travel, fantasy, or history to inspire any palate or taste.

Hours: Year round, daily, 9 a.m. to 5 p.m.

Travel north on I-94 from Chicago to downtown Milwaukee. Go west on I-94 from Milwaukee to the 22nd Street/Clymourn Exit. Go west 5 blocks to 27th Street and turn left on Domes.

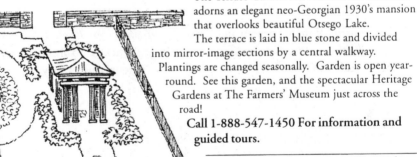

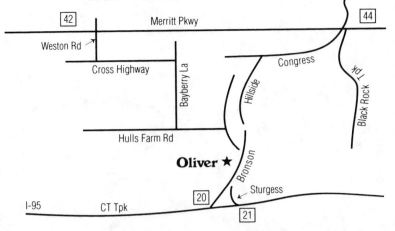

AUSTRALIA'S OPEN GARDEN SCHEME

MORE THAN 800 inspiring private gardens drawn from every Australian state and territory feature in our annual program.

Included are tropical gardens in the Northern Territory and Queensland, awe-inspiring arid zone gardens, traditional gardens in the temperate south, gardens which feature Australia's unique flora, and gardens designed by many of Australia's contemporary designers.

Our full colour guidebook is published each August by ABC Books and every entry includes a full description, map references and directions, opening details and amenities.

State-by-state calendars make it easy to plan a personal itinerary, and a special index identifies gardens with a particular plant collection or area of interest.

Also included are exhaustive listings of permanently open gardens around the country, as well as some of the many gardens which offer accommodation.

PRESIDENT: *Mrs Malcolm Fraser*
CHIEF EXECUTIVE OFFICER: *Neil Robertson*
Westport, New Gisborne, Victoria 3438
Tel +61 3 5428 4557
Fax +61 3 5428 4558
email: national@opengarden.org.au
website: opengarden.abc.net.au
Australia's Open Garden Scheme ABN 60 057 467 553

ABC
BOOKS

Providing Design Services
for Distinctive Gardens

RODNEY ROBINSON 🌿 LANDSCAPE ARCHITECTS

707 Philadelphia Pike

Wilmington, DE 19809

tel: 302. 764. 9554

fax: 302. 764. 4628

e mail: RRLA@rrlarch.com

Photo by Jeffrey E. Holder

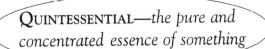

BRIDGE GARDENS TRUST ✳

Donna Paul for *The New York Times*

Bridge Gardens covers five acres, and features a large, meticulously-trimmed knot garden surrounded by beds of culinary, medicinal, ornamental, and textile and dyeing herbs. Another favorite attraction is a collection of 800 antique and modern roses.

Bridge Gardens is open to visitors on Wednesdays and Saturdays, 2-5 p.m., from Memorial Day weekend through September. Admission is $10.

36 Mitchell Lane
P.O. Box 1194
Bridgehampton, NY 11932

Telephone 631-537-7440
Facsimile 631-537-3667

gardener@bridgegardens.org
www.bridgegardens.org

INDEX

WITH OUR COMPLIMENTS

. . . .

Complete and return the free admission coupon offer below and we'll send you one free Open Days admission coupon. Discounted admission coupons are a great way to make garden visiting easier.

Admission coupons do not expire and may be used at any time during the Open Days Program to enter a private garden. However, they are not valid at Public Gardens listed unless otherwise noted.

Admission to each private garden is $5. Garden Conservancy members may purchase a book of 6 discounted admission coupons for $20 (that's 2 free admissions!). Non members may purchase 6 for $25.

Name _____

Address _____

City/town_____State_____Zip _____

Daytime phone _____

email _____

Where did you purchase your *Open Days Directory?*

To redeem, please return to:

> The Garden Conservancy,
> P.O. Box 219,
> Cold Spring, NY 10516.

Photocopies of this form will not be accepted. Limit 1 coupon per book.

Join the Garden Conservancy

If you have enjoyed our *Open Days Directory*, why not consider becoming a member of the Garden Conservancy? Your support will enable us to continue to identify and preserve exceptional gardens across the country, and to ensure that more of these treasures are opened for public enrichment and enjoyment. As a member, you will receive valuable benefits designed to enhance your appreciation of gardens, including:

- a subscription to our quarterly newsletter
- invitations to Conservancy-sponsored special events
- discounts on purchases of the *Open Days Directory* and admission coupons
- a personalized membership card and an automobile decal

With a gift of $100 or more, you will receive invitations to additional regional Conservancy activities and be acknowledged in our newsletter. With a gift of $1,500 or more, you will be enrolled in the Society of Fellows and have the opportunity to attend garden-study tours and special events highlighting America's finest gardens.

Please enroll me as a member of the Garden Conservancy at the level indicated below:

❏ $35 Individual ❏ $100 Friend ❏ $500 Patron ❏ $2,500⁺ President's Circle
❏ $50 Family ❏ $250 Sponsor ❏ $1,500 Society of Fellows

Open Days Discount Admission Coupons

Save on admission fees with discount coupon books. They make garden visiting easier and they do not expire. Use them at any Open Day garden (*private only*), anywhere.

Directories ($10.95 members, $15.95 nonmembers) $_____

Coupon Books—a $30 value ($20 members, $25 nonmembers) $_____

Add $4.50 for shipping & handling when ordering a Directory $_____

Add $1.50 for each additional Directory $_____

Membership contribution $_____

Total enclosed $_____

Please charge my credit card account: MasterCard _____ VISA _____

Account Number: _____ Exp. ___/___

Name _____

Address _____

City/town_____State_____Zip _____

Daytime phone _____

email _____

Please make checks payable to: *The Garden Conservancy* and send to: The Garden Conservancy, P.O. Box 219, Cold Spring, NY 10516, fax to (845) 265-5392. You may also order by calling us on our toll-free order line at (888) 842-2442 or logon to www.gardenconservancy.org.

The Garden Conservancy, Inc., is a tax-exempt organization under section 501(c)(3) of the Internal Revenue Code. Membership contributions are fully tax deductible. Purchases of *The Garden Conservancy's Open Days Directory* and/or coupon books do not constitute a charitable contribution and are therefore not

Notes